FIFTH EDITION

FUNDAMENTALS OF COGNITIVE PSYCHOLOGY

◆

HENRY C. ELLIS
University of New Mexico

R. REED HUNT
University of North Carolina

WCB Brown & Benchmark
P U B L I S H E R S

Madison, Wisconsin • Dubuque, Iowa • Indianapolis, Indiana
Melbourne, Australia • Oxford, England

Book Team

Editor *Michael Lange*
Developmental Editor *Sheralee Connors*
Production Editor *Kay Driscoll*
Visuals/Design Developmental Consultant *Marilyn A. Phelps*
Visuals/Design Freelance Specialist *Mary L. Christianson*
Publishing Services Specialist *Sherry Padden*
Marketing Manager *Steven Yetter*
Advertising Manager *Jodi Rymer*

Brown & Benchmark

A Division of Wm. C. Brown Communications, Inc.

Vice President and General Manager *Thomas E. Doran*
Editor in Chief *Edgar J. Laube*
Executive Editor *Ed Bartell*
Executive Editor *Stan Stoga*
National Sales Manager *Eric Ziegler*
Director of CourseResource *Kathy Law Laube*
Director of CourseSystems *Chris Rogers*
Director of Marketing *Sue Simon*
Director of Production *Vickie Putman Caughron*
Imaging Group Manager *Chuck Carpenter*
Manager of Visuals and Design *Faye M. Schilling*
Design Manager *Jac Tilton*
Art Manager *Janice Roerig*
Permissions/Records Manager *Connie Allendorf*

Wm. C. Brown Communications, Inc.

Chairman Emeritus *Wm. C. Brown*
Chairman and Chief Executive Officer *Mark C. Falb*
President and Chief Operating Officer *G. Franklin Lewis*
Corporate Vice President, President of WCB Manufacturing *Roger Meyer*

Cover design by Elaine G. Allen

Copyedited by Patricia Stevens

Consulting Editor Frank A. Logan

This book is dedicated to my wife, Florence, and to our children, Joan, Diane, and John Ellis

and to my parents, Nancy and Robert Hunt

CONTENTS

PREFACE

In this fifth edition of *Fundamentals of Cognitive Psychology* we have added many new topics, describing recent exciting developments in cognitive psychology while retaining the general objectives of prior editions. Users of the previous edition will recognize a slight name change from *Fundamentals of Human Memory and Cognition* to the present title, which more succinctly describes our book. We are gratified that many people found the previous edition a useful and enjoyable text and comments from faculty and students continue to reinforce our efforts in writing this text. Because of positive comments and reviews, we have retained the general organization of the fourth edition, while adding many new topics to keep the book timely.

The purpose of this book is to introduce the substantive fundamental issues of cognitive psychology. It is written with the conviction that students can be introduced to cognitive psychology so that its fundamental principles are revealed in bold relief. We want to portray cognitive psychology as an exciting, problem-solving enterprise which will engage and stimulate students. To accomplish these objectives, we have chosen to discuss basic conceptual issues in detail, believing that the reporting of data makes little sense unless the problems and issues are clear. We think this approach is very important in introductory cognitive psychology where, in many cases, the conceptual issues tend to be very abstract. Empirical work, however, is thoroughly covered. Our approach is to discuss in depth selected experiments and their implications for the conceptual issues rather than attempt an exhaustive survey of the empirical literature. Again, we have found this approach to be effective when introducing students to cognitive psychology. Detailed discussion of selected experiments allows students to appreciate the intricacies of problem-solving activity in cognitive psychology. We also think students can more readily grasp the relationship between theory and data if given extensive discussion of a few experiments rather than overwhelmed with a large amount of data. Following such an introduction, students should have a firm foundation on which to build additional knowledge and understanding in advanced courses.

The book is also written with the belief that the principles of cognitive psychology should be introduced in such a way that students see their direct pertinence to and potential impact upon human affairs. Illustrations and practical applications are liberally provided, with the hope that students will gain a fuller and richer understanding of the principles as they relate them to their personal experiences. These illustrations cannot, of course, perfectly reflect principles derived from laboratory settings, but they can approximate them, and thus, we hope, lead students to think of other illustrations as well as of potential exceptions.

This book is aimed principally at the undergraduate who is taking a basic course in Cognitive Psychology, in Memory and Cognition, or in Human Memory. It would also be appropriate as a text in an introductory graduate course when the students lack a background in Cognitive Psychology or Memory. Supplementary readings can be assigned by instructors who want more detail on specific topics. The book is written so that certain chapters can be omitted without disrupting the flow of topics. In this sense, the chapters can "stand alone"; however, interconnections among the chapters are made but can be understood by the prevailing context in each chapter. Finally, the text is written for the typical one-semester or one-quarter course.

This book can be used flexibly by instructors who wish to use certain portions of it and not others. For example, if an instructor teaches a comprehensive survey of Cognitive Psychology, all chapters would be appropriate. In contrast other combinations are possible. Here are a few of the possibilities:

	Chapters
Comprehensive Cognitive Survey	1–12
Memory Survey	1, 3–7, 9
Basic Cognition	1–8
Cognition Without Language and Comprehension	1–8, 10, 12

Chapter Title
1. Introduction to Cognitive Psychology
2. Sensory Register and Pattern Recognition
3. Attention
4. Short-Term, Working Memory
5. Encoding in Long-Term Memory
6. Retrieval Processes
7. Semantic Memory
8. Categorization and Concepts
9. Comprehension and Knowledge
10. Problem Solving and Reasoning
11. Language
12. Cognition, Emotion, and Memory

We have attempted to retain a *balance* between core concepts in cognitive psychology and newer "cutting edge" materials. Over sixty new and expanded topics have been introduced in this edition while retaining the important basic findings of cognitive psychology. Fundamental findings continue to be presented; at the same time new work on important topics such as autobiographical memory (Bahrick, Neisser), eyewitness identification (Loftus, McCloskey), connectionism (McClelland & Rumelhart), implicit memory (Schacter, Graf, Jacoby, Nelson, Roediger), working memory (Baddeley), schema theory (Brewer, Graesser), problem solving and reasoning (Holyoak), mood and memory (Hertel, Seibert), flashbulb memories (Pillemer, Neisser), language (Grice, Levelt), relational and distinctive processing (Einstein, McDaniel), and reality monitoring (Johnson) are presented.

We should also note some of the teaching features of this book which we believe are important. We have, as in previous editions, adopted an informal, at times conversational, style of writing in order to capture student interest. After the first chapter, most chapters begin with a familiar story, example, or illustration that gets students to think about their mental processes. These familiar, real-world settings help students to understand new concepts and make the material interesting. Each chapter begins with an outline, recognizing the importance of themes, prior knowledge, or advance organizers in helping students to better understand the material. Each chapter also contains a summary that highlights its main features. Practice test questions (multiple-choice, true–false, and discussion) are presented at the end of each chapter, beginning with chapter 2. A handy glossary is also provided for those who need a quick refresher and an extensive bibliography is provided.

Each major chapter ends with a set of examination items and explanatory answers. Students may use these items not only for review, but also for feedback in gauging their comprehension of the material. This, however, is not their only purpose, for we hope that the test items will stimulate students to raise new questions and to engage in additional thinking about the issues. Some of the questions are relatively straightforward, whereas others present issues from a somewhat different perspective to encourage students to stretch their imagination.

At the end of the book the Glossary describes the major technical terms defined in this book. The definitions are brief and do not, of course, provide all of the potential meaning of the terms. The Glossary provides a convenient refresher for students, but should not be relied upon exclusively. The understanding of technical terms and concepts comes when students can *use* the terms in the appropriate context.

An *Instructors' Manual* that contains multiple choice questions keyed to each chapter is available for instructors. Instructors need to ask their local Wm. C. Brown sales representative for a copy.

The book is generally organized around the information-processing framework of human cognition. Here are the principal features of each chapter, including the major changes and additions for the fifth edition.

Chapter 1. Introduction to Cognitive Psychology

This chapter provides a general introduction to cognitive psychology beginning with an explanation of cognitive psychology and its objectives. This is followed by a brief history of cognitive psychology and a discussion of mental processes. The approach of cognitive psychology, using experimental methods to analyze mental processes, and using inferences to build theory, is next outlined. New material includes a discussion of the usefulness of mental models as well as their limitations. Finally, we discuss the necessity for cognitive psychology to go beyond the information processing approach, using newer more sophisticated programs, such as parallel distributed processing, to model mental processes.

Chapter 2. Sensory Register and Pattern Recognition

This chapter retains an organization similar to that in the previous edition but adds important new material. The chapter organization focuses on the major topics of functions and characteristics of the sensory register, visual and auditory sensory register including modality effects, reading disability, pattern recognition and memory, template theory, serial and parallel processing, preprocessing, analysis-by-synthesis, and connectionism and parallel distributed processing. Particular emphasis is given to new material on connectionism and neural networks. The connectionist approach, as well as the assumptions underlying parallel distributed processing, is illustrated using McClelland and Rumelhart's theory of pattern recognition.

Chapter 3. Attention

The attention chapter contains a discussion of important topics including attention and consciousness, attention and pattern recognition, filter models of attention including the classic switch model and later attenuator models, late-selection filter models, capacity models of attention, secondary task procedure, and automatic processing, including automaticity and reading and the development of automaticity. The attention chapter was extensively revised in the previous edition so only minor changes were made here.

Chapter 4. Short-Term, Working Memory

This chapter provides a review of short-term memory research and theory and updates the topic with newer developments in working memory. The concept of working memory as developed by Baddeley is fully outlined, including its relation to capacity models of attention. The working memory subsystems of an articulatory loop and a visuospatial sketchpad are described and illustrated; and working memory is contrasted with earlier views of short-term memory. Studies of STM with amnesic patients are also described. Finally, the levels of processing approach is introduced as an alternative to earlier stage models of memory.

Chapter 5. Encoding in Long-Term Memory

This chapter provides a discussion of the major topics in encoding and long-term memory and begins with the issues of memory permanence and autobiographical memory, including Bahrick's now classic studies of people's memory for high school classmates. Problems with the levels of processing approach are described including revisions involving elaboration and distinctiveness. New material on organization, relational and distinctive processing, memory for personally relevant information, the generation effect, aging and memory, imagery, and neuropsychological studies of memory, including brain scanning, are introduced.

Chapter 6. Retrieval Processes

This chapter provides an overview of memory systems, retrieval mechanisms, implicit memory, forgetting, and state dependent effects. New in this chapter is an extensive discussion of memory systems including procedural and propositional subsystems of semantic memory. A thorough description of the new and exciting developments in implicit memory is provided, including a discussion of the significance of dissociations between direct and indirect tests of memory; included is Jacoby's work on perceptual identification. Two general theoretical explanations of memory dissociations are described: memory systems explanations and processing accounts. The importance of conceptually-driven and data-driven processes, as described by Roediger and others, is discussed. Finally, the importance of automatic vs. controlled processes in retrieval is reviewed.

Chapter 7. Semantic Memory

This chapter describes the role of knowledge in governing our actions, the task of describing semantic memory, and theories of semantic memory. In addition it describes semantic memory and its relation to pattern recognition and attention, semantic and episodic memory distinctions, implicit memory, and knowledge acquisition. Implications for separate semantic memory systems stemming from implicit memory research are discussed, including the important work of Mitchell, Brown, and Murphy. The chapter ends with a new discussion of knowledge representation issues.

Chapter 8. Categorization and Concepts

This chapter contains a description of types of concepts, the importance of natural concepts, the variety of categories, theories of categorization, and practical principles in forming concepts. A major new section on theories of categorization is introduced, including attribute, prototype, and exemplar theory. Priming and context effects in categorization are discussed, including the role of inductive inferences in categorization. The role of linguistic factors in forming categories, perceptual and semantic categories, family resemblances and basic-level categories is described. Finally, the material on traditional concept identification studies has been substantially reduced. This chapter has been moved so that it immediately follows the chapter on semantic memory in order that related issues are more easily seen by the student.

Chapter 9. Comprehension and Knowledge

This chapter retains its broad coverage of major topics in comprehension. The chapter has principal sections on integration and themes in comprehension, presuppositions and inferences, locus of constructive processes, schemas in comprehension and memory, schema theory, and prior knowledge and text processing. New material includes the role of presuppositions in eyewitness testimony, response bias and memory integration interpretations of eyewitness testimony research, including Loftus' and McCloskey's views, developments in schema theory including Brewer's and Graesser's theoretical approaches, and a useful student-oriented summary of schema theory. Finally, the role of knowledge in priming effects and reading comprehension is discussed.

Chapter 10. Problem Solving and Reasoning

This chapter provides the range of topics typical of research and theory on problem solving and reasoning. The importance of mental representation, stages in problem solving, processes in problem solving, practical tips on problem solving, theories of problem solving, and major issues in reasoning are discussed. Seven new topics are introduced in this chapter: creativity and evaluation, brainstorming and creativity, ill-defined problems, experts and novices, analogical reasoning, problem solving in the classroom, and reasoning errors.

Chapter 11. Language

The language chapter contains the same general structure as in the previous edition with four major sections dealing with the function of language, the structure of language, processes in language, and issues in language. However, it has undergone a thorough revision and updating including removal of some of the older topics. Important new material is found in the topics of speech acts and intentions, fuzzy boundaries in language and the role of word meaning, context and language, language production and Grice's maxims, and language and the brain, including brain disorders such as aphasia.

Chapter 12. Cognition, Emotion, and Memory

This chapter has the same general structure as in the previous edition but has a number of new topics. The chapter is organized around four main issues: the importance of cognition and emotion, experimental findings in mood and memory, theoretical interpretations, and specific issues in emotion and cognition. New topics in the chapter include research on the importance of focused attention in eliminating depressive deficits in memory, the role of irrelevant thoughts in explaining mood and memory effects, the role of emotional states in eyewitness testimony, flashbulb memory, personal memories, and anxiety and performance.

ACKNOWLEDGMENTS

We are indebted to many persons in the preparation of the fifth edition of *Fundamentals of Cognitive Psychology*. We wish to thank the following individuals who either carefully reviewed the fifth edition or who made very helpful suggestions in preparing the fifth edition. We especially thank Paul Amrhein who assisted us in the revision of the language chapter:

Paul Amrhein, *University of New Mexico*
Jane Ann Ausley, *University of North Carolina*
Gilles Einstein, *Furman University*
Paul Foos, *Florida International University*
Danalee Goldthwaite, *Cariboo College*
David Gorfein, *Adelphi University*
Paula Hertel, *Trinity University*
David Horton, *University of Maryland*
Stanley Klein, *University of California, Santa Barbara*
David Mitchell, *Southern Methodist University*
Douglas Nelson, *University of South Florida*
Roddy Roediger, *Rice University*
Pennie Seibert, *Boise State University*
Jeff Toth, *McMaster University*

In addition, we wish to thank the following individuals who have provided either useful feedback regarding previous editions, or who have thoroughly reviewed one of the previous editions or one or more chapters. We continue to appreciate all of their earlier suggestions.

Paul Amrhein, *University of New Mexico*
Janet Andrews, *Vassar College*
Jane Ann Ausley, *University of North Carolina*
Bernard Barrs, *SUNY, Stony Brook*
Brian Babbitt, *Missouri Southern College*

Charles Brewer, *Furman University*

Bruce Britton, *University of Georgia*

Fergus Craik, *University of Toronto*

Robert Crowder, *Yale University*

Tony DeCasper, *University of North Carolina*

Terry Daniel, *University of Arizona*

Harold Delaney, *University of New Mexico*

Gilles Einstein, *Furman University*

Paul Foos, *Florida International University*

William Gordon, *University of New Mexico*

Paula Hertel, *Trinity University*

Marcia Johnson, *Princeton University*

Peder Johnson, *University of New Mexico*

William Johnston, *University of Utah*

Joseph LaVoie, *University of Nebraska*

Leah Light, *Pitzer College*

Cheryl Logan, *University of North Carolina*

Frank Logan, *University of New Mexico*

Ruth Maki, *North Dakota State University*

Marc Marschark, *University of North Carolina*

David Mitchell, *Southern Methodist University*

John Mueller, *University of Missouri*

Jean Newman, *University of New Mexico*

Marcia Ozier, *Dalhousie University*

Frederick Parenté, *Towson State University*

James Pate, *Georgia State University*

Stan Parkinson, *Arizona State University*

Michael Scavio, *California State University, Fullerton*

Steven Schmidt, *Virginia Polytechnic Institute and State University*

Ronald Shaffer, *Western Washington University*

Blair Stone, *University of Utah*

Sherman Tyler, *University of Pittsburgh,* and

Eugene Winograd, *Emory University*

The people at Brown and Benchmark provided superb support and assistance throughout this project. We were especially fortunate in having the support and cooperation of a first-rate staff who were also encouraging and enthusiastic. We especially thank Ann Schaffer and Sheralee Connors, our editors, who have done everything possible to make our association with Brown and Benchmark Publishers an enjoyable experience. We also thank Kay Driscoll, production editor, who oversaw the complex job of getting the book through production and handled all of the numerous details that arose in this job. We thank Carla Aspelmeier, product manager, who did a superior job in preparing materials, and Michael Lange, senior editor, whose help was always available.

The secretarial staffs at the University of New Mexico and the University of North Carolina not only contributed their word-processing expertise but also gave us frequent words of encouragement. We are especially grateful to Mary Hungate, department editor, University of New Mexico and Rosemarie Andrews and Grace Martin, secretaries at North Carolina, for their help. Their skill and patience are most appreciated. Finally, we thank the students in our cognitive psychology classes who read and commented on earlier drafts of the manuscript.

1

INTRODUCTION TO COGNITIVE PSYCHOLOGY

The book that you are about to read describes some of the major issues and problems currently addressed in contemporary psychology. More specifically, the topics described in this book have arisen from a particular perspective on psychology which is known as *cognitive psychology*. The sole function of chapter 1 is to give you an orientation to this topic.

What is cognitive psychology? In part, this is a question we hope to answer throughout the book, but a preliminary discussion of the question will be helpful in gaining a perspective on what you are about to read.

Perhaps the most direct answer to the question is that *cognitive psychology is the study of mental process*. Several questions are begged by this answer such as what we mean by "study" and "mental processes." We shall answer these questions in this chapter. But the questioning might begin with the more fundamental issue of why do psychologists study mental processes.

Since the beginning of recorded history, people have expressed curiosity about the operation of the mind, largely because they believed that behavior, particularly voluntary action, is the result of mental processes. For example, how are we to understand the very behavior in which you are engaged at this moment, reading this book? At one level, we are interested in explaining your ability to comprehend what you are reading and in so doing, we are likely to appeal to processes of perception of words and computation of meaning. At another level, we might explain your motivation for reading in terms of your goals to complete this course which in turn is motivated by your goal of obtaining a college degree in order to follow some plan that you have for a career. The point is that your behavior of reading this book is determined in part by your intent to meet some goal and fulfill some plan. *Intentionality, goals,* and *plans* are mental phenomena that affect behavior. Further, the specific behavior, in this case reading, is understood by appeal to specific mental processes involved in perception and comprehension of text. In short, the study of mental processes is important because these processes are responsible for much of the behavior we find interesting.

Whose mental processes are studied? For much of the previously mentioned recorded history, the answer to this question simply would be normal, adult humans. Non-human animals were denied mental processes for a variety of reasons, the most famous of which is Descartes' argument that they lack language and therefore lack minds. Although it has not disappeared entirely, this species bias is on the wane today. Aspects of behavior of various species ranging from apes to bees are being subjected to cognitive analyses by animal behaviorists, and the exciting prospect of a true comparative cognition looms on the immediate horizon. Humans are biological creatures, and what we learn about other animals' minds may be important not only to our understanding of those animals, but for evolutionary reasons, also to an understanding of our minds. Nonetheless, the research we cover in this book derives from humans. Within human psychology, however, the study of mental processes should not be constrained by age or some definition of normality. Much can be learned from developmental analyses of cognitive functioning. Questions about how people of various ages perceive, comprehend, and remember are essential to understanding the establishment and change in mental processes. Moreover, similar questions about clinical populations are invaluable sources of information. An understanding of the normal operation of the mind is enhanced by observations of mental dysfunction. Consequently, we shall appeal to research from developmental and clinical studies throughout the book. Although much of the focus of this book is the normal, human adult, a full understanding of mental processes ultimately reaches into the study of other human populations and even other species.

Your appreciation for the activity of cognitive psychology can be increased by consideration of a few examples of everyday experiences that are also of theoretical interest to cognitive psychologists. Have you noticed the difficulty of simultaneously taking notes in class and understanding a lecture? How many times have you carefully proofread written work only to be embarrassed later by an obvious error you overlooked? When you dial Directory Assistance for a telephone number and do not have a pencil to record the number, why do you have to repeat the number until you have dialed it? And why do you have to repeat your call to Directory Assistance if someone talks to you before you dial the number? You may have heard a television commercial for aspirin claim, "You cannot buy a more effective pain reliever than our brand." Later you remember that this brand is the most effective pain reliever you can buy. Your memory of what was claimed is actually quite different from the assertion made by the commercial, a point we will address later in the book. Do you remember the experience of working on a problem or a puzzle which you were unable to solve, but after taking a break from the problem, you subsequently obtained a solution? These are just a few of the many examples of everyday experiences which are discussed throughout this book and which are directly relevant to the experiments and theory of cognitive psychology.

Two points about these examples should be considered as we attempt to gain an overview of cognitive psychology. First, all represent instances of difficulty or failure of mental processes. Interestingly, we tend to treat our mental functions or processes the same way we treat our automobile: We rarely think of them unless they fail to work. Failures of mental processes are immediately noticed because they can be frustrating, embarrassing, and sometimes even dangerous, and consequently, such failures become useful tools for the psychological analysis of mental phenomena. You should be alerted, however, to the fact that most of the analysis focuses upon the *successful* operation of the mental processes. Probably we tend to appreciate the successes less than we notice a failure, but adaptive success of the human intellectual machinery far exceeds its failure.

The second point is that cognitive psychology is interested in what is generally called *mental phenomena*. In this sense, the examples just discussed are consistent with the dictionary definition of cognitive psychology: "the scientific study of the mind." While it is hoped that the examples help clarify the definition, questions undoubtedly remain concerning how one goes about this "scientific study of mind." Such questions can be addressed by closely examining what is meant by *mind* and *scientific study*. Perhaps the best way to approach these issues is by briefly describing the historical origins of cognitive psychology.

A BRIEF HISTORY OF COGNITIVE PSYCHOLOGY

Psychology began as a scientific study of human knowledge and experience. The problem of what knowledge is has intrigued philosophers for centuries, and the formation of a separate discipline of psychology was marked by the application of experimental methods to the problem of knowledge. This "problem of knowledge" is an involved issue, but here is one example. As strange as it may seem, the certainty of your sensory "knowledge" is not at all clear. For example, can you be sure that the book you are reading is really there? What a stupid question, you may think; but consider the problem. The information you have about the book arises from the reaction of your receptors to the physical energy from the environment. The receptors then begin a process of nervous transmission to the brain where the interpretation of the physical energy culminates. So what you really "know" is that a certain pattern of activity occurred in the brain, not that a book is really there. Sometimes the interpretive processes are "fooled" as in the case of perceptual illusions, in which case what you see is not what is "really" there. The general point here is that what we "know" consists of our own perceptual or mental processes.

The first psychologists believed, just as you and I believe, that the physical energy from the environment is related to mental processes, or what we know. Consequently, psychology began as the experimental study of relationships between the environmental energy or stimuli and mental processes. Experiments generally involved manipulating some aspect of the environment in the form of a simple stimulus event followed by the subjects' report of their mental or psychological experience. The goal of psychology was to provide a theoretical description of the mind. In some cases, this took the form of trying to decide what elements make up the *structure* of the mind. In other words, what are the elements of psychological experience? Another important question focused on the operation of the mental processes. What can we learn about the processes of perceiving, attending, remembering, and thinking?

These early psychologists were then trying to provide a theory of mental elements and processes in much the same way that early physicists and chemists were developing theories of the elements of matter and the processes which affect matter. However, in the history of psychology, some theorists very quickly became impatient with this approach and set about to redirect the course of psychology. Rather than view psychology as the study of *mental experience,* these researchers shifted the subject matter to *overt behavior.* The champions of this new approach called themselves *behavioristic psychologists* and emphasized the idea that the proper study of psychology deals with directly observable behavior. Their primary concern was that mental processes cannot be reliably observed, and consequently the results of experiments are not always consistent. Since the cornerstone of the new science of psychology was the experimental approach, the lack of consistency in experimental outcomes was a serious problem. The proposed solution to this dilemma was to abandon the study of mental processes and to direct the effort toward something that can be measured reliably. That something was overt behavior, and by studying the relationship between environmental events and behavior, the behavioristic psychologists hoped to understand why human beings do what they do, without reference to mental processes. All of these fundamental conflicts arose between 1879 and 1920.

By 1930, however, some psychologists had begun to argue that even simple overt behavior cannot be understood without some reference to mental processes. In other words, the door was opened, at least partly, for the mental processes to become again the focus of interest in psychology. For example, consider the phenomenon known as the *goal gradient.* One instance of this phenomenon can be observed when a hungry rat learns to run down an alley to obtain food. The *goal gradient* refers to the observation that the rat runs faster the closer it gets to the goal. Why is this true? One straightforward explanation is that the animal "expects" to receive food, and the expectation becomes stronger the closer the rat gets to the goal. But *expectation* is a psychological concept, not an overt behavior. If expectation is necessary to the understanding of the behavior, we are then back to the study of psychological processes. At this point we are talking about a simple observation, even for rat behavior. Imagine how much more complex is the understanding of human behavior such as the use of memory or language.

Beginning in the 1950s, a variety of events occurred which led to a renewed and vitalized cognitive psychology. It is beyond the scope of this book to capture all this history, and interested persons are referred to an excellent treatment of the history by Lachman, Lachman, and Butterfield

(1979). A few highlights can be noted here. First, British psychologists interested in applied problems began to develop theories of human performance and attention. A leader in this movement was Broadbent (1958) who developed an early model of how human attention works. Other psychologists such as Miller, Galanter, and Pribram (1960) sounded a clarion call for "a new theoretical approach" to psychology which would allow for the study of plans, images, and other mental processes. In the same year in his presidential address to the American Psychological Association, Hebb (1960), described what he called "the American Revolution," a resurgence of interest in mental processes and cognitive psychology. Renewed interest in mental processes such as imagery (Paivio, 1969), search and scan processes in short-term memory (Sternberg, 1966), and organizational processes in memory (Mandler, 1967; Bower, 1970) served to bring cognitive psychology to the forefront. Developments in other areas of science also accelerated this trend. Rapid changes in linguistics, computer science, ethology, and other areas complemented developments in cognitive psychology. These changes can be but briefly sketched here. The important point to note is that the ferment and excitement during the period from roughly 1957 through 1970 led to renewed interest in cognitive psychology.

For the foregoing reasons psychology has again shifted course and returned to some of the earlier questions regarding the nature of *mental structures and processes*. Although the basic questions are quite similar to those of the early psychologists, the approach has changed in many respects. Among the more important changes are the conceptualization of mental processes and the techniques used to study these processes. The breath and scope of these issues are clearly revealed in such works as those of Izawa (1989), Roediger and Craik (1989) and many others. Moreover, the range of applications of cognitive psychology are fully portrayed in Izawa (in press).

MIND AND MENTAL PROCESSING

With minor exception, psychology has consisted of the scientific investigation of mental processes, as our brief review of the history indicates. To this point, however, all discussion of what psychologists mean by *mind* has been avoided. The current view of most cognitive psychologists is that *mind* and *mental processes* are ways of describing brain activity. That is, human mental functioning is not a mysterious, nonphysical event, but rather is the activity of the brain. Of course, brain activity can be studied physiologically, but cognitive psychologists use a different approach. Since the brain activity of interest cannot be directly observed (for example, we have no idea what happens in the brain when a person remembers a grandmother), we must infer the existence of these processes and then describe the processes in abstract language. Let us look more closely at these two aspects of the method cognitive psychologists use.

Approach of Cognitive Psychology

Cognitive psychology proceeds with its study of mental functioning through the scientific method, which is just a way of trying to solve problems through a combination of thinking and data gathering. Thinking is typically known as a theoretical enterprise and data gathering is accomplished by experiments. The exercise begins with an idea or theory about how a particular mental process works. The idea or theory contains certain implications, so that if the idea or theory is reasonable, then certain other events should follow. An experiment can then be set up to see whether these events actually do happen.

For example, consider one of the problems mentioned earlier: Why is it so hard to simultaneously take notes and understand a lecture? One theory suggests it is because we can attend to only one thing at a time, and when we are attending to one event, the information about other events is completely ignored. One implication of this theory is that when attending to one event, a person should have no memory of other events. As we shall see, experiments can be set up to approximate this situation and allow us to determine the validity of this particular theoretical idea.

An important aspect of the scientific process is inference; in this context inference is perhaps best defined as educated guessing. A situation in which we know the surrounding circumstances is established, and then the behavior of the person in this situation is observed. Based on our knowledge of the circumstances plus our observations of the behavior, we infer or guess what types of processes the person must use in order to respond in that fashion. The method is not unlike the problem-solving activity of everyday life. Suppose you try to start your car and it refuses to start. Those of us who are not mechanics usually try to isolate the problem through a series of observations allowing us to infer the nature of the problem. Is there gas in the tank? If the answer is yes, are the lights and radio functioning? If they are not, perhaps the problem is electrical. This sort of activity is continued until all possibilities are exhausted. Note that we often learn a great deal about the problem even though we may not have the vaguest notion of precise automobile mechanics. The work of inferring the nature of mental processes based on observations of overt behavior proceeds in much the same way.

An important aspect of this analogy is the knowledge we have about the system before we try to solve a particular problem. In the case of automobiles, most of us do know a little something about operating an automobile, like the necessity of fuel and electricity. But in the case of the human brain, so little is known that our ideas about what might be going on are based on *models*. A *model* is something we understand which seems to function similarly to the object we are trying to understand. In other words, we take what we know about the model and ask: Does the brain work in a similar fashion? One type of model is borrowed from the computer.

The Computer Model and Information Processing

Psychology has always used models as a means for understanding its subject matter. Freud proposed a hydraulic model of mental processes, and the behaviorists have long used a model of stimulus and response (adapted from physiology), just to name two. For the last thirty years, however, the computer has emerged as a prominent model for psychological processes. The computer is an appealing model for human cognitive processes because the computer accomplishes many of the intellectual tasks ascribed to cognitive functioning. The computer accepts incoming information, stores that information for further use, and uses it later for computation in solving problems.

The analogy between the general framework of computer functioning and human cognitive functioning is obvious. People take information in the form of environmental energy and store it for later use. Just as input is transformed into machine language, incoming information from the environment, we can reasonably assume, undergoes important transformations. We know that the brain cannot use electromagnetic energy, which is the physical energy involved in light. Electromagnetic energy is transformed into chemical energy and then into electrical energy in the course of transmission from the eye to the brain. The storage function of the computer is analogous to the process we normally think of as memory. The stored information can later be retrieved, used to solve a problem, and then expressed as output from the computer. Again, the analogy with a search process and problem-solving activities in human beings is striking.

Using the computer as a model, however, is far from suggesting that the human brain works like a computer. The brain processes which correspond to such activities as perception, memory, thinking, and language are much more complex than any existing computer. Rather, the computer model provides a general way of thinking about human cognitive functioning. This general framework is known as information processing. The basic model is depicted in figure 1.1. As you can see, in figure 1.1 cognition can be divided into three components: input processing, storage, and output. Although it is convenient to think of these components as sequential stages, this need not always be the case. For example, in figure 1.1 feedback from long-term memory to the perceptual processes is indicated. The three components may all contribute to ongoing activity at any point in time. Regardless, the information-processing approach is a very useful tool in the analysis of human cognitive functioning.

As useful as the information processing approach has been in generating ideas about the mind, a variety of criticisms and concerns have been raised about the computer model. Perhaps the most aggressive arguments are those of Herbert Dreyfus in his book, *What Computers Can't Do* (1979).

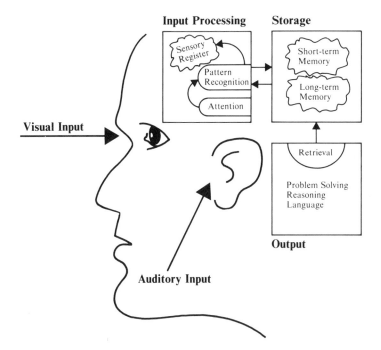

Figure 1.1 Sequence of information processing.

These arguments range from concerns about the relative inability of any computer program to perform general cognitive functions such as "understanding" to philosophical concerns about the relationship between levels of descriptive analysis. For example, the information processing approach might describe a situation as beginning with "olfactory stimulus input" that is "processed" and gives rise to the perception of "chocolate-chip cookies." Dreyfus' provocative argument is that this description seduces you to feel as if something has been explained when in fact it has not. Olfactory stimulus input literally is in the form of certain molecules that contact certain receptors in the nose. These receptors respond with electrical impulses that are transmitted in and responded to by the central nervous system. Where and how does the very real experience of smelling chocolate-chip cookies arise?

While critics such as Dreyfus argue that the computer is a bad model for the mind, a weaker criticism is that the model is not useful for some of the questions of interest. For example, a central issue in psychology is the function of consciousness, but is a computer conscious? If not, it cannot provide ideas about the function of consciousness; that is, the computer would be irrelevant to the question. Since the computer is not a biological entity and humans are, many important issues about the human mind may resist computer modelling.

Another important point is that ultimately all *models* in science are wrong. Very simply, a model is an analogy; it is not identical to the thing to be studied. Since the two things are not identical, differences exist between them. It is in this sense that the model is ultimately wrong. The computer and the mind may share some analogous operations, but ultimately they are two different things. Therefore, a complete understanding of the mind requires going beyond the computer model, just as it would with any other model.

As you read this book, you will see two reactions to these concerns about the computer model. One reaction is that our thinking needs to go beyond the information processing approach and base research on some other idea. The second reaction is to continue to use the computer model but to use much more complex and sophisticated programs to model the mind. Our discussion of parallel-distributed processing in chapter 2 is an example of this development. Thus, in spite of concerns about the computer model, some psychologists believe that advances in technology and information science are producing computers and programs that circumvent many of the criticisms and provide useful models. Regardless, as an educated person, the important point for you to understand is that the mind is not literally a computer and that there are probably important aspects of mental function that are beyond the capability of computer functioning. Nonetheless, you will see that the information processing approach has provided a number of useful ideas for cognitive psychology.

The Importance of Memory

Memory is the heart of human intellectual functioning and, consequently, is ubiquitous in the information-processing model. Memory is much more than a static storage bin of facts; indeed, the storage function, while important, is much less interesting than the dynamic functions served by memory. Ellis (1987) illustrates this point by encouraging you to imagine life without memory. Of course, without memory you would be completely incapacitated in the working world, unable to function in even the simplest situation and unable to communicate coherently with your colleagues. Much more serious, however, is the fact that your social life would be nonexistent. You would have no friends because you would not be able to recall a person or anything about that person from one encounter to the next. Most devastating would be the lack of personal identity or self-concept. With no memory for prior personal experiences, how could continuity exist such that you could answer the question "Who am I?" You literally would confront a stranger in the mirror.

Ellis (1987) notes an extremely important implication of memory loss which you may not have considered but which underscores the centrality of memory to human behavior. With no memory for the past, you would have no basis for predicting the future. We are not talking about crystal balls, but rather the commonplace phenomenon of setting goals and planning your actions toward those goals. You probably have some idea of what you are going to do when you finish reading this chapter. With no access to the past, you would not be capable of even this mundane level of planning, let alone grandiose schemes for your future. If you think about it for a moment, almost all your plans are based upon some experience you have had, and with no memory of that experience, development of plans would be impossible.

Endel Tulving (1985) reports a conversation that he had with a densely amnesic patient who had suffered severe head injury. The patient was incapable of remembering information for any extensive period of time, but of interest to Ellis's point about the future is the patient's response when Tulving asked him what he planned to do after the interview. The patient replied that he did not know what he would do. Tulving asked the patient to think about it, but still no plan came to mind. When asked what his mind was like when he thought about what he was going to do, the patient replied that it was very much like an empty room, a room with no furniture. Tulving's fascinating interview confirms the importance of memory not just as a repository of the past, but as an important basis for making plans for the future, plans which are essential to guiding our behavior.

You will see in this book the central role of memory in various aspects of normal behavior. As shown in figure 1.1, memory assists in the perception of your world and is an indispensable tool in reasoning and solving the problems confronting you daily.

OVERVIEW OF THE BOOK

This book begins with the origin of the information processing sequence, at that point of contact between the physical energy from the environment and the organism's receptors. The *sensory register,* the first concept discussed, stores the information received by the receptors. The sensory register is a memory system, but one whose properties are very different from those of long-term memory; the information lasts for a very brief period, and more important, the information has not been processed for meaning at this early stage. Consequently, the next step in the flow of information is meaningful processing. This processing is represented by the concept of *pattern recognition,* which extracts the information from the sensory store and matches that information with a representation in long-term memory. When this process is completed, the information has been recognized; that is, we know what it is. In this sense, the incoming information attains meaning.

It is important to realize, however, that not all of the information reaching the sensory register can be processed in pattern recognition. One consequence is that some process must guide or focus pattern recognition in selecting information. This function is served by the concept of *attention,* the process which determines which information will be processed in situations where all of the available information cannot be processed. As we shall see, a number of such situations arise involving processes in addition to pattern recognition. This discussion implies that human beings can do only one thing at a time, but we shall also see that this is an important and controversial assumption. How limited is the information-processing system?

The primary storage mechanisms in human information processing are the *short-term memory* and *long-term memory* systems. Some people think that memory for recent events operates differently than does long-term memory. Research thought to show structural differences between short- and long-term memory is discussed, and an argument that such distinctions may not be useful is presented. However, the need for a concept like short-term memory, in large part to understand the limitations of conscious thought, is also emphasized.

Included in the discussion of long-term memory are a number of important general issues, all of which focus upon the factors producing good memory. For example, what are the best circumstances for experiencing or studying something? This is a question of input processing, as are all of the concepts discussed to this point. Additional points are raised, however, including organization and distinctiveness.

Information in long-term memory is useful only if it is accessed, or retrieved. Thus, chapter 6 is devoted to understanding the process of getting to information in long-term memory.

The structure of long-term memory is also an important issue, and chapter 7 on semantic memory describes current research and thinking on the organization of knowledge stored in long-term memory.

Once information is accessed in memory, it may be used in a variety of ways. Chapters 8 through 12 discuss some of these situations. In particular, the processes of comprehension, language, concept formation and categorization, problem solving and cognition and emotion are considered. Thus, this book is designed to introduce you to the theory and research of cognitive psychology from the initial reception of information to the complex utilization of that information.

SUMMARY

Cognitive psychology is the scientific study of mental processes. Although psychology historically was established as a discipline devoted to such study, confusion concerning the meaning of *mental processes* diverted attention from the original goal. With the contemporary view that mental processes are synonymous with brain processes, psychology has returned to its original mission. Cognitive psychology proceeds through a combination of theory and experiment, as does all of science. Observations of performance are used to infer the psychological processes which must be necessary to produce the performance. With the help of the computer model, the cognitive psychologist develops ideas about the most important and interesting questions facing science: the structure and function of mental processes which account for human behavior.

2

SENSORY REGISTER AND PATTERN RECOGNITION

In chapter 2 the initial stages of information processing, beginning with the activation of sense organs by physical energy from the environment, are discussed. The goal is to understand how physical energy is translated to psychological experience. For example, visual recognition of an object is based upon the physical energy of light. Yet, the physical description of light waves bears little resemblance to the psychological experience of the object we see. The light waves are precategorical, which means that the physical energy has not been categorized or has no meaning. Psychological processes must interact with this physical energy in order to add meaning to sensory experiences. The following example helps clarify this point.

Imagine that you are playing a variation of the old game twenty questions. The game is very simple: one player describes an object to another player who must guess the object from the description. In our special version of the game, however, your description must be limited to the way the object looks. You can provide as cues only the visual attributes of the object. Does this sound simple? Try to describe an apple using only the properties which are available to vision so that another person will be able to guess that you are describing an apple. Do not use attributes which cannot be seen such as *tart, juicy, crunchy,* or *fruit.* This exercise will probably demonstrate that just providing the visual description of a common object is difficult enough, and that a person attempting to guess what the object is will probably require several tries. When we recognize an object in the environment, the information-processing sequence begins with the same type of raw sensory information. Nonetheless, we rarely experience difficulty in moving from sensory information to full identification of a familiar object. How does this commonplace but remarkable event occur? This example illustrates the central issue of *pattern recognition,* translating patterns of sensory signals into psychological experiences of recognizable objects. Before pattern recognition is considered, however, we must discuss the first step in information processing, the *sensory register.*

Let us return to the example of the modified twenty questions game. Why is it so difficult to identify an object when cues are based solely on visual description of that object? The difficulty is due, at least in part, to the fact that visual properties do not exhaust the *meaning* of an object. Indeed, the visual properties alone have very little meaning in the sense of precisely specifying an object for someone else. When we extract meaning from visual experience, we actually add information to that experience. For example, the visual properties of an apple somehow activate other knowledge of apples, such as their taste and smell and abstract information such as apples are fruit. This constellation of information then constitutes the meaning of apple, and activation of this information allows us to identify the visual experience as apple. Notice that we have now moved far beyond the visual information initially provided to the retina of the eye.

Critical for our present purpose is the realization that the enrichment of sensory information takes time. In the twenty questions game, some amount of time is obviously required to guess the object being described. During this time, the guesser is searching for objects which meet the description. Although visual information processing rarely requires such a lengthy period of deliberation, some real time elapses between reception of visual information and recognition of the object represented by that information. If this point is understood, the function of the sensory register is easily grasped.

THE SENSORY REGISTER

The sensory register is a memory system designed to store a record of the information received by receptor cells. Receptor cells are the specialized sense organs of the eye, ear, nose, tongue, and skin which respond to physical energy from the environment. Firing of the receptor cells begins the psychological processes of sight, hearing, smell, taste, and feeling. Once these receptor cells have been activated, the record of this activation is preserved or stored on the sensory registers. The stored record is known as the *sensory trace.*

Unlike the short-term and long-term memory traces, the contents of the sensory register are not open to introspection. That is, we cannot reflect upon and, indeed, are unaware of the sensory trace. You can gain, however, an appreciation for the existence of the sensory trace with the following exercise. Ball up your fist and then extend and contract your fingers as rapidly as possible. As you do this, watch your fingertips. If you observe carefully, you will see your fingers extended while they are already on the way back to making a fist again. You must observe carefully, because you will be able to see this for only a very brief period. You are seeing a record of what happened previously. Your fingers are no longer extended, but you still see them in that position. The visual system is responding to the memory or sensory trace of a previous event.

Information processing thus begins with the activation of sensory receptors, and this pattern of activity is stored in a memory system, the sensory register. Some persons think it is strange that the initial stages of information processing includes a memory system. Why do we need to store or maintain the sensory trace? Why not assume that the processing of receptor activity begins immediately, without the necessity for storage? Actually, the concept of the sensory register serves a very specific function.

Function of the Sensory Register

To understand why the sensory register is assumed to be important, let us again return to the example of the twenty questions game. Guessing the identity of an object from its visual description takes time. We now assume that "guessing" an object from the receptor activity also takes time. That is, processing the sensory information for meaning, adding information to the sensory pattern, is not accomplished instantaneously. Furthermore, we assume that we are limited in our ability to process multiple patterns of sensory information. In other words, we can determine the meaning of only one sensory pattern at a time. Imagine the impossibility of *simultaneously* guessing the identity of two objects from two different visual descriptions in the twenty questions game. These two assumptions now demand that we have a sensory register.

To understand this point, suppose that you are actually looking at an apple. While you are interpreting the information corresponding to "apple," a worm pokes its head out of the apple for a fraction of a second. The physical energy corresponding to the worm activates the sensory receptors, but the processing system is occupied interpreting the previous information corresponding to apple. What happens to the information about the worm? Does it simply fade away without being interpreted? Obviously such a situation would be very maladaptive; in this example, we would never know that the worm is in the apple. Of course, other more catastrophic events than eating a worm would result if we were unable to process much of the sensory information impinging upon the receptors. What is needed is a buffer or holding bin for the sensory information until the interpretive processes are free. This, then, is the function of the sensory register.

The sensory register maintains sensory information until other cognitive processes are capable of interpreting or adding meaning to it. With this initial memory system, we avoid losing present information while we are processing information which has just occurred. Each sensory modality has a corresponding sensory register, but in human beings the most widely studied systems are vision and audition.

The need for a sensory memory may be more acute in audition. For example, when we comprehend conversation, the extraction of meaning lags behind the rate of speech. That is, we do not compute the meaning of each word as it is spoken, but rather speech continues while we are determining the meaning of what was just said. Unless some means for storing the ongoing speech was available, we would lose much of what is currently being said while we determine the meaning of what was just said. The auditory sensory register then serves the purpose of briefly holding information which cannot be immediately processed.

The sensory register thus functions to maintain sensory information until it can be processed, but as we shall now see, this function can be served only if the sensory register has certain characteristics.

Characteristics of the Sensory Register

Three important characteristics of the sensory register allow the system to serve its storage function optimally. First, the information is stored in a *veridical* form. This simply means that the information stored should accurately reflect what happened at the sensory receptor. The second important characteristic is that the sensory register needs to be *relatively large*, at least large enough to store all of the information impinging on the sensory receptor. Both of these characteristics are necessary because the sensory trace is precategorical. The information has no meaning at this stage, so it must *all* be preserved in its *veridical* form to allow subsequent interpretation. Otherwise, the primary function of the sensory register, holding information for processing, would be defeated. The third important characteristic is that the information remain on the sensory register for a *brief* time. Since the sensory register stores all information from the sensory receptors and the receptors are continually receiving information, the sensory register must be cleared quickly to avoid superimposing information from two exposures. For example, the information on the visual sensory register would be blurred if two scenes were registered in quick succession. The resulting image would be difficult to interpret, much as a photographic double exposure supplies blurred images. One conceivable means of avoiding this problem is a rapid decay time for sensory memory. A second way in which the superimposition of two discrete events can be avoided is for the second event to erase the first. Incoming information might displace the existing information on the sensory register. These two mechanisms, rapid decay time and erasure, could clear the sensory register of old information to allow vivid representation of information.

Experiments have provided evidence for each of the three characteristics listed here. Since these studies provide the primary evidence for the sensory register, it is important that these experiments be discussed.

Size and Duration of the Sensory Register

Sperling's (1960) research on the visual sensory register illustrates the technique and data used to argue for the large but brief memory system we call a sensory register. Sperling's work is important not only because it addresses the size and duration of the sensory register, but also because it provides clever solutions to several difficult methodological problems. Understanding these problems and Sperling's solutions to them will help you understand the sensory register.

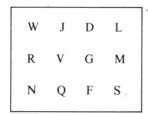

Figure 2.1 Example of a letter matrix used in a partial report experiment.

The first problem was the presentation of the to-be-remembered material. Since the sensory register stores information directly from the sensory receptors, a pure test of the system would measure retention from a single activation of the receptors. But how can material be presented such that the receptors are activated only once? In vision, the eyeball tremors or moves every one-fourth of a second to prevent a single receptor from receiving constant stimulation. The answer to this question is to present the to-be-remembered material at a rate more rapid than that of eye movement. Sperling presented the materials for 50 milliseconds (1 millisecond = 1/1,000 seconds), a rate you can approximate by closing your eyes and then opening and closing them again as rapidly as possible. In order to have such rapid presentation, special equipment is necessary to provide precise timing and to ensure that the subject is fixating upon the point at which the materials will appear. The stimulus materials were matrices of consonants, containing either nine or twelve letters. As you can see in figure 2.1, the matrices were arranged in three rows of three or four letters each.

With the issue of how to present the material resolved, Sperling could measure what a person remembers from a single glance at a letter matrix. Now, however, a second serious problem arises which basically questions the need for such an experiment. Prior to Sperling's research, it was a well-known fact that people could remember only about four letters from a set of nine or twelve letters. These data are inconsistent with expectations based on the sensory register. If all of the information from the receptors is stored on the sensory register, memory should be virtually perfect. Sperling argued, however, that the temporal characteristics of the sensory register prevent human beings from demonstrating how much information is actually available.

The sensory trace is assumed to fade from memory very rapidly, and consequently the time required to report a few items is sufficient to allow decay of the remainder of the sensory register. The problem now becomes one of demonstrating that subjects have perfect memory for the letter matrix without asking them to recall all of the letters.

The ingenious answer Sperling provided to this problem is based on a technique used by most teachers in assessing what students have learned. Rather than to ask for recall of all of the material, a procedure known as *whole report,* a person can be asked to report only part of the material. If the person does not know which part of the material will be tested, the only sure way to do well on the tested material is to know all of the material. Thus, the teacher can assume that the student's performance on the tested part of the material reflects knowledge of all the material.

The procedure just described is known as the *partial report technique* because the subject has to report only part of the information. Sperling used the partial report technique in the following manner. The letter matrix was shown for 50 milliseconds, and immediately upon termination of the matrix, a tone sounded. The tone was either high, medium, or low frequency and served as a signal for which row to report. The high tone indicated that the top row of letters was to be reported, the middle tone signaled the middle row, and the low tone signaled the bottom row. Thus, only one row of letters was reported on any trial, but the subject didn't know which row to report until the matrix disappeared. Thus, the responses had to be based on memory for the matrix.

With this procedure, Sperling found that the subjects were quite accurate, remembering almost 100 percent of a nine-letter matrix and about 75 percent of a twelve-letter matrix. With both nine- and twelve-letter matrices, the partial report technique suggests that the subjects have approximately nine letters available on the sensory register. This is a marked contrast to the whole report procedure where subjects are asked to recall the entire matrix, and they remember only three or four letters. The higher level of memory in the partial report condition suggests that all of the information in the matrix was available immediately on cessation of the stimulus, just as the reasoning about the sensory register suggests that it should be. Moreover, the difference in performance between partial and whole report performances suggests that the information in visual sensory memory decays very rapidly.

This latter point concerning the duration of visual sensory memory was examined more thoroughly by Sperling in the same experiment. On some trials the indicator tone was delayed following offset of the letter matrix. The delays ranged between 0 and 1 second. The delay conditions were added to see what happens to performance under partial report conditions when the report is not immediate. The results of the delay conditions, as well as the immediate partial report and whole report results, are shown in figure 2.2. Notice the high performance at 0 delay of the tone (immediate partial report). As the tone is delayed further, performance steadily declines to about 1 second. At this point, partial report performance is equivalent to

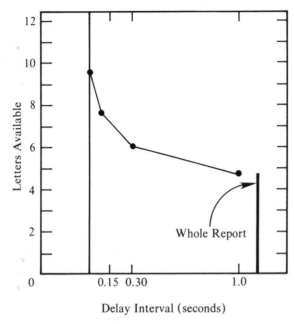

Figure 2.2 Number of letters recalled in Sperling's experiment as a function of delay between offset matrix and onset of partial report cue. (From "The Information Available in Brief Visual Presentations" by G. Sperling, *Psychological Monographs,* 1960, *74,* Whole No. 948. Copyright 1960 by the American Psychological Association. Reprinted by permission of the publisher and author.)

that of whole report. The rapid drop in performance across these short intervals is indicative of a very transient *trace.* Indeed, significant trace decay seems to have occurred following a 300-millisecond delay, which suggests that visual sensory memory has an effective life of about one-third of a second.

Supporting evidence for this conclusion has come from studies of *back-ward masking,* a phenomenon discovered by Averbach and Coriell (1961). Masking refers to the technique designed to erase the information on the memory register. For example, suppose a letter matrix is presented and immediately upon offset of the matrix a cue is given for the partial report. Rather than a tone, however, suppose the cue is either a bar appearing under the position formerly occupied by a letter or a circle surrounding the position formerly occupied by a letter. The subject's task is to report the letter indicated by the marker, a partial report task requiring the subject to report one letter. An example of the use of bar and circle markers is given in figure 2.3. Keep in mind that the markers occur following offset of the matrix.

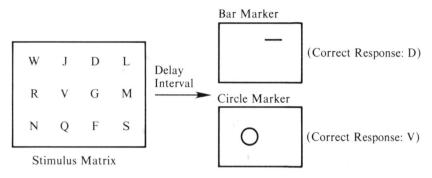

Figure 2.3 Example of the use of bar and circle markers, showing the input (stimulus) matrix followed by the marker.

The bar marker produces partial report performance similar to that found by Sperling. With the circle as a cue, however, performance is very poor. Why does a circle disrupt performance in the partial report situation?

The answer to this question appeals to the erasure of information from the sensory register. The circle appears in the same location as the letter and consequently may displace the letter on the sensory register. Since the bar marker is slightly removed from the location of the letter, it would not interfere with the letter's representation. The disruption produced by the circle is due to the masking or erasure of the letter. Since the circle occurs after the letter and its effect must operate backward in time, the technique is known as backward masking.

Estimates of the duration of visual sensory memory have been obtained using the technique of backward masking. Since the masking stimulus has its deleterious effect by erasing the sensory representation, the mask should be effective only as long as the information is on sensory memory. Once the information has left sensory memory, either through decay or selection for higher-order processing, performance following a masking stimulus should be no worse than following a nonmasking partial report cue. Thus, the duration of sensory memory can be estimated by systematically delaying the mask following the offset of the target stimulus. Studies using this method show that the mask disrupts performance if it is imposed between 0 to 300 milliseconds after offset of the target. Delays greater than 300 milliseconds seem to eliminate the negative effect of the mask. During the first 300 milliseconds following the offset of the target, an active representation is available, and the mask interferes with this representation. After 300 milliseconds, the mask is ineffective because the sensory representation has decayed. Thus, the estimates of visual sensory memory duration using backward masking have been very similar to those proposed by Sperling, on the order of one-third of a second.

Veridical Representation

The final characteristic of the sensory register is that the representation be veridical to the activation of the sensory receptors. The information on the sensory register reflects the pattern of receptor activity. Now recall the earlier discussion of the precategorical nature of receptor activity which described physical energy as precategorical. *Precategorical* means that the physical energy and corresponding receptor activity have not been categorized with respect to the object they represent. These patterns do not yet specify any particular object; further processing is necessary for object identification. The primary implication of the assumption of veridical representation is, then, that information on the sensory register will be precategorical. Can we demonstrate that the sensory information requires further processing to attain meaning?

Several studies have addressed this issue by using Sperling's partial report technique in a special way (e.g., von Wright, 1968). Suppose the stimulus matrix presented to the subject consists half of letters and half of numbers. For a partial report cue, you use letters or numbers; notice that this procedure conforms to partial report in that only part of the information must be reported. But an important difference exists between this partial report cue and the spatial cue used by Sperling. To label a visual pattern a letter or number requires categorization of the visual pattern. In other words, each symbol has to be processed to decide whether it is a letter or a number before that symbol is reported. If every symbol must be processed to use the partial report cue, the advantage of partial report is lost. Notice that sensory cues, such as spatial location, do not impose similar requirements. If the cue signals a single row to be reported, no other symbols in the matrix need be processed.

According to the previous discussion, the additional processing for categorization will take time and the sensory memory will decay. Thus, if the information in the sensory register is precategorical, any partial report cue which requires that the meaning of the information be processed to determine what is to be reported will produce very poor performance. On the other hand, if the sensory register contains meaningful information, a categorical cue, such as letters or numbers, should give the standard advantage of partial report over whole report.

The data from these studies are clear. A subject given a categorical partial report cue, such as "Report all the letters," does no better than a subject given whole report instructions. Apparently the processing time required to determine if information in the sensory register is a letter or number is great enough to allow remaining information to decay. The results of these studies strongly suggest a precategorical memory system.

So the picture which emerges from research on visual sensory memory is of a brief storage system which holds all of the information received by the receptors. The information is in precategorical form, awaiting further processing to allow interpretation of the information and to bring it to our awareness. In the absence of this further processing, the information will be totally lost, particularly if the external source of stimulation has ceased. But that portion of the information selected for further processing represents what we come to know about our world.

Auditory Sensory Register

The reasons for assuming an adaptive function for the sensory register are even more compelling in audition than in vision. As we have seen, the function of the sensory register is to maintain information if the central processing system is otherwise engaged. The need for such a memory in audition is even more acute than in vision. Audition generally requires the integration of information over time. For example, to understand a two-syllable word, the first syllable must be integrated with the second syllable, but obviously the second syllable occurs later in time than the first syllable. The same point can be made more dramatically with sentences. Comprehension of a sentence requires that the subject be related to the predicate, but some amount of time separates these two parts of a sentence. If anything, the auditory system may require a longer-lasting sensory memory than vision.

Preliminary evidence for auditory sensory memory, also known as *echoic memory,* was provided by studies comparing partial and whole report performance. As in studies of visual sensory memory, these studies presented more information than could be processed, and recall was prompted by partial or whole report cues. For example, Darwin, Turvey, and Crowder (1972) asked subjects to listen to three different messages, played simultaneously over three different speakers. In the whole report condition, the subject simply tried to recall as much as possible. Partial report required recall from only one of the three speakers. As with visual sensory memory, partial report performance was superior to that in the whole report condition. A number of other experiments have confirmed this partial report advantage in audition, suggesting that more information may be available initially than the person can report.

This duration is considerably longer than the estimates for visual sensory memory. But, as we have seen, the requirements of audition are different from those of vision. Vision takes in lots of information at once and integrates this information spatially. Audition requires integration over time, and thus the different temporal durations estimated for visual and auditory sensory memories mesh with the modality-specific requirements of the two systems.

Modality Effects

In an attempt to study further the characteristics of echoic memory, some researchers have taken advantage of a memory phenomenon known as the *modality effect*. The modality effect refers to the higher level of recall of the last few items of a list when presentation is auditory rather than visual. For example, subjects may be given a list of nine words, presented one at a time. One group of subjects sees the words and a second group of subjects hears the words. The people who hear the words recall the last two or three words at a higher level than the people who see the words. The same effect can be obtained even if both groups see the list, but one group is instructed to read the words silently and the other group reads the words aloud. The people who read aloud recall the last few words better than the people who read silently (Conrad & Hull, 1968; Murray, 1966). Since the superior recall of the last words depends upon the presence of auditory input, the modality effect has been attributed to information in echoic memory.

Suffix Effects

Explanations of the modality effect as the operation of echoic memory have been strengthened by another discovery known as the *suffix effect*. Suppose the nine-word list is followed by another word which the subjects have been told signifies the end of the list. The word can be any nonlist word, and the subjects have been told they need not remember the word. Under these circumstances, the last word of the list itself is remembered more poorly than in the case where the subject simply hears the nine-word list. This result is the suffix effect, and the redundant last word is the suffix. A depiction of the effect can be seen in figure 2.4.

The suffix effect occurs only when both the to-be-remembered words and the suffix are presented auditorily. A visual presentation of the suffix does not disrupt memory for auditorily presented words. Further, the extent of the disruption is determined by the physical similarity of the suffix to the target items. If the suffix word is read by a different voice than the target words, for example, the suffix effect is less than if the suffix and targets are read in the same voice. The semantic or meaningful relationship between the target and suffix has little effect upon performance (Crowder, 1976).

The relationship between the suffix effect and the modality effect is grasped easily if we assume the modality effect is due to the availability of echoic information which aids recall of the last items. If, however, a suffix word is appended to the list, the echoic information corresponding to the last list item is masked by the suffix. That is, the suffix is assumed to cause backward masking of the list item in echoic memory and thereby interferes with memory for the last word.

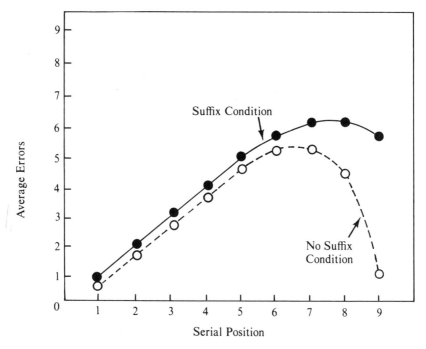

Figure 2.4 Schematic depiction of suffix effect. Note the data plotted are errors.

On the basis of this interpretation, one can use the modality and suffix effects to estimate the duration of echoic memory. For example, Watkins and Watkins (1980) asked subjects to remember a list of twelve words presented either auditorialy or visually. After the list was presented, the recall test was delayed for 20 seconds during which time the subjects engaged in a silent, verbal distractor task. Even after a 20-second delay, the last three list words were much better recalled following auditory than following visual presentation, indicating that the modality effect persists for at least 20 seconds. If an auditory distractor task is inserted in the delay interval, the advantage of auditory presentation is eliminated, but a visual distractor task has little effect upon the superior recall of the auditorially presented items. This last result is important in suggesting that the modality effect is modality specific. Because sensory memory is defined as a modality-specific memory, Watkins and Watkins's research corresponds nicely with interpretation of the modality effect in terms of echoic memory and suggests that echoic memory may persist for periods of up to 20 seconds.

Questions about Echoic Memory

In spite of the encouraging research described above, questions have been raised about the interpretation of this work. For example, Greene and Crowder (1986) have reported a modality effect when the to-be-remembered items are silently mouthed. Such a situation does not involve auditory sensory input, and if the modality effect was due to echoic memory, the effect would not be expected in situations which do not contain auditory stimulation.

It is unclear, however, that the modality effect obtained when the stimuli are silently mouthed is caused by the same psychological processes as the modality effect obtained when the stimuli are said aloud. In a series of experiments designed to make this point, Turner, LaPointe, Cantor, Reeves, Griffeth, and Engle (1987) discovered that only certain types of stimuli were susceptible to modality effects following silent mouthing. All of the stimuli they used showed modality effects when said aloud. This difference suggests that the modality effects in the two situations may be caused by different psychological processes and leaves open the possibility that the modality effect actually is due to echoic memory processes.

Another difficulty has been establishing the precategorical status of echoic memory. Remember that the partial report superiority is attributed to the additional processing time required in the whole report condition. The additional time is required because the whole report procedure requires that more items be processed than for the partial report. Although several studies have reported the partial report advantage in auditory sensory memory, the interpretation is complicated by difficulty in demonstrating that the auditory sensory trace is precategorical. The precategorical status of visual sensory memory was established by experiments such as the one discussed which compared partial report using letters and numbers versus spatial location as cues. Letters and numbers are categorical, and hence the additional processing required to use these cues should offset the partial report advantage. Unlike studies of visual sensory memory, categorical cues provide performance equivalent to spatial cues in auditory sensory memory (Darwin, Turvey, & Crowder, 1972; Massaro, 1975).

In summary, the research on echoic memory has produced less agreement about auditory sensory memory than there is agreement about visual sensory memory. This disagreement, however, has been an important impetus for continued research on echoic memory. Such research continues to be quite active and offers the promise of a better understanding of the initial phases of auditory information processing.

Visual Sensory Memory and Reading Disability

The sensory register operates at a preattentive level, which means we have no conscious control over its functioning, nor are we aware of its contents. Partially for this reason, the concept may appear esoteric and of little use in understanding real-world behavior. To the contrary, the sensory register has been applied to several problems of considerable importance.

A particularly interesting example is the use of visual sensory memory to study specific reading disability. *Specific reading disability* is a syndrome which has long been of interest to educators and psychologists because of its unique characteristics. Initially, the only obvious difficulty the person presents is in reading; no organic damage is present; the IQ score is in the normal range; and no intellectual deficits are apparent beyond the reading problem. The pattern, then, is of an otherwise perfectly normal individual who has great difficulty reading. Actually, only young children show this pattern, because beyond a certain level of formal schooling (roughly the sixth grade) the reading deficit begins to pose a serious obstacle to performance in other disciplines, including mathematics. Thus, if it is not detected early, specific reading disability eventually is disastrous to the academic achievement and maturation of an otherwise capable person.

For many years, the primary hypothesis concerning specific reading disability was the *perceptual deficit hypothesis.* In its simple form, the idea suggested that reading-disabled children do not see the same images as do normal readers. For whatever reason, the visual system of disabled readers was assumed dysfunctional such that the information available was distorted. This general hypothesis was rather disheartening in that it suggested some critical but unspecified organic difference between good and poor readers which could not be remedied in the classroom.

The data supporting the perceptual deficit hypothesis were based, by and large, upon simple perceptual tasks. For example, a child might be shown a single letter or a small set of letters and then asked to say or write the letters after they were removed. The reading-disabled child was likely to perform more poorly than the normal reader and to make mistakes such as letter reversal (mistake *b* for *d*) in these simple tasks. Since the test was administered very soon after termination of the stimuli, the task was assumed to measure the sensory information available to the child, not memory. With the advent of the information-processing framework, a new perspective on the simple perceptual task was available. Perhaps the reading-disabled children did see exactly the same images as the normal readers, but memory performance between the two groups differed. In other words, the good and poor readers may register the same information on visual sensory memory, but then differ in their *ability to process the information* off of the sensory register.

This idea was tested by Morrison and colleagues (Morrison, Giordani, & Nagy, 1977), using groups of good and poor readers from the sixth grade. The procedure used was a variation of Sperling's partial report in which the subjects were shown a circular array of eight symbols. Three types of stimuli were used: letters, geometrical shapes, and random shapes. The stimulus array was shown for 100 milliseconds and was replaced by a marker at the position of one of the eight symbols. The marker was presented at delays following offset of the array varying from 0 to 2 seconds. After the marker appeared, the child was shown a card containing several symbols. The child's task was to indicate which of the symbols on the card had appeared at the position of the marker on the original array. The test was thus recognition rather than recall. The primary questions addressed in this study were: Do poor readers differ from good readers? And if they do, is this difference a function of the delay interval? The perceptual deficit hypothesis would predict superior performance by good readers at all delay intervals.

The results, which are presented in figure 2.5, were quite striking. As you can see, there was no difference in the number of trials on which correct recognition occurred until the indicator was delayed by about 300 milliseconds. Beyond this point, the good readers recognized more items than did the poor readers. This outcome was consistent across all types of stimuli.

Using the previous estimates of the duration of visual sensory memory, Morrison's data clearly indicate that poor readers perform as well as good readers when the information is in sensory memory. It is at the point of *higher-order processing* that the poor reader is disadvantaged. The deficit may be a problem of translating visual information to phonetic information or it may be some confusion of the visual information, but regardless, Morrison's study shows that good and poor readers do register the same sensory information, contrary to the perceptual deficit hypothesis. This is important information in both the understanding and treatment of specific reading disability.

PATTERN RECOGNITION

Among the oldest and most fascinating questions facing psychology is the relationship between physical energy in the environment and psychological experience. What are the processes which govern the transformation of physical energy, such as light, into a meaningful psychological experience? Our ability to recognize patterns of physical energy is obviously an absolute necessity for survival. Perhaps not so obvious, however, is the flexibility and complexity of the pattern-recognition process. Consider first the enormous

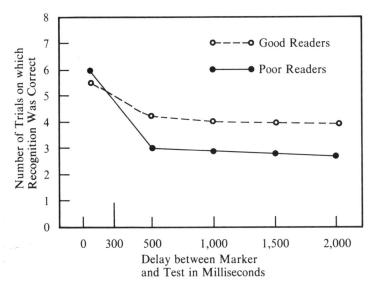

Figure 2.5 The number of trials on which correct recognition responses were given by good and poor readers following various delay intervals. Notice that both good and poor readers begin to differ only after a delay of 300 milliseconds. (From "Reading Disability: An Information Processing Analysis" by F. J. Morrison, B. Giordani, and J. Nagy, *Science,* 1977, *199,* 77–79, Fig. 2, 1 April 1977. Copyright 1977 by the American Association for the Advancement of Science.)

range of patterns which a person can recognize. The number of people, objects, and events which are immediately and effortlessly recognized by adults are virtually uncountable. You may have difficulty recalling the name of a particular person or object, but rarely do you have trouble recognizing the pattern as a person, or a tree, or an airplane. In fact, pattern recognition at this level is accomplished with such ease that the entire issue may appear trivial.

But the ability to recognize patterns of sensory information is neither simple nor trivial. The complexity of pattern recognition can be illustrated by considering some very common situations. You and a friend are standing by the ocean, and you see an object in the distance. You point out the object to your friend and remark on the danger of a swimmer being that far from shore. Your friend laughs and says that the object is not a person but is a sea turtle. You look again, and still see a person. A mild argument ensues. Cases of two people disagreeing about a pattern when both are receiving approximately the same physical information are notoriously common.

Figure 2.6 Example of the same pattern recognized as two different objects. (From "The Role of Frequency in Developing Perceptual Sets" by B. R. Bugelski and D. A. Alampay, *Canadian Journal of Psychology,* 1961, *15,* 205–211. Copyright 1961 by the Canadian Psychological Association. Used by permission.)

Indeed, you may be surprised to learn that you will frequently respond differently to exactly the same pattern of physical energy. For instance, examine the top row of figure 2.6, which is taken from an experiment of Bugelski and Alampay (1961). What is the fifth symbol in that row? Now examine the second row of figure 2.6. What is the fifth symbol? In the top row, the fifth symbol is easily recognized as a rat, but in the second row the same pattern is just as easily recognized as a face. The same auditory patterns can also give rise to different recognition responses. In normal conversation, the physical pattern of the utterance "new display" is the same as that of "nudist play." Rarely, however, would we fail to recognize the appropriate pattern in normal conversation. Our attempts to understand the apparently simple process of pattern recognition are then complicated by the ability to recognize appropriately the same physical energy as different patterns.

The other side of this coin also must be considered. Different patterns of physical energy are frequently recognized as the same pattern. Think, for a simple example, of the enormous variety of ways in which the letter *A* may be written: not only is everyone's handwriting different, but also infinite variations in size and shape are possible. In spite of the incredible variability presented by physical information, the psychological mechanisms respond consistently and accurately. This flexibility in the pattern recognition process is highly adaptive and again illustrates the complexity of the interface between physical energy and psychological experience. The flexibility of human pattern recognition has been extraordinarily difficult to simulate in machines. Computers can recognize patterns, but the input must be unambiguous. The bizarre numbers on credit cards are necessary for computer recognition because normal Arabic numerals are too similar for consistently accurate recognition by a computer.

Thus, the study of pattern recognition addresses a number of complex issues related to the process of extracting meaning from sensory experience. First, how are we to conceptualize the extraction of meaning from sensory information, capturing both the speed and accuracy of pattern recognition? Moreover, the conceptualization must account for the enormous flexibility of the pattern recognition process, including the influence of contextual information. The complexity of some of these issues is so great as to allow only a general understanding at present, but the discussion of the general conceptualization will lead to more specific ideas and research.

Pattern Recognition and Memory

Within the framework of information processing, pattern recognition is a process which interacts with the information on the sensory register. In a sense, information is read off of the sensory register through the process of pattern recognition. Remember that information on the sensory register is assumed to be *precategorical* or without meaning. Pattern recognition is the process by which meaning is derived. In general, pattern recognition is assumed to involve the match between sensory information and the corresponding representation stored in long-term memory. The sensory pattern is recognized as one of the patterns stored in the long-term system. Once this recognition occurs, the information associated with the pattern in long-term memory is available, and in this sense the sensory pattern acquires meaning. Pattern recognition, then, is a process which interprets sensory information by matching that information to previous experiences stored in long-term memory.

Within this general framework, more specific questions can be asked of the pattern-recognition process. For example, pattern recognition requires the interaction of two separate memory systems, sensory register and long-term memory. What is the nature of the memory codes which are to be matched between these systems? Moreover, how is the decision concerning the "goodness" of the match reached? In other words, the description must consider not only the nature of the codes to be matched, but also the processes which are responsible for the matching. In order to give a feeling for the necessary complexity of an adequate description, we shall begin with a very simple theory of pattern recognition.

Template Theory

Perhaps the most intuitive hypothesis of pattern recognition involves a direct match between the sensory experience and the literal copy of that experience. The literal copy, known as the *template,* is stored in long-term memory. The pattern presented by the sensory experience is compared to templates stored in long-term memory until a direct match is found. The matching or decision process is made on the basis of perfect overlap between the sensory pattern and the template, and once overlap is achieved, the pattern is recognized as the template. Template theory in this simple form is essentially a lock-and-key type of hypothesis. The match process continues until a template is found that fits the sensory experience.

The difficulties with the simple template hypothesis concern an understanding of the speed, accuracy, and flexibility of pattern recognition. For example, in day-to-day activities, most familiar patterns are recognized rapidly. Identification of familiar objects in the environment, such as a face, a type of car, and so forth, seems to occur instantaneously and with no effort. Although we now know from laboratory studies that pattern recognition does require measurable amounts of time, the brief period of time required does not seem perfectly consistent with the description of pattern recognition by template theory. A potential solution to this problem is to assume that the sensory experience is matched against all templates simultaneously, a process known as parallel processing.

Serial and Parallel Processing

According to template theory, the number of templates stored in long-term memory have to equal the number of patterns a person can recognize. This would be a very large number indeed if you consider all of the possible variations of all of the possible patterns you can recognize. If each sensory pattern is matched against each template, the process could be quite time-consuming. One solution to this dilemma is to make an assumption about the comparison process. Rather than match the sensory patterns to each template one at a time, which is known as *serial processing,* perhaps the match is made against all templates simultaneously. Matching the sensory experience against a number of templates simultaneously, known as *parallel processing,* would greatly enhance the speed of the matching process.

Although parallel processing is not intuitively plausible, probably because of the difficulty of doing two complex things simultaneously, Neisser (1964) provided some evidence in favor of parallel processing in pattern recognition. Neisser's experiment required that subjects scan a sheet of paper containing fifty lines of four letters each and press a button as soon as they detected a particular target letter. The target letter was randomly positioned among the letters on the sheet. In the first condition, the subjects were given only one target letter, but in the second condition, the subjects were told to respond to any of ten different letters. If we assume that the instructions concerning the target letter activate the template for that letter, the sensory patterns are then compared to the activated template. The critical aspect of the experiment for evaluation of serial processing and parallel processing is the number of templates against which the sensory pattern must be matched. If pattern matching is serial in nature, specifying one letter should produce faster recognition than specifying ten letters. With ten letters, each sensory experience, that is, each letter on the sheet, would have to be matched against ten templates one at a time, whereas the other condition requires only one match for each letter. Parallel processing, however, should produce no difference in match time as a function of the number of potential targets. All activated templates would be matched simultaneously against the sensory pattern such that the number of activated templates would be irrelevant to the decision time. The results of this experiment, and others since, have in fact shown no difference in the time to detect targets as a function of the number of targets. These data are consistent with ideas about parallel processing, and parallel processing offers a potential solution to one of the problems facing template theory. Unfortunately, other more serious problems exist.

Preprocessing

Yet another and perhaps more serious difficulty arises for template theory when we try to explain the ability to recognize patterns in spite of wide variation in their physical form. The most obvious position for template theory is to argue that a template exists for every recognizable variation of every pattern. Considering again only the numerous variations in the pattern that can be recognized as *A,* the number of templates necessary is very large. If all of the potential variations of all of the patterns a person can recognize are imagined, the required number of templates is staggering. The large number of templates requires massive long-term memory capacity and the ability to resolve ambiguity concerning which of two or more possible patterns an ambiguous or unusual sensory pattern represents.

One solution to this difficulty is to assume some *preprocessing* of the sensory pattern prior to the matching decision. Preprocessing essentially functions to "clean up" the pattern, for example, to place it in proper orientation, to reduce or expand its size, to remove extraneous information, and the like. For example, the pattern V might be rotated 180 degrees to form the pattern A prior to being matched with a template. The advantage of preprocessing is that it reduces the number of templates needed in long-term memory. A further logical problem now arises, however. In order for preprocessing to function efficiently, it seems that the pattern must already have been recognized. That is, to reorient or clean up the pattern, you may need to know what the pattern is; yet, this is the very process that preprocessing serves. In other words, how does preprocessing decide to reorient V to A as opposed to removing the extraneous horizontal line to form V?

A possible solution lies in the influence of contextual information; the context in which a pattern appears delineates the possibilities. For example, the context of V might be such that an upside-down A is more probable than a V, and hence preprocessing reorients the pattern rather than removes the horizontal line. Indeed, some evidence is available to indicate that reorientation does occur in contextually constrained situations.

If the task is to decide whether you are seeing the pattern R or its mirror image Я, and the pattern is presented in other than its normal orientation, for example, Я, the amount of time to make the decision systematically increases as the stimulus departs from its normal orientation (Cooper & Shepard, 1973). One interpretation of this finding is that the pattern is being *mentally rotated* prior to the match decision. Notice, however, that the alternative patterns have been specified in advance; the subjects *expect* particular patterns. This expectation or prior knowledge can be described theoretically as the activation of the long-term memory representation of the patterns prior to the presentation of the actual stimulus. Activation of the memory representation prior to presentation of the stimulus is under control of the instructions in this task, and these instructions serve as the contextual constraint. Preprocessing becomes possible under these circumstances because the sensory pattern, once it is presented, can be rotated or refined in other ways until it matches the activated template.

This situation is analogous to the rather common experience of looking for a particular person in a crowd, searching for a friend at a football game or large party. You know for whom you are looking; that is, the template for that face is activated. If the person for whom you are searching has changed in physical appearance (grown a beard, for example), it is still possible to clean up the pattern to match your memory of the person. Remember, however, the previous criticism of preprocessing. Preprocessing requires that the pattern to be recognized already be activated in long-term memory; while contextual constraints may serve this function, we certainly are capable of recognizing patterns in the absence of knowledge of which pattern is to be recognized. We recognize a face even when a person is unexpected.

Simple template theory has thus proved inadequate in describing the richness and flexibility of pattern recognition. Even when supplemented with concepts such as preprocessing, template theory leaves many questions unanswered. As is often the case in science, however, the inadequate theory is invaluable in raising questions for other theories to answer. It is to one of these other theories that we now turn.

Analysis-by-Synthesis

The general class of theories now discussed were initially proposed by computer scientists (e.g., Selfridge, 1959) interested in machine pattern recognition and subsequently were brought to the attention of psychologists by Neisser (1967). Although several versions of this approach are available, certain basic ideas are common to all, and we shall discuss these ideas under the general rubric of analysis-by-synthesis. The term *analysis-by-synthesis* describes the process by which pattern recognition is assumed to occur. The initial step in the process is analysis or breakdown of the pattern of sensory information on the sensory register. Recognition ultimately occurs through synthesis or reconstruction of the pattern from its component parts. The synthesis process involves the comparison of the sensory information with corresponding representations in long-term memory and a decision concerning the sufficiency of the match between the two. For example, the letter *A* might be analyzed into two oblique lines and one horizontal line, /, \ , −. The list of components are then *compared* to lists stored in long-term memory that represent patterns. During the comparison stage, several patterns having some of the features provided by the analysis are uncovered. For example, *M, N, R, V, W, X,* and *Y,* in addition to *A,* all have oblique lines. Horizontal lines are present in *A, E, F, H, I, J,* and *Z.* Thus, the comparison stage might generate several candidates from long-term memory, necessitating a *decision* concerning which is the best match for the sensory pattern. The decision stage determines the amount of evidence for a particular recognition response.

As can be seen from this overview, analysis-by-synthesis involves more complicated *processes* than the simple pattern match proposed by template theory. As will be discussed, the additional complexity adds explanatory power to the analysis-by-synthesis approach. It also should be clear from the outset that analysis-by-synthesis requires a different kind of long-term memory representation. Rather than holistic templates, analysis-by-synthesis assumes patterns are represented by component *features.*

Features

All patterns consist of a configuration of elements, and theoretically any pattern can be broken down into these basic elements. The basic elements or parts of a pattern are known as *features* of the pattern. For example, the letter *A* consists of the three features /, \ , and −. Angles might also be included as features, in which case *A* also has the feature obtuse angle. Any visual pattern thus can be described by listing its features. Likewise, acoustic patterns, the sensory information in speech perception, can also be analyzed as combinations of features. As lines and angles seem to be important visual features, speech contains basic units of sounds, called *phonemes,* which determine meaning. The sounds of *b, c,* and *h* in the words *bat, cat,* and *hat* are phonemes in that each of the distinct sound patterns changes the meaning of the word. Much of the exciting research in speech perception is currently devoted to identifying acoustic features.

If physical patterns of light and sound can be described in terms of their components, it then seems reasonable that long-term memory be composed of lists of features describing patterns. Thus, some theorists suggest that patterns are represented in long-term memory as *feature lists.* To recognize a sensory pattern, it then becomes necessary to transform that pattern into the same code as that of long-term memory, specifically, the pattern would have to be analyzed into its component features. The features are then compared to the feature lists of long-term memory to reach a recognition decision.

The concept of features may appear to complicate unduly the process of pattern recognition, particularly compared to the rather straightforward template hypothesis. What advantage does the concept of featural representation offer which could possibly justify the complexity?

The feature hypothesis handles several problems which are difficult for the template theory. For example, template theory is forced to postulate an enormous number of templates in long-term memory corresponding to each pattern we recognize. Feature theory, on the other hand, can reduce this load on long-term memory by assuming that only the finite set of features are represented in long-term memory. That is, the number of possible lines and angles of visual stimuli is large but not as large as the total number of patterns we can recognize. By assuming that any pattern can be described as some combination of features, long-term memory need only contain one complete listing of features, and each pattern is represented by the activation of some unique subset of the features. Thus, feature theory enjoys a conceptual advantage over template theory in terms of the burden placed on long-term memory.

Further justification for a featural representation is derived from studies demonstrating the psychological reality of features. Research from both physiological and behavioral perspectives yield results highly consistent with feature theory. For example, a number of physiological studies on a variety of animals have shown that specific cells in the visual system respond differentially to simple stimuli such as line orientation or angles (Hubel & Wiesel, 1962; Lettvin, Maturana, McCulloch, & Pitts, 1959). These cells seem to be specialized in detecting the simple visual stimuli which correspond to what have been called features of a pattern. Cells have even been identified in the frog's visual system which respond only to small, dark, moving objects. Perhaps these cells function as a lunch detector for the frog. Equally impressive are data demonstrating cortical cells in monkeys which fire only to the visual stimulus of a monkey paw! The important point here is that neural mechanisms fire to specific patterns, a fact which corresponds well with feature theory.

Behavioral data also have been offered in support of feature theory, particularly in the form of confusion matrices. Confusion matrices summarize the patterns of errors a person makes in making judgments about rapidly presented letters. For example, when the letter *A* is presented very rapidly and a mistake in judgment is made, the letter reported is likely to share visual features with *A*, such as do *H, K,* or *N*. If the process of recognizing these patterns entails the use of basic features, confusion among patterns sharing features would be expected. Feature theory thus helps us understand data from both behavioral and physiological research and therefore gains credibility. Armed with both logical and empirical justification for a feature code in memory, the analysis-by-synthesis approach describes a series of steps by which the sensory features of a pattern are matched in long-term memory.

The Process of Analysis-by-Synthesis

Essentially three steps are involved in analysis-by-synthesis. The *first* step is extraction of information from the sensory register. Unlike template theory, which assumes that the holistic sensory representation is lifted from the sensory register, analysis-by-synthesis assumes that the sensory representation is analyzed into component features. The first step is then to extract information from the sensory register through the featural analysis of the pattern. The identification of these features is the *second* step. Here, the features contained in the pattern are matched to features in long-term memory. As you can see, this stage of pattern recognition is very similar to template theory. Each sensory feature must be matched against what amounts to a template in long-term memory. In spite of this similarity, the advantage of feature theory is that the number of feature templates necessary to describe all patterns is assumed to be smaller than the total number of patterns. The *third* step is the decision process itself in which the set of features selected and identified in the first two stages are compared with feature lists in long-term memory. The best match in terms of the number of overlapping features is selected as the pattern represented by the sensory information. The pattern in long-term memory containing the most features in common with the sensory pattern is then selected as the recognition response. The process of analysis-by-synthesis thus proceeds from initial analysis of the sensory pattern into component features to identification of these features, to the final decision concerning what pattern is represented by the features. The final step represents a synthesis in that the separate features are now put together in the pattern decision.

As described thus far, analysis-by-synthesis appears to be completely *data driven*. That is, the entire process seems to be guided by the features of the sensory pattern. As we have previously seen, however, certain recognition decisions cannot be determined solely by the sensory data; the same sensory pattern may be recognized as a different pattern in a different context. Refer again to figure 2.6. Since the sensory data from the specific pattern are the same in the two situations, some other information and process must account for the recognition decision. The additional information is derived from the context in which the pattern occurs, and the context is assumed to affect recognition by activating conceptual information or *pre-synthesizing* the pattern.

Let us illustrate the effects of context and the process of presynthesis through an experiment by Reicher (1969) on letter recognition. Suppose that the word *BOOK* is presented at a very fast exposure rate. Immediately at the offset of the word, the subject sees _ _ _ ?, and the task is to report the letter which had appeared in the space occupied by the question mark, in this example, *K*. In order to estimate the influence of the word context upon letter recognition, it is also necessary to measure recognition in a non-word context. For example, the stimulus *OBOK* could appear, followed by the same test query, _ _ _ ?. Note that in both cases *K* is the pattern to be reported, but in one instance, *K* occurs in the context of a word and in the second instance, it occurs in nonword context. The results of such comparisons show both more accurate and more rapid recognition when the letter occurs in the context of a word.

This result, however, is not perfectly straightforward because the probability of guessing the correct letter is higher in the word context. That is, the subject may not have seen *K,* but only *BOO_*. Knowing the response should be a letter which completes the word beginning in *BOO* makes *K* a fairly obvious guess. Alternately, guessing in the nonword context is much less likely. Thus, the advantage provided by word contexts may have little to do with true recognition, but may result simply from a higher probability of guessing. It is possible, however, to control for guessing by changing the test to recognition with alternative choices, either of which would make a word. For example, the test alternatives for *BOOK* might be *K* and *T,* and the subject must choose the correct response. The same test is given following the nonword context. The important point is that any differences between the two conditions can no longer be attributed to guessing from the word context. With the guessing probability thus controlled, recognition of the final letter is still more accurate when that letter is presented in the context of a word.

How does the analysis-by-synthesis approach describe this facilitating effect of context? First, it should be apparent that context serves to narrow the possible choices among the incoming patterns. Whether we are talking about a letter, an object in the environment, or a face, the context in which a pattern occurs limits the possible choices. Another way of saying this is that the context establishes expectations concerning incoming patterns. Analysis-by-synthesis tries to capture this expectation through the concept of presynthesis. Remember that the final stage of recognition involves synthesis of the sensory features, in that the previously analyzed sensory features are compared to feature lists in long-term memory. Contextual information, however, could serve to activate the patterns in long-term memory prior to the appearance of the actual sensory representation of the pattern. In other words, the context leads us to expect a particular pattern, which may be constructed with minimal reference to the sensory information.

A competent reader, for example, certainly does not analyze each letter in each word. Indeed, reading seems to involve much in way of presynthesis or anticipation of patterns. Adult readers rarely notice the omission of articles such as *the* and *a*. Did you notice that the sentence before last omitted *the* prior to *way*? We seem to fill in the blanks with patterns which fit with the prevalent context. This process is an example of *conceptually driven* pattern recognition in which the final recognition decision is guided by long-term memory rather than by sensory information. The startling implication is that persons may "recognize" patterns *without* any sensory experience with those patterns!

Since presynthesis amounts to constructing a pattern based on expectation of what the pattern should be rather than on sensory information, certain situations are likely to lead to embarrassing recognition failures. A prime example of such a situation involves proofreading a paper. People commonly fail to detect misspellings or typographical errors when proofreading their own written work. In terms of the analysis-by-synthesis model, you usually know what you have written or at least what you meant to write. Consequently, in proofreading, you are likely to construct patterns on the basis of your expectations, and it is sometimes difficult to force yourself to check carefully the sensory pattern, the actual writing itself. Errors may thus go undetected even after "careful" proofreading of the material. If you understand that pattern recognition in normal reading usually proceeds with a great deal of presynthesis, you may realize that extra effort is required to avoid presynthesis or at least to force yourself to check the presynthesized pattern against the sensory information. An effective means of doing this is to get someone to help you proofread important material. One person reads the material aloud to the other person who follows along, using another copy of the material. By reading aloud, you can slow the normally rapid pattern recognition in reading and perhaps reduce the tendency to rely heavily on presynthesized patterns. By having a person unfamiliar with the material read along with you, you further increase the chance of detecting errors. Although this may seem to be a rather extreme measure just to correct minor errors (it certainly requires a good friend to tolerate the tedious task), you should not underestimate the impact minor errors can have upon supervisors, clients, or colleagues in whatever career you choose. You probably already know of professors' reactions to "minor" errors. The point is that the normal operation of the pattern recognition system can work to your disadvantage, and sometimes it is worth extraordinary effort to ensure that what you think you saw is really there.

Connectionism and Parallel Distributed Processes

A new development in pattern recognition is parallel distributed processing (PDP) which also is known as connectionism. PDP incorporates most of the ideas we have described in previous theories but also adds new assumptions that vastly increase the complexity of the framework. The PDP approach differs fundamentally from previous theories in that its model of pattern recognition is the *activity of the brain* rather than the activity of a computer. The important manifestations of this difference is that all processing is assumed to be parallel and that knowledge resides in the connections among units rather than the units themselves.

Parallel Distributed Processing

The parallel processing assumed by PDP is of two sorts. First, all of the information available to the sensory field is processed simultaneously. In the simple case of recognizing a word, the assumption is that the processing of each letter of the word begins simultaneously if all of the letters are in the visual field. This is in contrast to the possibility that each letter of the word is processed sequentially. The second sense of parallel processing is that the "parts" of the object are processed simultaneously with the "whole" object. This processing of "part" and "whole" is interactive such that, for example, the processing of a word influences the recognition of the letter. Advocates of PDP argue that massive parallel processing is required by the "neural model" of pattern recognition because neurons are so slow. Neurons operate on a time-scale of milliseconds whereas computer components operate on a time-scale of nanoseconds which is much faster than neurons. Given that the psychological processes to be modelled are often very complex and that the neurons are relatively slow, the assumption must be that the processes operate in parallel in order to accomplish their function in a reasonable time frame (McClelland, Rumelhart, & Hinton, 1986).

An illustration of parallel processing can be seen in figure 2.7. This illustration is taken from McClelland and Rumelhart's (1981) theory of pattern recognition. In this illustration the presented pattern is the letter T. The analysis begins with feature extraction that provides input to letter

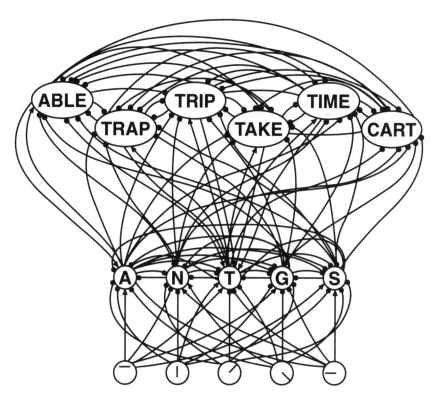

Figure 2.7 An illustration of the connectionist network proposed by McClelland and Rumelhart (1981). (From "An interactive activation model of context effects in letter perception: Part 1, An account of basic findings" by J. L. McClelland and D. E. Rumelhart. *Psychological Review*, 1981, *88*, 375–407.)

activation. But notice that the connections from all features go to all letters; the letters themselves are interconnected, and the letters and words are connected so that activation can proceed in both directions. On appropriate activation, all of this interconnected network can operate simultaneously. This is massive parallel processing.

Distributed Knowledge

The second assumption that is driven by the neural model is that knowledge resides in the connections, not the units connected. We have known for some time that most brain functions operate in accord with mass action; that is, the brain function is not localized to one exclusive structure such as a single neuron. Therefore, the assumption of most theories that the knowledge required for recognition and comprehension is localized to a single representation (node or proposition) is at odds with this fact of brain functioning.

Figure 2.8 A hypothetical set of features that might be extracted from the word WORK. (From "An interactive activation model of context effects in little perception: Part 1, Basic findings" by J. L. McClelland and D. E. Rumelhart. *Psychological Review,* 1981, *88,* 375–407.)

PDP models assume that the knowledge is distributed across the connections, and that knowledge is represented by these connections, not by the units.

Again consider the illustration in figure 2.7 from McClelland and Rumelhart (1981). The connections among the units can be excitatory or inhibitory. Excitatory connections in this example are indicated by an arrow at the terminal point and inhibitory connections by a dot. The eventual recognition of the presented pattern as a T is not modelled by the activation of a T-node but rather it is the sum of the activity, both excitatory and inhibitory, in the network that represents T. It is the activity of the connections that represent knowledge in the PDP framework. The connections and their valence, excitatory or inhibitory, are formed as the result of experience. Thus, the knowledge is the result of learning.

An Example of PDP and Pattern Recognition

Let us illustrate this general overview of PDP with a specific example from McClelland and Rumelhart. Suppose the word WORK has been presented to a subject, and the subject has extracted the features as shown in figure 2.8. All of the features of W, O, and R have been processed, but the features of the final letter are consistent with both R and K. Note that the situation is somewhat similar to the experiment by Reicher (1969) that we described previously. How does a connectionist framework lead us to recognition of the last letter as K?

At the word level of knowledge (refer to figure 2.7), a number of possibilities exist, such as *work, wear, word, weak,* but only *work* is consistent with the available evidence. Therefore, *work* will have the highest level of activation, and this activation of *work* will result in inhibition to the other words from *work.* The excitation these other words are receiving from their feature activation is dampened by the inhibition coming from the word *work.*

The excitation of *work* feeds back into *K* at the letter level, but notice, again referring to figure 2.7, that the activation of the letter *K* will continue to excite the word *weak* as well as the word *work*. The excitation of *weak* feeds back to the letter *K*. Even though the word *weak* is receiving inhibition from *work,* the letter *K* receives the excitation from the residual activation of *weak*. Over some relatively short period of time, the parallel activity in this interactive set of connections strengthens *K* to a level of activation that allows recognition of the word *work*.

This example illustrates the use of ideas from various other theories of pattern recognition such as feature detection, associative interconnection, spreading activation, top-down, and bottom-up processing. Added to these notions, however, are the important ideas of parallel processing and distributed knowledge. Application of PDP has provided successful simulation of various recognition phenomena when run on computers, and although questions have been raised about its importance to psychology (e.g., Pinker & Prince, 1988), this critical inhibition is not likely to dampen the excitement of researchers in this area.

SUMMARY

The emerging picture, then, is of a memory system in which the stimulus is available to the subject both during and immediately after cessation of the stimulus. This information decays very rapidly, however, and much of what is available will not reach meaningful processing. Since the information on the sensory register is assumed to be precategorical, it must undergo additional processing to attain meaning. During the brief time required for additional processing, the remaining information decays.

The implication of this situation is quite striking: the vast majority of the information that activates the senses goes totally unnoticed because of the time and effort required to process some minuscule portion of that information. Much of the information stimulating the receptors remains unknown. The ramifications of this conclusion are quite fascinating. What is *missed?* Even more important for cognitive psychology, how is information from the sensory register (which has no meaning) *selected* such that it is consistent with the meaning of what has been processed? As we shall see, this has been a major question in the study of selective attention.

Pattern recognition is the process by which sensory information is extracted from the sensory register. Through contact with long-term memory, the meaning of the sensory information is then derived. Adequate descriptions of pattern recognition require considerable complexity, as illustrated by the analysis-by-synthesis model. Analysis-by-synthesis assumes a featural representation of patterns in long-term memory, which in turn requires the assumption that sensory patterns are analyzed into features to match long-term memory. Moreover, context affects pattern recognition such that a pattern may be recognized with minimal reference to the sensory information. In some sense, context allows us to make a highly educated guess about a pattern, avoiding the more time-consuming analysis and synthesis of the sensory pattern. Presynthesis of the pattern may increase the speed of pattern recognition, but the potential for error is also increased because the sensory data may contribute minimally to the recognition decision.

More recently, parallel distributed processing and connectionism have entered the arena of theory in pattern recognition. This approach differs from analysis-by-synthesis in assuming explicitly that patterns are processed in parallel. That is, the recognition of letters and words is occurring simultaneously, and the processing of a letter or a word interacts with recognition of other letters and words. In this fashion, the activation of any letter or word is distributed in the form of inhibition or activation to other letters and words.

TO THE STUDENT

Beginning with chapter 2, a set of multiple-choice, true-false, and discussion items are provided at the end of each chapter. The answer to each multiple-choice and true-false item is given along with a brief explanation. These items sample some of the chapter content and thus provide some index of your comprehension of the material. The items are not, however, exhaustive of the content of the chapter and hence should not be relied upon exclusively for study and review. Some questions tap the factual information of the chapter, whereas others attempt to apply concepts and principles to new situations not directly described in the text. Thus the questions sample the types on typical examinations.

MULTIPLE-CHOICE ITEMS

1. The sensory register is an initial memory system which has the following characteristics
   a. large capacity and short duration
   b. small capacity and short duration
   c. large capacity and long duration
   d. small capacity and long duration

2. The primary function of pattern recognition is
   a. totally independent of the sensory register
   b. to add meaning to the sensory information
   c. easily described as a simple template matching
   d. to increase the duration of information on the sensory register

3. The property of the sensory register which makes pattern recognition absolutely necessary is

   a. its large capacity
   b. its short duration
   c. precategorical code

4. The sensory register functions
   a. to recognize information
   b. to supplement the other memory systems
   c. to hold information until it can be processed
   d. to process information for meaning

5. Backward masking studies have been very helpful in establishing
   a. the duration of the sensory register
   b. the size of the sensory register
   c. the type of code in the sensory register
   d. the relationship between pattern recognition and the sensory register

6. The primary problem for template theories of pattern recognition is
   a. the assumptions they make about the sensory register
   b. the requirements they impose on long-term memory
   c. preprocessing
   d. the results of physiological studies demonstrating the presence of features

TRUE–FALSE ITEMS

1. The reason we need the concept of sensory register is that people remember so much after such a short period of time.

2. The major advantage of a feature theory of pattern recognition is the smaller amount of information needed to recognize large numbers of patterns.

3. Long-term memory is very important in pattern recognition.

4. Partial report of a briefly presented matrix produces better performance than whole report.

5. The auditory sensory register seems to be much shorter in duration than the visual sensory register.

6. Presynthesis implies that a pattern may be recognized without any sensory input.

DISCUSSION ITEMS

1. Discuss Sperling's experiment and describe how the results indicate a short-duration but large-capacity memory system.

2. Why is template theory inadequate to describe the pattern recognition process? How does feature theory deal with these inadequacies?

ANSWERS TO MULTIPLE-CHOICE ITEMS

1. (a) The sensory register contains a large amount of information but only for a brief period.
2. (b) Pattern recognition is the concept which describes the process of determining the meaning of sensory information.
3. (c) Since the information on the sensory register is precategorical, an additional process is necessary to add meaning.
4. (c) The sensory register holds information until it can be processed for meaning.
5. (a) Backward masking studies have been used to confirm Sperling's estimate of the duration of the sensory register.
6. (b) The problem for template theory is that it requires a very rapid search through a large amount of information in long-term memory.

ANSWERS TO TRUE–FALSE ITEMS

1. (False) We need the concept of a sensory register because the processing of sensory information requires some time, and a memory system is necessary to hold sensory information until it can be processed.
2. (True) With a feature representation, an infinite number of patterns can be constructed from a finite number of features.
3. (True) Pattern recognition is assumed to involve a match between sensory information and long-term memory.
4. (True) Reporting only part of the matrix produces better performance than reporting all of it.
5. (False) The information on the auditory sensory register seems to last longer than information on the visual sensory register.
6. (True) Presynthesis is a concept describing the recognition of a pattern based on expectations rather than on sensory input.

3

ATTENTION

As class begins, you and your friends stop talking and begin listening to the lecture. Today's class is on the topic of attention and the professor is describing something called a *switch model*. As usual, you are trying furiously to take accurate notes. Suddenly the professor asks the class to predict how much unattended information would be processed according to the switch model. Although you have heard everything said thus far, as attested by your detailed notes, neither you nor your friends can answer the professor's question. This is somewhat strange, because the material is actually easy to understand. Once again you realize how difficult it is to simultaneously take good notes and follow the meaning of a lecture. The lecture continues with the professor relating a story about the year she spent in England at Oxford University and her study with a researcher named Broadbent. Your mind begins to wander to your date of the previous evening, and soon you are absorbed in thinking about an argument you and your date had. You are only vaguely aware of the professor's voice, and as you continue to be occupied with the disagreement of last night, you have little idea of what the professor is saying.

Common situations such as this illustrate phenomena central to the study of attention. At the heart of attention research is the issue of how many tasks can be done at the same time. Taking notes and understanding a lecture are two different activities. Why is it so difficult to do both simultaneously? Is it because one can process only one source of information at a time? If this is true, what happens to the unattended message? We know that the unattended material activates the sensory receptors and thus must appear on the sensory register. Does the unattended information simply decay from the sensory register because it was not selected for pattern recognition? The locus of attention, before or after pattern recognition, is a theoretical issue with important implications for the fate of unattended material. Thus, it is profitable to consider briefly the relationship among the concepts of sensory registration, pattern recognition, and attention.

ATTENTION AND CONSCIOUSNESS

When we refer to "fate of the unattended material," we are raising the question of possible unconscious influences upon behavior. Attention and consciousness have a close relationship that developed from the observation that conscious processing capacity is quite limited. For the moment, consciousness will be taken to be synonymous with awareness, and to say that conscious processing is limited is to say that we can be aware of only a few things at any one point in time. To seriously think about two things simultaneously—for example, your daydreams and a lecture—is virtually impossible. The psychological process of attention is assumed to select information for conscious thought, and since the amount of conscious capacity is limited, attention simultaneously prohibits other information from reaching awareness. The relationship between consciousness and attention is, then, one in which attention screens information before it reaches awareness, and to attend to information, therefore, is to be conscious or aware of that information.

But what happens to the *unattended* information? Does this information also get processed, or is it completely unavailable to affect behavior later? You now can see that this is the same question as the question, Does information of which you are unaware influence your behavior? Following Freud's terminology we shall refer to unattended information as *preconscious* rather than unconscious. Preconscious refers to processing of which you are unaware, but you later could become aware of preconsciously processed material. Unconscious information is a special designation reserved for material which has been repressed, and you cannot become aware of unconscious material without special help, as in psychotherapy. Preconscious processing means the same thing as what you may have heard called subliminal perception.

Does preconscious processing occur? Again, this is the same question as, Are people influenced by unattended information? The question is a consistent theme that we shall follow through the research on attention. Even though they may not always be explicit about it, all theories of attention take a position on this issue. However, as you will see, providing convincing evidence of preconscious processing is not an easy matter.

ATTENTION, SENSORY REGISTER, AND PATTERN RECOGNITION

As discussed in chapter 2, all incoming information is stored on the sensory register. Some small proportion of that information is then processed through pattern recognition. We must now confront the difficult issue of how information is selected for processing. Our ability to behave consistently and rationally depends upon selecting information from the sensory register which maintains continuity in meaning with what has gone before. The pattern-recognition process must be directed to sensory information consistent in meaning with previous information. Thus, the decision to select particular information for pattern recognition is critical, and the decision to allocate processing resources, such as pattern recognition, is what we mean by attention.

A major focus of research in attention has been the localization of attention in the pattern recognition process. Does the decision to process or respond to sensory information occur prior to activating the meaning of that information? For example, while you are concentrating on your day-dreams in a lecture, do you have any idea of the meaning of the lecture material or do you completely block out the unattended material? This question was thoroughly investigated within the framework of filter models of attention.

FILTER MODELS OF ATTENTION

When we use the word *attention* in everyday language, as when we say, "Johnny, pay attention," we are referring to the selective aspect of the at-tentional process. A classic example of the ability to attend selectively is the well-known cocktail-party phenomenon. Suppose you are at a large party, with much good conversation and perhaps even music. The result is a noisy situation. Yet, you have little difficulty "paying attention" to the conversation in which you are involved. More impressively, if someone far across the room should mention your name, you hear it and may even switch your attention to that conversation. Most people have had this experience, which requires ignoring the adjacent conversation and focusing upon a discussion some distance away. How do we accomplish this rather remarkable feat?

Early-Selection Filter Models

Perhaps you can understand this ability by assuming that only one source of information is allowed to reach the stage of meaningful processing. Perhaps unattended information is actively filtered or blocked early in processing such that it never competes for the scarce resources of higher-order processing. Maybe we can attend to one conversation at a cocktail party because all others are successfully filtered or blocked at the sensory level. Such a position is at the heart of what are called early-selection filter theories of attention. *Early selection* means that attention operates early in the information-processing sequence.

Switch Model

According to the early-selection model, attention operates like a simple on-off switch, a light switch, for example. Broadbent (1958) first proposed this model, which subsequently generated a tremendous amount of important research. Operating as a switch, attention serves to direct processing to one input message or channel. This message will be fully analyzed for meaning. Since the switch operates in an all-or-none fashion, however, any additional messages are completely blocked or filtered. At any given time, only one channel is "on." This simple idea explains how we focus on one message and ignore all others, but it also raises an immediate question concerning how we select the appropriate message.

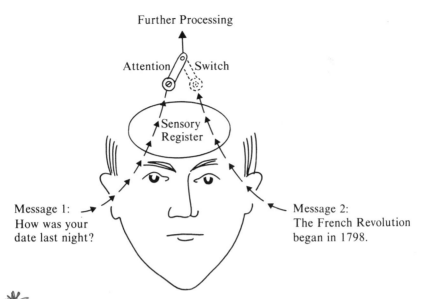

Figure 3.1 Schematic representation of the switch model in which Message 1 is attended and Message 2 is blocked.

Since we are receiving continuous sensory input or messages, it is important to explain what cues are used to set the switch. In other words, what information determines which message receives attention and, equally important, allows us to continue to attend to this message in the face of other messages? Broadbent suggested that attention is attracted and maintained by sensory or physical attributes of the messages. For example, your attention to various conversations at a cocktail party is controlled by the voice qualities of the people conversing.

One good reason for assuming that physical cues control attention is the relationship between attention, sensory register, and pattern recognition. The relationship between these three concepts is depicted in figure 3.1. Notice that the attention switch occurs prior to pattern recognition. Thus this is an early-selection model because attention operates early in the information-processing sequence, guiding the pattern-recognition selection from the sensory register.

Given the theoretical location of the switch, we can be quite clear that the switch model does not allow preconscious processing. If attention filters information at the sensory memory, unattended signals are not selected from the sensory memory register. Left in sensory memory, the unattended information will rapidly decay and never receive the additional processing required for longer-term retention. Consequently, there is no theoretical possibility of unattended information influencing later behavior. The early-selection switch model therefore denies the possibility of preconscious processing and assumes that behavior is influenced only by information of which we are conscious.

The early-selection idea of the switch model quickly became the focus of experimental tests. With a bit of reflection, we can see that the critical test concerns what is known about the unattended message. Since the switch is set at the level of physical analysis, human subjects should be able to report only physical features of the unattended message, not the meaning of that message. In order to perform such a test, however, some technique is necessary to ensure that the switch is set. Such a paradigm was available by combining dichotic input with a shadowing task.

Dichotic Listening and Shadowing

The experimental paradigm which proved quite influential in evaluating early-selection filter theories was introduced by Cherry (1953) and consisted of a combination of *dichotic listening and shadowing. Dichotic* means to present different messages to each of the ears at the same time. In the dichotic listening task, the subject is instructed to attend to one message presented to one ear and to ignore the other message simultaneously presented to the other ear, a situation similar to that of the cocktail-party phenomenon. What would Broadbent's switch model predict in the dichotic listening task? The most straightforward expectation concerns the unattended message; since the switch is set to the attended message, the only facts a subject can know about the message in the unattended ear are its physical characteristics. Suppose the two messages are prose passages, one read by a man and the other by a woman. After both messages have been presented, we would expect the subject to be able to report the contents of the message in the attended ear, and according to the switch model, knowledge of the information in the unattended ear should be restricted to the sex of the speaker, physical information. Nothing about the meaning of the unattended message should be available.

But suppose the subject can tell something about the meaning of the unattended message. Does this cause difficulty for the switch model? Not really. The dichotic listening task does not allow us to determine when attention is shifted, and because of the shifts between the attended ear and unattended ear, the subject may know something of the meaning of both messages. What we need is some means of determining on which message the switch is set. The shadowing task serves this function.

Shadowing is a procedure in which the listener is required to follow one of the dichotically presented messages by repeating that message as it occurs. The subject must repeat the shadowed message word by word immediately as each word occurs, a very difficult task, of which you will be convinced of by trying to shadow a friend's conversation. The very difficulty of shadowing provides its primary rationale; a subject effectively shadowing one message cannot possibly switch to the other message. Thus, shadowing switches the subject to one message. Furthermore, if the subject does switch attention to the unattended message, shadowing of the attended message is disrupted. Hence, shadowing not only forces the subject to attend to one message, but has the added advantage of allowing determination of when attention shifts. Shadowing in conjunction with dichotic listening provides an ideal technique to test the switch model. As long as shadowing is effective, the subject should know only about the shadowed message. If shadowing breaks down, the subject might know something about the unattended message at that point.

Experiments using the shadowing technique (e.g., Moray, 1970; Treisman, 1960) resulted in extensive revision of the switch model. The results were inconsistent with Broadbent's initial idea, in that subjects knew too much about the unattended message. The content of the nonshadowed channel was shown to influence performance, an event which should not occur if the nonshadowed message is blocked. For example, consider Treisman's experiment in which subjects received dichotic presentation of sentences and were required to shadow the message in one ear. Compound sentences were used: for example, *Swann caught the ball, and he ran for a touchdown,* or *Ronstadt sings marvelously, but her selection of music is strange.* The critical manipulation was that half of one sentence was presented to the shadowed ear and the other half presented to the nonshadowed ear. Simultaneously, the same thing happened to the other sentence. The result was as follows: *Swann caught the ball, but her selection of music is strange* occurred in one ear, while *Ronstadt sings marvelously, and he ran for a touchdown* occurred in the other ear.

According to Broadbent's all-or-none switch model, we should have no difficulty shadowing one of these messages and ignoring the other. In fact, people find it virtually impossible to shadow consistently the appropriate message. When the meaning of the shadowed sentence switches to the nonshadowed ear, shadowing is disrupted; the subject experiences confusion, and many times switches to the ear which is supposed to be nonshadowed. Instead of attending to the physical cue of location of the message, the subject follows the meaning of the message.

The critical point for Broadbent's model is that meaning of the nonshadowed message must be getting through to influence the subject's performance. This is a very important conclusion, which is counter to subjective experience. Although you are attending to one conversation at the cocktail party or to your daydreams during a lecture, you probably are detecting some aspects of the meaning of a second conversation at the party or of the lecture in class. Usually we are completely unaware that this is happening.

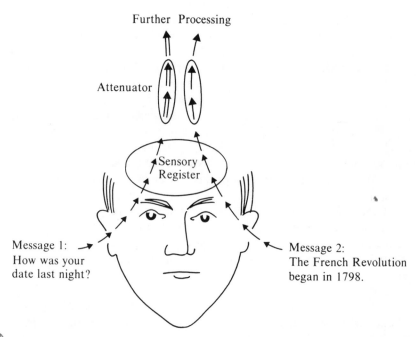

Further Processing

Attenuator

Sensory Register

Message 1:
How was your
date last night?

Message 2:
The French Revolution
began in 1798.

Figure 3.2 Schematic representation of attenuator model in which Message 1 is attended and in which some of Message 2 also gets through for further processing.

The question now becomes: How much of the unattended message is analyzed? One response is an alternative early-selection filter model, the attenuator model.

Attenuator Model

Treisman (1964) proposed a more flexible early-selection theory, based on a different kind of mechanical switch. Rather than a simple off-on mechanism, Treisman suggested that attention operates more like an attenuator. An attenuator is a switch that allows gradations in the amount of energy passing through it; the volume control on a radio or television receiver is an attenuator which can be adjusted to allow more or less of a signal through. If attention operates as an attenuator, then different amounts of information can come through each channel.

Attention thus becomes a matter of degree in the attenuator model. A schematic diagram of the attenuator model is provided in figure 3.2. Notice in this diagram that most of the information from the attended message is allowed through the attenuator. Simultaneously, some of the unattended message may also reach the level of pattern recognition. The attenuator model is still an early-selection theory in that attention filters information prior to meaningful analysis or pattern recognition. Unlike Broadbent's all-or-none approach, however, the attenuator model allows for the processing of more than one input at a time.

As with the earlier switch model, the attenuator theory must specify what cues attract and hold attention. Consistent with the switch model, Treisman suggests that physical cues are used to tune the attenuator such that changes in the physical cues can serve as the basis for adjusting the attenuation on various inputs. Unlike the switch model, however, the attenuator may also be influenced by the meaning of previously analyzed material. When the attended message switches channels, two events happen: the new information becomes incongruent with the previous information on the attended channel, and the previously unattended channel now contains information congruent with the previously attended channel since some of the meaning of the unattended message has been processed. Thus, attenuator control is exerted by both sensory and semantic information. Notice that the attenuator model can now explain the difficulty subjects have shadowing sentences whose meaning alternates from ear to ear.

Let us illustrate the operation of the attenuator model with a common situation which we will call the mini-cocktail-party phenomenon. Suppose you are one of a group of five people. Three of you are involved in the same conversation, while the other two are engaged in a separate discussion close by. If you think about this situation, you will realize that the conversation in which you are directly involved can usually be processed with little difficulty. You can attend to each of the other participants in turn and follow the continuity of the conversation. Assuming the meaning or content of the conversation remains consistent, the switching between the two speakers is accomplished primarily on the basis of physical cues, in this case the voice qualities of the participants. But what of the separate conversation occurring close by? In many cases, you have some idea of what the other people are talking about, although you do not hear everything they say. In terms of the attenuator model, some of the information in the unattended conversation has filtered through, even though the attenuator is set fairly high on this channel. The information picked up from the unattended channel allows you to enter the second conversation if you wish, with some idea of the topic.

Contrast to switch model

Although the attenuator model may appear more liberal on the question of preconscious processing than the switch model, the two ideas actually are identical on this question. The attenuator model differs from the switch model only in that the attenuator allows gradations of filtering rather than all-or-none selection. The two ideas are identical, however, in that the filtering occurs at the sensory memory level. While the attenuator permits some attention to multiple messages, it does not allow for any long-term effect of unattended information. Unattended information is left to decay in sensory memory and, like the switch model, the attenuator model thus assures that behavior is influenced only by conscious content.

To summarize early-selection filter theories, the revision from the switch model to the attenuator model represents loosening of the strictures on how many activities can be done at the same time. As the example illustrates, the attenuator model allows for the processing of more than one message for meaning. The attenuator model, however, was viewed by many theorists as too cumbersome. Furthermore, early selection theories of attention pose a logical problem in that the selection of information based on sensory signals seems to require recognition of information before it is processed. The decision to allocate processing capacity to one message and deny capacity to another message serves the goal of maintaining continuity in meaning. But how can we sift through various sources of information for continuity in meaning without determining the meaning of all inputs? The attenuator model attempts to deal with this issue by suggesting that partial analysis of all signals occurs. Some theorists view this solution as a half-measure. Why not assume that all incoming sensory information activates a meaningful representation? Selective attention then becomes a matter of deciding to which input to respond, which is the fundamental premise of late-selection filter models.

Late-Selection Filter Models

Certain theories, most notably those of Deutsch and Deutsch (1963) and Norman (1968), are known as *late-selection* filter models because selective attention is assumed to operate on response output. In contrast to the assumption that information is filtered or blocked prior to recognition, all information is assumed to activate its long-term memory representation. Very simply, the late-selection model proposes that all information is recognized. The human system, however, is assumed to be limited in the ability to organize a response to all of the sensory input. That is, we are unable to focus or concentrate upon all of the information activated in long-term memory and must select some fraction of that activated information to which we shall respond.

The difference between early- and late-selection theories would appear easy to test. Suppose we have dichotic input with subjects shadowing one of two messages. Why not simply ask the subjects, after both messages have been completed, what they can tell us about the nonshadowed material? In fact, several experiments have done just this and report that subjects know little about the nonshadowed message. However, late-selection theorists do not see these experiments as critical for at least two reasons.

First, a test for nonshadowed material following presentation of both messages requires a considerable delay between presentation and test of the information. During the delay, the nonshadowed material may simply have been forgotten. Even though all sensory information activates long-term memory, the nonshadowed information, which does not require an overt response at presentation, may be rapidly forgotten before the test. If this were the case, a slight modification of the proposed experiment would be more appropriate. Suppose the nonshadowed material is tested immediately after it occurs. That is, the shadowing is stopped at any point and the subject is asked what just occurred on the nonshadowed message. Should the immediate test not reveal some knowledge of the nonshadowed message?

Surprisingly, the late-selection model need not predict that the subject will be aware of unattended material, even if tested immediately. Perhaps a better understanding of this argument, and of the second reason that shadowing experiments are inconclusive in regard to late-selection theories, can be gained by examining a specific experiment. Treisman and Geffen (1967) designed what appeared to be a straightforward test of the late-selection model. Subjects heard two prose passages presented dichotically and were required to shadow one of the messages. In addition, the subjects were given a second task involving both the shadowed and nonshadowed passages. Certain words were designated targets, and anytime a target word occurred in either the shadowed or the nonshadowed message, the subject was to tap on a table. Treisman and Geffen (1967) found that the target words were detected 87 percent of the time in the shadowed message, but only 8 percent of the time in the nonshadowed message. The detection task required a response immediately upon presentation of the target word. Therefore, if all information is recognized, as the late-selection model argues, why are so few targets detected in the nonshadowed message?

The late-selection theorists argue that such results are due to the extraordinary demands of the shadowing task. Shadowing was initially devised for attention research because its very difficulty ensured that a subject focused upon one message. But if we assume that all information is recognized and that the limitation in our processing ability is in organizing responses, the difficulty of the shadowing task makes it impossible to determine how much a subject knows about an unshadowed message. Since only one response can be pursued, the subject cannot shadow one message and simultaneously perform *any* other response to indicate recognition of a nonshadowed message. Indeed, the late-selection theorists argue that awareness itself is a response, and if an integrated response such as shadowing is required for one message, the subject's ability to organize a second response to a different message, even as simple a response as perceptual awareness, will be sorely limited.

Preconscious Processing of Meaning

The foregoing discussion illustrates the position of late-selection theory on the possibility of preconscious processing. By locating the attentional filter at the point of response selection, all sensory input is allowed to activate its corresponding meaning, but we are aware of only the fraction of this information to which a response is organized. Marcel (1980) has reported an experiment, the results of which are quite consistent with the provocative position of late-selection theory.

Marcel's experiment takes advantage of an existing phenomenon known as *semantic priming.* In a simple laboratory procedure, the lexical-decision task, the subject sees a sequence of letter strings and must decide as rapidly as possible if the letter strings represent words. Semantic priming refers to the fact that if the stimulus preceding the current stimulus was semantically related to the current stimulus, the response to the current stimulus is affected by the preceding stimulus. For example, if the word *doctor* is presented and was preceded by the word *nurse,* the decision on *doctor* is much faster than it would have been if it were preceded by an unrelated word such as *peach.* The assumption is that the pattern recognition of the first word, *nurse,* results in the spread of activation to semantically related words such as *doctor* and thereby makes them easier to recognize when they are presented.

Marcel used a lexical-decision task in which the critical semantic relationships were among word triplets. For example, the subject might see *hand* followed by *palm* followed by *wrist.* An essential aspect of the experiment was the polysemous or multiple-meaning characteristic of the second word of the triplet. Thus, using the preceding example, a different triplet might be *tree* followed by *palm* followed by *wrist.* In the first case, the meaning of *palm* primed by *hand* is consistent with *wrist.* In the second case, the meaning of *palm* primed by *tree* is not consistent with the third word *wrist.* The final important aspect of Marcel's method was that the second word was pattern masked (refer to chapter 2 for a description of pattern masking) in one group of subjects and unmasked in a second group. The question of interest is, What effect will the second word have on decision time for the third word?

The surprising result was that the second word primed the third word when the two were consistent in meaning even if the second word was masked. That is, the time required to identify *wrist* as a word was faster if it was preceded by *hand—palm* than if the two preceding words were unrelated to *wrist,* but of particular importance is the observation that this priming was just as effective when *palm* was masked as when it was unmasked. As we saw in the last chapter, pattern masking seems to disrupt visual processing such that the subject is unaware of the masked stimulus. This was true in Marcel's experiment in that the subjects could not report the presence of the masked word. Nonetheless, the masked word produced the same level of semantic priming as the unmasked word of which the subjects were fully aware. The effect of the masked word strongly suggests *preconscious processing* of meaning in that the second word influenced responding to the third word but the subjects were unaware of the presence of the second word.

Of further importance to late-selection theory was the result obtained when the meaning of the second word was not related to the third word, the case of *tree—palm—wrist*. When the second word was unmasked, the incongruent meaning of *palm* did not facilitate responding to *wrist*. In the condition in which the second word was masked, response times to *wrist* were as fast as they were in the condition in which *palm's* primed meaning was congruent with *wrist*. The astonishing result is that semantic priming was equally effective for the congruent and incongruent meanings of the prime when the prime was masked!

Marcel interpreted these data entirely within the context of late-selection theory. The fact that masking the prime did not disrupt the priming effect suggests that the masked word was pattern recognized and that the activated meaning influenced semantically related words. Masking prevented awareness of the word. In this sense, Marcel argues that his data reflect preconscious processing. Information of which the subject was unaware had an effect upon later performance. Marcel goes on to argue that the function of consciousness is selectivity and thereby explains the different effects of an incongruent prime when it is masked and unmasked. Marcel argues that all meanings of a word are activated at the preconscious level but only one meaning can enter conscious awareness. In the unmasked condition, the meaning of *palm* reaches consciousness, but the meaning is the one biased by the prime. In the incongruent case, the meaning of *palm* is not related to *wrist*. In the masked condition, however, the meaning does not reach consciousness, and since all meanings of *palm* are activated preconsciously, the congruent meaning of *palm* is available to influence responding to *wrist*. Regardless of the accuracy of this interpretation, it is a prime example of late-selection theory. Attention operates after pattern recognition so that the activation of meaning is preconscious. However, attention operates to select among the activated meanings, allowing only a limited amount of information to reach consciousness.

Our extensive discussion of Marcel's experiment was designed to clarify the sense in which late-selection theory allows for preconscious processing. We also should be careful to note that the preconscious processing allowed by most late-selection theories is quite limited in its long-term effects. The extent of the preconscious effects is determined by the duration of the activity resulting from pattern recognition. Most theorists assume that this activity decays very rapidly unless the activated meaning is selected for conscious processing. Thus, most late-selection theories are in agreement with early-selection theories in denying long-term effects of preconscious processing upon later behavior, but the two theories do disagree over the possibility of short-lived effects of preconscious processing.

Impasse between Early-and Late-Selection Theory

The critical difference between early- and late-selection theories turns on the issue of preconscious processing. Evidence on this issue derives from studies of divided attention, particularly the question of what the subject knows about the unattended input. A quandary arises, however, in that the experimental conditions demanded by early-selection theory to assure that an input is unattended are likely to be conditions that late-selection theorists will argue preclude detection of the pattern recognition of the unattended information. Early-selection theories require a stringent response to the attended message to ensure that attention is not switched to the unattended message; late-selection theories argue that all messages activate meaning, but a response to two different messages is not possible. It thus appears impossible to design an experiment which would localize attention at the sensory level or at the level of response selection. This sort of dilemma in science typically produces attempts at compromise between the competing theories. In the study of attention, the compromise begins by assuming that perhaps both early and late selections contribute to the difficulty of doing two tasks simultaneously. Rather than view attention as a selective filter located at one point in the processing sequence, a new approach considers *limitation of the entire system* in relation to the particular task requirements.

CAPACITY MODELS OF ATTENTION

As we have seen, the primary question addressed by theories of attention concerns the limitation on our ability to deal with multiple input. Capacity models of attention (Kahneman, 1973) approach this issue by assuming that our psychological resources are finite; that is, we have a certain amount of *cognitive capacity* to devote to the various tasks confronting us. Different tasks require different amounts of this capacity, and the number of activities which can be done simultaneously is determined by the capacity each requires. If a single task demands intense concentration, no capacity will remain for an additional task. Within this approach, *attention is the process of allocating the resources or capacity to various inputs.* Attention then is important in determining which tasks are accomplished and how well the tasks are performed.

Secondary Task Technique and Cognitive Effort

The amount of capacity or effort required by one task will come at the expense of capacity that can be devoted to other tasks. With this assumption, measurement of the capacity demands of a task becomes possible. The technique is quite simple: the subject is instructed to perform a task and is given the impression that this primary task is the most important aspect of the experiment. Almost as an afterthought, however, instructions to perform a secondary task simultaneously with the primary task are also given. Estimates of the capacity required by the primary task are obtained on the secondary task. The harder the primary task, the poorer will be the performance on the secondary task (cf. Johnston, Greenberg, Fisher, & Martin, 1970; Britton & Tesser, 1982).

For example, consider an experiment from Ellis's laboratory. This experiment (Tyler, Hertel, McCallum, & Ellis, 1979) tested the proposition that memory for words will improve as the amount of *cognitive effort* devoted to the words increases. To vary the amount of effort or capacity exerted, the words were presented as anagrams and as missing elements in sentence-completion tasks. Anagrams are words whose letters are scrambled, such as *croodt*. Can you solve this anagram? How about a different anagram for the same word, *dortoc?* The second form is easier for most people than is the first. (The word, by the way, is *doctor.*) To vary effort, one group of subjects received hard anagrams and a second group received easy anagrams for the same words. To assure that the hard anagrams required more capacity, the subjects were required to perform a second task simultaneously with the anagram task. The second task was to press a button as rapidly as possible when a tone sounded. The speed of the response to the tone was taken as a measure of capacity required by the anagram task. The more capacity required by the anagram task, the less will be available to tone detection, and the slower will be the reaction to the tone.

A similar logic prevailed in the sentence-completion task. Subjects were given sentences in which, in some cases, the word was clearly implied. For example, this sentence, "The girl was awakened by her frightening _____," clearly implied the word *dream*. In this two-choice task in which two words are presented (*dream* versus *table*) the word *dream* is easy. Other sentences contained words in which the implication was not obvious and hence were more difficult.

Tone detection indeed was slower in the hard-anagram condition than in the easy-anagram condition. This outcome then permitted an interpretation of the memory data in terms of differential capacity requirements. Hard anagrams produced better memory for the words than did easy anagrams, presumably due to the greater effort required by hard anagrams.

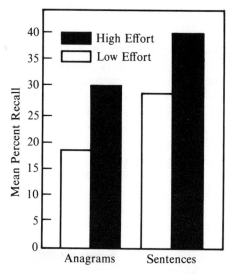

Figure 3.3 Recall of words in high-effort and low-effort anagrams and sentences. (From "Cognitive Effort and Memory" by S. W. Tyler, P. T. Hertel, M. C. McCallum, and H. C. Ellis, *Journal of Experimental Psychology: Human Learning and Memory*, 1979, *5*, 607–617. Copyright 1979 by the American Psychological Association. Reprinted by permission of the publisher and authors.)

Similarly, words that did not easily fit in the sentence (high-effort condition) were better recalled than those in the low-effort condition. The basic results are shown in figure 3.3, which plots recall as a function of cognitive effort.

The remaining issue is how to explain the effects of cognitive effort on recall. Two reasonable possibilities are that the allocation of capacity or processing resources leads to a more elaborated memory trace and/or to a more distinctive memory trace. Since this issue concerns the nature of encoding, we shall return to this topic in chapters 5 and 12. Our purpose in mentioning it here is simply to call your attention to the question of interpretation. The point of this experiment, for present purposes, is that the capacity demands of various tasks differ in measurable ways. Some tasks may require so much capacity that performing other tasks simultaneously is very difficult. Alternatively, some tasks, such as solving the easy anagrams, require little capacity. Indeed, some tasks seem to require no central processing capacity. Such tasks are said to be *automatic.*

Automatic Processing

Automatic processing is a very important concept within the capacity model. *Automaticity* refers to the apparent lack of central capacity requirements for a particular task. This is an important development because tasks that are performed automatically leave resources for other tasks; other tasks can be performed simultaneously with a task that is automatic. Driving a car has probably become automatic for you. Rarely do you have to concentrate on steering or braking, and you can leave processing capacity for carrying on conversation, listening to the radio, and thinking about other things.

The secondary task technique is used to study automaticity in the laboratory. Again, the rationale of the secondary task method involves measuring the amount of interference between two tasks. If a particular task can be performed as well with another task as it is alone, that task is assumed to require no capacity.

A very nice demonstration of automaticity is provided in an early experiment from Posner's laboratory (Posner & Boies, 1971). The primary experimental task was letter matching; the subject had to decide, as quickly as possible, whether two letters were the same or different. The letters were presented successively and were preceded by a warning signal. Specifically, the warning signal occurred to alert the subject to an upcoming letter, half a second later the first letter appeared, and one second later the second letter followed. As soon as the second letter appeared, the subject was to judge whether it was the same as the first letter. In addition to the letter-matching task, a tone-detection task was also included. The tone could occur at any stage of the letter-matching task, which allowed use of the reaction time to the tone to estimate the capacity requirements of each aspect of the letter-matching task.

Reaction times to the tone are shown in figure 3.4 as a function of the stages in letter matching. First, note that responding to the tone becomes faster after the warning signal than before the warning signal. Presumably, the subject becomes more alert and concentrates more at the onset of the warning signal. Next, you see in figure 3.4 that the reaction to the tone is not slowed by presentation of the first letter. This is the important result for our purposes. During pattern recognition of the first letter, responses to the tone are not disrupted, a clear case of two activities being done at the same time. The tone is not filtered or blocked, as filter theory might suppose, but rather both visual pattern recognition and auditory-detection tasks are performed simultaneously. We shall return to this point after a brief discussion of the remainder of the data presented in figure 3.4. Following

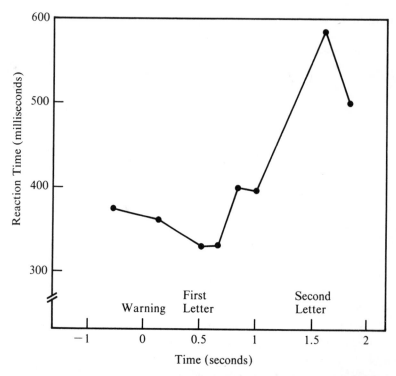

Figure 3.4 Reaction times to tone as a secondary task to letter matching. (From "Components of Attention" by M. I. Posner and S. J. Boies, *Psychological Review*, 1971, *78*, 391–408. Copyright 1971 by the American Psychological Association. Reprinted by permission of the publisher and authors.)

the first letter, reaction time to the tone increases substantially. This result is reasonably interpreted as due to rehearsal of the first letter. Rehearsal does require capacity, which disrupts responding to the tone. Reaction time increases even further following the second letter, the stage at which the decision about the letters is made. The decision process occupies even more capacity than rehearsal, which leads to this further increase in reaction time.

The major point of this experiment is that recognition of letters does not disrupt reaction time to auditory signals. Processing of the letter is automatic; little of the cognitive resources is required for this task. Of course, this result holds for college students who have had much practice in letter recognition. Imagine a young child just learning the alphabet. Letter recognition is likely to require much more effort, and only after considerable practice will it develop to an automatic skill.

In an important paper, Hasher and Zacks (1979) have extended the concept of automaticity to a variety of memory processes. The interested student should consult this important paper for further discussion of effort and automatic processing.

Automaticity and Reading

You can easily see that the development of automaticity is important for normal functioning in everyday tasks. The Posner experiment, for example, is directly applicable to reading. Reading requires rapid access to the meaning of verbal units such as paragraphs, sentences, and words. Yet reading presumably begins with letter recognition. If each letter recognition required much effort, reading would be painfully slow. Not only is letter recognition automatic, but access to word meaning appears to occur with little effort. The primary evidence for this assertion comes from studies of the *Stroop effect.*

The Stroop effect occurs in a special kind of dual-task situation. For example, suppose you are given a list of color names, *Red, Blue, Green,* and *Orange,* but each word is printed in an ink color different from the color word. *Red* is printed in blue ink. Your job is to name the ink colors as rapidly as possible. The task in no way requires processing or even noticing the word. Nonetheless, incongruent word and ink color, *Red* printed in blue, produces slower responses than congruent conditions, *Red* printed in red. Word meaning appears to be processed and then interferes with color naming, even though the task does not require word processing. Word meaning is automatically processed and cannot be ignored.

Data such as these have led to the argument that automaticity is a very important step in learning to read. But how is it that a task becomes automatic?

Development of Automaticity

Some psychological processes never require central processing capacity. Initial sensory registration and feature analysis, for example, are always automatic processes. Neisser (1967) called these "preattentive processes" because they never require conscious effort. Beyond this initial stage of processing, however, we have seen that more complex tasks, such as driving and accessing word meaning, develop from effortful activities to automatic tasks. How does this happen?

Although the precise mechanisms underlying the development of automaticity are unknown, the critical ingredient in automatization clearly is practice. The importance of practice has been clear in the examples we have used thus far, driving and reading. Many other tasks, typing for example, also become automatized with sufficient practice. You must realize that we are talking about more than just increasing performance or skill with practice. Certainly good practice (not just practice per se) does make performance better, if not perfect, but automatization refers to performance of the task with fewer cognitive resources. A well-practiced golf swing is not only likely to be better, but it also requires less thought.

Some tasks may never become automatic, but practice still improves performance. The task posed by college courses, which we assume is the comprehension or understanding of certain material, will not be automated, but it does become easier with effective practice. We all know that you "learn how to study" as you progress through the college years. Perhaps this ability is due in large part to focusing processing capacity on the task at hand. You become more proficient at extracting salient materials from lectures and readings, not so much because "you learn what to look for," as because your ability to focus or concentrate on material sharpens. Thus, your general understanding of the material improves, with the typical result that you earn better grades as a senior than as a freshman even though you may spend less time with the books. So effective practice is important to tasks that require processing capacity, even those which do not become automated. There is no trick, nor is there necessarily a shortcut; if you want to become proficient at intellectual or motor-skills tasks, you must practice well.

Preconscious Processing and Automaticity

The concept of automaticity appears to place the capacity model in complete sympathy with the possibility of preconscious processing. Indeed, Hasher and Zacks (1979) list lack of awareness as one of the criteria of automaticity. However, does this mean that an automated task occurs without attentional influence? The data from the Stroop task appear to support this contention in that the response to ink color is influenced by a word's meaning even though the instructions are to attend to ink color. In spite of these instructions, word meaning is processed automatically. Does this mean that activation of word meaning, and tasks such as reading which require meaning activation, are uninfluenced by attention?

To answer this question, Kahneman and Henik (1981) devised a modified Stroop task in which a square and a circle appear unpredictably on either side of a fixation point. Within the square and the circle are printed respectively the words *red* and *house,* and both words are printed in green ink. The subjects' task is to name the ink color in the circle. An illustration of the stimulus configuration is presented in figure 3.5. Since the subject is fixating at a center point between the square and the circle, the quality of the sensory information within the square and the circle is the same. Thus, the word *red* within the square activates the sensory receptors, and if activation of meaning is automatic, the activation of *red* should produce the normal Stroop interference when naming the incompatible ink color in the

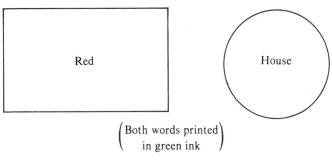

Figure 3.5 Example of Kahneman and Henik stimuli. Both the circle and square fall on the visual field. The subject must name the ink color. Instructions to name the ink color in the square produce No stroop effect, but significant interference is produced when the ink color in the circle must be named.

circle. Although the time to name the ink color in this case is slightly slower than in the case of two color-neutral words appearing in the circle and square, the interference produced by the color word in the square upon naming the ink color in the circle is minimal compared to the case in which the incompatible word *red,* printed in green ink, also appears in the circle. That is, a color word incompatible with the ink color produces minimal interference if the word and ink color are spatially separate. This result should not occur if the activation of meaning were automatic. How are we to interpret these results?

Kahneman and Treisman (1984) suggest that these results contradict the notion that the Stroop effect itself and, by inference, the process of reading, occur without attentional control. Their suggestion is that selective attention operates to filter irrelevant objects, such as the square and its contents. Thus, although the word *red* may fall on the sensory receptors, central attention successfully filters this information when the instructions were to name the ink color in the circle. Attention focuses upon the object, the circle. The psychological processes engaged by the circle do not distinguish among the task-relevant and -irrelevant properties. That is, if the word *red* printed in green ink appears in the circle, all properties of the object are processed. Thus, Kahneman and Treisman draw an important distinction between perception of different objects and perception of the properties of a given object. The former is a process under attentional control while the latter may be automatic.

The importance of this distinction is that it suggests that perception of the properties of an object may occur without intent, or perhaps even awareness, and in that sense, the processing of those properties is automatic, and perhaps preconscious. However, the processing of the properties of the object requires attention to that object, and central attention operates to select objects for perceptual processing. The implication is that not all information reaching the sensory receptors is preconsciously processed.

Rather, attention selects objects for perceptual processing, an affair which may be quite conscious and intentional. The subsequent processing of the attended objects may include many properties of the object that are irrelevant to a task. Attention does not filter processing of properties of the attended object. Thus, object discrimination is a capacity-consuming, attentional task. Properties of the attended object, however, may be preconsciously processed.

SUMMARY

The description of attention and its relationship to perception provided by Kahneman and Treisman (1984) uses elements of all three theories of attention, early-selection, late-selection, and capacity theories. The implication is that all three ideas capture some important aspect of cognitive functioning, but no one of the theories alone can completely describe performance on tasks as simple as Kahneman and Henik's (1981) modified Stroop test. Common behavior, such as being distracted from reading by a song on the radio, may involve early-selection, late-selection, and automated processing, and as we have seen in this chapter, each theory appealed to different types of laboratory procedures for its support. In some sense, the restriction to particular kinds of tasks probably limits the ability of any one theory to completely explain behavior in other situations.

Early-selection theory is designed to protect conscious processing from an overload of sensory information. Selective filtering of the sensory information was presumed to provide this protection, and the laboratory experiments designed to study this process required the subject to select and process one of several competing messages. These early studies indicated that people were quite capable of focusing upon one message but were severely handicapped in dividing their attention among several messages, all leading to the conclusion that perceptual processing required attention.

Late-selection theory is designed to insure that coherent action can be taken upon the available sensory information. Attention serves to filter perceptually processed information into consciousness such that responding can be directed to the most important perceptual information and that competing responses to other material do not paralyze adaptive action. The laboratory experiments designed to study these processes generally required the subject to detect a target, of which they were forewarned, amidst distractor items. The results of these experiments generally show some influence of the "unattended" events upon the target event, leading to the conclusion that attention does not influence perception but rather limits the entry of perceived material to consciousness.

Capacity theory extended late-selection theory in the sense that certain responses were assumed to be beyond attentional control. These "automatic" responses required minimal conscious processing for either the perceptual data or response organization. In this theory, attention serves to allocate the conscious processing capacity to various tasks, and laboratory experiments provoked by the theory primarily study cost-benefit trade-offs of performing multiple tasks. The results of these experiments generally suggest that multiple tasks can be processed in accord with the conscious-processing demands of each task and that some tasks seem to demand little, if any, conscious processing.

Perhaps we can summarize the current state of affairs by agreeing with Kahneman and Treisman (1984) that each of these approaches has some merit. To focus upon some aspect of the environment may require selective filtering of sensory information corresponding to other aspects of the environment. If you really listen to the song on the radio, you really can no longer read for comprehension. In that sense, selective attention does affect what is perceived. Within the selected information, however, elements may be perceived which are not the focus of attention. You may try intentionally to concentrate upon the lyrics of the song but also perceive the rhythm. In that sense, perception may occur for unattended elements of the *attended* event.

In this rather complex relationship between perception, attention, and consciousness, the message is that selective perception requires attentional filtering, as mandated by early selection theory. Certain aspects of the selected perception may be processed without awareness or intent, as described by late-selection theory and capacity theory. In all of this, however, those aspects of the situation which are attended become the substance of consciousness, and on that, all theories agree. Attention is the gateway to consciousness.

MULTIPLE-CHOICE ITEMS

1. Which theory of attention is least flexible in allowing us to do more than one task at a time?
   a. early-selection filter theory
   b. late-selection filter theory
   c. attenuator theory
   d. capacity theory

2. Experimental tests of early- and late-selection theories are very difficult because
   a. the difference between the two theories is slight
   b. the primary task required by the late-selection theory is too rigorous to allow early selection to occur
   c. early selection would then rule out any possibility of late selection
   d. the tasks required by early-selection theory to occupy attention will also occupy attention according to late selection

3. Studies of dichotic listening show that
   a. nonshadowed material is not processed for any meaning
   b. nonshadowed material is processed for some meaning
   c. shadowed material is not processed for meaning
   d. shadowed and nonshadowed material do not differ in degree of meaningful processing

4. In the secondary task technique, capacity is measured by
   a. the sum of reaction times to primary and secondary tasks
   b. the difference in reaction time to primary and secondary tasks
   c. reaction time to the primary task
   d. reaction time to the secondary task

5. The primary determinant of automaticity is
   a. the material
   b. the other tasks required
   c. the amount and kind of practice
   d. genetic

TRUE–FALSE ITEMS

1. One of the reasons why we need the concept of attention is to guide selection of information from the sensory register.

2. Capacity theory of attention argues that it is difficult or impossible to do two activities at the same time.

3. If we are allocating attention or capacity to a task, we are then also aware of that task.

4. The difficulty of shadowing makes it a useful technique for testing switch models, but also makes it useless for late-selection models of attention.

5. The late-selection theory of attention suggests that we are aware or conscious of all sensory input.

6. The Stroop effect suggests that access to word meaning may be automatic.

DISCUSSION ITEMS

1. Describe the relationship between sensory register, pattern recognition, and attention. Be careful to include a discussion of why attention is necessary within this framework.

2. Discuss the development of capacity models of attention from the research on early- and late-selection filter models.

3. Discuss the effect that the complexity and difficulty of a task have on attention.

ANSWERS TO MULTIPLE-CHOICE ITEMS

1. (a) According to early-selection filter theory, unattended information receives no processing, and it would not be possible to do anything with the unattended information.

2. (d) Tests of early- and late-selection theories are difficult because early-selection theory requires a stringent shadowing task to ensure attention is paid to one message, and the task then makes it impossible to organize a response to unattended material, according to late-selection theory.

3. (b) Shadowing studies have shown that some of the unattended information is processed for meaning.

4. (d) The capacity required by the primary task can be measured by the reaction time to the secondary task.

5. (c) Automaticity results primarily from extensive practice of a task.

ANSWERS TO TRUE–FALSE ITEMS

1. (True) Since the sensory register contains more information than can be processed, some mechanism is needed to selectively process from the sensory register.

2. (False) According to capacity theory, the number of tasks which can be performed simultaneously depends on the amount of capacity required by each task.

3. (False) Some tasks, such as walking, require such small capacity that we rarely are aware of performing these tasks.

4. (True) A difficult task is required to ensure attention within a switch model, but a difficult task prevents the organization of a response to unattended material, according to the late-selection theory.

5. (False) Although all input reaches the level of pattern recognition, according to late-selection theory, only the attended information reaches the level of awareness.

6. (True) The Stroop effect suggests that the meaning of words is automatically activated even when some other aspect of the word, such as ink color, is attended.

4

SHORT-TERM, WORKING MEMORY

Short-term memory is the first concept we encounter that is designed to explain events occurring at the conscious level. Consequently, the characteristics of short-term memory will be easily recognized as part of our everyday experience. How many times have you been introduced to a small group of people, and as soon as the introduction is completed, you turn to the first person introduced and simply cannot remember the person's name? Equally frustrating is the experience of obtaining a telephone number from Directory Assistance and having no pencil or pen to record the number. What do you do? Usually, most of us repeat the number rapidly until we dial it, but if anyone talks to us or we even think of something other than the number before it is dialed, we must make another call to Directory Assistance. A different characteristic of short-term memory emerges when you undertake a grocery-shopping errand. If the grocery list includes only a few items, you have little difficulty remembering the items, perhaps supplementing memory with some repetition. If the list is longer and has approximately five items or more, an energy-conscious shopper writes the items down.

As with the other conscious memory phenomena, we are most aware of short-term memory when it fails, as each of these examples illustrates. Failures, however, are quite instructive for students of memory in understanding the system. These examples, for instance, illustrate the two cardinal attributes of short-term memory. First, information is retained briefly, as shown in the instances of introduction to new people and receiving a number from Directory Assistance, unless the information is maintained by repetition. Second, short-term memory has quite limited capacity; long lists cannot be easily maintained.

The principal question for psychologists has been, How are we to understand the differences between short-term and long-term memory? Are these two different memory systems, obeying different principles, perhaps occupying different locations? Or do the differences reflect different states of essentially the same information? William James (1890) exemplified this latter position with the distinction between primary (short-term) and secondary (long-term) memory. James described primary memory as the contents of consciousness; that is, short-term memory referred to information under active consideration at the moment. As such, the contents of short-term memory would be subject to the limitations of conscious span, which we discussed in the last chapter, and since thought processes are constantly changing, the contents of consciousness would be fleeting. Thus, for James, short-term memory was information in the active conscious state, subject to the capacity and duration limits of conscious thought. The primary source of the information in short-term memory was long-term memory. Long-term memory was not a different place but rather was information in an inactive state. Very simply, all of the things about which you could think, but currently are not thinking, constitute the contents of long-term memory. For example, assuming you are not presently thinking about the Fourth of July, that is inactive information. Of course, as soon as we mention the Fourth of July, you think about it, transforming the information to an active, conscious state. James's idea is one which distinguishes short- and long-term memory as active and inactive memory. We shall return to this idea later in the chapter because it has been revitalized with the renewal of interest in consciousness and awareness.

A somewhat different conceptualization of short- and long-term memory emerged with the information-processing approach in the 1960s. This view became extremely influential and represented a more elaborate theoretical approach to the differences between short- and long-term memory than just the state of the information. Short-term and long-term memory were to be considered completely different memory systems. One manifestation of this type of distinction is that we tend to think of the two as located in different places. Although the spatial separation is not necessarily entailed by the approach, the important point is that the principles governing memory would be completely different. That is, variables affecting retention—such as the time between input and test, the meaningfulness and organization of the material, perhaps amnesia—should exert different effects upon short-term and long-term memory. If so, the two types of memory require different theories; that is, they are different systems.

We shall begin by discussing a particular theory of short- and long-term memory as different systems. Then we shall examine the data for and against this theory and conclude the chapter by returning to the relationship between short-term memory and conscious contents.

THE MODAL MODEL OF MEMORY

Richard Atkinson and Richard Shiffrin proposed a view of the entire memory system in 1968, which subsequently became so influential that it is known as the "modal" or typical information-processing model of memory. It is also known as the stage model of memory because it proposes that the flow of information moves in stages through the memory processes. Their model is particularly pertinent at this point, because it concentrates heavily upon short-term memory, including the relationship between sensory register, short-term memory, and long-term memory. A schematic view of the model is presented in figure 4.1.

According to Atkinson and Shiffrin's model, incoming information flows from the sensory register to short-term memory to permanent storage in long-term memory. The transfer of information from the sensory register to short-term memory is controlled by attention, described in chapter 3 as

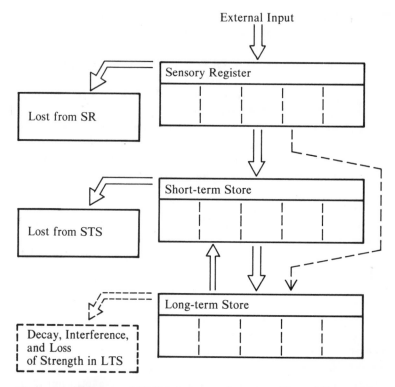

External Input

Sensory Register

Lost from SR

Short-term Store

Lost from STS

Long-term Store

Decay, Interference,
and Loss
of Strength in LTS

Figure 4.1 Atkinson and Shiffrin's stages of memory. (From "Human Memory: A Proposed System and Its Control Processes" by R. C. Atkinson and R. M. Shiffrin, in K. W. Spence and J. T. Spence, Eds., *The Psychology of Learning and Motivation: Advances in Theory and Research,* Vol. 2. New York: Academic Press, 1968. Copyright 1968 by Academic Press. Used by permission.)

the decision to allocate the pattern-recognition process to sensory information. Once in short-term memory, the information is subject to *control processes,* which are operations serving a variety of memory functions. For example, the most important control process is *rehearsal.* Rehearsal serves two functions: to maintain information in short-term memory and to transfer information from short-term memory to long-term memory.

Other control processes include *coding,* which involves attaching appropriate information from long-term memory to the short-term information. For example, a telephone number is easier to remember if it is coded into larger units than dealt with as single digits: 1-800-555-1212 becomes one, eight hundred, five fifty-five, twelve, twelve. The rules for transforming the single digits are retrieved from long-term memory and applied to the string of single digits in short-term memory. The strategies for retrieving information from long-term memory are another important short-term memory control process. For example, if you are asked this question, "Who is the primary author of the switch model of attention?" your strategy may be to activate long-term information concerning "names associated with the psychology of attention." These names are then brought to short-term memory where you decide which is the correct answer.

You should now see that the concept of short-term memory entails much **more** than just memory for information after a short period of time. *Short-term memory is a conceptual system which not only stores information, but also serves as a work space for rehearsing, coding, retrieving, and decision making.* An important feature of the Atkinson and Shiffrin model is that the short-term memory system has a severely limited capacity. This implies not only that a small number of items can be stored, but also that the control processes require some of the limited capacity. Rehearsal, for example, may guard some information against loss from short-term memory, but this gain comes at the expense of other items. Only so much can be rehearsed at one time, as can be proved by trying to repeat rapidly the numbers 58615294 while simultaneously reading this text. In general, the control processes expedite the processing of some information, but facilitation comes at the expense of other information. This event is another instance of the assumption of limited-processing capacity discussed in chapter 3.

Much of the research surrounding short-term memory has the ultimate goal of establishing the characteristics of short-term memory, particularly to demonstrate that these characteristics differ from those of long-term memory. Such research is essential to establishing a distinction between short- and long-term memory systems, because elaborate theoretical descriptions of two different memory systems would be unnecessary if there were no evidence for two different types of memory.

CHARACTERISTICS OF SHORT-TERM MEMORY

Three basic characteristics have been proposed to distinguish short-term memory from long-term memory. These characteristics, *trace life, storage capacity,* and *nature of the code,* also distinguish short-term memory from the sensory register. Remember that the sensory register is characterized by a very brief trace, stored in a veridical form in a large-capacity system. As the information moves on to short-term memory, the trace life increases somewhat, although it is still brief by the standards of long-term memory. The information is transformed into a phonetic code in short-term memory, and the capacity of the system is considerably smaller than either the sensory register or long-term memory. We shall now briefly consider the evidence for these characteristics, evidence which is crucial to any conceptual distinction between short- and long-term memory systems.

Duration of Short-Term Memory

Among the modern classics of experimental psychology is the research claiming to demonstrate a short-term trace. Very similar experiments were reported almost simultaneously by Brown (1958) in England and Peterson and Peterson (1959) in the United States. The experimental procedure, now known as the *Brown-Peterson paradigm,* is quite simple. Subjects are shown three items consisting of nonsense syllables or words for three seconds. Memory for these triads is then tested following a retention interval which varies from 0 to 18 seconds. Such a task does not seem to be particularly difficult: How hard can it be to remember three simple items over a period as short as 18 seconds? Indeed, the task would be no challenge at all if the subjects were allowed to repeat the items during the retention interval. This is not the case, however, because a *rehearsal prevention* task is inserted between presentation of the material and the recall test. A rehearsal prevention task is an activity which prohibits the subject from repeating the test items. For example, the subject may be required to count backward by threes from a designated number, a task which is sufficiently difficult that rehearsal becomes impossible. We are then in a position to examine memory in the absence of rehearsal.

The typical results of a Brown-Peterson experiment are shown in figure 4.2. The critical aspect of these results is the rapid forgetting that occurs over the very short retention interval. Notice that after 18 seconds, only about 10 percent of the material is remembered. Such a poor memory after such a brief period of time was a startling finding which later served as one basis for claiming a separate, short-duration memory system.

When these data first appeared in the late 1950s, they were strikingly in contrast to what was known about forgetting, mainly from studies of long-term memory. At that time, forgetting was seen as a gradual process occurring as the result of *interference.* Interference is produced by the intervention of other material between the presentation of a to-be-remembered event and the memory test. For example, suppose you have a history class immediately after your psychology class. Your memory for the material learned about psychology is subject to interference from the material learned about history. We shall discuss theories of forgetting at a later point, but it is critical at the moment to notice that interference implies that memory failure results from competition among stored information. Forgotten material does not go away, but rather loses in the momentary competition for expression.

The rapid forgetting in the Brown-Peterson paradigm challenged a unitary view of interference as the cause of forgetting. Not only did massive forgetting occur in a very short time, but also the source of interference in the Brown-Peterson task was not initially apparent. Some theorists then

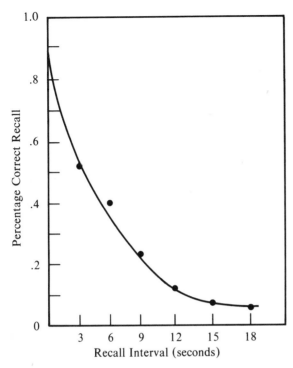

Figure 4.2 Percentage of items correctly recalled after various retention intervals. (From "Short-Term Retention of Individual Verbal Items" by L. R. Peterson and M. J. Peterson, *Journal of Experimental Psychology,* 1959, *58,* 193–198. Copyright 1959 by the American Psychological Association. Reprinted by permission of the publisher and authors.)

claimed that short-term memory is subject to *decay* of information, a position on forgetting which differs substantially from interference. Decay results from disuse, failure to rehearse in this situation, and implies that the forgotten material has disappeared from memory altogether. The important point to note here is that the Brown-Peterson data not only suggest a brief trace in short-term memory but also seem to imply completely different principles of forgetting in short-term memory and long-term memory. It is the claim for different principles in forgetting that established these experiments as controversial in the attempt to describe memory as being successive, separate stages.

The Brown-Peterson paradigm also establishes the importance of rehearsal in maintaining information in short-term memory, a point later emphasized by Atkinson and Shiffrin's inclusion of rehearsal among the important control processes. Rehearsal not only serves to counteract the short-term trace, but also serves as the mechanism of transfer to long-term memory. In this regard, a useful distinction can be drawn between two types of rehearsal.

Rote or *maintenance rehearsal* functions primarily to keep information active in short-term memory. Maintenance rehearsal corresponds to simple repetition of information. *Elaborative rehearsal* involves relating the information to other known information, a process involving meaning. For example, if the words *dog, tree,* and *cat* are to be remembered, elaborative rehearsal might involve the construction of a relationship among the words, even to forming a visual image of a dog chasing a cat up a tree. Elaborative rehearsal functions to quickly transfer information to long-term memory. Thus, the two types of rehearsal extend the trace life of short-term information but in different ways. In either case, you also should keep in mind the trade-off between rehearsal and capacity. The rehearsal process may increase the duration of some information, but rehearsal requires some of the limited capacity which is then unavailable to other items. We now turn to a discussion of studies designed to demonstrate the limitations on capacity of short-term memory.

Capacity of Short-Term Memory

In an influential paper Miller (1956) argued that the capacity of short-term memory ranged from five to nine items, with the average being seven items. These estimates were obtained from Miller's study of immediate memory span performance. Immediate memory span is measured by presenting a list of items, digits, letters, or words and determining how many items can be recalled in their correct serial order immediately after presentation. In this task, Miller noticed that most people remembered between five and nine items, which suggested that short-term memory has quite limited capacity. It is no accident, by the way, that the standard telephone number is seven digits; the telephone company takes Miller's estimate quite seriously in its effort to reduce the number of calls to Directory Assistance.

Seven items may seem an unrealistically small number, especially when we consider that short-term memory must funnel vast amounts of information from the sensory register into long-term memory. Notice, however, that "item" has not yet been defined. An item is a *chunk* of information ranging from a single letter to an idea expressed by a paragraph. At this point, another of Atkinson and Shiffrin's control processes becomes important. As information arrives in short-term memory, relationships may be detected among individual items which allow the items to be organized or "chunked" into a single unit. Simple examples of chunking include grouping individual letters, *c-a-t,* into a single unit, *cat.* More complex chunking involves detailed linguistic descriptions that are organized into single idea units. For example, this description, "The man, whose skin was wrinkled and leathery, had silver-white hair and supported his slow, limping walk with a cane," might be reduced to a single idea, "The man is old."

Regardless of the complexity of chunking, the process of integrating or organizing discrete items into larger units is actually an example of elaborative rehearsal. To form a coherent unit, it is necessary to detect a relationship among the discrete items based on what is known about the items. What is known about the items is stored in long-term memory. Thus, chunking must require retrieving information from long-term memory to aid organization of items in short-term memory.

Chunking is a useful process which can serve to offset the extreme capacity limitations of short-term memory. More information can be stored by increasing the information in each unit, thus making the limited number of chunks rich in information value. As with rehearsal, however, the chunking process consumes short-term memory capacity, and the advantage of chunking certain information comes at the cost of other information, which may be lost due to lack of rehearsal. To illustrate this point, consider the difficulty of coding 7-3-1-9-8-0 as a single number while simultaneously repeating or rehearsing the words, *horse, justice,* and *green.* Again, we see that critical decisions concerning allocation of processing capacity must be made in short-term memory.

The limited capacity of short-term memory contrasts sharply with the large storage capability of long-term memory. Everything we know is assumed to be stored in long-term memory, a very large amount of information indeed. This marked difference in storage capacity is then taken as additional evidence for separate systems of short-term memory and long-term memory.

Coding of Short-Term Memory

Another distinction between short-term memory and long-term memory is the memory code of each system. Long-term memory is assumed to be based on a semantic code, and short-term memory is acoustically or phonetically coded. Information is stored in long-term memory in terms of its meaning, whereas sound patterns are remembered in short-term memory. Research supporting these assumptions has demonstrated greater confusion among semantically similar words in long-term memory and greater confusion among acoustically similar words in short-term memory.

For example, Baddeley (1966, a, b) describes experiments in which subjects were asked to remember either a five-word list or a ten-word list. The shorter list is within the capacity of short-term memory, while the longer list exceeds short-term capacity and must reflect the operation of long-term memory. In both the five-word and ten-word lists, all of the words either sounded alike (e.g., *bat, hat, cat*), had a similar meaning (e.g., *tiny, small, little*), or were unrelated (e.g., *bat, desk, tiny*). The five-word lists were poorly recalled when all of the words sounded alike, but similarity of meaning produced recall much like that of unrelated words. With the ten-word list, however, semantic similarity produced poor recall, and acoustically similar words were recalled as well as were the unrelated words. This outcome can be understood by assuming that similar memory codes produce confusion among the items. Since acoustic similarity but not semantic similarity disrupted memory for short lists, Baddeley argues that short-term memories are acoustically coded. Semantic confusion in the longer lists suggests the existence of a meaning code in long-term memory. Thus, studies such as Baddeley's are offered as further evidence that different kinds of information are stored at different stages in the retention interval. If it is valid, such a conclusion would suggest a useful distinction between short-term memory and long-term memory.

Additional Evidence for Short-Term Memory

Short-term memory has a brief trace and small capacity and is acoustically coded, whereas long-term memory is assumed to be permanent, to have a large capacity, and to be semantically coded. These characteristics are the primary distinctions between short- and long-term memory systems. These distinctions, however, can also be used to interpret other situations, and to the extent that the interpretation is reasonable, additional evidence is provided for the short-term–long-term distinction. Simply stated, if a particular phenomenon can be better understood by the assumption of a difference between short-term memory and long-term memory, we have another reason for accepting the distinction.

The Serial Position Effect

A good example of this approach is to apply the short-term–long-term distinction to the *serial position curve*. The serial position curve depicts the accuracy of recall of an ordered list as a function of the input position of an item in the list. Early items are recalled well and so are the last items, but the middle items are remembered poorly, resulting in a U-shaped function such as that depicted in figure 4.3. Examples of the serial position effect are quite common. Consider a young child learning the alphabet; *A B C* and *X Y Z* are not a problem for the child, but the middle letters are the last added to the child's knowledge. Many children in the initial stages of alphabet learning even treat *L M N O P* as a single letter. Knowing about the serial position effect can help you prepare for serial rote memory tests. Whether you are faced with remembering a long grocery list or the names of the bones in the hand for a biology test, you can be sure that the first

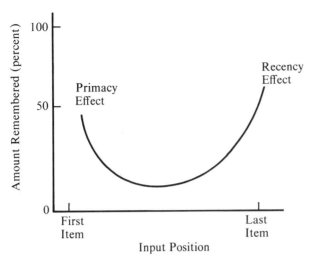

Figure 4.3 An idealized version of a serial position curve showing memory as a function of the input position of the material.

and last items will be best remembered. Thus, you may want to give special attention to the middle items in preparing for a test involving serial retention.

Why does the serial position effect occur? One explanation is based entirely on the distinction between short- and long-term memory systems. The early items are recalled well, which is called the *primacy effect*, because they are the first to enter short-term memory and thus allow adequate opportunity for rehearsal and subsequent transfer to long-term memory. The middle items, however, enter short-term memory while the first items are being rehearsed, and hence little capacity is available to rehearse the middle items. Therefore, the middle items are not likely to be transferred to long-term memory. The last items in the list are also well remembered, a finding called the *recency effect*, presumably because these items are still in short-term memory at the time of recall.

This explanation of the serial position curve was tested by Glanzer and Cunitz (1966) in an experiment which demonstrated that the primacy and recency effects can be manipulated independently. In one condition, subjects were given a list of twenty words to remember, but after the words were presented and before the memory test, the subjects were required to perform a *rehearsal prevention task*. After the rehearsal prevention activity, the normal recency effect did not occur, presumably because rehearsal prevention allowed time for the last items to decay from short-term memory prior to the recall test. The primacy effect was unchanged by rehearsal prevention as should be the case if the early list items are recalled from long-term memory. In the second part of the same research, the primacy effect was reduced by increasing the rate at which the items were presented. Faster presentation rates decrease the time available for rehearsal and thus should reduce the probability of items entering long-term memory. Since the primacy effect is due to the early list items reaching long-term memory, the decrease in primacy effects with faster presentation rates is consistent with interpretation of the serial position curve as the joint operation of short-term memory and long-term memory.

Amnesia

Studies of patients suffering from amnesia have been used as another source of indirect evidence for the distinction between short-term and long-term memory. Serious head injuries and some diseases, such as Alzheimer's disease, produce a memory impairment known as anterograde amnesia. Anterograde amnesia refers to the inability to remember events following an injury or disease.

In some cases, the patient has a normal memory span for recent events, but cannot retain the information for long periods (e.g., Baddeley & Warrington, 1970; Milner, 1970). Such a pattern suggests that short-term memory itself is intact, but the mechanisms for transferring information from short-term to long-term memory have been disrupted. In effect, these patients were thought to be incapable of learning anything new because information could not be transferred from short-term to long-term memory.

In other cases of anterograde amnesia, the immediate memory span was far below normal (e.g., Shallice & Warrington, 1970; Warrington, Logue, & Pratt, 1971). In at least one instance, the patient had an immediate memory span of one item! Performance such as this is easily interpreted as disruption of the short-term memory store. Thus, the pattern of memory loss in anterograde amnesia can also be interpreted by using the distinction between short-term and long-term memory, particularly by assuming that injury and disease can disrupt the brain processes corresponding to short-term storage and transfer from short-term to long-term memory.

SUMMARY OF THE SHORT-TERM–LONG-TERM DISTINCTION

To this point what emerges from the theory and research is the suggestion of two distinct memory systems which obey different principles and produce differential retention. Immediate memory for new events is very fragile because short-term memory decays rapidly and has small capacity. In contrast, the information which progresses through short-term memory is stored permanently in long-term memory. Long-term memory has a huge capacity, storing all of the knowledge we have of the world. Whatever forgetting occurs in long-term memory is the result of interference produced by intervening events. The rapid forgetting in short-term memory occurs due to decay or disuse, a condition which can be prevented with constant rehearsal. Rehearsal, however, requires a code which is easily repeated. Sound patterns satisfy this requirement, and therefore a phonetic code in short-term memory becomes highly adaptive. It is much more difficult to imagine rote repetition of visual images and of meaning codes, yet these codes would be quite efficient in long-term memory where decay is no problem and rehearsal is unnecessary.

In summary, the stage model assumes that a different set of principles is required to understand both short-term memory and long-term memory. Since the major demarcation between the memory systems is the length of time after presentation of the material, the laws of memory would differ as a function of the length of the retention interval. As plausible as this theory seems, it is not perfectly clear why the memory system would operate completely differently for recent versus past events. Therefore, concern over this issue led to critical reexamination of the evidence for separate short- and long-term memories.

ONE MEMORY SYSTEM OR TWO MEMORY SYSTEMS? —Objections to Stage Model.

The examples of short-term retention given at the beginning of the chapter are real enough, and the experimental work just discussed may seem to require separate short- and long-term memory systems. If we accept this distinction, we must then try to establish at least two, and probably three, completely different sets of principles governing memory, one each for the sensory register, short-term memory, and long-term memory. Furthermore, we also need to try to understand the relationships among the systems. It is not difficult to imagine what a complicated activity this becomes. Consequently, psychologists have carefully examined the short-term–long-term distinction to ensure that it provided the best description of memory. *As a result, many theorists now contend that two separate systems are unnecessary and propose an alternative which assumes only one memory system.* Let us now examine the arguments against separate memory systems or stores. We will see serious objections to the stage model and to the idea of distinct memory systems.

Forgetting in Short-Term Memory

We have seen that a major distinction between long-term memory and short-term memory is the duration of the trace. The Brown-Peterson data show rapid forgetting for recent experiences if rehearsal is prevented, and this rapid forgetting is explained by assuming that unrehearsed information decays rapidly. Long-term memories, however, remain available in the absence of any use or rehearsal, as is evident by consulting any of myriad facts we know but have not thought about recently. Decay, then, must not be operating in long-term memory; consequently, some other principle of forgetting must control failure of long-term memory. Thus, we now see that the differences in the duration of short- and long-term memory traces point to a more fundamental difference: the principles of forgetting in the two systems. This fundamental difference in the laws of forgetting was proposed as a major distinction between short- and long-term memory systems.

If we look more closely, however, we see that the original decay interpretations of forgetting in the Brown-Peterson paradigm were influenced by the inability to identify interfering events. *Interference* is forgetting caused by events intervening between exposure to the to-be-remembered material and the test for that material. If such interfering events could be identified in the Brown-Peterson paradigm, differences in forgetting from short-term memory and long-term memory would be less apparent, and an important basis for the distinction between the two systems would be undermined.

As we discussed the Brown-Peterson paradigm and the issue of interference and decay, you may have already identified the rehearsal prevention task as a potential source of interference. Counting backward, or any of the other activities used to prevent rehearsal, intervenes between exposure to the material and the memory test and may induce forgetting through interference. Decay theorists argued that the rehearsal prevention activities do not produce sufficient interference to account for the enormous forgetting normally found in the Brown-Peterson paradigm. This argument is based on the fact that interference increases with the similarity between target (to-be-remembered) and interfering materials, and the similarity between the target and the rehearsal prevention task is minimal. Counting backward requires the use of numbers which are not similar to the words the subjects are to remember. Nonetheless, the suspicion that the rehearsal prevention task may cause interference remains. You should also notice that a real *dilemma* is introduced when we try to decide between decay and interference theories. *To establish a situation in which decay can occur, rehearsal must be prevented, but anything done to prevent rehearsal may actually introduce interference. Hence, it becomes extremely difficult to decide whether the forgetting is due to interference or to decay.*

In addition to the rehearsal prevention task, another source of interference in the Brown-Peterson paradigm was identified by Keppel and Underwood (1962). In the typical Brown-Peterson experiment, the subject faces a number of recall trials. After the very first trial, each succeeding trial is subject to interference from the preceding trials. If only memory on the first trial is examined, the length of the retention interval seems to make little difference. Only after a long series of trials does the decline in performance over the 18-second retention interval appear. Thus, it appears that interference is present in the experimental situation.

Some ideas about forgetting in short-term memory represent a compromise between interference and decay. For example, Reitman (1971, 1974) suggests that we think of retention of recent experiences as being similar to the detection of a signal against a background of noise. For example, your ability to hear the radio is obviously related to the amount of additional noise in the immediate surroundings as well as to the loudness of the radio. If we consider the to-be-remembered event as the signal and interference as the background noise, we see that memory will be determined by the strength of the memory trace and the amount of interference. Moreover, the strength of the trace declines as the length of the retention interval increases, a statement of the decay principle of forgetting. As the retention interval lengthens, the memory trace weakens and becomes more difficult to detect. Detection, of course, depends upon the existing level of interference, but a constant level of interference has different effects, depending upon the decay of the target signal. In this way, Reitman argues that short-term forgetting involves the principles of both decay and interference. Just as the ability to hear the radio depends upon both how loud the radio is and how much other noise is around, so the ability to remember a recent experience depends upon both how long it has been since the event was experienced and how much interference is present.

Reitman's theory exemplifies the increasing complexity in ideas about forgetting as we learn more about memory. Simple descriptions of forgetting in short-term memory and long-term memory as due, respectively, to decay and interference no longer seem adequate. We therefore question whether the theoretical distinction between short-term memory and long-term memory is really necessary.

The Question of Different Codes

Another of the primary distinctions between short-term memory and long-term memory which has been seriously questioned is the nature of the code. Remember it is assumed that short-term memory is stored as a phonetic code, whereas long-term memory is stored semantically. While both of these assumptions are possible, recent evidence clearly indicates that *no one code exclusively characterizes either short-term memory or long-term memory*. Some experimenters report that short-term memory can be based on visual codes. In the discussion of pattern recognition in chapter 2, we mentioned the experiment on mental rotation. A letter is shown briefly and the subject then has to decide whether the normal orientation or the mirror image of the letter is shown. Since the decision must be made rapidly, such an experiment qualifies as short-term retention. If, as the accepted inter-pretation implies, subjects do rotate mental images to reach their decisions, the short-term code is the visual image of the target letter. In addition to other reports of visual codes in short-term memory, some investigators have even reported the existence of semantic codes in short-term memory.

Long-term memory also can be coded in less rigid ways. Abundant evi-dence is available to suggest the presence of visual codes in long-term memory. For example, consider this question: In your room is the doorknob on the left or right as you exit the room? To answer this question, most people claim to retrieve "a picture" of the door. Phonetic codes also are much in evidence in long-term memory, as is clear from our ability to re-member any of a range of sound patterns as well as from the evidence of experimental work.

Again, as with the distinction between the types of forgetting, short- and long-term retention cannot be neatly distinguished on the basis of codes. The ability to remember material may well depend upon whether we attend to the way it looks or sounds or to its meaning, but certainly we are not constrained to code recent experiences in one way and longer-standing memories in some other way.

Additional Evidence on Serial Position Effects

We saw that one source of support for the distinction between short-term memory and long-term memory is the way the stage model interprets the serial position curve. Particularly convincing is the research showing that recency effects are reduced by adding a rehearsal prevention task to a serial recall test and that primacy effects are reduced by increasing the rate of item presentation. If recency effects are due to recall from short-term memory, rehearsal prevention should eliminate the recency advantage; if primacy effects are attributed to the amount of rehearsal devoted to initial list items, increasing the rate of presentation should reduce the time for rehearsal and consequently the primacy effect. Equally important are the facts that rehearsal prevention does not affect primacy nor does rate of presentation reduce recency effects, which suggests that information is in either short-term memory or long-term memory but not in both.

More recent research raised several difficulties for this interpretation of serial position effects. For example, a number of researchers found re-cency effects in situations where short-term memory should be eliminated, an event that should never happen according to the stage model. Further problems are posed by the research of Bernbach (1975) who showed that under certain circumstances rate of presentation reduces recency effects. One simple situation producing such results occurs when subjects do not know the length of a list. Denied such knowledge, the subjects continue rehearsing all items, but when they know how long a list is, rehearsal can be stopped near the end of the list and immediate recall of the last items can occur.

The results of Bernbach's experiments are obviously inconsistent with the stage-model interpretation of the serial position curve. His idea is that the strategy the subject adopts determines the serial position curve. This idea foreshadows what can be described as the major alternative to the stage model, namely, *memory can be best understood in terms of what a person does to incoming information.*

What Does the Amnesic Remember?

Exciting new experiments on amnesic patients have revealed memory performance far exceeding expectations. The key element of these new experiments is a technique which actually grew out of Freudian theory. The trick is to test a person's memory for an experience without the person being aware that his or her memory is being tested (called an implicit test), the same idea underlying such techniques as free association, dream analysis, and Rorschach tests in psychotherapy. Under such conditions people suffering from anterograde amnesia, who were previously considered incapable of transferring information to long-term storage, perform as well as healthy people.

The experiments are quite easy to follow as illustrated by a study from Peter Graf and Dan Schacter (1985). Subjects were shown a list of unrelated word pairs and asked to construct a sentence containing each word pair. This task was designed to induce semantic coding of the word pairs. Following the study session, an *implicit* memory test was administered in which the subjects were shown a long list of word stems; the word stems were the first three letters of words. The subject was instructed to complete the word stem to make a word. No reference was made to the fact that some of the word stems corresponded to words in the original study list, encouraging the subject not to treat the stem-completion test as a memory test for the study words but as a test of ability to think of a word beginning with the three letters given. Following the stem-completion test, a standard cued recall test was administered in which one member of each of the original word pairs was presented and the subject was asked to recall the other member of the pair. The cue word was also present in the stem-completion test. Subjects in Graf and Schacter's experiment included college students as well as patients with anterograde amnesia caused by head injuries, strokes, and disease.

The results of the second experiment reported by Graf and Schacter (1985) for unrelated word pairs are shown in figure 4.4. The cued recall performance of amnesic patients and college students is shown in the left

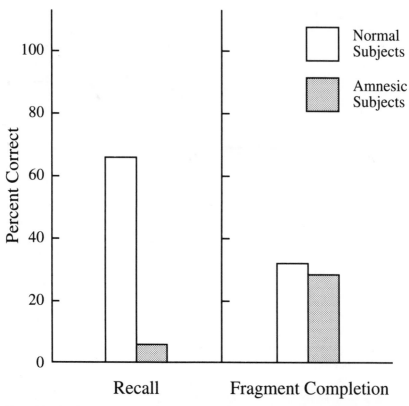

Figure 4.4 Performance of normal subjects and amnesic patients on a cued recall test and a fragment completion test. (From "Implicit and explicit memory for new associations in normal and amnesic subjects by P. Graf and D. L. Schacter. *Journal of Experimental Psychology: Learning, Memory, and Cognition,* 1985, *11,* 501–518. Copyright 1985 by the American Psychological Association. Reprinted by permission of the publisher.)

panel of figure 4.4. You can see that the amnesic patients recalled very few of the words, actually about 2%. This is not surprising; after all, amnesics cannot remember. Or can they? The right panel of figure 4.4 shows the stem-completion performance. The amnesic patients completed about 35% of the stems with list words, which was about the same level of performance as college students. Considering that people who had not seen the study list completed the test stems with only 12% of the study words, the performance of both the amnesic patients and the college students represents a signifi- cant influence of the study session on the stem completion test. *The important point is that the amnesic patients benefitted just as much as the college students from this experience.*

Results such as these indicate that anterograde amnesia is not due to the failure of information to be passed from short-term to long-term memory. In this sense, the stage model's explanation of amnesia appears to be wrong. What the more recent research suggests is that amnesic patients seem to be unable to retrieve past experiences when they must exert conscious effort to memory. When circumstances allow these past experiences to be activated without conscious intent to remember, the amnesic performs as well as you and I.

SUMMARY OF OBJECTIONS TO THE STAGE MODEL

The fundamental premise of the stage model is that memory is determined by *where* the to-be-remembered information is in the processing sequence. Each of the stages (sensory register, short-term memory, and long-term memory) has characteristics which theoretically determine the probability of remembering information. Chief among these characteristics, of course, is duration of the trace. Thus, all other things being equal, the probability of retention increases as we move through the system because each succeeding stage has longer trace life. If retention is determined by the stage in which the information resides, the question now becomes: What factors determine in which stage the information will be?

The two critical factors seem to be the length of time after presentation of the material and the type of processing performed on the material. For example, incoming information may be in the visual sensory register for up to 250 milliseconds after presentation, but only moves on to short-term memory if it is selected by the process of attention. Information may remain in short-term memory for up to 30 seconds, but rehearsal must occur to move the information to long-term memory. If we now consider this system, we realize that the length of time after presentation is much less critical for memory than is the *activity or process* imposed on the material. Transfer from one stage to another is always determined by a process, never by mere passage of time. Moreover, memory for information within a system is also under the influence of processes. Rehearsal allows information to be maintained in and recalled from short-term memory. Recall from long-term memory requires, among other factors, the operation of the retrieval process. The point to see here is that, even from the view of stage models, memory is primarily a function of the processes imposed upon the information.

We must now ask why various stages should be considered, rather than concentrate solely on processes. The only reason to propose discrete stages of memory would be if each stage included different processes. This was the original assumption of the stage model—that certain processes occur only at a particular stage. For example, semantic coding occurs only in long-term memory. However, we have just reviewed evidence contrary to this assumption; identifying the stage as best we can based on the length of the retention interval, neither the principles of forgetting nor the type of coding seems to differ. *What again emerges is that memory is determined by what is done to the information, but now the important point is that what is done does not seem to be constrained by how long it has been since the information was presented.* Hence, there seems to be little compelling reason to think of memory as occurring in stages. Thus *memory is determined by what is done to the information, not by where the information is.*

Arguments of this type have convinced most researchers that the stage model is not quite as useful as once thought. Nonetheless, the stage model made a real contribution to theories of memory by focusing upon short-term retention, which clearly has characteristics that must be explained. We now shall consider two alternatives to the stage model, with the full realization that these alternatives build upon the foundation laid by the stage model: working memory and levels of processing.

WORKING MEMORY

The stage model was proposed to account for certain fundamental facts, and if we reject the stage model, we must provide an alternative account for these facts. Among the basic facts, two important issues stand out. The first fact concerns our awareness of the contents of memory; we are usually aware or conscious of immediate experiences. In other words, certain events occupy our thought processes at any given moment, but at the same time, many other facts are also known but not thought about, although they could be. In a sense, this is the distinction between currently active and inactive memories, and historically, active memory has been ascribed to short-term memory and inactive memory to long-term memory. If we abandon the short-term—long-term distinction, we must have an alternative account for the active-inactive memory phenomenon.

The second fundamental fact is the limitation on retention of recent experiences, which was discussed extensively. Even if we cannot find convincing differences between the principles of forgetting, the limitations on short-term retention are real enough, as evidenced by both experimental work and everyday experiences. In the absence of a short-term memory system, how are we to account for this important observation?

The Idea of Working Memory

Alan Baddeley has championed an idea to meet these needs. Beginning with Baddeley and Hitch's 1974 paper, Baddeley has been developing the concept of working memory (Baddeley, 1986; 1990). Like short-term memory, working memory is assumed to be a limited capacity system containing transient information. Unlike short-term memory, however, the function of working memory is less a matter of a storage way-station to long-term memory than of holding information used for other cognitive work. The assumption is that working memory is a critical part of many important activities such as problem solving, reasoning, and comprehension. For example, if the problem is to add 63 + 18 "in your head," carrying operations and partial sums must be retained until the final solution is reached. Even this simple addition problem places considerable demands on conscious capacity as is evident if you reflect on how difficult it is for you to do this problem and think about anything else at the same time.

You may notice some similarity between working memory and capacity models of attention. This connection is made explicitly by Baddeley's assumption that working memory includes a *central executive* that is the controlling, decision-making mechanism of working memory. The functions of the central executive are to recruit and perform operations required by the current task and to allocate capacity in other working memory subsystems, functions very much like attention. It is therefore not surprising that the dual-task technique described in chapter 3 has been used in laboratory studies of working memory. The question of capacity limitations in working memory can be approached by asking, What sorts of mental tasks can be performed concurrently? and, Do different types of tasks interfere differentially with other types of tasks?

Among the first observations was that in many instances concurrent tasks can be accomplished, albeit at some cost to each task. For example, Baddeley and Hitch (1977) showed that simple reasoning problems could be performed while simultaneously maintaining a string of digits for immediate recall. As the digit string became longer, the time to perform the reasoning task increased but the errors in reasoning did not. The importance of this observation was to suggest that working memory is not a single, limited capacity store like the older short-term memory. If it were, both tasks would be impaired. Rather, Baddeley suggests that different subsystems exist in working memory for different tasks.

Working Memory Subsystems

The two subsystems that have received some research effort are the *articulatory loop* and the *visuospatial sketch* pad. An illustration of the articulatory loop and the visuospatial sketch pad along with their relationship to the central executive is shown in figure 4.5. Visual-spatial material is stored and manipulated by the visuospatial sketch pad whereas speech-based material is stored and manipulated by the articulatory loop. These subsystems are controlled by the central executive. Each subsystem is essentially

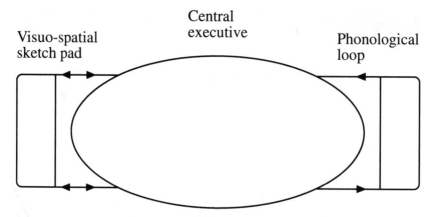

Figure 4.5 A simple sketch of the working memory system. (From *Human Memory: Theory and Practice* by A. D. Baddeley. Boston: Allyn and Bacon, 1990).

a modality-specific storage/work space, an idea generated from the results of the previously mentioned research using dual-tasks. The results that led to the proposed distinction between the articulatory loop and the visuo-spatial sketch pad came from experiments showing more interference from secondary tasks involving the same modality as the primary task.

Consider, for example, an experiment by Loggie and Baddeley (1987). The focus of this study was the simple but basic cognitive process of counting objects or events. Counting seems to involve subvocal articulation of the numbers in a sequence as well as short-term storage of the running total. These functions would be served by the articulatory loop in the scheme of working memory. If so, a secondary task requiring the use of speech-based material should interfere with simple counting while a secondary task that does not involve speech should interfere less with counting. Loggie and Baddeley (1987, Experiment 2) examined this prediction by asking subjects to count the number of times a square appeared on a computer screen. In a given trial, the square would appear between 1–25 times, and the subjects' task very simply was to count the number of times the square appeared. In some instances, however, the subject also had to rapidly repeat the word *the* throughout the presentation of the sequence. This was the secondary task designed to occupy the articulatory loop. In other cases, the subjects were asked to rapidly tap their fingers during the presentation sequence, a secondary task not requiring articulation. Finally, a control condition was included for which no secondary task was required.

The errors in counting are shown in figure 4.6 as a function of the type of secondary task and the length of the counting sequence. As you can see, the subjects required to repeat a word while simultaneously counting performed more poorly than other subjects. This result is evidence that counting

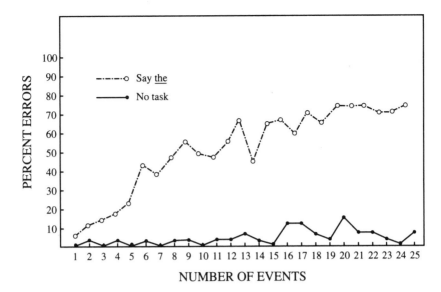

Figure 4.6 The percentage of errors made in the counting task as a function of the secondary task. (From "Cognitive processes in counting" by R. H. Logie and A. D. Baddeley. *Journal of Experimental Psychology: Learning, Memory, and Cognition,* 1987, *13,* 310–326. Copyright 1987 by the American Psychological Association. Reprinted by permission.)

requires the articulatory loop, presumably for subvocal articulation of the consecutive numbers and for maintenance of the running total. Concurrent articulation of a word during this activity competes with counting for the capacity of the articulatory loop, resulting in errors. A secondary task such as tapping your finger does not occupy the articulatory loop, and thus fewer errors in counting accrue to this task. Note that tapping does produce more errors than no secondary task, suggesting that tapping occupies capacity of the central executive.

In summary, Baddeley's concept of working memory is an idea containing elements of previously discussed notions. At a general level, working memory describes the contents of current conscious thought, much as James' description of primary memory. Working memory is limited in capacity, and allocation of the limited capacity is controlled by a central executive, reminiscent of Kahneman's description of attention as a decision to allocate processing capacity.

As an alternative to short-term memory, working memory does not propose separate principles for long- and short-term memory systems. All retention is determined by the amount and type of processing devoted to the material. New events require extensive processing, and as extensive processing produces awareness, we are likely to be conscious of memory for recent events. Since processing capacity is limited, however, a limitation is imposed on the amount of new information which can be retained. Thus, the concept of working memory deals effectively with the basic facts of retention of immediate experiences and is compatible with the general view that retention is a function of processing.

LEVELS OF PROCESSING

The emphasis on cognitive processes apparent in the concept of working memory was initiated by the idea of *levels of processing* (Craik & Lockhart, 1972). Levels of processing had a different goal than working memory. Working memory was an elaboration of the concept of short-term memory. Levels of processing was conceived as an alternative to the entire stage model. As we have just mentioned, the stage model focused its explanation of retention on the structural characteristics of each stage of memory. Levels of processing abandons the idea of discrete stages; that is, it does not refer to different memory systems, but rather concentrates on the types of processes associated with different levels of retention. The goal here is to replace the stage model by explaining the facts of retention without proposing different memory systems.

Assumptions of Levels of Processing

Levels of processing is based on two fundamental assumptions. The first is that the memory trace is a by-product of perception and comprehension. What you remember will be the things to which you attended. If, when introduced to a person, you devote your attention to their clothes, you will not remember their name because the perceptual processes were not allocated to the name. Another subtle but important implication of the first assumption concerns the role of *intent to remember*. The implication is that intent to remember is not crucial. We do not go through our day *trying* to remember the things that happen to us, but rather we try to understand the experiences we have. For example, think of all the things you can remember from yesterday. Now, how many times yesterday did you say "I have to remember this"? Probably not many, yet you can remember a large proportion of yesterday's events. Conscious intent does not seem critical, as might be the case from the stage model with conscious intent to rehearse. Rather, memory results from perception and comprehension of events.

The second assumption of levels of processing concerns the differential retention of an event depending upon what is encoded. Very simply, semantic processing is assumed to produce better memory than nonsemantic processing. If what you notice or encode is an aspect of meaning, you will remember the event better than if what you notice are superficial aspects of the event. Semantic processing is assumed to be "deep" processing and nonsemantic processing "shallow," hence the designation "levels of processing."

Experimental Tests of Levels of Processing

The two fundamental assumptions are easily captured in an experiment requiring special processing of each individual word in a list. The special processing comes in the form of an *orienting task*, which is a simple activity performed on each word. For example, the subject is told to rate each word for its pleasantness. Alternatively, the subject might be asked to write the middle letter of each word. The first task is designed to direct attention to the meaning of the word, a semantic task. Consider making a pleasantness judgment of the word *rape*. Most persons rate this word as quite unpleasant. Why? It is not a particularly ugly-looking word, and its sound is very much like *grape*, a word usually rated as quite pleasant. Clearly, the unpleasantness of *rape* stems from its meaning. Thus, pleasantness ratings serve as a semantic orienting task because a pleasantness judgment requires determining the meaning of a word. Writing the middle letter of a word, however, does not require determining its meaning and hence is a nonsemantic task. Any task that can be performed without determining the meaning of a word is nonsemantic orientation. Nonsemantic tasks usually require a judgment about the letter patterns or sound patterns of a word, such as estimating the number of rhymes for a word.

The orienting task is designed to control the subject's attention. (For a discussion of the effectiveness of orienting tasks in controlling attention, see Hunt, Elliott, & Spence, 1979.) Regardless, levels of processing argues that memory is based on what is attended to, and furthermore that attention to semantic attributes produces better memory than attention to nonsemantic attributes. In addition, these experiments are usually conducted under *incidental memory* instructions. Incidental instructions mean that the subjects are not told to remember the words, but rather are led to believe that the purpose of the experiment is something other than to test memory, usually something to do with their orienting response. After all the words have been seen, a surprise memory test is administered. The incidental instructions are designed to strengthen the attentional control of the orienting task.

Imagine that you are a subject in one of these experiments and are given a nonsemantic orienting task. For example, you are told to check all of the *e*'s in the words you see and are given memory instructions that are *not* incidental but *intentional*. That is, in addition to checking *e*'s you are told to remember the words. In all probability, you will not restrict your attention to the letter *e*, but will also engage in processes you normally use to remember. In this situation, we have no assurance that what you remember is under the control of the orienting task. However, when you are not told of the memory test but rather are told that the interest is in how quickly and accurately a person can detect particular letters, our confidence is greater that the orienting task affects your attention. You have little reason to attend to anything other than the orienting task if you are not told of the impending memory test. In summary, the subject in these experiments sees a list of items—words, pictures, even sentences—and is asked to perform a task on each item, either a task requiring that the meaning of the item be detected or one that does not require the meaning to be detected. The sole purpose of the experiment is to determine whether more items are remembered following semantic orientation than following nonsemantic orientation.

The answer to this question is a resounding yes! Regardless of the semantic task, be it pleasantness rating, free association, sentence completion, or whatever, semantic orienting tasks produce better memory for the items than do nonsemantic tasks. Using pictures of human faces, Bower and Karlin (1974) showed that judgments of honesty produce better memory than do judgments about physical features of faces. The honesty judgment is seen as a semantic orienting task. This experiment is widely cited as evidence that levels of processing applies even to memory for faces. But why should semantic tasks produce better performance than do nonsemantic tasks?

Craik and Lockhart's original answer was that semantic information lasts longer than does nonsemantic information. Notice the similarity to the stage model where phonetic (nonsemantic) information is assumed to be stored in short-term memory and semantic information in long-term memory. Short-term memory has a shorter duration than does long-term memory. In spite of many other differences between the descriptions of encoding, the stage model and levels of processing agree that storage duration in nonsemantic information is briefer than in semantic information. Unfortunately, this particular assumption appears to be incorrect.

At this juncture, there are two important points about levels of processing. *The first is that it is an idea designed as an alternative to the stage model as an explanation of memory.* The crucial difference is the emphasis on mental processes rather than mental structures. *The second point is related in that levels of processing is the beginning of an attempt to describe the mind as process rather than structure.* We shall develop this controversy over the next two chapters as we examine the study of long-term memory.

IMPROVING MEMORY FOR RECENT EVENTS

Let us now briefly consider some practical applications of what we have been describing.

William James, a distinguished American psychologist, many years ago claimed that attention is the key to better memory. Assuming attention to be the allocation of processing capacity through rehearsal or semantic elaboration, James's suggestion has considerable merit for improving memory of recent events. Take the simple case of meeting new people and remembering their names shortly after an introduction. First, be sure you hear each name. Many times we simply do not listen carefully when a name is mentioned. Look at the person being introduced and then use his or her name immediately when expressing your delight at meeting the person. After that, continue to use the name frequently when addressing remarks to that person. As simple as this technique is, most of us rarely use it and all too often find ourselves in the embarrassing situation of forgetting a name immediately after an introduction. If you should forget, ask the name again; most people would rather be asked than be addressed impersonally. People want you to know and use their names, and in some professions such as sales, it is an important skill.

Other techniques for improving long-term retention will be discussed in chapter 5. A final hint concerning retention of recent experience is suggested here. Now that you are aware of the limitations on processing capacity, be prepared to write long lists of items and events you know you are going to have to remember. A complex event or a long list of items is impossible to remember with complete accuracy when you are only briefly exposed to it. Knowledge of the limitations of memory is a very important step toward better retention, because with this knowledge you can take appropriate steps to supplement your memory with written records.

SUMMARY

Memory for recent experiences characteristically is quite fragile. We seem to remember only a small proportion of this information, and the information is remembered for a short period of time. Observations such as these have led to the concept of short-term memory, which some researchers regarded as a system separate from long-term memory. The implication of this distinction between short-term and long-term memory systems is that different processes determine retention in the two systems. If this is the case, it should be possible to discover that the same variables will have different effects upon memory, depending upon where the information is in the system. Thus, in chapter 4 we reviewed a good deal of research which was designed to argue for differences in the capacity, duration, and nature of the codes in the short-term and long-term memory systems.

We also saw that the primary determinant of retention, even within the modal model of memory, is what is done to the information. A strong delineation of short-term memory and long-term memory is then necessary only if it is believed that the processes which can be imposed on the material are different for the short-term and long-term memory systems. More recent research questioning this assumption was then reviewed. Consequently, the current view of short-term memory is that it is much less like a separate storage system, distinct from long-term memory, and more like a work space during which information may be elaborated upon. Hence the change from short-term memory to working memory.

We concluded with a discussion of levels of processing which is very different from the stage model. Levels of processing does not encourage you to think about different memory systems but rather different memory processes. Retention is described as a function of semantic and nonsemantic processing. In the next chapter we shall take up the study of long-term memory where we shall see discussion of other types of processes that affect memory, and we shall also see the introduction of another idea about memory systems.

MULTIPLE-CHOICE ITEMS

1. The characteristics which best describe short-term memory are
   a. large capacity and long duration
   b. small capacity and long duration
   c. large capacity and short duration
   d. small capacity and short duration

2. The results from the Brown-Peterson paradigm were important in establishing
   a. temporal limitations of short-term memory
   b. capacity limitations of short-term memory
   c. coding characteristic of short-term memory
   d. physiological distinctions between long-term memory and short-term memory

3. The fundamental objection recently expressed to the distinction between short-term memory and long-term memory is based on
   a. the failure to replicate the Brown-Peterson data
   b. the lack of attention to processing assumptions in the modal model
   c. the lack of any convincing evidence that the principles of memory differ as a function of the retention interval
   d. the failure to locate precise physiological mechanisms corresponding to the two memory systems

4. Rehearsal represents a trade-off in short-term memory because
   a. it can use either maintenance or elaborative rehearsal
   b. it extends the trace life, but also requires capacity
   c. it reduces both the primacy and recency effects
   d. it requires different physiological mechanisms than does chunking

5. The serial position curve has been important in distinguishing short-term memory and long-term memory because
   a. the primacy effect may be explained as long-term memory and the recency effect as short-term memory
   b. chunking explains the primacy and recency effect
   c. rehearsal is very important in explaining both the primacy and recency effects
   d. memory for primacy and recency items is about the same, but the middle items are poorly recalled

6. The two fundamental facts associated with memory for recent events which must be explained by any theory of memory are
   a. primacy and recency
   b. awareness and poor retention
   c. rehearsal and chunking
   d. phonetic codes and small capacity

TRUE–FALSE ITEMS

1. The primacy effect in the serial position curve is due to short-term memory.

2. In the theoretical analysis of memory, the process imposed on the material is more important than the amount of time elapsed since the material was seen.

3. Working memory is more similar to the concept of long-term memory than to that of short-term memory.

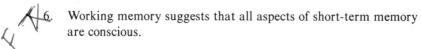

4. The different trace life in short- and long-term memory systems was thought to implicate different principles of forgetting in the two systems.

5. Considering all available research, it is now clear that only phonetic codes are available in short-term memory.

6. Working memory suggests that all aspects of short-term memory are conscious.

DISCUSSION ITEMS

1. Describe the argument for separate systems of short- and long-term memory.

2. Why have many theorists become increasingly skeptical of the structural distinction between short- and long-term memory?

ANSWERS TO MULTIPLE-CHOICE ITEMS

1. (d) The short-term trace lasts for a brief period, and the limits of capacity are quite small.

2. (a) The Brown-Peterson paradigm shows very rapid forgetting.

3. (c) The distinction between short-term memory and long-term memory requires different processes operating at different times after presentation, and the evidence for this assumption is quite limited.

4. (b) Rehearsal helps by extending the trace life, but the help comes at the expense of capacity.

5. (a) The short-term–long-term distinction provides an explanation of the serial position function, which lends credibility to the distinction.

6. (b) Memory for recent events is different from memory for less recent events in that we tend to be thinking about the recent events, but the information is poorly retained relative to long-term memory.

ANSWERS TO TRUE–FALSE ITEMS

1. (False) The primacy effect is due to the operation of long-term memory.

2. (True) Memory seems to be determined by what is done to the material regardless of how long it has been since the material was seen.

3. (False) Working memory is a concept designed to account for many of the characteristics of short-term memory.

4. (True) The differences in trace life simply indicates there are different rates of forgetting.

5. (False) Evidence exists suggesting both visual and semantic codes in short-term memory.

6. (False) Much of the activity of working memory may be conscious, but not all.

5

ENCODING IN
LONG-TERM MEMORY

Much of the previous discussion centered on the fragile status of short-term memory. At one level, we have all experienced the frustration of failure of short-term memory. At another level, performance of even the most mundane activities, tying a shoe or preparing a simple meal, requires memory for events and information that occurred in the past. Indeed, our very survival depends upon long-term memory. Thus no matter how limited short-term memory is, a lot of information must survive from past experience to form the basis of long-term memory.

Long-term memory is the concept which represents the vast store of knowledge we have about the world, ranging from everyday events such as how to use a knife and fork to more esoteric information such as axioms of geometry. In addition to the concept of the vast amount of information in long-term memory, many researchers hold the assumption that long-term memory is permanent: that is, once information enters long-term memory, it remains there. Any forgetting which occurs is due to inability to retrieve the information and not to a decay process. The permanence assumption was, however, questioned by Loftus and Loftus (1980). They suggest that memory for prior events can be modified by subsequent events. In some cases, a subsequent event even may replace the prior event.

These suggestions are based largely on Elizabeth Loftus's research demonstrating that intervening events change a subject's memory for the original event. For example, Loftus (1977) showed subjects complex scenes on slides involving several people, one of whom was a man reading a book with a green cover. Later, subjects were exposed to information suggesting the book cover was a different color. Subsequent memory tests for the details of the slides asked the subjects to pick the color of various objects seen in the slides. The subjects were allowed to make two choices for each object. When subjects were wrong on their first choice, they were likely to select the color suggested by the intervening information. More importantly, when the subjects did this, their second choice of color was no better than chance. These results suggest that the intervening information actually replaced the original information rather than just becoming a higher probability response. The original color was not likely to be given even as a second choice on the test.

Elizabeth Loftus's research has been very useful concerning the practical issues of eyewitness testimony and also is provocative on the question of permanence of long-term memory. On the other hand, other research programs have provided evidence more consistent with the traditional assumption of permanence of long-term memory.

MEMORY PERMANENCE: STUDIES
OF AUTOBIOGRAPHICAL MEMORY

As you think of all the times you have forgotten things, the very idea of a permanent memory may seem ridiculous. We must be careful to realize, however, that the assumption of a long-term memory does not preclude the possibility of momentary forgetting. In certain circumstances, we may fail to remember something we are sure we know, a person's name for example, but the fact that the name is *inaccessible* at the moment does not mean that the name is permanently *unavailable*. Perhaps the cues present at the moment are inappropriate, a topic discussed in detail in the next chapter, and on a later occasion with different cues, the name will be remembered. In short, the assumption that long-term memory is permanent does not preclude momentary forgetting, but rather implies that such forgetting is due to transient retrieval failure, not the loss of information.

Studies of autobiographical memory have found high levels of memory for personal events. In an ambitious study, Marigold Linton (1982, 1986) recorded at least two events that happened to her every day for six years. Once a month she tested her memory by looking at a brief description of the event and then deciding if she could recognize and date it. Over the six years of her study, Linton discovered that only about 5% of the real-life events were lost each year.

Even longer retention periods have been explored in Harry Bahrick's studies of autobiographical memory. For example, Bahrick, Bahrick, and Wittinger (1975) tested people's memory for their high school classmates by using pictures from old yearbooks. In the most extreme case, the subjects in the experiment had graduated from high school 48 years earlier. These people still could recognize correctly over 60% of their classmates! In further studies, Bahrick and Hall (1991) have demonstrated that surprisingly large portions of high school Spanish and algebra are available 50 years later. Such demonstrations are not designed to argue that *all* of your prior experiences are available *all* of the time, but rather that the possibility of permanent long-term memory may not be as far-fetched as our intuitions suggest. The goal of long-term memory research is to describe conditions separating successful and unsuccessful retention as well as to offer theoretical explanation of why these conditions have their effect.

In pursuing this goal, we return to the discussion of memory processes that concluded the last chapter. It is important to keep in mind that the processes under discussion are those that occur at the time of the experience; that is, these are the processes of perception and comprehension of experiences that form the basis for subsequent memory. These processes are referred to as *encoding* processes to long-term memory. Processes occurring at the time memory is tested will be discussed in chapter 6. These are *retrieval* processes, and we shall see that forgetting from long-term memory is largely a matter of retrieval failure.

Let us now return to the theme we left at the end of the last chapter with discussion of further developments in levels of processing. Remember that levels of processing attempts to explain retention without reference to memory systems but rather suggests that good memory results from semantic processing. Also remember that the reason semantic processing produces good memory is because semantic information was presumed to last longer than nonsemantic information. It is this latter assumption that was wrong.

DOUBTS ABOUT DEPTH

Research from levels of processing demonstrated that semantic orienting tasks produce better memory for items than nonsemantic orienting tasks, but the question now becomes, Why? Does semantic information last longer than nonsemantic information? One of the nonsemantic tasks frequently used in laboratory studies is rhyming, and the fact that rhyming tasks produce poorer memory than semantic tasks is interpreted to mean that phonetic information does not last as long as semantic information. Such an interpretation appears inconsistent with some facts about real world memory. For example, can you recite the nursery rhyme "Jack and Jill"? How about the counting-out rhyme "Eenie-meenie-meini-mo"? These and other materials such as songs are remembered over long periods in spite of the fact that in some cases it is not even clear what the meaning might be. What is salient is the rhyming character of the material.

David Rubin at Duke University has made these points in his interesting research program on the oral tradition (Rubin & Wallace, 1989; Wallace & Rubin, 1988). This research focuses on the characteristics of orally transmitted materials. Rubin has studied epic poems, ballads from the mountains of North Carolina, rhymes we learned as children, and memory for popular songs. In all cases, he finds that rhyming is an important aspect of the material, and this is particularly true when rhyme and meaning work together. For example, in telling the lines "she rode a dappled bay . . . one hour before day," the word *bay* may change to *gray* and back again over many tellings, but the meaning constrains the word choice such that you will not tell, "She rode a dappled Oldsmobile." It is a horse she rode and the rhyme further constrains the choice such that it will be a "dappled gray or bay" but not a "dappled palomino" (Rubin & Wallace, 1989). Rubin's careful studies of the oral tradition clearly show that rhyme information can be very important to long-term memory.

In many respects, Rubin's research followed from the systematic experiments of Douglas Nelson of the University of South Florida. Nelson, from whose article the title of this section was drawn (Nelson, Walling, & McEvoy, 1979), has shown that memory benefits from the use of rhymes as cues under certain circumstances. Nelson's research program has been directed to understanding the relationship between conditions of encoding and types of retrieval cues and has resulted in his own recent theory of the operation of memory (Nelson, Schreiber, and McEvoy, 1992). This theory draws heavily on his earlier research from which Nelson concluded that "sensory information activated by a stimulus event is not accurately described as shallow, evaporating quickly in the sunshine of semantic encoding" (Nelson, Walling & McEvoy, 1979, p. 43). In short, nonsemantic attributes are retained and used.

A good example of the persistence of nonsemantic information can be seen in an experiment by Barry Stein (1978). In this experiment, subjects were given a list of words in which one letter in each word was capitalized. After each word, the subject had to make a yes-no decision requiring either semantic or nonsemantic information. The semantic decision was to judge whether the word fit in a sentence frame. For example, with the word *roCk*, the sentence frame was, "The _____ rolled down the hill." The nonsemantic decision required a yes-no response to a statement such as, "The letter *c* is capitalized." After presentation of all the words, subjects were given a recognition memory test to tap their semantic or nonsemantic retention. The semantic test required that the subjects select the words on the original list from a larger group of words. The nonsemantic test required that the subjects select the version of the original word which had the same letter capitalized: for example, "Among *Rock, rOck, roCk,* and *rocK,* which one was presented earliest?" Subjects whose orienting task required a semantic decision performed better on the semantic recognition test, but subjects who performed the nonsemantic orienting task did much better on the recognition of capital letters.

The important message of this experiment is quite clear. Nonsemantic information is retained as long as is semantic information. Consequently, the superior retention for words following semantic orientation cannot be due to more rapid decay of nonsemantic information. Again, why does semantic orientation produce better memory than does nonsemantic orientation?

Elaboration Hypothesis

One answer is a modification of the depth hypothesis proposed by Craik and Tulving (1975). They suggested that semantic processing produces more *elaborate* encoding than does nonsemantic processing. Elaboration is a process of relating the to-be-remembered event to other information that may be known about the event. Elaboration serves to broaden the stored information of the to-be-remembered event. The elaboration hypothesis was actually proposed to explain the effects of different semantic orienting tasks.

In particular, the phenomenon known as the *congruity effect* posed some difficulty for the original depth hypothesis. Many of the earlier experiments using the levels-of-processing paradigm presented semantic orienting questions which were either true or false. For example, the subject was given a sentence such as, "A DOG is an animal," or, "A STONE is an animal," and asked to respond yes or no, depending upon whether the statement was true. Later, the subject was asked to remember all of the capitalized words. Memory in this situation was much better for all the sentences to which the yes response was given. Why should this happen? Both true and false sentences require semantic processing of the target word. In order to say no to the assertion that "A STONE is an animal," you must determine the meaning of *stone*. The difference in memory cannot then be solely a matter of depth or semantic processing.

Craik and Tulving argue that the true statements leading to the yes response are more congruent than are the false statements. That is, the elements of the true sentence make sense, while the elements of the false sentence are incongruous or nonsensical. Congruent sentences provide elaboration on the basic meaning of the target word, whereas incongruous sentences do not. Semantic processing then produces better memory than nonsemantic processing because the semantic encoding is more elaborate, but within the realm of semantic processes, certain situations can produce more elaborate encodings than others.

The heart of elaboration is embodied in the suggestion that something is remembered better if it is related to other known facts. Certainly this suggestion can be appreciated by reflection on personal experiences. For example, material in a totally new course may be difficult, not only to understand but also to remember. The reason for this is not surprising; very little about the material is known and little related information is available. Most introductory courses devote a great deal of time to definitions of basic concepts in order to provide the foundation upon which more advanced courses may elaborate. But let us return to the original question: Why does semantic processing, now in the form of elaboration, improve memory?

Perhaps elaboration comes closer to providing the answer than does depth. Relating material to a number of other known facts increases the number of potential retrieval cues. Elaborate processing may improve memory, because the number of events which may remind us of the target item have increased. This explanation of the influence of elaborate encoding on subsequent retrieval is quite plausible, but it implies that the encoded information is widely spread, perhaps to the point of not specifying the to-be-remembered event clearly. That this need not be the case is illustrated by yet another idea about why semantic processing and elaboration aid memory.

Distinctiveness Hypothesis

Suppose we take quite literally the first assumption of levels of processing, that the memory trace consists only of the attended portion of an event. That is, what is encoded and remembered is that collection of attributes, only a subset of the total number available, that is concentrated upon during the experience. At the time the event must be recalled, only what is available can be worked with, and the entire event must be reconstructed from the encoded subset of features. The ability to reproduce faithfully the original event will depend in large part upon how well the encoded features specify that event. A simple example clarifies this suggestion. Suppose you are asked to remember a list of words, one of which is *elephant*. If the task requires a semantic orientation, the encoded trace might contain information corresponding to "very large, gray animal with large ears and trunk living in Africa and India." If you retrieve this information at the time of recall, *elephant* is an obvious response. However, if your task is nonsemantic orientation, for example, to check all the *e*'s in the word, the encoded trace might contain information that the word has two *e*'s. Reconstructing the word *elephant* from just that information seems to be quite unlikely. Most of us know a large number of words which contain two *e*'s.

This illustration is designed to introduce the distinctiveness hypothesis. *According to the distinctiveness hypothesis, memory is determined in part by how well the information encoded specifies the event being reconstructed.* As in the earlier discussion of pattern recognition, it is as if the cognitive system were playing a game of twenty questions. What is required here is the best guess possible, based on all available information concerning the event. In the case of event memory, part of the available information is what was encoded at input. Semantic information is likely to be much more specific and thus much more useful than nonsemantic information, as illustrated in the example of remembering *elephant*. Nonsemantic information such as letter combinations and sound patterns are considerably more redundant than semantic information. Simply put, the meanings of different words are less likely to be shared than are the letter combinations or sound patterns. Semantic orientation then produces superior performance because semantic features more distinctively represent the event. Semantic features are simply more useful in the game of twenty questions with past events.

The distinctiveness hypothesis shares with levels of processing the assumption that the memory trace is a by-product of attention and pattern recognition, but the two ideas differ in their descriptions of what constitutes effective information. Rather than semantic information, the distinctiveness hypothesis emphasizes distinctive information.

This difference has interesting implications, among which is the prediction from the distinctiveness hypothesis that nonsemantic information can be useful in memory (Hunt & Elliott, 1980). If the nonsemantic information is distinctive, attention to that information should facilitate memory. Consider an experiment by Eysenck (1979). Subjects were asked to attend to the sound patterns of words as an orienting task. In one condition, however, the subjects were given very unusual, atypical pronunciations of the words. Since these pronunciations are not likely to be shared by other words, the distinctiveness hypothesis predicts that they should facilitate memory. In fact, subjects attending to atypical pronunciations remembered the words as well as did a group given semantic orientation. This should not happen if nonsemantic information decays more rapidly than does semantic information, as originally supposed by the depth hypothesis. The distinctiveness hypothesis, however, predicts that *unique features* aid memory for an event, regardless of whether the features are semantic or nonsemantic. Thus, Eysenck's results are more consistent with a distinctiveness explanation.

Distinctiveness may be preferable to depth, but what about elaboration? Elaboration, with its concern for the spread of encoding, seems diametrically opposed to distinctiveness, with its concern for highly specific encoding. For example, consider an experiment by Winograd (1981) on memory for faces. This experiment asked the question "Is memory for faces better if you encode the most distinctive feature?" To induce elaborative encoding of a number of features, subjects were asked to scan the pictures and rate the most distinctive feature. In the process of scanning, the subjects presumably would encode a large number of features. For the distinctive encoding condition, Winograd had a group of people rate the pictures prior to the experiment and select the most distinctive feature. Subjects in the experiment then focused on this feature of each picture, be it eyes, nose, mouth, and so forth. Thus subjects in the elaboration group encoded a number of features, while subjects in the distinctiveness group encoded only one feature. As it resulted, both groups were equally proficient at recognizing the faces. Winograd interpreted this finding as indicating that the function of encoding a number of features is to increase the distinctiveness of the encoding. One feature will do as well *if* it is highly distinctive. *This interpretation suggests that elaboration is effective because it produces distinctiveness.*

A bit of reflection may persuade you that this position is sensible. As Craik and Jacoby (1979) suggest, the more elaborate the encoding, the more will be remembered about an event. Not only does elaboration increase the probability of sampling a single distinctive feature, but also the more that is known about something the less like other things it will appear. For instance, if all you can remember is that one of the words in a list was an animal, you may have trouble producing the precise word. If you have more elaborate information, such as "a large gray animal with large ears and trunk living in India and Africa," you will have little trouble producing the correct response. Elaborate information increases the distinctiveness of any event *because the more that is known about something, the less like other things it will seem.*

ORGANIZATION

Another important encoding process is *organization.* Organization is the process of grouping discrete, individual items into larger units based on a specific relationship among the items. Organization differs in an important way from the previously discussed process of elaboration. Elaboration refers to relationships between the to-be-remembered event and additional information that is not to be remembered. Organization describes relationships among to-be-remembered events.

A simple example clarifies this distinction. Suppose you are given the common laboratory task of remembering a list of words. Some of the words refer to *animals: dog, cat, camel,* and *tiger.* You detect the relationship among the four words and *organize* them under the category *animal.* In addition, however, you also may encode information about each word that is not relevant to the other words. For example, you may elaborate *tiger* by including such information as *stripes, India,* or maybe *nickname of football team.* Elaboration, then, *adds information unique* to the individual item. In both processes, organization and elaboration, the *meaning* of the word is being encoded; that is, facts we know about *tiger* include: it is an animal, it lives in India, and it has stripes. The distinction between organization and elaboration, however, is that with organization what is encoded is information shared by the meaning of the to-be-remembered events, whereas with elaboration what is encoded is information unique to the meaning of one of the events. As with elaboration, a considerable amount of research supports the importance of organization.

Psychologists long have recognized the importance of organization in perception, and by 1970, Gordon Bower would say "A modest revolution is afoot today within the field of human learning, and the rebels are marching under the banner of cognitive organization" (p. 18). However "revolting these rebels" may have been, it is certainly true that the ubiquity of organization in perception and comprehension had come to be appreciated. In simple terms, we tend to be confused by or fail to understand situations where "something does not fit." A person acts "out-of-character" if some aspect of their behavior cannot be related to other things we know about the person. A text is incomprehensible if the parts cannot be related. The discovery of a new plant or animal is immediately followed by attempts to classify it with existing species. A major diagnostic marker of psychosis is speaking in "word salad", that is, uttering sentences that are apparently unrelated to one another or even clauses within sentences that are unrelated. In short, the cognitive process of detecting relationships and grouping on the basis of the relationships is fundamental to the coherence of perception and comprehension. It is therefore not surprising that these organizational processes have consequences for memory.

Material-Induced Organization

The majority of laboratory studies of organization and event memory use *categorized* word lists. The lists consist of words drawn from the same natural category, such as *dog, cat, horse, pig,* and *cow* from the category *animal.* In most experiments several categories are used to represent the words; for example, a list might contain twenty words having four words from each of five categories. Compared to uncategorized lists, subjects remember categorized lists very well.

Furthermore, categorized lists are better remembered when presented in *blocked* form than when presented *randomly.* Blocked presentation refers to the order in which all items from a particular category are presented one after another before items from another category are presented. With random presentation, the items from different categories are mixed in the presentation order. The superior memory for blocked presentation again suggests the important role of organization in memory, because blocked presentation is much more organized than is random presentation.

Further indication of the importance of organization is obvious from the finding of active rearrangement of randomly presented lists. Even though items from various categories are presented in random order, subjects group the items into their appropriate categories at recall. That is, the items are recalled by category in spite of having been presented randomly. This regrouping is known as *clustering in recall.* Clustering is an important indication of the active encoding process of organization in that the materials are rearranged from the random presentation order to an organized output order.

The importance of the relationships among separate elements also has been illustrated with nonverbal materials. Palmer (1975) has shown that simple line drawings of parts of the face are difficult to recognize when presented separately. Examples of these drawings are presented in figure 5.1. The same drawings, however, are quickly recognized when presented in the context of a face. Additional information is provided by the context, the face in this case, which aids the recognition of each separate element. Again, organization in the form of relationships among elements is important to the encoding process.

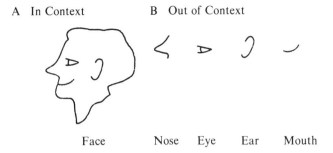

A In Context   B Out of Context

Face   Nose   Eye   Ear   Mouth

Figure 5.1 Materials used by Palmer to assess memory for facial features following presentation of certain features of the face in context (*A*) and out of context (*B*). (From *Explorations in Cognition* by Donald A. Norman and David E. Rumelhart and the LNR Research Group. W. H. Freeman and Company. Copyright © 1975.)

Subjective Organization

Organizational effects are obvious when categorized lists are compared to uncategorized lists, but careful examination of performance on uncategorized lists also reveals persuasive evidence of organizational activity. When subjects are asked to remember lists of words unrelated in any obvious way, they find idiosyncratic relationships which result in consistent output groupings. Although clustering scores based on some category grouping cannot be obtained from uncategorized lists, Tulving (1962) outlined a method for detecting organization of presumably unrelated lists. Tulving's measure of *subjective organization* requires multitrial recall. That is, the subjects receive several presentations and recall tests of a list. Subjective organization is measured by the *consistency of output order* over the recall tests. As the tests progress, the order in which the words are written on the tests becomes progressively more consistent. The particular order differs for different individuals, since the groupings are based on idiosyncratic relationships. Nonetheless, subjective organization is a more impressive indication of the prevalence of organizational activity in encoding than is material-induced organization. It is important to remember that even when the words appear to be unrelated and the input order changes on each presentation, the output becomes highly organized.

Subjective organization is yet another example of using previous knowledge to interpret a current situation. Individual experiences allow us to relate the apparently unrelated words and to bring order to an otherwise chaotic event. Analogous situations exist in everyday experiences, perhaps more commonly than not. When we are confronted with actions which seem to make little sense, most of us try very hard to bring whatever information possible to bear on such situations to interpret and organize them. Consequently, the discrepancies among different persons' memory for the same event are not at all surprising. Based on differences in knowledge of it, an event may be organized and remembered in very different ways by different observers, just as unrelated lists are subjectively organized in very different ways by different persons. This phenomenon is enlarged on later when comprehension and memory are discussed. For the moment, it is important to see the pervasiveness of organization in memory, which is perhaps best illustrated by subjective organization.

Locus of Organizational Effects

The question of how organization affects memory is a very important and also a very complex one. In studies of both material-induced and subjective organization, good memory is accompanied by good organization, but measures of memory and measures of organization are measures of two different processes. Memory is measured by recall and organization by clustering or subjective organization. When these two measures are correlated, that is, good memory is accompanied by high clustering, it is tempting to assume that organization causes good memory. We must consider, however, that the relationship is correlational, and we cannot be absolutely sure that organization *causes* good memory. Indeed, the relationship may indicate just the opposite: good memory may cause organization. How can this be? Very simply, the more you remember the more capable you are of detecting the relationship among the items at output. In other words, as you recall a lot of the items, you see the relationships among them and organize them according to those relationships in the test. This interpretation of the relationship between clustering and recall implies that memory leads to organization. Although such a view cannot be completely dismissed, it just does not make much sense. Why would organization be so prevalent? What is the function of organization? Why should we bother to organize the information *after* we remember it?

In the absence of persuasive answers to these questions, the relationship between recall and clustering becomes much more sensible if *it is assumed that organizational processes contribute to good memory*. With this assumption, it now becomes important to ask how organization affects memory. Why does organization improve memory? Two related answers to this question have been offered.

On the one hand, Mandler (1967) suggested that organization is effective because of *economy of storage*. Organization of discrete units into one holistic unit reduces the number of items to be stored. *Dog, cat, horse, pig,* and *cow* can be stored in the category *animal,* just as *eggs, bacon, juice,* and *coffee* can be stored in the category *breakfast items.* Reminiscent of the short-term memory work on chunking, Mandler then argues that organization improves memory because the amount of information per stored unit is increased. This approach assumes that the organization occurs as the information comes in and thus occurs during encoding.

Alternatively, Tulving argued that oganization benefits memory because of its *effect on retrieval*. Tulving agrees with Mandler that organization occurs as an encoding process of integrating separate items into holistic units; the benefit to memory, then, derives from the ability to access the whole unit at retrieval. Once the unit is accessed, all of the information within the unit can be retrieved. For example, while viewing a categorized list, you may notice that some words are categorized as *animals,* some as *vehicles,* and so on. At retrieval you remember seeing *animals* and *vehicles,* which gives you access to all of the individual items. Organization then is assumed to work because the integrated unit formed at encoding can be retrieved with all of the information of the individual units.

Tulving's retrieval argument is not really at odds with Mandler's encoding position. In fact, Tulving assumes that organization occurs at encoding as Mandler does, only Tulving goes further to suggest why organization at input facilitates output.

Many questions remain concerning the precise mechanisms of organizational effects. For example, how are the similarities among items detected and why does organization improve retrieval? In chapter 9 on comprehension and knowledge we shall see that organization is very important to understanding what is read and heard. Even though we may perfectly understand an individual sentence, we must be able to detect the relationships among the sentences in order to understand the passage or conversation. Thus, organization is one of the most important processes in human cognition, and its effects can be seen throughout the system from perception of visual scenes to comprehension of prose passages and discourse.

THE PARADOX OF ORGANIZATION AND DISTINCTIVENESS

We now have discussed research indicating that memory benefits from distinctive processing and that memory benefits from organizational processes. These facts are well-established and perfectly consistent with our intuitions, but on close inspection, these facts appear paradoxical. Distinctive processing refers to the encoding of differences among events, and organization refers to the encoding of similarities among events. Distinctiveness and organization seem to prescribe diametrically opposed prescriptions for good memory.

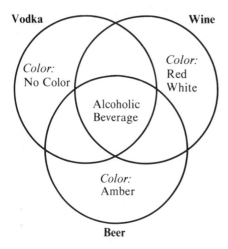

Figure 5.2 Representation of shared information (*alcoholic beverage*) and distinctive information (*colors*) among the concepts *beer, wine,* and *vodka.*

One resolution of this apparent dilemma is to assume that *both types of information* are important to memory (Einstein & Hunt, 1980; Hunt & Einstein, 1981). Some evidence indeed suggests that this is the case. Consider the following experiments reported by Epstein, Phillips, and Johnson (1975) and by Begg (1978). Subjects were given either highly related word pairs (*beer-wine,* for example) or unrelated pairs of words (*beer-dog,* for example). For each pair the subjects had to list either the similarities between the members of the pair or the differences between the members of the pair. Memory for the pairs was then tested. Related pairs were better remembered when subjects oriented to the differences between the words, and unrelated pairs were better remembered when similarities were processed. Why should this be? It appears that both similarities and differences are important. Related pairs command attention to similarity, but the similarity may produce confusion in memory. Subjects may remember "alcoholic beverage," but be unable to decide whether they saw *beer, wine, vodka,* or *scotch.* Noticing the differences among similar items aids in this discrimination. The opposite problem occurs with unrelated items. The differences are obvious, but no relational structure is available to help generate the items. This relational structure or similarity among events seems to be very important in initiating the retrieval process. Remembering an event, whether it be a word in a list or what was done last Tuesday, seems to start at the general level of shared information, such as "words in the list" or "events of last Tuesday," and proceed to finer discriminations.

This interaction between similarities and differences is illustrated in figure 5.2. If each of the circles represents what is known about a word, the overlap or intersection of the circles represents their shared meaning and the nonoverlapping portions represent the meaning of each that is not shared. For example, *beer, wine,* and *vodka* all share *alcoholic beverage* as part of their meaning, but we also know that they have different colors. Color, then, is part of the information which does not overlap.

Thus, the encoding process involves attention to certain aspects of events. Some of this information will be shared among the events and some of the information will differ. Optimal verbatim memory requires both, a point that will be more appreciated when retrieval is discussed in chapter 6.

MEMORY FOR PERSONALLY RELEVANT INFORMATION

In an interesting variation on the levels of processing paradigm, Rogers and his colleagues have shown that the personal relevance of information has a powerful effect on memory. Rogers, Kuiper, and Kirker (1977) asked subjects to perform orienting tasks on lists of adjectives. In addition, to the now familiar semantic and nonsemantic tasks, the subjects were asked to rate how descriptive the word was of them. When later asked to recall the rated words, the words rated for personal descriptiveness were better recalled than those on which a semantic orienting task had been performed. The more self-relevant the event, the better the memory.

Why does self-relevance of an event enhance memory? At one level of description, Stanley Klein and Judith Loftus (1988) of the University of California, Santa Barbara have suggested that the assessment of self-relevance increases both the relational and distinctive processes at encoding. Relational and distinctive encoding influences performance as suggested by Hunt and Einstein (1981). But why should self-relevance enhance relational and distinctive encoding? In all probability, events that we perceive as personally relevant attract more attention than events that are perceived as less relevant. Part of what we mean by "attract more attention" is that more processing is devoted to those events, consistent with the capacity model of attention discussed in chapter 3. It is this additional processing that influences memory, but it is the perceived personal relevance that attracts the additional processing.

Regardless, self-relevance is an important influence on encoding. Not only is this fact evident from laboratory work, but also from your ability to recall the events of yesterday. If you try to do so, you will see that you remember an amazing amount of what happened to you, and most of this information is personally relevant. We now turn to another influence on encoding that revolves around self-involvement, the generation effect.

SELF-GENERATION EFFECTS IN MEMORY

Folk wisdom has it that you will remember something better if you do it yourself than if you watch someone else do it. Perhaps you received this advice from your parents or teachers. Well, as it turns out, they were absolutely right. Recent laboratory work has demonstrated conclusively that information you generate is better remembered than information you see or hear. This finding was labeled the *generation effect* by Slamecka and Graf (1978).

The experiments Slamecka and Graf performed are quite straightforward. In the most simple case, one group of people is asked to generate some words according to a specified rule. For example, each person may be told that they will see a list of words, each followed by a single letter and some blank spaces. Their task is to generate a word that begins with the letter given and contains as many letters as blank spaces. The generated word should be an antonym of the first word. Thus, the person might see FAST-S ___ , and generate SLOW. A second group of subjects sees a list of word pairs which are exactly the same as the words seen and generated by the first group, such as FAST–SLOW. This second group does not generate any words but rather simply reads the list. Notice that the two groups ultimately receive exactly the same words. Subsequently, when asked to remember the second word of each pair, the group that generated the words remembers many more than the group that read the words. This result is the generation effect.

We now know the generation effect occurs under a wide range of circumstances. A number of different generation rules, including rhyme, category, and associative rules, produce the effect. Different types of memory tests, such as recognition, free recall, and cued recall, all yield generation effects, and we also know the effect can be obtained with materials other than single words. The point is that memory for self-generated materials is a very general phenomenon, raising the possibility that the process of self-generation has effects on memory unlike those of to perceptual processes.

In an attempt to assess the importance of the generation *process* itself, Glisky and Rabinowitz (1985) performed an experiment to contrast the effects of the process versus the product of generation. In other words, is the generation effect best explained in terms of the special character of the generation process or in terms of the special character of the trace produced by the generation process? To ask this question, subjects either generated the completion of word fragments or read words during the study task. The memory test was an unusual version of recognition memory in which the subjects saw both words and fragments. The test fragments were to be completed and then a recognition decision was made about the completed word

Table 5.1

Illustration of the study tasks (Read or Generate) and the various conditions of recognition memory at test in Glisky and Rabinowitz's (1985) experiment.

Study Task		Test Task
Read: Elephant		Read & Recognize: Elephant
	or	
		Generate & Recognize:—lep— —nt
Generate: —lep— —nt		Read & Recognize: Elephant
	or	
		Generate same & Recognize: —lep— —nt
	or	
		Generate different & Recognize: E— —p—ant

as a member of the study list. The complete words on the test simply had to be recognized. Some of the words on the test had been presented as fragments at study and some of the fragments on the test had been presented as words at study. Table 5.1 depicts the combination of study task and test task conditions. The purpose of this manipulation was to manipulate reading and generating at study and test such that some items were read both times, some were generated both times, some were read at study and generated at test, and some were generated at study and read at test. Furthermore, for those items generated at study and at test, some had the same fragments and some had different fragments at study and test. The point here was to determine the specificity of the generation process effects. The results showed that generating an item at study led to better recognition of the item than reading at study regardless of the test. This is the standard generation effect. The new finding was that recognition was better for items generated at both study and test than for items generated at study and read at test. This outcome suggests that the generation process contributes to memory over and above the effect of a generated product. Moreover, the effect is very specific as suggested by superior recognition of items generated to the same fragment at study and test in comparison to items generated to different fragments at study and test. *Glisky and Rabinowitz's data clearly indicate that the psychological process of generation is at least as important as the structural representation produced by the process in accounting for generation.*

Another indication of the importance of the *process* of generation in contrast to the trace left by generating is a study by Slamecka and Fevreiski (1983). In this study, subjects were asked to generate a word in response to a dictionary definition. For example, the subject might hear "an astronomical instrument used in computing angular distances, especially by sailors," and the task was to generate the word defined. In the read condition, a definition was followed by presentation of the word. The interesting aspect of the experiment was those cases in the generation condition where the subject was in a tip-of-the-tongue state. Tip-of-the-tongue is the state in which you feel as if you know a word and may even be able to say things about the word such as its first letter, the number of syllables, etc., but cannot actually produce the word. Cases such as these in Slamecka's and Fevreiski study represent attempts to generate that result in failure. But what happens to these words on a subsequent memory test? Astonishingly, these "generation failures" not only are better recognized but also better recalled than read words. Keep in mind that the words in question were never successfully produced at study, but nevertheless were better remembered. Since no "product" was produced by generation of study, this experiment strongly suggests that *the process* of generation is crucial.

McDaniel, Wadill, and Einstein (1988) proposed that the generation process can be explained *as enhancement of relational and distinctive processing,* which we already have discussed as important contributions to memory. Their theory assumes that generating information is analogous to problem solving, and that the subjects use whatever clues are available to solve the problem including cue words, word fragments, and even other read or generated words in the study list. In the course of solving the generation problem, the task focuses the subject on relational or distinctive aspects, or both, of the material to-be-remembered. If the memory test requires the use of the relational or distinctive processing emphasized by the generation task, memory will benefit from generation. This theory has received support from research by McDaniel, Riegler, and Waddill (1990), and the idea has additional appeal because it can explain some important cases in which generation does not facilitate memory (Begg & Snider, 1987; Slamecka & Katsaiti, 1987).

A final important point about McDaniel, Wadill, and Einstein's theory is that self-generation does not involve *different* processes than perception. Relational and distinctive processes have been invoked to explain memory of externally provided information as we saw earlier in this chapter. The advantage of self-generation, when it is advantageous, is the consistency with which the processes are applied. That is, generated items *must* be processed at study because you have to do something to them. Read items may or may not receive the consistent relational and/or distinctive processing, just as you may or may not really be concentrating on this material as the words cross your eyes. Whatever theory finally emerges as best, the data are very clear that generation is very important in memory because of the processes involved.

IMAGERY

Think about your room when you were ten years old. As you left the room, was the doorknob on the left or right side of the door? In answering this question, many people report that they visualize the room including the door. The answer requires information from long-term memory, and the visual representation reported by many people suggests that long-term memory may store *images*. Imagery is an instance of an *analogue representation*. Analogue representations directly mirror the world; analogues contain a point-for-point correspondence with the object they represent. For example, a photograph is an analogue; a verbal description of the same object is not an analogue. Considerable debate has arisen over the existence of analogue repesentations in memory, particularly as they refer to visual memory.

The question at issue here is whether or not some representations in long-term memory are functionally equivalent to visual perception (Solso, 1991). Be careful to understand two things about this question. First, the controversy is not over the question of "imagination" per se but rather concerns the existence of images in long-term memory. That is, few cognitive psychologists would quibble with the belief that visual imagination can be an important element of intellectual functioning. For example, if you have a number of errands to run on a busy day, you may plan your schedule by visually imagining the most efficient routes for all of the stops you must make. The controversial question is: Was this visual information retrieved from memory or alternatively, was the information retrieved in some non-visual form and then converted to a subjective visual experience?

The second point to note about the question is the functional equivalence of images and visual perceptions. Since we have no way to directly determine if a representation in memory is *identical* to a visual perception, the research strategy is to establish conditions under which imagery theoretically should be a factor and then determine if performance is analogous to what would happen if the person actually were "seeing" the event. In this fashion, arguments can be made that the image functions equivalently to visual perception. This strategy guides all of the research we shall now discuss.

Evidence for Imagery

The old saying that a picture is worth a thousand words has considerable validity when applied to memory. Pictures are much better remembered than are words in recognition tests. Of the many experiments demonstrating this fact, consider the work of Standing, Conezio, and Haber (1970). Subjects were shown 2,560 pictures of complex visual scenes, each picture

Figure 5.3 A map used in the studies of mental travel. (From "Visual Images Preserve Metric Spatial Information" by S. M. Kosslyn, T. M. Ball, and B. J. Reiser, *Journal of Experimental Psychology: Human Perception and Performance,* 1978, *4,* 47–60. Copyright 1978 by the American Psychological Association. Reprinted by permission of the publisher and the authors.)

available for inspection for only 10 seconds. In the recognition test the subjects were able to remember correctly 93 percent or a total of 2,380 pictures. This remarkable level of performance is much higher than is usually obtained with verbal materials. Moreover, the rapid rate of presentation and the complexity of the visual scenes make it unlikely that the pictures were verbally recoded. One interpretation of these data, then, is that pictures are stored in a visual form which somehow facilitates memory.

Further evidence for direct storage or visual information comes from Kosslyn's work on "mental travel" (Kosslyn, Ball, & Reiser, 1978). Subjects are shown a simple map containing several important landmarks. The map is drawn so that the distance between the points differs, and these distances are labeled, for example, A to B = 10, B to F = 20, F to A = 30. An example of such a map is shown in figure 5.3. Subjects are asked to remember the map, an easy task given its simplicity. With the map absent, the subjects are then asked to go from one point to another based on their memory of the map. The request is for mental travel, and when the person reaches the designation point, a button is depressed to signify the end of the journey. The button actually stops a clock which was started when "travel" began. The measure of interest in this research is the amount of time to mentally travel the map as a function of the actual distances listed on the map. Interestingly, the times are directly correlated with the distances. If A to B = 10 and B to F = 20, the subjects take much longer to mentally scan from B to F than from A to B. Kosslyn suggests this result indicates that subjects actually use visual representation to perform this task, much as a person might visualize a familiar route when giving directions. As with the previously mentioned picture superiority in memory, Kosslyn's work, along with the mental rotation phenomenon discussed in chapter 2, suggests that visual stimuli may be stored in a visual form.

The argument for an active imaginal encoding to memory, however, is easily illustrated with materials other than pictures. For example, do we imagine an object or scene represented by words and then store the visual scene in memory? If this is so, imaginal encoding would be a very active process of converting an abstract symbol, the word, into a completely different representation. Paivio (1971) has vigorously pursued this issue with a very interesting research program. At the basis of Paivio's research is his discovery that concrete words are better remembered than are abstract words. Concrete words refer to real-world objects and are words such as *cigar, bicycle,* and *dog;* abstract words have less clear real-world referents and are words such as *belief, justice,* and *knowledge.* Paivio and students clearly demonstrated that concrete words are better remembered than abstract words. What does this fact have to do with imagery?

To illustrate Paivio's answer to this question, close your eyes and attempt to visualize *cigar.* Most people find it rather easy to obtain a vivid image of cigar. Now close your eyes and try to get a mental picture of *knowledge.* This is a much more difficult matter, and whatever you may imagine, the image is likely to be hazy and only related to *knowledge* in some fashion. There really is no single concrete instance of knowledge. Abstract words, then, are more difficult to encode in an imaginal form. Paivio suggests that this fact may account for the difference in memory for concrete and abstract words. The more important question now becomes, How does imagery influence memory? Paivio's dual-code theory provides one answer to the question.

Dual-Code Theory

Paivio suggests that information in memory may be stored in two forms, *verbal codes* and *imaginal codes.* Any event or object which can be described may be stored in a verbal code, and any event or object which can be visualized can be stored in an imaginal code. Thus, most events can be remembered through either a verbal code, an imaginal code, or both. For example, a picture can be labeled and remembered as the verbal code implied by the label. Alternatively, the picture can be remembered through the image code, which Paivio argues will produce better memory because the visual image retains more detail than does the verbal code. Thus, superior memory for pictures is due to the ease with which they are visually stored and the amount of detail maintained in the image.

With words, a verbal code may be more probable, but words may also be transformed in encoding to a visual image code. If a word is remembered both by verbal code and image code, the probability of retrieving one of the codes is higher than if only one code is available. Very simply, two codes are better than one. Abstract words, which are difficult if not impossible to code visually, will then be at a disadvantage compared to concrete words. Concrete words can be encoded verbally and visually, whereas abstract words can only be encoded verbally.

As plausible as Paivio's ideas are, a great deal of controversy developed around the concept of imagery. No one doubts the validity of the experimental effects of imagery on memory. Rather, the dispute centers on the idea of a visual long-term memory. Let us briefly examine these arguments.

Are Visual Images Stored in Memory?

Among the most persistent critics of imagery is Pylyshyn (1973), who is, interestingly enough, a colleague of Paivio's at Western Ontario University. The thrust of Pylyshyn's argument is that the experiments just discussed *do not require* a mental imagery interpretation. Furthermore, Pylyshyn and others do not believe that memory contains anything resembling a "picture." For example, consider the work on rotation of mental images. Pylyshyn points out that beliefs and knowledge can affect the way this task is performed, but beliefs and knowledge exert little effect on the rotation of an actual physical picture.

In the same vein, Richman and colleagues (Mitchell & Richman, 1980; Richman, Mitchell, & Reznick, 1979) have criticized Kosslyn's work on visual memory for maps. In a series of papers entitled "Reservations on Mental Travel" and "Confirmed Reservations on Mental Travel" they argue that the correlation between reaction time and distance in Kosslyn's work reflects the subjects' perception of the task demands. That is, the subjects guess that the experimenter expects longer distances to require more time to traverse, and they comply with the expectation.

Again, the argument is that human beings do not really store "pictures" of the world in memory. Neisser and Kerr (1973) provided the opportunity to directly confront this question experimentally. If the mental image is like visual perception, an object hidden in the image should not be remembered. If you are actually looking at a piano and a ball is hidden behind it, you will not see the ball. By the same token, you should not be able to "see" hidden objects in a mental image if the image is like visual perception. Neisser and Kerr instructed people to visualize scenes described by sentences such as, "A harp is hidden inside the torch of the Statue of Liberty." Later the subjects were given a cue such as "torch" and asked to recall the sentence. Will they remember *harp* which should be concealed in the torch? In fact the subjects remembered *harp* as well in the hidden condition as they did in conditions where the harp was blatantly exposed "on top of the torch." Neisser and Kerr conclude that mental images, whatever they are, cannot be two-dimensional snapshots of the world.

More recently, however, Keenan and Moore (1979) repeated Neisser and Kerr's experiment with much stronger instructions about hidden objects. Keenan and Moore report that their subjects remember fewer of the hidden objects than of the exposed objects. Such results, of course, suggest that the image may be like visual perception.

If, however, the images stored in long-term memory were the same as visual perception, then we would not expect people who cannot see to benefit from manipulations of imagery. Nancy Kerr (1983) has performed this experiment with congenitally blind subjects, people who were blind at birth. In fact, Kerr's blind subjects performed exactly as sighted subjects on the memory test. Instructions to imagine objects as spatially contiguous produced better memory than did imagining objects as spatially separated for both blind and sighted subjects. These results suggest that imagery effects upon memory do not depend upon prior visual experience nor does the remembered "image" seem to be the same thing as a visual perception.

The critics of imagery offer an alternative account of encoding processes which involves a common, underlying propositional code. A *propositional code* is an abstract representation (some theorists call it the language of thought) of both verbal and pictorial materials. According to this approach, all types of incoming materials are encoded in the propositional code. Certainly we do experience images, but not because images are stored in memory. Rather the images are generated or created from the underlying propositional representation. How would this position account for some of the data on imagery, for example, the difference in memory between concrete and abstract sentences? As it turns out, abstract sentences are more complex and difficult to understand than concrete sentences. One effect of this additional complexity may be increasing difficulty with propositional encoding, leading to poorer memory.

Regardless of the outcome of the continuing disagreement over imagery, the debate represents a healthy concern for understanding the effects of variables such as pictures, concrete words, and instructions to image upon memory. Again, there is no disagreement that these variables can help to improve memory, as can be illustrated with mnemonic techniques. The argument is in how *to conceptualize* these effects.

Neurocognitive Studies of Imagery

As you now can see, obtaining evidence for the existence of images in long-term memory is more difficult than you might have supposed. Part of the problem lies in the indirect inferences from behavioral data to theoretical concepts about the mind, allowing alternative theories to explain the same behavior (Anderson, 1978). It is tempting, therefore, to believe that questions such as the imagery debate can be decided more directly by obtaining evidence about brain functioning. If imagery and visual perception are functionally equivalent, then the same brain activity should underlie both. The advent of technology allowing brain scanning has opened the door to this research and produced provocative data on the question of imagery.

For example, it is possible to measure the relative amount of blood flow in various parts of the brain. Assuming that greater blood flow signifies greater activity, one can ask if the same parts of the brain are active during visual perception as during imagination. Roland and Friberg (1985) discovered that blood flow during visual imagery of walking through the neighborhood was most apparent for the same regions of the cortex that are responsible for higher visual procesing. Further, these regions are different than those parts of the cortex that are maximally active when doing simple mental arithmetic. The research of Roland and Friberg (1985) suggests that the brain activity associated with mental imagery is the same as with visual perception, both of which are different from nonvisual cognitive tasks.

A number of other investigators have reported similar correlations between imaginal tasks and neurophysiological data, and this information is important to our understanding of the brain. How conclusive these data are on the psychological dispute over imagery is less certain. In spite of appearances, measures of brain responding are no more direct indices of psychological concepts than are behavioral measures. That is, cerebral blood flow (and other neurophysiological measures) is no more directly related to imagery than is number of items recalled. Inferences about the relationship between the brain measure and the psychological concepts still must be made, leaving open alternative possibilities just as with behavioral data. Neurocognitive experiments thus provide a different source of evidence on the imagery debate, but the data are no more useful than behavioral data in the debate over imagery. In fact, the studies conducted thus far really are correlating *imagination* per se with brain activity whereas, as mentioned earlier, the theoretical argument in psychology is about the representation in long-term memory, not the process of imagination. It may well be that the subjective experience of visual imagination and visual perception are functionally equivalent and are subserved by the same brain processes, but this still leaves open the possibility that memory from which the imagination was constructed is not visual.

Although the functional equivalence of imagery in memory to visual perception has not been resolved, there are reasons to believe that neither the memorial image nor even the process of imagination are functionally equivalent to visual perception. Among the best of these reasons is that true functional equivalence of imagination and perception would produce hallucinations for *all* imaginations. If we could not discriminate our perception from our thoughts or memories, behavior would be severely disrupted, as is the case for psychotic patients. Although the mechanisms for this discriminitive ability are not known, research is available indicating the power of these processes in healthy people.

Reality Monitoring

Among the interesting issues which surrounds the concept of imagery is the question of discrimination between our thoughts and our perceptions. Suppose long-term memory does contain images which are very much like visual perceptions. When such an image is retrieved, do we know it is a visual memory rather than a current perception? Such a question may appear foolish, but remember that people who suffer from hallucinations are not capable of making the discrimination. The point is that the human system sometimes makes gross errors in distinguishing fact from fantasy, and phrased in a slightly different form, we can see that the question is reasonably asked of those of us who are not mentally ill.

Rather than ask if a memory can be discriminated from a perception, the question is: *Can memory for an event which actually happened be discriminated from memory for your imagination of that event?* For example, people commonly are confused about whether they actually locked the door or just thought about locking it, actually turned off the oven or just imagined turning it off. The question concerns the ability to discriminate memories for one's perceptions and actions from memories for one's thoughts, a question which could be particularly pertinent if long-term memory of events is stored visually.

The ability to discriminate memory for perceived events from memory for thought has been called *reality monitoring* by Marcia Johnson of Princeton University (e.g., Johnson, 1988). Reality monitoring is different from the clinical term *reality testing,* which refers to the ability to discriminate current thought from current perception. In a highly systematic research program, Johnson and her colleagues have studied reality monitoring and discovered that people are extraordinarily capable of discriminating between memory for thought and memory for perception. The paradigm used is quite simple. A long list of items is presented, with each item occuring several times. However, the subject must do different things with the item. For example, one of the items may be *apple*. On some occurrences, the subject is instructed to imagine an apple and on other occurrences, a picture of an apple is shown. After presentation of the entire list, the subject's task is to estimate the number of times the picture occurred and the number of times an apple was imagined. Even in the absence of prior instructions, people are highly accurate in this discrimination. Johnson has demonstrated that this discriminative ability applies to a wide range of decisions, such as imagining an action versus performing the action, imagining saying something versus actually saying it, and imagining another person saying something versus the person actually saying it (e.g., Foley & Johnson, 1985). Further, high levels of performance have been obtained across wide age ranges from children to the elderly.

Perhaps the only evidence of very poor reality monitoring has been obtained from Alzheimer's patients. Mitchell, Hunt, and Schmitt (1986) found that patients could remember some words from a list but they could not remember whether the words had been generated or read. Such confusion corresponds to certain aspects of Alzheimer behavior. For example, one of the patients in this study recently had written and mailed a check for the same bill ten different times! He could remember that the bill had to be paid but could not remember if he had paid it or just thought about paying it. Schacter, Harbluck, and McLachlan (1984) also have reported serious confusion over source of a memory among amnesic patients.

Otherwise, as Johnson's research has demonstrated, our ability to monitor the source of our memories is quite good. Such an ability is fundamentally adaptive for the individual (consider your fate if you confused thinking about eating with actually having eaten), but the mechanisms of this cognitive precision are not well understood. Among other things, however, the ability to discriminate between memory for imagined events, and memory for perceived events suggests that if images are stored in long-term memory, images of perceived events are not the same as images of imagined events.

Imagery Mnemonics

Almost everyone who claims to have new tricks for better memory will encourage the use of an imagery mnemonic. One of the oldest uses of this technique is known as the *method of loci* and was used by early Greek orators. The method of loci involves associating certain ideas and points with certain parts of the room in which a speech is made. The method can be modified for remembering lists of things by imagining a familiar walk, say from your room to a classroom. Imagine notable landmarks along the walk: a fence, a particular tree, a rock, and so on. Now take the list of things you want to remember—grocery items, chemical elements, names of people doing imagery research, or whatever—and place one item at each of the familiar landmarks. When the time for memory comes, you take a mental walk along the route, noticing each landmark and the associated item. Regardless of whether images are visual or propositional codes, the method of loci is an effective technique for improving memory.

MEMORY AND AGING

Everyone is now aware of the new demographic change in the age of the population. Perhaps for the first time in human history, a significant proportion of the population is elderly, and this trend poses new challenges for society. Among those challenges is an understanding of cognitive changes with aging, particularly changes in memory. The ability to reside independently demands functional memory, to the point that serious memory disturbance is sufficient reason for institutionalization as in the case of Alzheimer's disease. While the risk of memory-threatening disease accompanies aging, many people remain quite healthy well into their 80's. Does memory ability deteriorate with healthy aging?

The answer to this question seems to be "yes." Many laboratory studies have demonstrated that people over 60 years old perform more poorly on recall and recognition of words and sentences than do younger people. Moreover, studies of memory for common, but important, everyday activities have shown deficits associated with aging. For example, Morrell, Park, and Poon (1989) have shown that adults have poorer memory for information from medicine labels than do younger people. As with any situation involving memory deficits, the most certain route to remediation would come from an understanding of the cause of the deficit. Unfortunately, the source of age deficits in memory is not yet clear, although a number of hypotheses are under investigation.

In her thorough review of research on memory and aging, Leah Light (1991) delineates four general hypotheses about age-related memory deficits: 1) Failure to employ effective strategies for remembering due to insufficient knowledge about memory; 2) Defective encoding of experiences due to deficits in comprehension; 3) Deficiencies in deliberate retrieval; and 4) Encoding deficits due to reduced cognitive processing capacity. As Light points out, evidence exists for each of these ideas but inconsistent data also abound for each of the general hypotheses. Thus, research to date has demonstrated a decline in memory ability with aging, but the explanation for this decline is not yet clear. Research in this area, however, continues to accumulate, and the picture will clear as the effort goes forward.

SUMMARY

Encoding processes are the psychological activities which determine the type of information available for later memory. Encoding generally involves the transformation of the incoming information, either through addition or deletion of information. An important source of additional information is the relationship between an event and other known facts. The relational information can serve to organize a set of discrete events into a single, higher-order unit by detecting similarities among the events. This, of course, is the encoding process described as organization. Relational information can also serve to elaborate a single event with additional information not contained in the episode. Such elaboration serves to enrich memory for the given event, probably by making it distinct from other events. Finally, encoding may involve the transformation of information from one form to another, for example, from verbal to visual form or vice versa.

Encoding processes are important to understand because they determine what is *potentially* remembered about an event. What is *actually* remembered, however, is determined by the ability to access or retrieve the information stored in encoding. The effect of any variable on encoding must also be explained through its impact on retrieval, which is the topic of chapter 6.

MULTIPLE-CHOICE ITEMS

1. The difference between semantic memory and episodic memory is
   a. semantic memory is short-term and episodic memory is long-term
   b. semantic memory is event memory and episodic memory is general knowledge
   c. semantic memory is less likely to include images
   d. semantic memory is memory for general knowledge and episodic memory is for specific events

2. A consistent ordering in the output of unrelated items is referred to as
   a. material-induced organization
   b. subjective organization
   c. elaboration
   d. distinctiveness

3. It is difficult to decide conclusively whether organization causes good memory because
   a. clustering scores and recall scores can only be correlated
   b. organization does not always improve memory

c.   we do not know how retrieval is influenced by organization

d.   we do not know whether organization affects short-term memory or long-term memory

4.   The primary difficulty for the original levels-of-processing hypothesis was

a.   nonsemantic processing normally does not lead to poorer memory than does semantic processing

b.   orienting tasks really do not control encoding

c.   nonsemantic information does not decay more rapidly than does semantic information

d.   semantic information is usually less distinctive than is nonsemantic information

5.   The relationship between distinctiveness and organization suggests that

a.   neither are important to memory

b.   both are important to memory

c.   organization is more important to memory

d.   distinctiveness is more important to memory

6.   The most direct experimental evidence on the question of whether images are stored in memory comes from studies on

a.   imagination of hidden objects

b.   concrete versus abstract words

c.   mental travel

d.   words versus pictures

TRUE–FALSE ITEMS

1.   Encoding processes are an important determinant of retrieval.

2.   Material-induced organization requires no psychological process because the organization is in the material.

3.   The experiments on clustering and recall clearly show that organization occurs only during encoding or input.

4.   Semantic orienting tasks *always* produce better recall than do nonsemantic orienting tasks because semantic information lasts longer.

5.   The distinctiveness hypothesis predicts that under some circumstances nonsemantic information can produce better memory than can semantic information.

6.   There is much disagreement about whether imagery effects occur in memory.

DISCUSSION ITEMS

1. Describe the relationship between organization and distinctiveness.

2. Why is the research on hidden objects in images crucial to the question of images in memory?

3. Trace the development of the levels-of-processing approach to memory.

ANSWERS TO MULTIPLE-CHOICE ITEMS

1. (d)   Semantic memory refers to general knowledge, while episodic memory refers to specific events.
2. (b)   Subjective organization is a consistent grouping in the output of unrelated words.
3. (a)   All we know is that high clustering usually accompanies good recall. We do not know that clustering causes good recall.
4. (c)   Studies such as Stein's show that nonsemantic information is remembered reasonably well.
5. (b)   Organization may be quite helpful in generating information from which an appropriate response may be selected if the response is distinctively encoded.
6. (a)   If snapshotlike images are stored in memory, a hidden object should not be remembered.

ANSWERS TO TRUE–FALSE ITEMS

1. (True)   Only those things which have been encoded can be retrieved accurately.
2. (False)   The process of organization detects or imposes the structure of the material.
3. (False)   Clustering may also occur at retrieval.
4. (False)   A number of studies have shown that nonsemantic information may last as long as does semantic information.
5. (True)   Distinctiveness, regardless of whether the information is semantic or nonsemantic, is a very critical factor for retention.
6. (False)   Imagery effects clearly occur in memory; the disagreement is over how to explain these effects.

6

RETRIEVAL PROCESSES

A nswer the following question: What were you doing at 10:00 A.M. on November 21, 1990? At first glance, this may appear to be a difficult question, but we shall give you a clue and let you think about it. November 21 was the Wednesday before Thanksgiving Day. Now can you answer the question? You may remember that, since November 21 was the day before the Thanksgiving holiday and you had decided to leave school early, you were traveling at 10:00 A.M. on that day. Or you may remember that at 10:00 A.M. on Wednesdays during the fall term you were in English literature class. Regardless of the situation, most people can provide an answer when clues are given and they use a little thought. This simple example illustrates some of the fundamental characteristics of retrieval from memory.

When memory is used to answer questions such as the one just posed, we generally have the sense of narrowing a set of alternatives until we arrive at the answer. Even to begin this process, however, *cues* are necessary to delineate the general set of events from which to sample. Imagine how ridiculous a question such as, "What did you do?" is without context. The questioner must provide some cue as to when or where the activity occurred. Given the importance of cues to retrieval, we begin with a discussion of the effect of cues on memory.

WHAT MAKES A CUE EFFECTIVE?

If the retrieval process is critically dependent upon the use of cues, what is an effective cue? The obvious answer is that a good cue is any information which helps us remember. Equally obvious is that this suggestion is not very helpful. If we must wait until the time of a memory test to see what sorts of cues are useful, we have no way of predicting the level of memory performance and, even worse, no way of facilitating memory in ourselves or others. Thus, an idea about the effectiveness of cues becomes essential not only in understanding the retrieval process, but also in improving memory for events. Two such ideas have dominated thinking about cue effectiveness in event memory: *associative strength* and *encoding specificity.*

Associative Strength Theory of Cue Effectiveness

The basic premise of associative strength theory is that a cue is effective if it has occurred frequently with the to-be-remembered event in the past. Such cues are said to be strongly associated with the event. For example, *whistle* frequently occurs with *train,* and *whistle* is a very good cue to help remember *train.* To determine how strongly associated two words are, free-association norms are used. Free-association techniques were popularized by Freud who, interestingly enough, used free association for roughly the same purpose as does the cognitive psychologist, to study the structure of memory. In free association, a person simply responds with the first word which comes to mind when given the target word. For example: I say *grass*. You say _____ ? Associative strength is determined by the number of persons giving a particular response. The greater the number of persons who give a common response, the higher the associative strength becomes.

A substantial number of memory studies have shown that strongly associated cues produce better memory than do weakly associated cues. In these experiments, subjects are typically shown pairs of words in a study or input session, some of which are strongly associated *(whistle-train)* and some of which are weakly associated *(black-train)*. At the time of the memory test, the cue *(whistle* or *black)* is provided, and the subject must produce the other member of the pair *(train)*. Again, the strongly associated cue is more effective than is the weak cue, and this is true even when the cues are not present at input but only in the test.

Associative-strength theory works on a memory structure consisting of an associative network interrelating all of the items in memory. Retrieval begins with the "activation" of the representation of the cue itself. As John Anderson (1983), a prominent associative theorist, has noted, "activation" refers to the transfer of information from long-term to short-term memory. In other words, activation is a concept describing the transformation of information from a latent state to a conscious state. An important feature of the activation of the cue's representation is that the activation then spreads through portions of the associative network. Anderson's apt analogy is of water coursing through irrigation ditches. Each memory representation is analogous to a small pool at the end of a ditch. As the pool fills, the water spills out to ditches connected with that pool. Eventually, the available water is insufficient to spill over and the spread stops.

Spreading activation is a crucial concept in the associative view of retrieval. As the activation spreads from the cue's representation, each additional representation which receives activation is a candidate to be remembered. The strength of association between a cue and another item is represented by the distance between the two in the associative network. Strongly associated items are closer together. Thus, strength of association is fundamental to retrieval because the activity spreads from the cue to associated items, and items close to the cue are most likely to receive activation before it dissipates.

How does associative strength develop? Historically, the consensual answer to this question has been the frequency of previous pairing of two events. After many pairings, the occurrence of one event quickly and automatically brings the other to mind. Thus, a fundamental premise of the associative-strength theory of cue effectiveness is that the number of previous encodings of two events will determine the cue effectiveness of one for the other. This certainly sounds reasonable, but surprisingly, Tulving disagreed and proposed a competing idea.

Encoding Specificity Hypothesis of Cue Effectiveness

Tulving does not quarrel with the premise that past experience is very important to current performance. Virtually all psychologists agree with this principle. Tulving's argument, however, is the interesting suggestion that any given event occurs only once. A particular event does not occur several times, allowing frequent pairings with other events, but rather every event has one and only one episode. You can only have one "first bicycle" to remember just as there can only be one "last night's dinner." If this point is true, and at some level it must be, associative-strength theory with its emphasis on frequency of past occurrence must be inadequate.

Tulving's alternative is to suggest that effective retrieval cues are those which were present when the event occurred. That is, *a cue will be effective if it was specifically encoded with the target event*—hence the name *encoding specificity.*

Tulving and Thomson (1971) provided evidence for encoding specificity in contrast to associative strength. Subjects were given a list of weakly associated pairs, for example, *black-train,* at input, and then the subjects were divided into two groups at output. One group was given the list of weakly associated cues seen at input. The second group was given strongly associated cues not present at input. The issue is, which group can remember the best? The results of this experiment demonstrated that the cues present at input or encoding are more effective, even though they are weakly associated. Tulving and Thomson suggest that these results provide support for encoding specificity over associative strength.

The primary difference between encoding specificity and associative strength is the role of past co-occurrence of both the cue and the target event. Tulving suggests that a given event occurs only once, and hence cues that occur with that event are the most effective. Yet, there are certainly situations in which the associative strength of the cue is important. When given the cue *salt,* you are likely to think of *pepper;* when given the word *dog,* you are likely to think *cat.* These are strongly associated word pairs which frequently co-occur, but unlike the previous situations, the information retrieved here is not of a specific event but of general knowledge. Tulving (1972) argues that encoding specificity does not apply to the retrieval of general knowledge, and this argument now becomes the basis for the distinction between episodic memory and semantic memory.

MEMORY SYSTEMS

Episodic and semantic memory were proposed as distinct systems, meaning that they operate on different principles and serve different functions. The initial reason to suggest these different systems was the observation that sometimes encoding specificity seemed to explain cue effectiveness and sometimes associative strength seemed to be the explanation. Encoding specificity seemed to apply to retrieval of specific episodes and associative strength to retrieval of general knowledge, and from this speculation rose this characterization of memory as having distinct structural systems.

Episodic memory refers to memory for specific events that only happen once. *Semantic memory* refers to general world knowledge that is not specifically time tagged. "What did you have for dinner last night?" is a question requiring episodic memory. "What do Eskimos eat for dinner?" is a question drawing on general knowledge of the world, or semantic memory. Retrieval from semantic memory is not governed by encoding specificity. For example, the specific events that occurred when a person initially learns that George Washington was the first president of the United States are not necessary to retrieve *George Washington* in answer to the question "Who was the first president of the United States?"

More recently, Tulving (1983) has suggested that semantic memory be subdivided into *procedural* and *propositional* subsystems. Procedures are skills, like tying a shoe, riding a bicycle, or using a knife and fork. Skills are learned procedures, and procedural memory refers to memory processes required to retrieve information underlying skilled performance. Notice, based on the examples described above, that procedural memory is characterized by absence of thought. A skilled bicycle rider does not "try" to retrieve "bicycle-riding" information. Indeed, conscious attention to procedural information can disrupt performance of the skill, as most athletes know or you can see by trying to describe how to tie a shoelace.

The propositional subsystem of semantic memory contains world-knowledge, not skills, as described above. This knowledge is generic and context independent, such as the color of rubies, Ronald Reagan's vice president, and the meaning of "dinner." Retrieval from this system does not depend upon encoding-specificity because the information is not about a particular encoding episode. The information is "context-independent" in that it does not refer to a particular event in time or space.

Episodic memory is the system that represents these particular events, and the cues to retrieve them from episodic memory must have been part of the original experience. Remembering what you had for dinner last night is episodic memory and is defined by the unique event of "last night's dinner." Given the context-dependency of this information, the cues must be some part of that context. Unlike the semantic system, the operation of episodic memory is accompanied by the conscious feeling of remembering.

The distinction among these memory systems derives from the different uses of prior experience and is grounded in the belief that different retrieval processes characterize the systems. This thinking has been applied to other issues in memory, particularly the fact that the effects of a given variable differ as a function of the type of memory test. We shall discuss research on two aspects of this issue, the first being the difference between recall and recognition memory.

RETRIEVAL PROCESS: ONE OR TWO?

The issues we just have reviewed are concerned with the question of what makes a cue effective. This is an important issue and as we have seen, leads us to more general questions concerning the very structure of memory. On the other hand, the question of cue effectiveness does not directly address the question of the *processes* of retrieval. What happens when an effective cue is presented? Does the person automatically produce the desired item or is there an additional process of decision about the information? This question characterizes the two alternative views that have been adopted about retrieval processes.

In the first case, which we shall call single-process theory, the psychological process of retrieval is simply a matter of producing an item to the cue. Encoding specificity theory of cue effectiveness is consistent with this simple process view in that a cue encoded with the desired information will be effective. No other aspects of processing at retrieval are specified. The alternative view, which we shall call the generate-recognize process, suggests that two processes are involved in retrieval in *recall*. The first process is the generation of an item which is the same as the single process view, but in addition, a second process of recognizing the generated item is proposed. The research arena in which these alternatives have battled is the comparison of recognition and recall tests. The reason that comparisons of recognition and recall are important is clear if we think a bit about the generate-recognize process.

Generation-Recognition Model of Retrieval

The generation-recognition model suggests that the output process in recall, where information must be reproduced, involves, first, the activation of potential answers and, second, the decision concerning the accuracy of the response. For example, when we are involved in conversation, we may think of things to say, and then reject some as inappropriate or inaccurate.

In recognition, however, the generation stage is unnecessary. A recognition test does not require reproduction but only the decision concerning whether a particular event was or was not present at input. In other words, generation of the original event is not necessary because the event is present on the test. Thus, the generate-recognize view argues that recognition memory and recall memory tests differ in their retrieval demands. Recall is more complex, requiring *both* generation and the recognition decision.

Recognition only requires the recognition decision. One-process theories argue that retrieval occurs in the same way in both recognition and recall. Hence, experimental tests of one- versus two-process theories have focused on differences between recall memory and recognition memory.

How Similar Is Retrieval in Recognition and in Recall?

Generate-recognize theory contends that retrieval operates differently in recognition and in recall, whereas single-process theory suggests that retrieval is the same in both processes. How do we decide between these theories? Obviously we look for differences between recognition memory and recall memory, but we shall see that simple differences between the two are not sufficient to decide the issue. For example, recognition has long been known to be easier than recall. Knowledge of this fact is demonstrated by the preference of most persons for multiple-choice examinations as opposed to essay examinations. Multiple-choice examinations are recognition tests and are generally easier, although this need not be the case if the incorrect alternatives are very similar to the correct response.

One interpretation of the greater difficulty of recall is that recognition does not require generation. This is, of course, generate-recognize theory. Single-process theory, however, can also explain the relative ease of recognition in several different ways. One way is to assume that retrieval cues are important in both recognition and recall, and recognition is at an advantage because it always has the best possible cue, the old item itself. The point is that a more subtle means of deciding between these views is necessary.

The research strategy adopted is actually fairly straightforward in conceptualization. If we want to know whether recognition includes a generation process like that in recall, we can try to manipulate some aspect of a *recognition test* identified as affecting generation in recall. If we get the same effect in recognition as we do in recall, we may assume that generation must have been operating in recognition. For example, the frequency with which words are used in the language is assumed to affect their accessibility, and indeed, high-frequency words are better recalled than are low-frequency words. Examples of high-frequency words are *house* and *people,* and low-frequency words are exemplified by *cider* and *loon.* What happens in recognition? Low-frequency words are usually better recognized. This theory would make sense if it is true that recognition does not require generation but is based on discriminative decision. Low-frequency words are unusual or rare and hence are quite distinctive in a recognition test. Findings such as these are strong support for the generate-recognize theory.

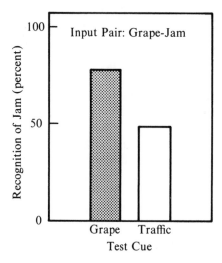

Figure 6.1 Summary of results from a number of studies showing the effect of recognition accuracy of changing a cue from input to test so that the test cue biases a different meaning for the target noun. (From "Recognition Memory and Degree of Semantic Contextual Change" by R. R. Hunt and H. C. Ellis, *Journal of Experimental Psychology,* 1974, *103,* 1153–1159. Copyright 1974 by the American Psychological Association. Reprinted by permission of the publisher and authors.)

Using the same technique, however, the one-process theorists generated evidence in their favor. As just discussed, retrieval cues are one of the most powerful variables affecting retrieval in recall. If retrieval cues are changed from input to output, recall memory suffers. If *grape-jam* is seen at input, changing the test cue to *traffic-_____* makes it difficult to retrieve *jam.* By the same token, if a person's name is associated with his face and then at a later meeting the face has changed, say there is now a beard, the name may be more difficult to recall. The difficulty engendered by the change in cues is generally attributed to failure to generate the response.

Do cue changes affect recognition memory? Certainly they do. A change in the physical appearance of a face can affect recall and may also result in complete failure to recognize the face. If a subject sees *grape-jam* at input and the recognition test pair is *traffic-jam,* recognition of *jam* is quite low (Hunt & Ellis, 1974; Light & Carter-Sobell, 1970). Since the cue is presumed to influence generation, the detrimental effect of cue changes on recognition suggests that generation may be as important in recognition as recall. These data, examples of which can be seen in figure 6.1, support a single-process view of retrieval.

Further evidence for a single process of retrieval in recognition and recall comes from the paradigm developed by Tulving and Thomson (1973) which produces the phenomenon known as *recognition failure of recallable words.* The subject is given several presentations and several recall tests on a cue-target word pair, for example, *glue-chair.* After a few such trials, recall of *chair* in the presence of the cue *glue* is very good. Without warning, the next test is a recognition test for *chair* in the presence of a new cue, for example, *table.* Recognition of *chair,* which previously was recalled with high probability, is now very poor. How can this happen if recall requires the recognition decision and recognition does not involve generation? The words were recalled, and for the generate-recognize theorists this means that the words were both generated and recognized in recall. But if they were recognized in recall, should they not easily pass the same recognition decision in the recognition test? Why should recognition fail for recallable words? The single-process theorist's answer is clear: recall and recognition both require the generation process and the new cue in recognition disrupts this process. Here we have another example of evidence taken to support a relatively uncomplicated single-process view.

Summary of Generation-Recognition Model

What, then, are we to make of retrieval of event memories? Before addressing the differences between the two major theories, we should not lose sight of the useful information gained from confrontation between the two ideas. We now know that good event memory depends upon the similarity of cues at input and at output, regardless of whether the test is for recognition or for recall. You can put this powerful piece of information to work by concentrating on developing good cues for material you know you will have to remember. For example, some observers recommend that some study time should be spent in the very room in which the examination will be held. The reasoning is that the room itself can be a useful cue, and this advice can be surprisingly helpful.

Let us briefly return to the nature of the retrieval process. Perhaps there is less difference between the single-process and generate-recognize views of retrieval than initially apparent. If we return to the conceptualization of retrieval as a process of narrowing down the possibilities or of making increasingly fine discriminations, we can see merit in both positions and perhaps find some reconciliation between them. Consider, for example, how to answer the question of what you did in the afternoon two days ago. Usually you initiate the answer by generating fairly general information: "Let's see, two days ago was Tuesday." Then you use the general information to generate more specific information: "On Tuesday I had lunch, and then I went to anthropology class, and I had coffee with friends after class, and we discussed the exam." When generated, such information may lead to finer-grained information about what you did two days ago. This example illustrates what is meant by event retrieval being a *process of narrowing down the possibilities,* and in this particular example, the approach appears similar to the generate-recognize model of event memory. You generate a possibility, consider it, and report it when it is correct and withhold it when it is incorrect.

Sometimes, however, possibilities do not seem to be generated and considered, but rather the event in question is retrieved immediately. Perhaps memory for the event is quite distinctive and cues are so powerful that access is automatic. For example, "Two days ago I took the worst anthropology exam ever" might be an automatic response to the question about what you did two days ago, and response to the question "What is the date of your birth?" might also be automatic. The point is that some events may be so distinctive and the cues so effective that no decision is needed. For more normal day-to-day occurrences, however, this is not likely to be the case. Usually the strategy of narrowing down the events from most general to more specific is employed. In short, some instances of retrieval seem to conform to the generation-recognition model and other instances to the single-process model.

Retrieval: Organization and Distinctiveness

Finally, we can relate the general process of retrieval to the previous discussion of organization and levels of processing in encoding (Einstein & Hunt, 1980; Hunt & Einstein, 1981). Organization at encoding produces the general information being described in the retrieval process. Organization is the extraction of shared information from among a variety of events. Such information as "all events on Tuesday" and "all events in anthropology class" results from organizational encoding and can be a useful starting point in retrieval. Information specific to each event within the more general organization is also extracted at encoding. This specific or distinctive information is necessary if we are to move from general organization to specific event memory in retrieval. The principle here is simply that what can be retrieved is only what has been stored, and what has been stored can be retrieved only under appropriate circumstances. We can learn more about the interaction between encoding and retrieval as well as about the circumstances appropriate for retrieval by examining retrieval failure.

The power of highly distinctive retrieval cues has been demonstrated dramatically by Timo Mantyla (1986). Subjects in this experiment were asked to generate one or more properties for each word seen. Subsequently, the subject was given the properties as retrieval cues for the words they studied. In one case, subjects who were given the three properties they generated for each studied word were able to recall 90 percent of the 600 words they studied. Relative to most laboratory studies of recall memory, performance in Mantyla's experiment was phenomenal. Apparently, the critical difference in procedure which produced this extraordinary memory was the use of distinctive, personal cues.

If you think about it for a moment, Mantyla's experiment seems to model the conditions of much of "real-world" memory. Perception and encoding always occur in the context of an individual's own idiosyncratic knowledge system. Some large proportion of day-to-day memory probably is cued by self-generated cues which, according to Mantyla's data, would produce extremely accurate memory. Given all of this, what is the purpose of more general cues? Is the emphasis upon general cues, cues which are common to a number of discrete elements, simply the product of laboratory obsession with organization with no correspondence to real-world memory?

One answer to this question is rather obvious. Quite often in the real world retrieval cues are provided by someone else. Indeed, this is almost always the case when you take examinations or even when you are involved in conversation. Someone else's idiosyncratic, distinctive cues are unlikely to be the same as those you have encoded, and following the principle of encoding specificity, someone else's distinctive cues may be of little use to you. Indeed, Mantyla's experiment included test conditions in which he switched people's cues and found that someone else's self-generated properties were not nearly as effective as the subject's own properties.

The principle suggested here is very simple. Suppose your friend says to you, "I thought I would die when I saw his tie." Such a statement sometimes produces utter perplexity for the listener. You respond: "What in the world are you talking about?" Your friend says: "You remember psychology class on Thursday. That horrendous tie Dr. Hunt wore." At this juncture, the cue information, psychology class, is more general and may provoke some memory. Perhaps you may be able even to reconstruct information about the tie. Nonetheless, the point is that a distinctive element of a situation for your friend may not have been a distinctive element for you. Therefore, your friend's distinctive cue serves little retrieval function for you. More general cues, however, are likely to be shared and hence may well be more useful than distinctive cues when someone other than the rememberer is providing the cues. That is, not only is a general cue shared by more target elements, general cues also may be shared by more people than distinctive cues. Thus, in accord with encoding specificity, someone else's general cue may be more effective for you than someone else's distinctive cue.

IMPLICIT VERSUS EXPLICIT MEMORY

The theories we have just described were proposed to explain the differences in performance on recognition and recall tests. Both recognition and recall are *direct* memory tests in that they explicitly direct the subject to produce something from memory. The influence of past experience also can be indirect in that past experience is used for current performance without trying to remember. For example, if you are well acquainted with your campus, you do not recall the way to class each day. You simply go to class; yet, it is indisputable that your ability to get to class depends upon prior experience, and in that sense, depends on memory. Such use of prior experience is known as an implicit or an *indirect* memory test because memory is not the direct object of the test. In the indirect test, the task is to solve some problem for which a particular past experience is relevant, but the task does not direct you to consider that past experience. (See Roediger, 1990)

Dissociations between direct and indirect memory tests have become a fertile source of speculation about retrieval processes in memory. Dissociation refers to the fact that a variable has a different effect on performance depending upon the type of test, much as we already have seen with recognition and recall and with short- and long-term memory. An example of the dissociation between direct and indirect tests was discussed in chapter 4 when we described Graf and Schacter's research on amnesia. Graf and Schacter showed that relative to normal subjects, amnesic patients performed poorly on recall, a direct memory test, but that the same patients performed just as well as normal subjects on a test of stem-completion, an indirect memory test. Actually, this type of dissociation was reported much earlier by Warrington and Weiskrantz (1968) who found that amnesic patients showed as much benefit from prior experience with a word on a test requiring identification of highly fragmented words as did normal subjects.

Notice that the same variable, amnesia, has a different effect depending upon the type of memory test. In recall, amnesia results in poor performance, but in the case of stem-completion or word-fragment completion, amnesia has no effect. Since the obvious difference between the situations is the test, these results suggest very different retrieval processes.

Numerous factors producing dissociations have been identified. Study variables such as semantic vs. nonsemantic orienting tasks or generation vs. reading that are known to produce large effects on direct memory tests exert a very different effect on indirect tests. For example, Jacoby and Dallas (1981) used a *perceptual identification* test to study the effects of generation on indirect memory. Perceptual identification is a test that simply requires the subject to identify a word under degraded conditions; usually, the word is flashed very briefly on the computer monitor and followed by a backward mask. Prior to the test, subjects read a list of words, all of which subsequently appear on the test along with an equal number of words that were not previously read. Perceptual identification is considered an indirect memory test because the subjects are not told to try to remember the study words during the test, yet identification of the studied words is much better than identification of nonstudied words. Jacoby and Dallas (1981) required subjects to generate some of the words at study and read others. On a direct test of recognition memory, the standard generation effect was obtained; that is, generated words were better recognized than read words. Perceptual identification showed the opposite effect. Read words were better identified than generated words. Again, both tests were influenced by the prior experience of the study list, but the effect of a particular variable, generation in this case, was different on the two tests.

Dissociations between direct and indirect memory tests offer an interesting opportunity to understand further the psychological processes of retrieval. Something about the differences between the tests engages very different retrieval processes. Explanations of the dissociations have focused on different dimensions of the test demands to argue for various theoretical alternatives. The most salient differences between the direct and indirect tests are: 1) direct tests can be completed correctly only by referring to a particular prior experience, but indirect tests do not require reference to a particular experience; 2) the cues on direct and indirect tests are different; and 3) direct tests instruct people to remember intentionally, but indirect tests do not request intentional retrieval of prior experience.

Memory Systems Explanation

The dissociation between direct and indirect tests has been explained by Tulving's distinction among memory systems. The starting point of this explanation is the identification of particular test demands with particular memory systems. For example, a recall test demands that you produce a specific prior event, an obvious case of episodic memory. A stem-completion test demands that you complete the three-letter stem with a word, any word you know. Since the word does not have to be a particular word from the study list, this test is driven by semantic memory. Or consider the perceptual identification test. The demand is to read a word. Reading a word is a matter of general knowledge and hence semantic memory. *In general, the memory systems explanation of these test dissociations begins with the assumption that direct tests draw on episodic memory and indirect memory tests draw on one or another of the semantic subsystems.* Since the different systems operate according to different principles, it is not surprising that a given variable has different effects on the different tests. For example, see Schacter (1992) for a recent discussion of a cognitive-neuroscience version of this approach.

For example, semantic orienting study tasks produce better recall and recognition than nonsemantic tasks, but as Graf, Squire, and Mandler (1984) have shown, stem-completion performance is not affected by the orienting task. Keep in mind that the study experience does increase the probability that a study-list word will appear on stem-completion. The memory systems explanation appeals to different retrieval processes to account for these data. Direct memory tests are subject to encoding specificity since they test episodic memory. Semantic orienting tasks encourage elaborative encoding, broadening the range of cues at encoding that then potentially will be effective at retrieval. Indirect tests, such as stem-completion, are governed by associative strength since they operate from semantic memory. The association in question is between the three-letter stem on the test and the word that comes to mind in response to the stem. During the study experience, the semantic memory representation of the word is "activated" if the word is read. Since both the semantic and nonsemantic tasks require reading the word, they both result in semantic memory activation. The greater the activation, the more likely the word is to come to mind. Thus, the stem cues in the stem-completion test elicit the study words rather than some nonstudied words because the studied words have been activated at study. But there is no difference between semantic and nonsemantic study tasks because they both activate the semantic memory representation. Thus, the memory systems view ultimately relies on different principles of retrieval to explain the dissociations between direct and indirect tests.

Processing Account of Dissociations

A somewhat troublesome fact for the memory systems explanation of dissociations is the *modality effect on indirect tests*. If the study list is presented in one modality, visually for example, and the test items are presented in a different modality, auditorially for example, the beneficial effects of the study experience are reduced or eliminated. This modality effect has been reported in tests of fragment completion (Roediger & Blaxton, 1987) and perceptual identification (Jacoby, 1983). Direct memory tests such as recognition and recall are not subject to the modality effect. This dissociation is not easily managed by the memory systems approach. Since the semantic representation for the word should be activated at study regardless of study modality, the benefit of this activation should be apparent in the test regardless of test modality. Such is not the case. About the only recourse for the systems approach is to postulate additional memory systems to hold modality specific input. This tactic would be awkward because the prior distinction between semantic and episodic memory is blurred. Modality information is contextually specific and semantic memory is supposed to be context free. Thus, one would expect modality information to be episodic, but the tests that are subject to the modality effect are those drawing from semantic memory.

In the face of this type of argument, an alternative explanation of dissociations has emerged. Known as the *processing* account (Roediger, Weldon & Challis, 1989) *this approach generally argues that the effect of a prior experience on a subsequent test depends on the match between the mental processes engaged by the study experience and the mental processes required by the test.* To the extent that the mental processes required at study overlap with those at test, test performance will be improved.

Mental processes are very specific. Reading the word CAT requires different mental processes than reading the word DOG. Reading the word DOG involves different mental processes than hearing the word DOG. Thus, the modality effect is explained as a mismatch of processes. That is, hearing a word at study does not provide as much benefit when you see the word at test because the mental processes are less similar than if the word occurs in the same modality on both occasions.

Clearly, the fundamental principle of retrieval for the processing approach is comparable to encoding specificity. In both cases, the necessary factor is overlap of what happens at study and at test. The principle of encoding specificity, however, was the first step to Tulving's memory systems; the processing approach does not make distinctions between systems, but rather distinguishes among memory processes. The upshot is not only a different interpretation of dissociations but also a different view of memory in general. We can see the implication of these differences by examining two versions of the processing approach.

Conceptually-Driven and Data-Driven Processes

A distinction has been drawn between mental processes that are *data-driven* versus processes that are *conceptually driven* (Roediger & Blaxton, 1987; Roediger, Weldon & Challis, 1989). Data-driven processes deal with the physical features of the presented information whereas conceptually-driven processes are related to meaning rather than physical features. Jacoby (1983) recommended this distinction to explain the results he obtained in perceptual identification following a generate-read study task. Recall that in this experiment, Jacoby discovered that read words at study were better identified than generated study words, a reversal of the generation effect obtained in recognition and recall.

Jacoby suggested that reading a word at study relied on processing of physical features of the word. The generation study task in his experiment required subjects to produce an antonym to a cue word plus the first letter of the target (e.g., *hot-c...*). Since the target antonym cannot be processed through the physical features of the presented information but rather must be retrieved from memory based on its conceptual relation to the cue, generation was classified as a conceptually-driven task. Perceptual identification is a test that essentially requires the subject to read the test word, albeit

Memory System

		Episodic	Semantic
Type of Processing	Data-Driven	Graphemic Cued Recall	Word Fragment Completion
	Conceptually Driven	Free Recall Semantic Cued Recall	General Knowledge

Figure 6.2 The design of Blaxton's (1989) experiment comparing data-driven/ conceptually-driven distinction with semantic-episodic distinction. (From "Investigating dissociations among memory measures: Support for a transfer-appropriate processing framework" by T. A. Blaxton. *Journal of Experimental Psychology: Learning, Memory, and Cognition,* 1989, *15,* 657–688. Copyright 1989 by the American Psychological Association. Reprinted by permission.)

in a degraded form. Thus, the test requires data-driven processes and consequently, performance is better following reading than generation at study. The conceptually-driven processes of generation are appropriate to direct memory tests such as recall where the test requires processes other than those driven by the physical features of the target because the target is not presented in a recall test. In this fashion, Jacoby explained the reversal of the standard generation effect on perceptual identification by distinguishing between conceptually-driven and data-driven processes.

This explanation has been extended by Henry L. Roediger and his students as a general account of dissociations between direct and indirect tests. The idea is that most indirect tests require data-driven processes and most direct tests require conceptually-driven processes. Therefore, a variable affecting data-driven processes will not affect a direct test and a variable influencing conceptually-driven processes will not affect an indirect test. A better understanding of this approach can be gained by examining an experiment by Teresa Blaxton (1989) that was designed to pit the processing approach against the memory systems approach. The study conditions were the same as Jacoby's, a read task and a generate task. Four different kinds of tests were given. As illustrated in figure 6.2, these tests were selected so that the memory systems classification would predict different outcomes than the processing classification. The graphemic cued recall test was a test in which the cue shared many letters with the target (e.g., *bushel-bashful*). Free recall was a request to recall as many words as possible. Word fragment completion was a test that required completion of fragments (e.g.

b..sh..u..). The general knowledge test required an answer to a question (e.g. "Which of the seven dwarfs comes first alphabetically?"). The memory systems view would group graphemic cued recall and free recall as episodic tests; fragment completion and general knowledge would be grouped as semantic tests. The processing view would group graphemic cued recall and word fragment completion as data-driven tests because the physical features of the cues in these tests drive processes similar to those of the studied target. Free recall and general knowledge tests are grouped as conceptually-driven because the physical features of the cues do not overlap with the target. By "grouped," what we really mean is that the study variable of generation will affect the tests the same way.

Blaxton's results showed that performance on graphemic cued recall and word fragment completion was better following read study than generate study. Performance on free recall and general knowledge tests was better following generate study than read study. In short, the dissociations clustered as would be predicted by the conceptually-driven/data-driven classification, but not in accord with the memory systems classification.

The distinction between data-driven and conceptually-driven processes is a broad classification of mental processes that is based on the task requirements. Consequently, this approach classifies test tasks as data-driven and conceptually-driven. Notice that other classifications such as episodic versus semantic or implicit versus explicit are irrelevant. The only consideration is that the test demands match the study demands so that retrieval processes required by the test benefit from the use of the same processes at study.

Some evidence exists contrary to the data-driven/conceptually-driven approach. In particular, some studies have shown that a study variable that should influence data-driven processes has effects on tests that should be conceptually driven and that a study variable that should influence conceptually-driven processes affects tests that should be data-driven (Hunt & Toth, 1990; Toth & Hunt, 1990). Such results suggest that the data-driven/conceptually-driven classification of tests may be too broad to identify the appropriate mental processes, even though the test classification has proved useful to researchers. The distinction between data-driven and conceptually-driven tests clearly captures some important dimension of the psychological processes underlying these tests.

Automatic versus Controlled Retrieval Processes

Larry Jacoby of McMaster University has proposed a different version of processing theory. At the heart of Jacoby's idea is a distinction between automatic and controlled retrieval processes. Automatic processes essentially operate without conscious control whereas controlled processes are conscious monitoring invoked by intent to remember. The distinction between automatic and controlled processes has obvious relevance to explaining the dissociations between direct and indirect tests because the instructions for direct tests are to intentionally remember a prior event, and indirect test instructions make no mention of memory for the prior event. The situation, however, is more complicated than simply suggesting that direct tests involve automatic processes. Jacoby (1991) reasonably suggests that both controlled and automatic processes could underlie both direct and indirect tests; that is, the tests are not process pure. Therefore, an understanding of automatic and controlled retrieval processes requires a research strategy that goes beyond the simple comparison of direct and indirect tests.

Let us borrow two examples that Jacoby often uses in his public lectures to illustrate the operation of automatic and controlled retrieval processes. In both examples, automatic processes are involved, but in the first example there is no experience of memory because of the way the controlled processes work. It is quite common at the beginning of a term for students to complain that the professor is lecturing too fast. The students will maintain that they cannot keep up with the notes and have trouble comprehending the material because the instructor talks too fast. Later in the term the students often thank the professor for slowing down, expressing an ability to understand more easily because the professor is no longer talking so fast. The fact is that the professor rarely slows his or her rate across the term! Jacoby suggests that the students' perception of speech-rate is a function of automatic retrieval of prior experience. Initially, the psychological process of comprehension is difficult because you have little prior experience with the course material. As the course progresses, you gain some understanding of the subject and that prior experience facilitates your comprehension of the subsequent material in the course. So it is true that the material usually is easier to understand as you move through the course, but rarely is it because the professor has changed speech-rate. The automatic or unconscious retrieval of prior experience influences the current process of comprehension but the increased fluency of comprehension is not attributed to prior experience. Rather the controlled or conscious process *mistakenly* attribute the improved comprehension to the professor's speech rate.

Consider now a second example in which the automatic processes operate in the same way but the controlled processes attribute the effect to memory. Suppose you are shopping in a crowded grocery store. You see dozens of people as you cruise the aisles but there is nothing remarkable about this. Suddenly, as you scan the array of chocolate-coated cereals, a person walks by and you experience a rush of familiarity. You know you have seen this person before but when or where is not clear. You forget the cereal and concentrate on solving this mystery. Eventually you realize that the person is a clerk in the video store where you occasionally rent tapes.

Jacoby's analysis of this rather common situation is that prior experience again exerts an automatic effect on psychological processes, in this example the perceptual processes of face recognition. The perceptual processing of the video-store clerk's face is more fluent than the processing of the faces of strangers because of prior experience with the clerk. The immediate effect of this enhanced fluency is a feeling of familiarity at which point conscious retrieval processes are engaged to attribute the familiarity to some specific prior event. In other words, the controlled processes are engaged to search for the previous event that would underlie the current feeling of familiarity. Unlike the first example in which the ease of comprehension was misattributed to speech-rate, this second example illustrates a correct attribution of the influence of automatic processes to prior experience, the situation we normally call memory.

The examples illustrate what Jacoby means by automatic and controlled processes. The idea essentially is that prior processing of some event facilitates later processing of the same event. Basically this is the repetition effect, and its influence is automatic; it cannot be consciously controlled. Whether this automatic effect is attributed to the prior experience or to some other source is the responsibility of controlled retrieval processes. The controlled processes operate consciously and are heavily influenced by the task demands. Further understanding of the relationship between automatic and controlled processes can be gained by considering a typical experiment from Jacoby's laboratory.

In this experiment (Jacoby, Woloshyn, & Kelley, 1989) subjects are shown a list of names and told to remember those names. Further, they are told that none of the names are of famous people. The relevance of this instruction will be clear in a moment. After studying the names, the subjects see an even longer list of names some of which were in the original list. The instructions are to indicate whether or not the person in this second list is famous. Some of the nonstudied names in this second list are moderately famous people (e.g., Satchel Paige, Minnie Pearl, Christopher Wren). After the fame-rating, the subjects are shown a third list of names again containing the names from the original study list plus an equal number of nonstudied names. The purpose of the third list is to provide a recognition memory test; that is, the subjects are told to indicate which of the names in the third list were in the original study list.

The interesting results of the experiment involve the relationship between fame-rating and recognition of the names from the original study list. Briefly, an old name from the study list was very likely to be called nonfamous in the fame judgement task if it was also recognized as an old name in the recognition test. If the old study name was not correctly recognized as an original test item in the recognition test, the name was very likely to be judged as famous in the fame task, particularly compared to the nonfamous names that were not on the study list.

How do you acquire fame so quickly and easily? Jacoby's explanation appeals to the opposing effects of automatic and controlled processes. First, the exposure to the names in the study list enhances the fluency of processing of those names in the subsequent test lists. Thus, the effect of the prior experience from the study list automatically produces more fluent processing of the studied than the nonstudied names on the fame judgement task. This automatic effect of the prior experience is manifested as a conscious feeling of familiarity, much as in the example of the video clerk in the grocery store. The cognitive system then determines why the name is familiar. If the controlled retrieval processes provide evidence that the name was in the study list, the familiarity is correctly attributed to the prior experience. If this happens, that is the subject recognizes the name as a study item, the name will be judged as nonfamous because they were told that the study names were nonfamous. If, however, the controlled retrieval processes fail to provide evidence leading to correct recognition, the familiarity of the name is attributed mistakenly to the person being famous. The conscious recollection processes fail, and the automatic effect of the prior exposure is then mistakenly ascribed to the fame of the person. Notice that the task demand, fame judgement, has influenced the attribution of familiarity when memory fails. So the easy road to fame is to be seen but not remembered!

All of the examples described contain an indirect memory test in that some prior experience influences current performance, be it judging a professor's speech-rate, the feeling of familiarity on seeing a person in the grocery store, or judging the fame of a recently encountered name. Jacoby's approach, however, is to assume that both automatic and controlled processes can be involved in the indirect test performance, and the same would be true of a direct test. The fame rating experiment illustrates the potential for both automatic and controlled processes to occur on an indirect test and also illuminates Jacoby's strategy of placing the two types of processes in opposition to one another. That is, the increased fluency of processing the name on the fame rating test is an automatic influence of reading the name on the study list. The familiarity of the name is a consequence of this automatic processing. The indirect test of fame-rating is affected not only by the automatic process but also by controlled processes. If the subject can remember seeing the name on the study list, the fame-rating will be low, but if conscious memory of the name does not occur, the fame-rating will be high. The experiment is designed to place the effects of the automatic and controlled processes in direct opposition to one another. Using this strategy, Jacoby has developed an alternative procedure to the direct-indirect test comparison and has effectively argued that it is the difference between conscious and unconscious retrieval processes that produce the test dissociations that are the topic of this section.

Summary of Implicit and Explicit Memory

The discovery of dissociations in performance on implicit and explicit memory tests has produced a flurry of research activity and more importantly, several alternative ideas about the nature of retrieval processes. The primary distinction between the ideas is whether one talks about memory systems or memory processes. The systems view entails different mechanisms in that an episodic test will engage different processes than a semantic test, but to date, the systems approach has devoted relatively less attention to the nature of these processes than to the identification of various tests with various systems. One version of the processing approach, the distinction between data- and conceptually-driven processes, essentially has done the same thing with tests, suggesting that retrieval processes can be distinguished on the basis of the type of test cue. An alternative processing view suggests a distinction between automatic and controlled retrieval processes and essentially advocates an understanding of retrieval as either unconscious or consciously controlled.

This research on retrieval processes is continuing at a rapid pace and influential new developments appear with encouraging regularity. These developments are indicative of the importance of research on implicit and explicit memory for our understanding of retrieval. The importance of retrieval itself will become even more salient to you as we now move to discuss retrieval failure, otherwise known as forgetting.

OVERVIEW OF RETRIEVAL FAILURE: FORGETTING

Rarely is memory for events noticed until that memory fails. Human memory is so important for our survival that the system is quite efficient, and when it fails, the results are usually frustrating and sometimes serious. Forgetting causes problems ranging in severity from simple inconvenience of a second trip to the store due to forgetting to get some items, to potential death due to forgetting to add brake fluid to the braking system of an automobile. Forgetting then becomes a major practical problem for individuals as well as for organizations and industry. As interested as we are in providing solutions to practical problems, we are perhaps more concerned with the basic question of why memory fails.

We first must understand that not all problems we call forgetting are actually due to memory failure. Many times we fail to provide an appropriate answer, not because we forget, but rather because we have never known the information. An examination may be missed because of not paying attention on the days the examination was announced. These instances are not properly forgetting but represent lack of storage or failure to input the event to long-term memory. How some of these storage problems may arise were discussed in the earlier chapters on displacement from the sensory register and short-term memory and capacity limitations on attention. The term *forgetting* is reserved for cases of *failure to access information that is stored.* Why does forgetting occur?

Decay Theory

We discussed two general classes of theories in chapter 4 on short-term memory: decay and interference. Recall that decay theory suggests that information simply weakens or is lost over time if it is not used. You may also recall that decay theory has not been very popular, although at the levels of sensory register and short-term memory it has advocates. Few researchers, however, maintain that long-term memory decays. This aversion to the decay theory is due in part to the fact that natural events are influenced by factors other than the passage of time. For example, if left in a complete vacuum, iron does not rust over any period of time. As a natural phenomenon, memory should therefore not go away due only to the passage of time. Something does happen over time to cause forgetting, but does forgetting result from the complete loss of long-term memory, as implied by the decay theory? Evidence from several sources has long suggested that this is not the case, but rather that long-term memory is permanent. For example, Penfield (1959) suggested that electrical stimulation of certain parts of the brain can activate memories not thought to be available. Patients undergoing neurosurgery are sometimes given only a local anesthetic because the brain has no pain receptors, and once the brain is exposed, very little pain is involved. These patients can talk and report the sensations they are having. Thus, when Penfield stimulated certain parts of the brain, the patients reported memories such as smells and songs from their childhood. This finding is often cited as strong evidence for the permanence of long-term memory, but we should also note the recent criticism of this conclusion by Loftus and Loftus (1980).

Regardless of the ultimate fate of decay theory, we do know that available information sometimes cannot be immediately accessed. How many times do we try and fail to remember something only to remember it later? The fact that the information is remembered later suggests that it was available but something interfered with its access. Let us examine the sources of the interference and the conditions in which it occurs.

Retroactive Interference	Proactive Interference
Encounter To-Be-Remembered Material	Encounter Interfering Material
Encounter Interfering Material	Encounter To-Be-Remembered Material
Memory Test for To-Be-Remembered Material	Memory Test for To-Be-Remembered Material

Order in which Events Occur — 1, 2, 3

Figure 6.3 Sequence of events in retroactive interference and in proactive interference.

Retroactive and Proactive Interference

Two sources of interference to disrupt memory for certain to-be-remembered (target) information are available. *Retroactive interference* is produced by material encountered after the target event is encoded. For example, information acquired in a sociology class may disrupt memory for the information learned in an earlier psychology class. The prefix *retro* means "backward in time," and remembering this fact makes it easy to remember that retroactive interference results from interfering material that occurs after the target material, which thus exerts its interfering effects on information encountered before the interfering event.

Proactive interference is produced by material occurring prior to the target information. In the previous example (psychology class before sociology class) material learned in psychology class might interfere with information acquired later in sociology class. The prefix *pro* means "forward" and therefore remember that proactive interference results from material exerting an interfering effect on material learned later. A schematic representation of situations producing retroactive interference and proactive interference is shown in figure 6.3.

Material that occurs either before or after the event being remembered can make memory difficult. We call one proactive interference and the other retroactive interference, but so far they are just labels for two situations in which forgetting occurs. They do not tell us why some of the events that occur before and after an event cause forgetting. This is the role of *interference theory.*

Interference Theory

During the 1940s and 1950s, when experimental psychology was domi- nated by the concern with associative learning, the closest approach to the study of memory was called *verbal learning*. All of human learning, in- cluding verbal learning, was assumed to be a matter of establishing asso- ciations between units known as *stimuli* and *responses*. The degree of learning of an association was described in terms of associative strength, and the primary concern in verbal learning was the fate of associative strength over time. Decrease in associative strength presumably accounted for forgetting. Interference theory developed as the account of changes in associative strength over time (e.g., McGeoch, 1942).

Interference theory proposes two basic mechanisms underlying for- getting, *response competition* and *unlearning*. Response competition occurs when the same cue is associated with two different responses. Suppose that the concept of *behavior* is defined differently in your psychology class than in your sociology class. Assume also that your psychology class meets before the sociology class. If *behavior* is defined in your psychology class, and then in your sociology class the definition for *behavior* is different, the first def- inition will be in competition with the second definition. The stimulus *be- havior* elicits two different responses, the definitions, only one of which is correct. Response competition leads to the second basic mechanism, unlearning.

When the response to the stimulus is incorrect, a likely event in re- sponse competition, the incorrect response is not reinforced. That is, we learn that it is wrong, and this lack of reinforcement weakens the associ- ative strength of that response. The problem is that different responses to the same stimulus may actually be appropriate, each in a different context. For example, both the sociological and psychological definitions of *behavior* are appropriate responses to the stimulus *behavior,* but in different con- texts. However, when you are asked for the definition of *behavior* in soci- ology class and you respond with the definition from psychology class, you will learn that you are wrong. The association between the psychological definition and *behavior* is weakened. You are now likely to forget the psy- chological definition. Notice that the material you acquired later, the so- ciological definition, interferes with the earlier event. This is then a case of retroactive interference.

Through the two basic mechanisms of response competition and un- learning, interference theory attempts to explain how retroactive interfer- ence and proactive interference cause forgetting. Elaboration of its basic concepts continues to enrich interference theory (Postman & Underwood, 1973). In spite of the refinement of interference theory, alternative ac- counts of forgetting have begun to emerge from the information-processing framework. The basic premise of one of these ideas is that all forgetting can be analyzed as failure of retrieval cues. Let us briefly examine how this approach explains proactive and retroactive interferences.

Cue-Dependent Forgetting

As discussed previously, many theorists believe that long-term memory is permanent. Once information is stored, it remains. This does not mean, however, that forgetting never occurs. Rather, failure to remember information stored may occur because of inability to gain access to this information. The major reason for access failure is that the cues are inappropriate or ineffective. Forgetting thus becomes a matter of *retrieval failure attributable to poor cues.*

For example, this type of problem was suggested in the discussion of levels of processing and encoding. Nonsemantic orientation leads to poor memory for a word, but not because the nonsemantic information is unavailable in memory. Rather the nonsemantic information is not very useful for reconstructing the semantic unit of a word. Morris, Bransford, and Franks (1977) labeled this problem inappropriate test strategy, but the general difficulty is that the nonsemantic information is inappropriate to retrieve the word. Tulving's encoding specificity principle of retrieval makes exactly the same point. Cues present at input are effective, whereas other cues are less appropriate. Forgetting then occurs because a cue which was not present at input fails to access the stored information.

Tulving's (1974) advocacy of encoding specificity led him to view forgetting as basically a problem with retrieval cues. He and his students argued that both retroactive interference and proactive interference are better understood as cue-dependent forgetting than as unlearning and response competition.

For example, Tulving and Psotka (1971) have shown that retroactive interference can be reduced when appropriate retrieval cues are provided. Retroactive interference was induced by giving subjects a series of categorized lists, each list containing different instances of the same category. The first list might include *dog, horse, cow, shirt, shoes,* and *hat* and the second list *cat, pig, lion, coat, pants,* and *tie.* After five such lists were presented, recall of the earlier lists was much poorer than recall of the later lists, a clear instance of retroactive interference. Furthermore, the decline in performance on earlier lists was due solely to the forgetting of entire categories. Subjects failed to recall a single instance from some categories, while they recalled a substantial number of items from other categories. The later lists seemed to cause complete failure to access some of the categories in earlier lists. In a final memory test, however, the subjects were given the category superordinates, for example, *animal* and *clothes,* as retrieval cues. On the final cued recall test, recall for items from the first list was as good as recall for items from the last list. Providing the cues eliminated retroactive interference. Tulving and Psotka suggest that retroactive interference occurs because the interfering materials result in failure to access the stored information. When the cues are provided, access can be achieved. Clearly, the information is not lost, as implied by either decay or unlearning, but rather is inaccessible due to cue-dependent forgetting.

Although the idea of cue-dependent forgetting is appealing in several respects, many questions remain to be answered. For example, why do subsequent materials interfere with retrieval of entire categories of previous materials? In some respects, Tulving and Psotka's (1971) experiment demonstrates that retrieval cues can be interfered with, but does not tell us a great deal about how this happens. Moreover, all forgetting does not seem to be due to failure to generate the correct event. In many cases, we are able to generate the event information but are confused or indecisive about its correctness. For example, remember times on an examination when you wanted to include the name of a particular research scientist, thought you knew the name but were not sure, and finally omitted it rather than risk being wrong. Here, you retrieved or generated the information, but did not respond due to indecision. Nonetheless, the result is something that can be called forgetting. This type of confusion is a frequent cause of forgetting and is more consistent with the failure of a two-process decision component. Nonetheless, the view of forgetting as cue-dependent retrieval failure promises to clarify certain aspects of forgetting, and after much additional research, it may lead to better understanding of memory failure.

HOW TO MINIMIZE FORGETTING

In this section techniques based on the principles of both encoding and retrieval, which minimize the forgetting of events, are discussed. Let us illustrate these principles in the context of study habits that can be developed, but you are warned at the outset that we know of no fancy tricks. On the other hand, developing facility in memory is not particularly complicated; you just need to concentrate on certain basic points.

Indeed, concentration is the first step. What was not stored cannot be remembered, and perhaps the major failure to perform is due to lack of initial storage. In the context of studying, *pay attention* to the lectures. Compulsive note takers may have to return to their notes after class since it may be difficult both to take notes and to think about the lecture. Notes for one day can usually be covered adequately in 10 to 15 minutes, so always try to cover notes on the same day as the class. Adequately covering notes, as well as reading the text, is an important aspect of encoding. As we have seen, encoding involves more than simply allowing the eyeball to pass over words. An important aspect of encoding is to develop *organization* or relationship between discrete parts of an event. This can be done during study by always relating the topic of the day's lecture to the previous class. The same is true of reading assignments where organization is inherent in the text. Most books have various headings and are divided into chapters. Be sure you can relate each subtopic to the next level. These activities are not usually hard to do but do require considerable concentration.

In addition to organization, *elaboration* and *distinctiveness* can be important parts of studying. Relate the material not only to the additional material but also to other known facts. You can decide whether you really understand a concept by trying to state its meaning in your own words. Then try to use the concept with an example of your own. For example, discuss both the meaning of encoding and provide an example of distinctive encoding. Next, increase the distinctiveness of the material by thinking about how it differs from other concepts in the same area. For example, see not only the similarities between *organization* and *distinctiveness,* but also the differences.

In addition to encoding processes, memory can be improved by concentration on certain principles of *retrieval.* Foremost among the principles is the *development* and *use of good cues.* During the course of good studying, persons are likely to develop good cues without intending to do so. The organizational structure of the material once encoded can serve a powerful cuing function. Unfortunately, many people do not take advantage of the cues at the time of a test. A decent examination question, for example, usually contains cues which should direct attention to the appropriate memory. Too many students, however, spend too little time reading and thinking about a question.

Another important consideration is to *practice retrieval.* Practice in retrieval is better for memory than are additional input trials. One way to incorporate retrieval practice in studying is to pause after each paragraph and without looking at the text repeat the main idea of that paragraph in your own words. This technique not only allows retrieval practice, but also provides a check on how carefully you are reading. Another possibility is to construct your own questions and then answer them. The point again is to practice retrieving information, even if you simply rehearse the material in your free time.

You now see that the practices we suggest are not particularly tricky and certainly are not difficult. They do, however, require time, and studying should be scheduled on a consistent basis. These kinds of techniques cannot be used the night before an examination, if for no other reason than the concentration required will make it difficult to study for long periods of time. On the other hand, we think implementing these techniques in your study habits will improve your performance considerably.

STATE-DEPENDENT MEMORY

In this section we turn our attention to the idea of state-dependent effects in memory. Just as memory is dependent upon the effectiveness of retrieval cues, it is also somewhat dependent upon a person's "state" when the information was originally encoded. The general notion of state dependency refers to the idea that the "states" or conditions under which an event is learned may be strong and important cues in retrieving particular information. For example, if information is processed while a person has a few drinks, it might be that later recall of the information would be best if the person had a few drinks at the time of recall. This is an instance of alcohol state dependency. There is, in fact, considerable evidence for drug-induced state dependency in memory (Eich, 1980). State-dependent memory is a special case of context effects and the role of context in memory is both important and complex (Bjork & Richardson-Klavehn, 1989, Smith, 1988).

State dependency is a relative concept. In the example just given, if the person can recall the information *only* after a few drinks, and not otherwise, his memory will then completely depend upon restoring the "semi-alcoholic" state present at the time of original learning. Fortunately, memory is usually not this dependent upon perfect and full restoration of the original state. What is usually the case is that memory is only partly dependent on a particular state. A particular state may be the amount of alcohol consumed or the presence of other drugs in the body. Other states may be the emotional mood conditions under which learning takes place (Eich, 1989, to be discussed in Chapter 12).

SUMMARY

In chapter 6 a variety of issues concerned with the output process from memory were raised. One of the obvious facts about memory is that cues are helpful. Indeed, memory cannot be addressed in the absence of some sort of cue. What is less obvious but equally important is what makes a good cue. Associative strength and encoding specificity are two ideas concerning cue effectiveness. More generally, both of these ideas imply an automatic and uncomplicated retrieval process.

A slightly different general idea is that retrieval entails both search and decision stages, which is the more complicated generate-recognize view. The differences between single-process and generate-recognize views of retrieval were explored in a number of experiments comparing recognition memory and recall memory tests.

Another area of research on retrieval processes is that of implicit and explicit memory tests. Performance dissociations on these tests have produced ideas about retrieval ranging from differences between memory systems to differences in conscious control of psychological processes.

Forgetting, which is the failure of retrieval, was discussed and various theories concerning the process of forgetting were considered, including decay and interference and cue-dependent forgetting.

Practical tips on increasing the probability of retrieval were suggested. Foremost among the suggestions were the development and utilization of effective cues and practice in retrieval.

Finally, a new concept, state-dependent effects on memory, was discussed, and recent research in this area will be described in chapter 12.

MULTIPLE-CHOICE ITEMS

1. Which of the following are the two major theories of cue effectiveness?
   a. levels of processing and associative strength
   b. imagery and encoding specificity
   c. associative strength and encoding specificity
   d. encoding specificity and proactive interference

2. The primary determinant of the associative strength of a cue is
   a. the encoding specificity
   b. the number of times a cue and target are paired
   c. the number of people giving the response to a cue
   d. the length of the retention interval between cue and target

3. The primary determinant of encoding specificity is
   a. the number of times the cue occurs with the target
   b. the associative strength of the cue and target
   c. the amount of time between cue and target
   d. the presence of the cue at encoding of the target

4. Encoding specificity is an example
   a. of the retrieval process
   b. of the generate-recognize model
   c. of a complex retrieval model
   d. of a single-process model

5. The similarity of recognition memory and recall memory is important to the generate-recognize model of retrieval because
   a. they should be the same according to this model
   b. they should be different according to this model
   c. recall should be easier according to this model
   d. all single-process models focus on this issue

6. The view of forgetting which is most compatible with the encoding specificity hypothesis of retrieval is
   a. cue-dependent forgetting
   b. proactive interference
   c. retroactive interference
   d. decay

TRUE–FALSE ITEMS

1. Strongly associated cues normally produce better memory than do weakly associated cues.

2. Encoding specificity does not apply to semantic memory.

3. Recognition memory is normally better than recall memory.

4. The interference theory of forgetting assumes that the forgotten material is available in memory.

5. Proactive interference results from material intervening between the to-be-remembered material and the memory test.

6. The major cause of forgetting is failure to store the materials in the first place.

DISCUSSION ITEMS

1. Describe the experiments used to support the encoding specificity hypothesis over the associative strength hypothesis of retrieval cue effectiveness.

2. Discuss the difference between single-process and generate-recognize models of retrieval, describing the importance of recognition and recall comparisons in this issue.

3. Describe the differences between a systems view and a process view of test dissociations. Discuss experiments that provide evidence for each view.

ANSWERS TO MULTIPLE-CHOICE ITEMS

1. (c) Associative strength and encoding specificity are the two major theories of cue effectiveness.

2. (b) The number of times the cue and the target occur together determines the associative strength.

3. (d) According to encoding specificity, a cue is effective if it is specifically encoded with the target.

4. (d) The only important consideration is the single process of the cue present when the target is encoded.

5. (b) The generate-recognize model suggests that retrieval processes are different in recognition and recall.

6. (a) Failure to remember, according to encoding specificity, is attributable to poor retrieval cues, and this position is the same as cue-dependent forgetting.

ANSWERS TO TRUE–FALSE ITEMS

1. (True) All other things equal, a strongly associated cue leads to better memory than does a weakly associated cue.

2. (True) The distinction between semantic memory and episodic memory is based on the assumption that encoding specificity does not apply to semantic memory.

3. (True) Recognition is usually easier than recall.

4. (True) In order for something to interfere with something else, both must be present.

5. (False) Proactive interference results from material which occurs before the to-be-remembered material is experienced.

6. (False) Forgetting refers only to cases in which the material was stored.

7

SEMANTIC MEMORY

L ong-term memory encompasses not only specific past events but also general knowledge of the world. As previously mentioned in the discussion of the distinction between episodic memory and semantic memory, semantic memory refers to general knowledge which cannot be traced to a single event. Rather, general knowledge seems to be the abstraction of common elements from a variety of previous episodes. For example, can you remember the circumstances under which you first learned the meaning of the symbol (Stop) ? Although you have encountered this event numerous times, you probably have few, if any, highly specific memories of the episodes. Nonetheless, you know what to do when confronted by the event, regardless of whether you encounter it driving a Mercedes in New York City or a pickup truck in Dubuque, Iowa. You have the concept or knowledge of this event. Notice that the knowledge you have about even this simple event reaches far beyond just "stop." It includes the action to be taken as well as the consequences of failing to take that action. In short, knowledge of even a simple concept consists of a wide range of information.

This example, of course, represents only a tiny fraction of the vast knowledge that all human beings possess. Psychologists have historically been interested in the acquisition and utilization of knowledge, and recent advancements in ideas and techniques bring renewed activity to this area. In chapter 7 some of the theories and experiments on semantic memory are described. First, however, let us examine the function of knowledge: What can a knowledgeable person do that a less knowledgeable person cannot? The answer to this question can provide a basis for constructing our theories of semantic memory, as well as instruct us as to the interaction between semantic memory and other cognitive processes. The best way to examine the difference between high- and low-knowledge performance is to compare persons who are experts on a topic with persons who are less expert.

EXPERT PERFORMANCE

When we speak of high-knowledge individuals, we refer to the highly developed skills these persons have in a particular area, not to their general intell... the belief of some, most of us are good at something ... mobile repair, golf, or social interaction. Psychologists ... ert performance have generally studied games (chess and (...) for several reasons. As a matter of convenience, most gam ... duration and can easily be adapted to laboratory situati ... portant, games have a clear set of rules and a clear goal state ... ate is to accomplish a specific action, such as checkmating a kin ... g points, and to do more of this action or do it more quickly than ... ent. It is then possible to present subjects with the partial account of a game in progress, such as a game of chess in which several moves have already been made, and assess various aspects of their knowledge. Furthermore, the unambiguous rules and outcome state of games make identification of experts easier. While other fields such as teaching, auto mechanics, and medicine clearly have experts, identification of these persons takes longer, and the criteria for labeling a person an expert are more complex. The hope is that what is learned about the function of knowledge by studying experts at games will apply in some general way to other domains of knowledge. Let us see what this approach might tell us about semantic memory by examining the work of James Voss at the University of Pittsburgh on knowledge of baseball.

In a series of experiments (Chiesi, Spilich, & Voss, 1979; Spilich, Vesonder, Chiesi, & Voss, 1979), Voss and colleagues reported interesting differences on a variety of measures between people who knew a lot about baseball and people who knew less. Baseball knowledge was assessed by a prior test, and two groups of subjects were identified as high- and low-knowledge groups. Everyone then was given an account of one-half an inning in the middle of a fictitious game. Subsequently, all subjects received a variety of tests on the material, beginning with straightforward memory tests. Not surprisingly, the high-knowledge individuals remembered much more of the passage than did the persons who knew less about baseball. Moreover, the recall of the baseball experts was more ordered and contained more detail relevant to the outcome of the game. High-knowledge persons were likely to have the events in proper sequence and to recall relevant information about the progress of the game. Low-knowledge subjects were more likely to remember less relevant information, like the time of day the game was played.

Finally, the subjects were asked to write what they thought would happen next in the game. For example, suppose the team at bat is behind 5 to 2 in the seventh inning. Runners are on second base and third base with one out. The scheduled batter is the pitcher and the opposing pitcher is left-handed. What is likely to happen next? If you know a good bit about baseball, you can construct a reasonable scenario for ensuing events. If you know little about baseball, your story is likely to be less detailed and accurate. This is exactly what happened in the experiment.

THE FUNCTION OF KNOWLEDGE

We suspect that there is very little of surprise in Voss's research, but careful consideration of the experiments shows that they are quite instructive. What sorts of activities does knowledge allow? First, the more that is known about a topic, the better new information related to the topic is remembered. Perhaps memory is so good because the knowledge provides a *framework* for interpreting and organizing the material. Second, the ordering of recall by the high-knowledge group is consistent with the assumption that knowledge aids organization. Third, a much more fundamental role for knowledge is implicated: namely, experiences are interpreted through the existing knowledge base. That is, the meaning of events derives from the information the event activates in semantic memory. The meaning of a particular event seems to be a multidimensional affair. In other words, the meaning of a concept includes perceptual information, conceptual information, and functional information. For example, the meaning of *apple* might include "red, round, fruit, and eat." An important point to note is that the concepts are defined in terms of other concepts, just as words are defined in terms of other words.

This leads to the final important observation from the baseball experiments concerning the function of knowledge. Knowledge, sometimes in conjunction with specific event memory, allows projection into the future. Based upon what is known, plans are laid and schedules made. Just as the high-knowledge subjects in Voss's experiments could project the probable action in the baseball game, so knowledge in other domains allows us to predict what will happen and to plot a course of action. This point is discussed later in relation to academic work and social interactions.

In summary, the functions of the concept of knowledge are to interpret incoming information, to provide the meaning of events, and to allow projection into the future.

THE TASK OF DESCRIBING SEMANTIC MEMORY

Psychologists interested in the study of knowledge have as part of their goal the description of the *structure* of semantic memory. By structure is meant an abstract, theoretical description of the organization of world knowledge. This description must capture the relationships among concepts and in so doing describe the richness inherent in the meaning of concepts.

A prominent view of human cognition is that of a computational system, in which the processes of perception, memory, thinking, and reasoning require calculation to obtain a particular outcome. In order to perceive a boat on the horizon, for example, the perceptual system calculates or computes the information available to arrive at the conclusion "a boat." Any computational system must have a data base from which to perform calculations. The system we know as arithmetic has numbers as its data base. While much formal training in arithmetic concentrates on the processes or rules of calculation, something must also be known about the structure of the data base. For example, even if we rarely think about it, we know that the interval between two adjacent numbers is equal regardless of the size of the numbers. The distance between 99 and 100 is the same as the distance between 0 and 1. As trivial as this fact appears, the description of the structure of the number system is critical to consistently applying computational rules. You know that the difference between 100 and 99 is the same as the difference between 1 and 0 because of the rules of subtraction and because of the structure of the number system.

In a similar fashion, semantic memory serves as the data base for the computational processes of the cognitive system. The content of semantic memory provides the raw data for perception, memory, and thinking, and thus it becomes quite important to know something of the structure and content of semantic memory. Primarily for this reason, the major goal of research in semantic memory has been to describe the structure of knowledge.

THEORIES OF SEMANTIC MEMORY

The ideas that we discuss concerning semantic memory can be distinguished on two levels. The first concerns the types of general structures proposed for knowledge. Here, two types of structures, network models and feature models are described. The second distinction is the level at which the knowledge is represented. Here, the primary difference is between structures designed to reflect single concepts, best described as words such as *dog, frog,* or *justice,* and more complex structures which reflect higher-order idea units, best described as phrases or sentences such as, "The young couple went barefoot in the park." The second idea generally proposes a concept known as the propositional representation.

The differences between these structures will become clear as we discuss the various ideas, and further, certain differences between the retrieval processes proposed by the various theories are described. The discussion begins with consideration of one of the first and simplest ideas about semantic memory, associative network models.

Associative Network Models

When you hear the word *green,* what is the first word that comes to mind? Many persons will say *grass* with no hesitation. Like many other questions, such as, "What is your name?" the answer seems to occur automatically. Further, the answer almost feels as if it were linked to the question in the mind. As soon as the question is heard, the answer appears. This situation suggests that the concepts involved are strongly related, perhaps to the extent that one is part of the other's meaning. The theoretical link between concepts has historically been called an *association,* and the associative network model of semantic memory is one in which all of the concepts, all of general knowledge, are interrelated through associations of various strengths. To give you a clear idea of the associative network model, let us begin by discussing one of the first contemporary models of semantic memory, which serves as the basis for more recent associative models.

Teachable Language Comprehender (TLC)

The first major theory of semantic memory was actually designed as a computer program to understand language. This program, proposed by Quillian (1968, 1969), was called the Teachable Language Comprehender (TLC). Quillian's strategy was to develop a memory structure for a computer which would allow the computer to answer questions and if the structure was successful for the computer, to explore whether it had testable implications in human beings for the use of knowledge. So the first challenge was to devise a method of representing knowledge so that even a machine could demonstrate some of the flexibility inherent in human knowledge. For example, questions which seem to be based on inferences rather than on directly known information are easily answered. Does a canary have skin? Assuming that you can answer this question, how do you know? Have you ever had direct experience with canary skin? Have you ever been taught explicitly that canaries have skin? Probably not. The answer to this question is inferred, based on other things known about canaries, and part of the task confronting Quillian was to capture this inferential ability.

The structure proposed by Quillian is actually quite simple. It is a hierarchically organized system in which related concepts are connected by associations. *Hierarchical conceptual organization* means that superordinate concepts are at a higher level and are connected to subordinate concepts. Figure 7.1 provides an example of a limited portion of the structure. Notice that the superordinate *animal* subsumes subordinates *fish* and *bird*. This then represents the knowledge that both mammals and birds are animals. Similarly, *bird* is superordinate to *canary* and *ostrich* as well as to all of the other facts known about birds. Furthermore, notice that each node or concept has associated with it certain properties characteristic of that concept. Animals have skin and they eat and breathe. Birds have feathers and wings and they fly. Canaries are yellow. At this point, the question of why the properties are not listed at each node might be raised. After all, canaries have feathers and birds breathe. This question brings us to the assumption of *cognitive economy*.

The properties of any concept are stored at the highest possible node. For example, if all animals have skin, then *skin* is not stored with the concept of each animal but is stored with the concept of *animal*. This assumption provides obvious economy of storage in that information is not duplicated unnecessarily within the structure. But if this is the case, how do we answer the question, Does a canary have skin?—a question which now takes us to the process of accessing knowledge in the TLC.

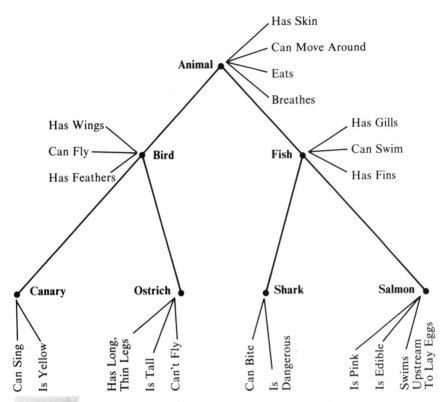

Figure 7.1 A portion of the teachable language comprehender (TLC) model of semantic memory. (From "Retrieval Time from Semantic Memory" by A. M. Collins and M. R. Quillian, *Journal of Verbal Learning and Verbal Behavior,* 1969, *8,* 240–247. Copyright 1969 by Academic Press. Used by permission.)

The process of retrieving knowledge is quite straightforward. The concept for which knowledge is to be accessed is activated by presentation of a question. The information linked to that concept is also activated by tracing the associative network. For example, the question "Is a canary a bird?" activates the concept *canary* and the association is traced to *bird.* Once the concept *bird* is found in association with *canary,* a yes response can be given to the question. The question "Does a *canary* have skin?" activates the canary node, and the network is traced directly to *animal* where the property "has skin" is found. Since *canary* is a subordinate of *animal,* it is now possible to respond that "Yes, canaries have skin." We can now see that TLC allows us to generate or infer facts not directly stored with a concept. Further, it is evident that knowledge of a concept is represented both by the concept node and by the relationships or associations between nodes. Thus, TLC describes the knowledge of a concept in terms of the representative node and concepts and properties associated with the node.

Tests of TLC   The importance of Quillian's computer program for psychology lies in its ability to generate interesting predictions about human performance. One such prediction is quite clear from the model, and the experiments based on this prediction created an explosion of research in semantic memory. The prediction is of a *category size effect:* that is, larger categories require more time for search than do smaller categories. *Animal* is a larger category than *bird;* very simply *animal* includes *bird* as well as a number of other concepts. Within TLC, the superordinate of a large category is farther from an instance in the associative network than is the superordinate of a small category. In other words, in figure 7.1 *canary* is farther removed from the larger category superordinate *animal* than it is from the smaller category superordinate *bird.* From the premise that traversing the network requires time, it should follow that verifying canary as a bird would require less time than verifying canary as an animal. This is known as the category size effect.

Notice that the measure of performance is not accuracy, as in many memory experiments, but rather is reaction time. The reason is fairly obvious. The questions posed to the subject are designed to tap the knowledge base. In order to examine the structure of knowledge, we must ask questions for which a subject knows answers. Because accuracy will be near perfect, another measure of performance is needed. Let us see how reaction time serves as that measure.

In a series of experiments, Collins and Quillian (1969) asked subjects to respond yes or no as quickly as they could to a series of statements such as, "A canary is a canary," "A canary is a bird," and "A canary is an animal." Based on the TLC model's prediction of a category size effect, reaction time should increase in the order that the statements are listed here. Collins and Quillian's results, which are presented in figure 7.2, are consistent with this prediction. The smaller the category is, the less time is required to verify an instance as a member of the category.

More impressive were the results on sentences stating property relations. For example, the TLC model predicts a regular increase in reaction time to verify the sentences "A canary can sing," "A canary can fly," and "A canary has skin." Again, the information required is stored at different levels of the hierarchy, and on the assumption of cognitive economy, reaction time should be faster to "sings" than to "flies" and faster to "flies" than to "has skin." Figure 7.2 shows that the results of Collins and Quillian's experiment were again consistent with the predictions from TLC.

The initial predictions were quite bold, and the results from this experiment were highly favorable to the model. As is often the case with a promising new approach, however, the work of Collins and Quillian initiated a line of research destined to modify their ideas.

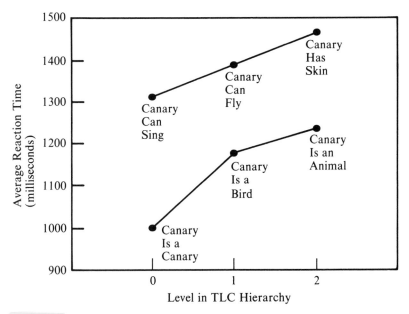

Figure 7.2 Reaction time to verify statements from different levels of TLC hierarchy. (From "Retrieval Time from Semantic Memory" by A. M. Collins and M. R. Quillian, *Journal of Verbal Learning and Verbal Behavior,* 1969, *8,* 240–247. Copyright 1969 by Academic Press. Used by permission.)

Problems for TLC The fundamental difficulty with the TLC is in the relationships between various concepts and between concepts and their properties. That is, a strictly hierarchical relationship between concepts is inconsistent with information now available, and the assumption of cognitive economy in the representation of concepts does not seem to be completely accurate.

Conrad (1972) questioned Collins and Quillian's original interpretation of the reaction times to property judgments. Rather than assume that the times to verify "A canary sings" and "A canary has skin" reflect differences in hierarchical storage, Conrad argued that these properties are experienced with different frequency. That is, it is quite common to experience singing and canary together, so that when we think of *canary,* we then think of "singing." But very few of us have any direct experience with canary skin and are unlikely to think "skin" when we think *canary.* To explore these ideas, Conrad collected production frequency norms; she gave subjects a concept such as *canary* and asked them to write all of the facts which came to mind when they thought of *canary.* She was then able to arrange the properties of various concepts in order of how many subjects listed each property. For example, a large number of subjects gave the response "moves" to *animal* but very few responded "has ears." It is important to note, however, that in the hierarchical model of Quillian both properties are listed at the *animal* node and should produce the same reaction time.

By pitting the frequency of responses against their position in the TLC hierarchy, Conrad performed an experiment whose results seriously questioned the strict view of cognitive economy. That is, the speed with which properties are verified was determined by the *frequency* with which they are listed rather than by their location in the hierarchy. Conrad then suggested that the properties are stored directly at the level of the concepts, regardless of the duplication involved.

Although Conrad's data raise serious problems for the cognitive economy of TLC, the idea of direct storage seems a bit implausible. Can it be that "has a backbone" is among the information most of us store for every person we know? This certainly seems unlikely. The problem is that Conrad also seems to be assuming a rigid hierarchical representation, where all concepts are represented in some strictly logical fashion. In fact, these data may be as critical of this type of hierarchical model as they are of the assumption of cognitive economy.

A related, and perhaps more serious, problem for a strict hierarchical network such as TLC is the relationship of various subordinates to a common superordinate. The hierarchical model treats all subordinates of a superordinate as equal; that is, all of the subordinates are directly related to the superordinate. But we know that all subordinates are not equally related to the superordinate. Not all birds are equally good examples of the concept of *bird,* nor are all dogs equally good instances of the knowledge of *dog.* (This point is developed more fully in chapter 8, Categorization and Concepts.) Again this fact is known from the production norms described previously. When asked to provide instances of the concept *bird,* persons are most likely to respond with *robin, wren,* and *sparrow* and much less likely to say *ostrich* or *egret,* even though they know these animals are birds. In short, some subordinates seem to be more closely related to the superordinate than do others. This phenomenon is known as the *semantic distance effect.* The failure of early associative network theory to handle this effect adequately provoked revisions in the theory.

Spreading-Activation Model

One idea about semantic memory is a direct revision of Quillian's TLC. This model, proposed by Collins and Loftus (1975), is known as the *spread of activation* model. Collins and Loftus retain the associative network of the earlier Quillian model, but take out the strict hierarchical structure which led to some of the problems described previously. In its place is a

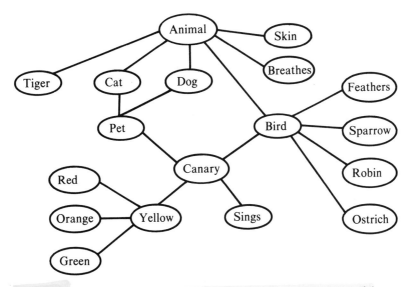

Figure 7.3 Representation of *canary* from the spreading-activation model. Contrast this representation with the *canary* portion of the TLC model in figure 7.1.

more complex structure designed to capture the degree of relationship between various concepts and to deal with the semantic distance effect. Indeed, the major change in structure from TLC is that instances of a superordinate concept are connected to that superordinate by associations of different lengths. As you can see in figure 7.3, *canary* is closer to *bird* than is *ostrich,* and when this model is compared to the original version of TLC represented in figure 7.1, it is evident that the change in associative distance is a major revision.

The various lengths of associations are designed to represent the strength of the relationship between the concepts. *Collie* is closer to *dog* for most persons than is *Afghan* or *basenji.* How do we know? Once again the length or distance between concepts is determined from the production frequency norms. The more persons giving a particular response to a particular concept, say *collie* when given *dog,* the closer the instance will be to the concept. Within associative network models, length of association nicely captures the strength of the relationship because verification or access to semantic memory is assumed to be a matter of traversing the network. This process is assumed to take time, and the farther there is to go, the more time will be required. This fact, then, predicts the result of faster verification of more strongly related pairs. When we discuss feature-set theory, however, we shall see that length or distance is not the only way to represent strength of relationship.

In addition to the structural revision, the spreading-activation model assumes a more complicated retrieval process than does the TLC. Rather than suggest a simple process of moving from one node to another, Collins and Loftus assume that activation of a given concept spreads to related concepts, much the same way that the activation of a tuning fork spreads to other nearby tuning forks. Activation of one node activates the next node, which in turn activates the next node, until the activation spreads through a considerable portion of the network. The strength of the activation decreases as it spreads, so that concepts farther from the originally activated node are less likely to be activated than are closer concepts. This, of course, is sensible because distance represents the semantic relationship among the concepts.

What does all of this mean? A very simple example (it will help to refer to figure 7.3) is to think of the concept *canary*; the *canary* node is now activated. Activation spreads to adjacent nodes with decreasing strength as the nodes become farther removed. In other words, when you think of *canary*, you are also likely to think of *sings* and *yellow*. You are also likely to think of *bird* and *feathers*. You may also think of *pet* and *animal*, but perhaps you may not because these concepts are farther removed from *canary*. You may even think of *green* and *orange* since they are close to the concept *yellow* which was activated. *Skin* is unlikely to occur to you, because activation would have to proceed some distance through several intervening nodes.

The spreading-activation model solves several of the problems in the TLC. In particular, the problem of representing semantic distance is resolved by moving away from the strict hierarchical associative network. The instances of a general concept vary in how close they are to the superordinate, and this structure combined with the process of spreading activation explains why some instances come to mind more readily than do others.

Although the spreading activation model succeeds in dealing with problems for TLC, difficult issues for associative network models such as spreading activation and TLC remain. Particularly troublesome is research showing clear violations of the category size effect. Smith, Shoben, and Rips (1974) reported that people verify sentences such as, "A cow is an animal" more rapidly than sentences such as, "A cow is a mammal." Likewise, the response to "Scotch is a drink" is more rapid than the response to "Scotch is an alcoholic beverage." In both examples, the first sentences require search of a larger category than do the second sentences; nonetheless, reaction times for the first sentences are faster. This outcome is in clear violation of category size predictions which prescribe faster reaction time for smaller categories. Any associative network theory which argues a logical conceptual structure for knowledge will have difficulty with these data. In such a structure, smaller categories must intervene between instances and the larger category. For example, *mammal* must logically intervene between *cow* and *animal* in the network, and thus, verification of "A cow is a mammal" should always be faster. The data indicating reliable violations of the category size effect thus have had a profound effect upon thinking about semantic memory, producing theories fundamentally different from the associative network models.

Feature Set Theory

Smith, Shoben, and Rips's (1974) research was used as the springboard for their theory of semantic memory which proposes a radically different structure than do the associative network models. Their theory, which is called *feature set theory*, was designed to account for semantic distance effects, category size effects, and violations of the category size effect. To encompass all of these effects, Smith, Shoben, and Rips suggest that we think of knowledge of various concepts as consisting of features. In a sense, the contents of semantic memory would be the attributes of the objects. Rather than propose a node for each concept, knowledge of the concept is represented as a set of features.

The features can be viewed as component parts of the objects, much the same as were the physical features described in chapter 2 on pattern recognition; more precisely, features are values on a dimension. The dimensions may be perceptual, such as shape, size, and color, in which case the features will be particular colors (e.g., red), or shapes (e.g., round), or sizes (e.g., small). Dimensions can also be functional characteristics and abstractions: mode of locomotion, a feature of which might be "flying"; or eating habits, a feature of which might be "worms"; or even abstractions such as honesty and beauty, features of which might be "deceitful" and "gorgeous." Knowledge of any concept then consists of all of the features comprising that concept. This view is considerably different from the assumption that knowledge of a concept is represented by a set of interconnected nodes.

To appreciate the power of the feature set model fully, the distinction between two kinds of features, *defining features* and *characteristic features,* must be considered. Defining features are central to the meaning of a concept; to be called a particular type means that the object has the defining features. To be classified a *bird,* the object must have certain features shared by all of those objects known as *birds.* Perhaps the critical features are feathers, wings, and two feet; we cannot say for sure what they are, but this is not critically important. What is important is that some set of the features define an object as a member of a particular class, be it *bird, automobile, house plants,* or *college professor.* All objects in the class share the defining features.

The second type of feature is characteristic of the object, but not necessary to its definition. For example, we characteristically associate pipe smoking with college professors, but we also know that pipe smoking is not a defining feature of college professors. Plenty of pipe smokers are not college professors, and plenty of college professors are not pipe smokers. By the same token, we characteristically associate flying with *bird,* but flying cannot be a defining feature of *bird.* Very simply, some of the creatures we know as *birds*— ostriches and chickens, for example— do not fly. So while we may think of "fly" when we think of *bird* (most birds do fly), "fly" is not an attribute that defines an object as a bird.

The meaning of a concept is then represented by the entire bundle of features, both defining and characteristic. When we think of the concept, all of the information contained in these features is activated. If we must call on knowledge to answer a question such as, "Is a robin a bird?", the features of both robin and bird are activated, and the decision process begins. The decision is a two-stage process of matching the features of the two concepts. In the first stage, all of the features, both characteristic and defining, are matched. If there are a large number of features in common, the question can quickly be answered yes. If there are very few features in common, the question can quickly be answered no. For example, "Is a robin a bird?" receives a quick yes response and "Is a turnip a bird?" receives a quick no response. Some concepts, however, share an intermediate number of features—"Is an ostrich a bird?"—and then the second phase of the decision process occurs. In the *second phase,* only the *defining features* are matched. The second phase then requires more time in order to produce an answer.

This process of differentially matching characteristic and defining features allows the feature set model to describe the category size effect as well as the anomalies associated with that effect. Furthermore, the model also accounts nicely for semantic distance effects. Understanding how this works begins with the realization that the degree of relationship is determined largely by the total amount of feature overlap. Using this basic premise, let us briefly describe how the model applies to the various empirical findings.

Beginning with the category size effect, persons require more time to verify that a *robin* is an *animal* than that it is a *bird,* the assumption being that *robin* shares more total features with *bird* than with *animal.* The retrieval and comparison processes for *robin* and *bird* can thus be completed in one stage, but the lack of overlap between *robin* and *animal* necessitates the second stage of comparing defining features.

Precisely the same analysis is applied to the semantic distance effect. Persons more quickly verify *robin* as *bird* than *chicken* as *bird,* because *robin* shares more features with *bird* than does *chicken.* To verify *chicken* as *bird* requires matching defining features. Furthermore, the same mechanism is applied to anomalies from the category size effect, cases in which instances are more rapidly verified as members of large than of small categories. *Scotch* is more quickly classified as a *drink* than as an *alcoholic beverage* and *dog* is more readily verified as an *animal* than as a *mammal,* because the instance shares more features with the large category superordinate than with the smaller category superordinate.

Although the feature set model seems to explain semantic distance effects and category size effects, the immediate reaction may be skepticism, because it appears that the explanation is provided after the fact. To counter this criticism, Smith, Shoben, and Rips (1974) suggest that the number of features shared by an instance and its superordinate can be determined by *typicality* ratings. *Typicality* refers to how well a particular instance represents knowledge of the concept, and ratings of typicality are easily obtained by simply asking persons questions like, "On a scale of 1 to 10, how typical is *robin* of *bird*?" "How typical is *ostrich* of *bird*?" and so on. We know that two concepts, such as *robin* and *bird,* share defining features when persons classify one as an instance of the other. The typicality ratings then provide an estimate of the number of characteristic features shared by an instance and a superordinate.

According to the feature set theory, the time required to verify an instance as a member of a category should be inversely related to its typicality. That is, highly typical instances should be verified quickly because they share a large number of characteristic features with the superordinate. Atypical instances are verified less rapidly because they share fewer characteristic features and require the second phase of the decision process, matching defining features. In a test of this idea, Smith, Shoben, and Rips (1974) found that typicality ratings nicely predicted relative reaction time. Consistent with their idea, typical instances were verified more rapidly than were atypical instances.

Another interesting ability of the feature set model is its account of commonly used linguistic *hedges. Hedges* are statements which are qualified in some respect such as, "*Technically speaking,* a bat is not a bird." From the standpoint of the feature-set model, the idea communicated is that bats and birds share many characteristic features but do not share defining features. Similar knowledge is communicated in such statements as, "*Loosely speaking,* a bat is a bird."

As you can see, the feature model differs in both process and structure from associative network models, and in part because of these differences, the feature model nicely explains some of the phenomena which cause problems for the network model. Of course, the feature model also has the advantage of being formulated to account explicitly for some of these problems, particularly the violations of category size effects. Nonetheless, the feature model is also capable of generating interesting predictions, such as the correlation between typicality and reaction time, which have been confirmed. In spite of these successes, the feature model has its troublesome side. Since Smith, Shoben, and Rips's initial proposal, very little development has occurred. This is unfortunate because the model leaves so many questions unanswered. For example, how are the features selected for the match process? Are all features selected? If they are not, what determines which features enter a decision? Much more thinking is required on these and other issues.

Another problem of the feature model is the long-standing criticism of the feature approach to knowledge: specifically, what constitutes a defining feature? Take any concept, *dog* for example, and try to think of one feature which can be removed from an instance so that it no longer is recognizable as a member of the concept. If you see a dog with no tail or no legs, or for that matter no head, is it still clearly a dog? The problem here is that the critical defining features of many concepts are not immediately obvious.

The criticism of featural representations has a long history and is based on the argument that no feature, or perhaps set of features, is necessary and sufficient to define a concept. The example of *dog* in the last paragraph illustrates the lack of necessity and sufficiency in that no matter what you remove, the thing is still identified as *dog*. Thus, whatever is removed must not be necessary to identify *dog,* and whatever remains must be sufficient to identify *dog*. Since we cannot think of things which when removed would obscure the identity of *dog,* serious questions arise concerning the existence of features which are necessary to identify a concept and which, when present, are sufficient to identify a concept.

In summary, it is not necessary that a thing fly in order to classify it as a *bird* (witness penguins) nor does the fact that a thing flies suffice to classify it as a *bird* (witness airplanes). Equivocation over necessary and sufficient (defining) features has provoked an important modification of feature set theory. Rather than maintaining that our knowledge consists of defining features, Larry Barsalou (1982) has proposed that certain features of a concept are *context independent*. That is, certain aspects of our knowledge will be activated upon every occurrence of the concept, regardless of the context in which the concept occurs. For example, "four-legged" is an aspect of your knowledge of *dog,* and if "four-legged" is a context-independent feature of *dog,* everytime you think of *dog,* whether it be in the context of chasing cats or aiding the visually impaired, part of what you think is "four-legged". Other aspects of your knowledge of *dog* may be quite sensitive to context. These *context-dependent* features represent things you know but will think about only in certain contexts. For example, "snarls" is something you know about *dog,* but when you happen upon a well-trained, seeing-eye dog at work, "snarls" is not likely to be activated. Alternatively, as you observe a dog vigorously pursuing a cat, "snarls" may well be part of your knowledge which is activated.

To say that a feature is context-independent is not to say that the feature is necessary to define that concept. Although an unlikely event, you could identify a dog with no legs as a dog. Thus, "four-legged" may be something you think of each time *dog* is activated but it is not something which must be present in order to classify an object as *dog*. Barsalou's distinction between context-independent and context-dependent features averts a major criticism of feature representations of knowledge. The distinction also provides an obvious avenue for contextual biasing of nuances of a meaning.

The feature model is an interesting contrast to the associative network model. Perhaps the most fundamental difference is the way the two types of models capture semantic relationships. In the network model, the relationship between meaning of concepts is expressed in terms of *distance,* whereas in the feature model the same relationship is expressed *as number of overlapping features.* On the other hand, the two types of models are similar in describing knowledge at the level of the single concept, virtually a description of the knowledge represented by a single word. More recent approaches to the representation of knowledge have recommended higher-level structures.

Propositional Network Theories

Perhaps the most popular current theories of knowledge representation are *propositional network theories*. These theories, and there are a number of variations (Anderson, 1976; Anderson & Bower, 1973; Norman & Rumelhart, 1975), are basically associative network models but have a *basic proposition* represented at each node. A *proposition* is the smallest unit of knowledge which can be asserted. Propositions are also the smallest units about which it makes sense to decide whether they are true or false. In a sense, propositions are "idea units" which represent relationships among events or objects.

The best way to understand what is meant by a proposition is through example. A sentence of any complexity is likely to contain several propositions. For example, the sentence "Sam sells fresh vegetables to Guido, who owns a restaurant" can be divided into at least the following propositions or idea units:

1. Sam sells vegetables to Guido.
2. The vegetables are fresh.
3. Guido owns a restaurant.

Notice that each of these propositions expresses a separate idea, any one of which can be true or false. Propositional theories of semantic memory argue that the basic unit of knowledge is best represented as an individual proposition.

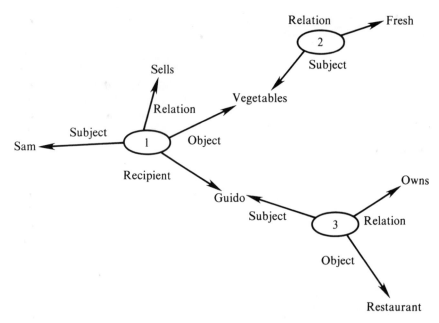

Figure 7.4 Schematic representation of a propositional network.

As pointed out in the discussion of the associative network models, knowledge is more than just individual propositions; it also includes the *relationships* among propositions. Taking the knowledge expressed in the sentence in the preceding example, we know the information in each proposition, such as "Sam sells fresh vegetables to Guido" and "Guido owns a restaurant." When the propositions are linked in a network, we know even more. Namely, we know, or at least infer, that Guido serves fresh vegetables in his restaurant. If the two linked propositions were "Sam sells fresh vegetables to Guido" and "Guido owns a canning factory," then this knowledge is in some respects quite different. The propositional network, then, like the associative network, describes knowledge in terms of basic propositions and the connections among them.

It is possible to list the propositions, as was just done, and they can also be schematized in a propositional network, much as an associative network model. A schematic representation of the propositional network of the previously used example is presented in figure 7.4. Following custom, the three propositions are represented by ellipses with the subjects and predicates connected to the ellipses. In addition, the information relating the subjects and predicates are connected to each ellipse and labeled relational information. For example, "vegetables" is the predicate or object of the subject "Sam" and the relationship between "Sam" and "vegetables" is "sells." Again, this relationship expresses knowledge in the sense that there are a number of activities Sam can do to or with vegetables such as "cook," "grow," "eat," "hate," and so on. But we *know* that Sam sells vegetables, and this particular knowledge is represented by this particular subject-relation-predicate.

From figure 7.4, it can be seen that the information contained at each node has changed, even though an associative structure is maintained. With associative network models, each node represents a concept, but the nodes of a propositional network are the entire proposition. Rather than "Sam," "sells," and "vegetables" being separate nodes, "Sam sells vegetables" is the basic unit of knowledge. This fact reflects the belief of propositional theorists that knowledge is stored in larger units than single concepts. The question then becomes: How do we describe knowledge of single concepts? One answer is to create a propositional network for each concept. You can imagine that the completed product would then be a very complex network indeed, but the complexity may simply mirror the nature of human knowledge.

The complexity of a propositional network may make one doubt the probability of determining whether human beings actually behave in accord with the model. Although there is no extensive evidence as yet, a number of experiments have provided results consistent with the propositional theory. First, the propositional network model easily accounts for all of the reaction time data of the verification experiments. The propositional nodes contain all of the information contained in the nodes and properties of Quillian's TLC and Loftus and Collins's spreading-activation model, and hence the explanation of the reaction time data would be the same in all of these situations. More direct tests of the psychological reality of propositions comes from several sources, particularly from the research of Walter Kintsch.

For example, Kintsch and Glass (reported in Kintsch, 1974) compared memory for sentences consisting of the same number of words but having different numbers of propositions. A sentence such as, "The settler built the cabin by hand," expresses one proposition, much as does the previous example, "Sam sells vegetables to Guido." An example of the two-proposition sentences in this study is "The horse stumbled and broke a leg." The propositions are "The horse stumbled" and "The horse broke a leg." Both of these sentences contain four content words, words which are not articles, prepositions, or conjunctions. Subjects showed clear differences in memory for the complete sentences, with much better recall of the one-proposition sentences. Furthermore, partial recall of a sentence was much more likely in the multiple-proposition sentences. Keeping in mind that the number of content words were equated, these data suggest that the number of propositions in a sentence affects the ability to remember the sentence. In particular, it appears that sentences are segmented into semantic units which correspond to propositions. More is said about propositional analysis of comprehension and memory in chapter 9. Data such as these from Kintsch suggest that the analysis of knowledge in propositional units may be quite fruitful.

Summary of Theories of Semantic Memory

Three basic types of ideas about semantic memory which can be distinguished on the basis of theoretical structures were described. Beginning with the historically prestigious TLC model, we discussed associative network theory as it has evolved to the spreading-activation model. Associative network theory proposes a vast system of interconnected nodes, each node representing a basic-level concept. Activation of a particular node or nodes conceptually describes the psychological experience of "knowing" or understanding; the richness of this experience is described or modeled by the spread of activity from the activated nodes to other associated nodes. Thus, when we think of "Santa Claus," we not only know this concept, but also a host of other facts, "presents," "snow," "evergreens," come to mind.

A different way of modeling semantic relationships is proposed by the second type of model. The feature model suggests that the basic concept is represented in terms of its component features or attributes, and the relationship among concepts is determined by the number of overlapping features.

A third type of idea discussed, the propositional model, also prescribes an associative structure for knowledge, but the propositional model differs in an important respect from the associative network model. Propositional models suggest a different structure at the level of the individual node. Nonetheless, the relationships among concepts are described in terms of associative connections, with the degree of semantic relationship directly related to the length of the association.

In summary, the structural differences among the various ideas are designed to account for different kinds of data. Human knowledge is an extraordinarily diverse and complex system, and the theories with which we now work can be expected to evolve considerably. Exciting developments will undoubtedly occur in this area as major research efforts uncover new facts to guide theoretical development.

SEMANTIC MEMORY AND COGNITIVE PROCESSES

This chapter began with a brief discussion of the function of knowledge, and we now return to that issue by examining the role of semantic memory in other processes discussed. The importance of semantic memory becomes clear when we see just how pervasive is the influence of knowledge on simpler processes.

Semantic Memory, Pattern Recognition, and Attention

Semantic memory played the central role in the discussion of pattern recognition, although at the time it was called, simply, long-term memory. Remember it was suggested that the process of pattern recognition is a matter of activating a representation in long-term memory, a process we can now say is the activation of semantic memory. Not only does the process of pattern recognition entail the activation of semantic memory, but also activation of semantic memory can give rise to the recognition response independently of sensory input corresponding to the pattern. This process, which is called *presynthesis* or *top-down processing,* is responsible for filling in gaps in pattern recognition and resolving ambiguity in the sensory information. Semantic memory is then fundamentally involved in the basic perceptual process of interpreting physical energy from the environment.

Semantic memory was also intimately involved in the discussion of attentional processes. If a limited processing capacity is assumed, it is important to direct processing capacity in such a way that continuity in meaning is maintained. One description of how attention operates is that expectations guide the continued allocation of capacity to a particular message. The expectations, as discussed, are basically the activation of the knowledge system by the preceding context, and capacity is then allocated to ensuing information to the extent that it remains consistent with the knowledge of what should follow. In this sense, semantic memory becomes indispensable as a guide to the process of attention.

Semantic Memory and Episodic Memory

Perhaps the relationship between semantic memory and episodic memory is at once more obvious but also more complex. Episodic memory is commonly viewed as the by-product of perceptual activity, or in other words, what is remembered about an event are the patterns that were recognized and allotted processing capacity. Since we have just seen that pattern recognition is the activation of semantic memory, this must mean that episodic memory, as the by-product of pattern recognition, is really the activation of semantic memory. If this is true, is there any point in distinguishing between semantic memory and episodic memory?

We discussed Tulving's answer to this question in the form of the episodic-semantic distinction. Tulving suggested that semantic memory and episodic memory are two different systems in that different principles govern their operation, particularly in retrieval. Events are dated in memory and as such can occur only once, but semantic memory or knowledge is a representation that is not time tagged. A particularly sensitive issue is how knowledge is acquired if semantic memory and episodic memory are totally different systems. We shall return to this issue momentarily.

More recently, a different view emerged suggesting that no distinction should be made between episodic memory and semantic memory. This approach finds support in several experiments which show that certain experimental manipulations have the same effect upon both semantic memory and episodic memory (Anderson & Ross, 1980; Lewis & Anderson, 1976; McKoon & Ratcliff, 1979). These results suggest that episodic memory and semantic memory share the same representation and that event (episodic) memory is the activation of some portion of semantic memory. Even this position, however, implies a distinction between semantic memory and episodic memory, at least to the extent that episodic memory is only a portion of the semantic representation. For example, memory of "seeing a bear in a circus" entails only a fraction of the knowledge of bears. Yet this view does differ from Tulving's by stopping short of suggesting that episodic memory and semantic memory obey different principles.

Tulving's thinking has been influenced by the data and arguments offered in opposition to his original idea. Tulving (1983) has suggested that episodic memory is a subsystem embedded within semantic memory and that semantic and episodic memory do interact. For example, semantic memory information may be useful in cuing episodic traces. At the same time, Tulving continues to argue for important differences between the two systems. These differences are not only the functional differences which we have described in the preceding chapter on retrieval, but also differences in neurophysiology and developmental priority. The later difference refers to Tulving's speculation that semantic memory is phylogenetically and ontogenetically prior to episodic memory. That is, the semantic memory system of some nonhuman animals and of human infants is better developed than their episodic memory system. The controversy continues, however, as McKoon, Ratcliff, and Dell (1986) argue that a single memory system is a better approach to understanding knowledge and memory. Tulving (1986) counters with the suggestion that the differences between knowledge and episodes are sufficient to require a theoretical classification of those differences. Obviously, debate on this issue continues.

Dissociations Revisited

Research demonstrating dissociations of memory tests has been offered as strong evidence of the existence of separate semantic memory systems. We discussed this research in the last chapter but shall return to it here to make some additional points. Research on dissociations, as you will remember, demonstrates that certain variables have different effects on different kinds of memory tests. You also will recall that these effects are relevant to the distinction between episodic and semantic memory because many of the *indirect* memory tests can be completed with responses that are context independent, the very criteria presumed to define the abstract knowledge stored in semantic memory. Most *direct* memory tests correspond to episodic memory because the test requires production of a particular prior event. Thus, the fact that the two tests respond differently to the same variable is in good agreement with the idea that semantic and episodic memory are different systems.

Consider another example of this argument from the research of David Mitchell and Alan Brown of Southern Methodist University. The experiments involve presentation of pictures of common objects. The subject sees 100 pictures presented one at a time and must name each picture as it is presented. In a second session, the subjects again see 100 pictures, half of which are from the first session and half of which are new. In this second session the subjects again have to name the pictures and also make a recognition decision about whether the picture appeared in the first session. In the second session, the time to name the picture is measured, a measure known as picture naming latency. To the extent that naming a picture in the first session influences the time to name the picture in the second session, a determination of which can be made by comparing the time to name old pictures with the time to name new pictures in the second session, picture naming latency can be used as an indirect test of memory. Thus the paradigm provides a comparison of direct (recognition memory) and indirect (picture naming latency) tests of memory.

Several interesting dissociations have been produced by the paradigm. For example, Mitchell, Brown, and Murphy (1989) found that older people are less accurate on recognition of the pictures than college-age subjects but that picture-naming latency did not differ as a function of age. The older subjects showed as much increase in speed of naming in the second session as the younger subjects. The dissociation of the effect of age on direct and indirect tests has been reported for both elderly subjects and children.

Another example of dissociations between recognition memory and picture naming latency is from Mitchell and Brown (1988). In this study, the second session (or tests) occurred either 1, 4, or 6 weeks after the first session. As you can see from the data depicted in figure 7.5, recognition memory performance declined over the 6-week retention period, a rather standard forgetting function. Picture-naming latency did not decline; the benefit of the first session practice on second-session naming-latency remained constant over the 6 weeks. Other investigators also have found that the decline in performance over time on indirect tests is less severe than on direct tests. Sloman, Hayman, Ohta, Law, and Tulving (1988) discovered that facilitation from single study trial continued to produce benefits to fragment completion performance as long as 16 months later! Here, then, is another dissociation between direct and indirect memory tests.

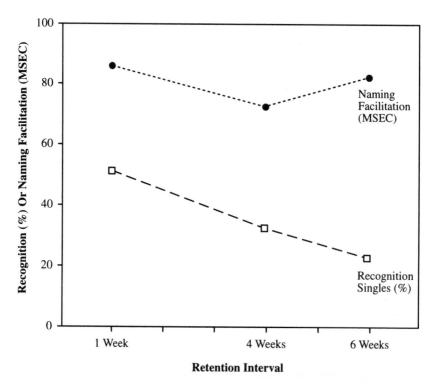

Figure 7.5 The effect of prior study on picture naming latency and recognition memory as a function of retention interval in Mitchell and Brown's (1988) experiment. (From "Persistent repetition priming in picture naming and its dissociation from recognition memory" by D. B. Mitchell and A. S. Brown. *Journal of Experimental Psychology: Learning, Memory, and Cognition*, 1988, *14*, 213–222. Copyright 1988 by the American Psychological Association. Reprinted by permission.)

The relevance of these data to the question at hand, namely the relationship between episodic and semantic memory, lies in the theoretical interpretation of the dissociation. From the view of memory systems, tasks such as naming pictures tap semantic memory, and the dissociation of picture naming performance and recognition memory is easily interpreted as the operation of different memory systems. Specifically, Mitchell, Brown, and Murphy's (1989) results would mean that episodic memory functioning declines with age, but semantic memory functioning does not. Mitchell and Brown's data would indicate that semantic memory is less susceptible to forgetting over time than is episodic memory.

Exemplar Theory

Not all of the research on dissociation is so easily interpreted in the context of memory systems. One example is a study by Jacoby and Witherspoon (1982) that simply required subjects to spell words. Knowledge required to spell a word presumably originates in semantic memory, and spelling performance presumably is governed by principles of semantic memory. That is, spelling does not appear to require access to a specific prior episode but rather access to general knowledge abstracted over a number of episodes. If so, a single, specific prior episode should have little influence on the simple task of spelling a word. If, for example, you have to spell the word *sale,* whether you had just encountered an advertisement for discounts at your favorite haberdashery or seen the famous Arthur Miller play should make little difference to your performance.

But, in the vein of this example, what if someone *said* to you, "Spell the word *sale,*" just as you were watching a yacht race? The point, of course, is that *sale* and *sail* are homophones, words which sound alike but are spelled differently. Most homophones have a dominant sense; that is, one meaning and spelling of a homophone will have a higher probability of occurring when the word is presented out of context. Taking advantage of this situation, Jacoby and Witherspoon (1982) examined the influence of a single prior exposure upon the spelling of homophones.

The pertinent portion of Jacoby and Witherspoon's experiment is simple but ingenious. First, homophones were presented in a biased context by asking subjects to answer some simple questions such as, "Name a musical instrument that employs a *reed.*" Reed is the low-probability interpretation of the homophone *read/reed.* After answering the questions, the subjects then were asked to spell a list of words which included the homophones from the questions. No instructions mentioned the relationship between questions and spelling. Interest here was primarily in the spelling of a homophone given a low-probability bias at input. In fact, the biased, low-probability spelling (*reed*) was more than twice as likely as the dominant spelling (*read*) for subjects who had answered the initial questions. The point is that following a single experience (question answering), the preferred spelling of a homophone was drastically altered. How could this happen if these preferred spellings resulted from semantic memory which is structured from hundreds of episodes?

The issue here is not about the existence of knowledge but rather about the *nature* of knowledge. The theories of semantic memory we have described in this chapter assume that knowledge is abstracted from previous experience. It is abstract in that the information represented as knowledge does not include the contextual particulars of the previous experience. Your knowledge of "George Washington was the first president of the United States" was acquired through numerous experiences, but the abstract representation of this knowledge does not include information about the particular episodes from which the knowledge was abstracted. Herein lies the fundamental difference between the episodic and semantic systems. The contextual particulars of prior experience are episodic memories, and semantic memory is abstract knowledge. The surprising aspect of Jacoby and Witherspoon's data is that a single experience could alter radically the preferred spelling of a homophone that had been acquired over numerous prior experiences.

A similar problem was raised in the previous chapter when we discussed the modality effect on indirect memory tests. To the extent that indirect tests draw on semantic memory, highly specific aspects of context such as modality of prior experience should not influence performance. The fact that the match between study-test modality is important to performance on many tests that are presumed to rest on abstract knowledge raises serious theoretical questions.

A more extreme alternative idea denies the existence of semantic memory by claiming that all knowledge is episodic. This position, which we shall call the *exemplar* theory, does not deny the existence of knowledge but rather attempts to explain the use of knowledge without reference to abstracted representations of general information. Knowledge is *specific* past experience. For example, comprehension of *dog* is not a matter of activating general knowledge of *dog* abstracted from your numerous previous encounters with dogs. Rather, *dog,* is comprehended by retrieving a particular episode involving a dog. In other words, when you think of *dog,* you do not think of some generic canine but of a specific dog. Prominent advocates of this idea have been Lee Brooks (1978) and Jacoby and Brooks (1984).

Discrete prior episodes actually do affect performance that could be guided solely by an abstract rule. Allen and Brooks (1991) asked subjects to learn to categorize two fictitious creatures, one called Builders and one called Diggers. The animals could be classified on the basis of a simple rule. The Builders (shown in the upper left panel of figure 7.6) always would have at least two of the following three characteristics, long legs, angular bodies, and spots. Anything else was a Digger. The subjects in the experiment learned this rule and practiced applying it with training examples such as those shown in the left panel of figure 7.6. The training session was 40 trials of classifying the examples as either a Builder or a Digger. By the end of training, the subjects possess a simple, well-practiced rule. The situation is designed to be as life-like as possible. For example, you probably behave in accord with rules such as: If it is cloudy and the forecast is for rain, take an umbrella. The point is that the rule appears to be abstract in

Rule: At Least Two of (Long Legs, Angular Body, Spots) —▶ Builder

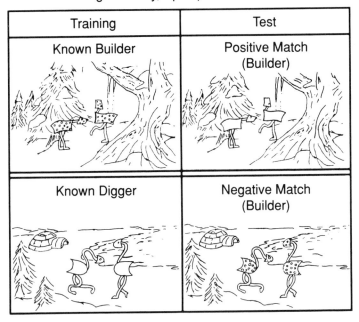

Training	Test
Known Builder	Positive Match (Builder)
Known Digger	Negative Match (Builder)

Figure 7.6 An example of the study and test, figures from Allen and Brooks's (1991) study of concept acquisition. (From "Specializing the operation of an explicit rule" by S. W. Allen and L. Brooks. *Journal of Experimental Psychology: General,* 1991, 20, 3–19. Copyright 1991 by the American Psychological Association. Reprinted by permission.)

that its application is not influenced by the prior episodes under which it was learned. In the Allen and Brooks experiment, the simple, well-practiced rule for defining Diggers and Builders should be applied to new examples without any influence from the specific training examples.

In a clever test of this intuitively plausible hypothesis, Allen and Brooks gave a classification test of new examples that had not been seen in the training session. Examples of these test items are shown in the right column of figure 7.6. Notice that the test examples are not identical to a training example but all test items can be correctly classified by applying the simple rule. Some of the test items, however, looked like a particular training example, and that training example was from the incorrect category. The animal in the lower right panel of figure 7.6 is clearly a Builder because it has spots and long legs; it conforms to the rule defining a Builder and should be classified as a Builder. Yet, this Builder has irrelevant features that are identical to one of the training examples of a Digger. This one training example is analogous to a single prior experience in the course of learning an abstract rule. The important result of the experiment was that performance on these Negative Match test items was less accurate and less rapid than on Positive Match test items. The only way this could happen was because a particular instance in training influenced the classification of the test items. Behavior that appears to be guided by an abstract rule actually is influenced by a very specific prior event. The general point is that knowledge may correspond to specific prior events rather than to abstract representations.

Summary of Knowledge Representations

The question of knowledge representation is a venerable issue, dating at least to the writings of Plato. Modern psychology has brought the methods of science to bear on this problem but as yet, no clear solution is forthcoming. One position is that all knowledge is abstract and if so, must be different from what we call "memory" because memory involves particular prior events. Consequently, memory and knowledge must be different systems, as, for example, episodic memory and semantic memory. Alternatively, the position just described as exemplar theory argues that what we take to be abstract knowledge is in reality the effect of a particular prior episode. The truth may lie somewhere between these extremes but by casting the alternatives in these extreme forms, empirical work on this important question moves forward.

You will appreciate the importance of the issue when we discuss this debate again in Chapter 8 in the context of concepts and concept acquisition. All of our concepts, after all, are exactly what most people mean by "abstract knowledge." As a preview, let us briefly consider the question of knowledge acquisition in the context of semantic memory.

Knowledge Acquisition

How does semantic memory develop? This question is in part an issue of how we acquire concepts and, as such, will be briefly discussed in chapter 8. For the moment, we wish to raise some fundamental questions pertinent to the role of semantic and episodic memory in knowledge acquisition.

Consider first our previous discussion of the interactions between semantic memory, pattern recognition, and attention. If perceptual experiences result from the activation of semantic memory, as is assumed by many theorists, meaningful perceptions obviously are not possible prior to the development of semantic memory. That is, very young infants presumably would perceive the world as "blooming, buzzing confusion" until they had sufficient experience to develop an organized semantic memory. Well, how does experience influence the development of concepts or semantic memory?

The typical answer to this question is that having a variety of experiences with a class of things, dogs for example, allows for the abstraction of common elements among the diverse experiences, and these commonalities form the core of the concept. Notice, however, that we are now in big logical trouble because we began with the premise that semantic memory functions to make sense of perceptual episodes, but we now have argued that semantic memory develops from the accretion of episodes. Theoretically, the episodes cannot be interpreted until there is semantic memory, and therefore episodes cannot be the basis upon which semantic memory develops.

Historically, the escape from this dilemma is to assume that even the youngest infant has some rudimentary or core knowledge which can be used to interpret experience and build a semantic memory structure. Among the implications of this position is that young infants remember their experiences, and indeed, exciting new evidence indicates that even prenatal experiences are remembered. DeCasper and Spence (1986) asked pregnant women to read a story to their unborn child each day for the last two weeks of pregnancy. The mother determined when the fetus was awake and then read the story aloud. Acoustical properties of the womb are well established, and we know that the physical energy to stimulate auditory processes is available. DeCasper and Spence then tested the infants within three days of birth to determine if they would choose to listen to the story. The procedure for the test allows the infant to hear one of two stories over headphones. The infant "chooses" a story by the rate at which he or she sucks a nonnutritive nipple. Sucking at a certain rate turns on one of the stories and changes in sucking rate switch stories. Infants in the experiment maintained a sucking rate which allowed them to hear the story their mothers had read to them before birth in preference to new stories. These results suggest that prenatal experiences influence postnatal behavior, and in that sense, memory for experiences begins very early in development.

Such discoveries do not implicate a developing semantic memory, but rather allow us to assume, if we wish, that the processes necessary to perceive and remember particular experiences are available to the fetus. By making this assumption, we circumvent the problem raised earlier about how episodes are interpreted prior to the existence of any substantial semantic memory. Of course, infant memory data may simply reflect the fact that knowledge is stored as discrete episodes.

The problem for this view is different but no less complex. If all knowledge is actually in the form of wholistic episodes, how do we classify and categorize our experiences? That is, if our knowledge is in the form of a list of events, how do we come to compare and contrast the events? The answer may appear very simple, namely, current experiences are compared to similar past experiences. But two things are not similar until they are compared, so it will not do to say that we call the Bernese Mountain dog that we see today a dog because it is similar to the cocker spaniel we saw two days ago. To know that the two things are similar requires that the current perception be compared with memory, and upon this comparison, a similarity judgment can be made. But how is the relevant memory selected? Not by similarity, because similarity is unknown until the comparison is made. In the absence of any extraction of commonalities, which would require generic representations, it is unclear how a child would learn to classify and categorize its world.

These are not new issues but are important questions of human intelligence which have been raised again in the context of knowledge and memory. The difficulty of these questions should never persuade us to avoid the issues because, if nothing else, an appreciation of the difficult questions gives us a fuller understanding of disagreements concerning the representation of knowledge.

SUMMARY

In chapter 7 the area of research known as semantic memory was discussed. Semantic memory refers to what is generally called knowledge, and the discussion began by exploring the research showing what knowledgeable persons or "experts" can do that less knowledgeable persons cannot do. Several theories of semantic memory were then examined and the differences in memory structure proposed by these theories was closely considered. It was stressed that each theory generated interesting research in support of its position, but each theory also has its shortcomings. Finally, consideration of the relationship between semantic memory and other cognitive processes, particularly episodic memory and perception, was begun.

MULTIPLE-CHOICE ITEMS

1. Which of the following is not a function of the concept of knowledge?
   a. interpret incoming information
   b. limit capacity of the system
   c. provide meaning of events
   d. allow projection into the future

2. In the TLC model, cognitive economy is
   a. the storage of properties at the highest possible node
   b. the second stage of the retrieval process
   c. the shortest distance between two nodes
   d. the duplication of defining and characteristic features

3. The fact that "a robin is a bird" can be verified more rapidly than can "a robin is an animal" is an example of
   a. a propositional model
   b. a difference in defining features
   c. the cognitive economy
   d. the category size effect

4. The difference between the spread of activation theory and TLC is
   a. the assumption about number of nodes
   b. the assumption about defining features
   c. the assumption about hierarchical organization
   d. the assumption about propositions

5. According to Smith, Shoben, and Rips's feature model, "Scotch is a drink" is verified faster than is "Scotch is an alcoholic beverage" because of
   a. differential overlap of characteristic features
   b. differential overlap of defining features
   c. differential length of associations
   d. differential complexity of propositions

6. The basic difference between the propositional network and the associative network model is
   a. the connection between nodes
   b. the retrieval process
   c. the assumption about typicality effects
   d. the type of information at each node

TRUE–FALSE ITEMS

1. Among other factors, an "expert" or high-knowledge person is able to predict what will happen in the future better than is a low-knowledge person.

2. A major implication of cognitive economy is that much of knowledge is not directly acquired but must be inferred.

3. Feature models and associative network models both assume that the similarity of meaning among concepts is represented by distance.

4. The biggest problem with propositional models is accounting for reaction time data generated from simpler models.

5. The more propositions a sentence contains, the harder it is to remember.

6. The reason to make a distinction between semantic memory and episodic memory is that we know semantic memory develops from episodic memory.

DISCUSSION ITEMS

1. Why did data on cognitive economy and typicality effects pose such general difficulty for hierarchically organized models?

2. Describe the retrieval process a person would likely use to verify "a robin is a bird" and "an ostrich is a bird" according to the Smith, Shoben, and Rips's feature model.

ANSWERS TO MULTIPLE-CHOICE ITEMS

1. (b) The capacity limitation is fixed and not a function of knowledge.
2. (a) Cognitive economy refers to storage of information at the highest node.
3. (d) The category size effect is faster verification time for smaller categories and "bird" is smaller than "animal."
4. (c) TLC assumes a hierarchical organization and spread of activation does not.
5. (a) Scotch is both "a drink" and "an alcoholic beverage" and thus has defining features of both. The difference in reaction time is due to the number of characteristic features.
6. (d) Associative network models represent simple concepts at each node, whereas propositional models represent propositions at each node.

ANSWERS TO TRUE–FALSE ITEMS

1. (True) The research on knowledge of baseball demonstrated that experts are very good at predicting what will happen next.
2. (True) Storing information at the highest possible node implies that we infer that this information applies to subordinate nodes.

3. (False) Feature models assume that similarity of meaning is represented by overlap among features.

4. (False) Propositional models can account for the reaction time data.

5. (True) Kintsch and Glass showed that the more propositions in sentences, even with total number of words equated, the more difficult the sentence was to remember.

6. (False) We do not know that semantic memory develops from episodic memory, and if episodic memory is interpreted through semantic memory, it is hard to see how this could be true.

8

CATEGORIZATION AND CONCEPTS

Concepts provide us with a certain kind of stability in interacting with the environment. Concepts allow us to rise above the specific details of the environment and to treat events that have common properties as members of a class. For example, in forming the concept of *dog,* young children learn to classify a variety of specific instances as members of a set. They learn that the label *dog* may be applied to specific instances, but more important they learn that *dog* refers to a *class of instances* which have certain properties or features in common.

If children apply the concept of *dog* only to a specific dog, such as their own, they have not really developed the concept of *dog.* It is only when they can apply the term to a number of specific instances in a reasonably accurate fashion that we say they have acquired the concept. Moreover, it is important not only that they apply the term appropriately in the presence of instances, but also that they recognize other events or objects that are properly not part of the concept. Thus, for example, they must properly exclude instances such as cats, rabbits, and other animals. Thus, the formation of concepts refers to *both* the *selection* of appropriate instances and the *rejection* or exclusion of inappropriate instances.

The development and refinement of some concepts take place over an extended time period. Moreover, the forming of many concepts involves progressing from some gross, diffuse state to a highly refined condition in which fine-grain distinctions can be made. Thus, students may have only general concepts about some things and very precise concepts about others. In addition, they may be in the process of refining some of their more vague concepts. In the course of formal learning, students' concepts of abstractions such as "justice," "freedom," and "integrity" constantly grow and change as they are exposed to new experiences and knowledge. Similar is the situation in which understanding of a particular concept sharpens and expands with additional experience, advanced training, or new knowledge.

A great deal of teaching is directed toward the development of concepts because they are necessary for more complex behaviors such as the learning of principles, problem solving, and symbolic activities such as thinking. One of the principal objectives of formal education is the teaching of basic concepts that enable individuals to function in society in conjunction with the teaching of the notion that concepts can be revised, altered, and amended on the basis of new knowledge and experience. The ability to handle concepts as they currently exist and to deal with them in a flexible and changing fashion is a joint objective of school learning.

TYPES OF CONCEPTS

Psychologists have used a wide variety of stimulus objects in the study of how concepts are formed and how things are classified. These stimuli range from natural objects in the environment such as trees, plants, and so forth, to useful objects such as furniture and automobiles, to artificial stimuli constructed in the laboratory. In much laboratory research on concept formation during the period 1955–70, artificial concepts were typically used. These concepts possess a certain convenience because their precise features are specified. A stimulus is usually either a member of the concept or not a member.

Logical Concepts

Logical or artificial concepts are used in tasks in which subjects are presented varied stimulus patterns not normally experienced in their everyday environment. The stimuli are constructed so as to vary systematically along certain dimensions. Typically, the laboratory researcher constructs visual patterns varying in size, shape, or color. Thus the stimuli consist of such things as red squares, green circles, blue triangles, and so forth. The concept to be learned is arbitrarily selected, such as large green objects. This category includes, then, all stimuli that are large and green regardless of their shape. Stimuli which cannot be placed in this category are not instances of the concept. Stimuli consisting of both positive instances (exemplars) and negative instances (nonexemplars) are presented. They vary in several *dimensions,* one or more of which are relevant to the concept, whereas others are irrelevant. Each dimension may take on two or more *values.* For example, we may have shape, size, and color as dimensions, with two values for each dimension: circle and square for shape, large and small for size, and red and green for color. This arrangement produces eight stimuli, as shown in figure 8.1.

The particular concept to be learned is arbitrarily determined by the experimenter. If the concept to be learned is *square,* then the green and red instances enclosed by the dotted line are positive instances of that concept. A similar arrangement can be made for the size concept. Moreover, various combinations could be used such as *small red* and *large green* objects, which designate a more complex kind of concept.

We can increase the number of instances dramatically simply by increasing the number of attributes. If the three dimensions (shape, size, and color) are each represented by three attributes, we have twenty-seven instances rather than eight. Figure 8.2 shows this set of instances. Note that the attributes for *shape* are square, triangle, and circle; for *size* they are small, medium, and large; *color* is represented by three different shadings.

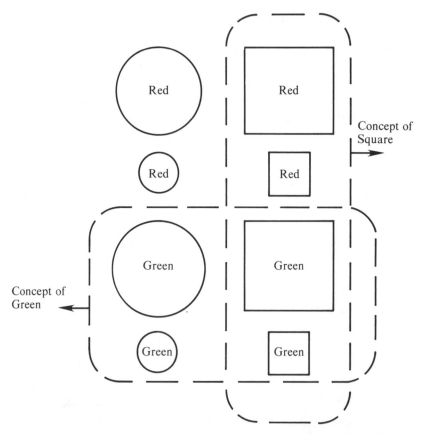

Figure 8.1 Schematic diagram showing instances of objects relevant to the concept *square* and to the concept *green*. (From *Fundamentals of Human Learning, Memory, and Cognition,* 2nd ed., by H. C. Ellis. Dubuque, Iowa: Wm. C. Brown Company, 1978.)

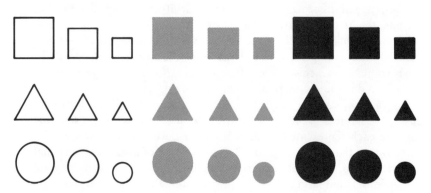

Figure 8.2 Set of instances generated from three stimulus dimensions, each represented by three attribute values.

Traditional Concept Identification Studies

A number of procedures have been developed to study how people classify objects and events. One procedure which has been used extensively is the concept identification procedure. In laboratory research using logical concepts, two basic paradigms have been used: the reception paradigm and the selection paradigm. In the *reception paradigm* the stimuli are presented in some random or predetermined order by the experimenter and the subject classifies each stimulus as it is presented. Following classification the subject is given informative feedback, that is, is told whether the classification is correct. Usually only one stimulus is presented at a time; thus subjects are required to depend on their memory of the events over a series of trials. In the *selection paradigm,* subjects select the stimuli, one at a time, from a set of stimuli placed before them. The subject is presented the entire set of stimuli at the onset of the experiment and selects each stimulus, trial after trial, on which feedback is desired. An obvious advantage of the selection paradigm is that the experimenter can observe how the subject goes about solving the problem.

The laboratory-constructed or artificial concepts have two important features: attributes and rules. We have already noted that these concepts have attributes, which are the characteristics of the stimuli relevant to the concept. Simple concepts may involve only a single attribute, such as *color.* Or they may have two attributes such as *sweet* and *sour,* which are essential aspects of the Chinese dish sweet-and-sour pork.

Attributes may be combined in several different ways to define a conceptual rule. In the preceding example, the Chinese dish consists of sweet *and* sour pork, that is, *both* the attributes of sweetness and sourness along with pork must be present. In this case we have an instance of a conjunction (joint presence) rule.

Humans adopt strategies when they attempt to focus on the relevant attributes of a concept. Suppose that a subject is presented with a set of stimuli varying in size, shape, and color, each with three values, for a set of twenty-seven stimuli. How can the subject go about selecting the relevant attribute most efficiently? The manner by which subjects go about selecting attributes is not a random or haphazard process, at least for most subjects. Rather, human beings frequently show a systematic approach to attacking this problem which is called a strategy. Strategies were first clearly described in classic studies by Bruner, Goodnow, and Austin (1956).

One type of strategy is called *conservative focusing.* Consider the case in which a subject has just been told that a large red square is a positive instance of the to-be-discovered concept. Conservative focusing requires that the subject's initial hypothesis include all three attributes of the stimulus in the hypothesis. The subject might then select a large red triangle as the next stimulus. If he is told he is correct, he then knows the shape is an irrelevant dimension. He might then select a small red square; if he is again correct, he knows that size is irrelevant, but that color is the relevant feature. Thus the important aspect of conservative focusing is that only one feature is changed at a time until the concept is identified. In general, human beings do better with conservative focusing than with any other type of strategy.

A more risky strategy is *focus gambling*. With focus gambling a person takes a chance and varies two or more attributes at a time in trying out hypotheses. If this strategy is successful, learning can then take place quickly. Using the stimuli in the example just given, the subject first selects a large red square, and if the strategy of focus gambling is followed, the subject might then select a small red triangle, changing both size and shape. If, in fact, blue is the relevant feature, the subject would have then learned the concept in one trial. On the other hand, if the subject fails in the gamble, learning is then slower.

Natural Concepts

As noted, a great deal of laboratory research has been done using logical concepts. They are defined on the basis of certain relevant dimensions which are combined according to a rule. Once the concept is figured out, all new exemplars presented can be categorized correctly. Thus, the concepts are tightly defined and the instances are unambiguous instances of exemplars or nonexemplars of the concept, which is to say that logical concepts are *deterministic*.

In recent years objections have been raised to the use of these concepts. Rosch (1973a, 1975) expressed concern over their appropriateness and argued for the use of *natural concepts*. *Artificial* (logical) concepts are not representative of the kinds of concepts encountered in the everyday world. The world is not so neatly divided into instances and noninstances, so Rosch notes. Indeed, the majority of concepts in everyday world experience do not fall into neatly defined categories. Many concepts have fuzzy boundaries with some uncertainty. For example: Is a tomato classified a fruit or a vegetable? Many *natural* concepts fit the situation of having fuzzy boundaries. And some examples of natural concepts are considered to be better examples than others. For instance, a chair is a very typical example of the concept of *furniture,* whereas a beanbag is a less representative example. In addition to the criticism that natural or real-world categories differ from logical, deterministic categories, some psychologists have argued that the concept identification procedures using artificial concepts do not represent the way people learn concepts. As a result, this approach is much less used today being superceded by studies of categorization to be discussed shortly.

Color concepts are an interesting example of natural concepts. The color spectrum is divided into a fairly similar manner in different cultures. Try visualizing a perfect blue, or red, or yellow. Persons tend to agree on what colors best represent each. But consider a color halfway between blue and green. When asked to identify it, some persons call it blue, others call it green, and a few are unsure of the color.

The point in noting the distinctions between logical and natural concepts is to emphasize that natural concepts are not defined in terms of clear, distinguishing attributes and precise rules. These concepts or categories are characterized by possessing certain features, some of which are more typical than others. We call these *prototypical concepts*. For example, *chair* is considered a very good (representative) example of furniture, whereas a *chest of drawers* is regarded as being a less typical or representative example. More generally, a prototype refers to the best representative of a category.

Natural concepts are also frequently *probabilistic*. They possess some uncertainty. For such concepts the relationship between the attributes and the concept is less than perfect. For example, high grades in high school do not automatically mean high grades in college. There is, of course, some probability that high grades in high school predict similar performance in college, but the correlation is far from perfect. We do not know all the relevant variables that predict college success, and we thus must deal with a probabilistic situation.

VARIETIES OF CATEGORIES

We can further distinguish a variety of ways in which human beings categorize objects and information. How are categories defined? On what basis are stimuli grouped and organized? Probably the most general way categories are defined is by the sharing of common attributes. Things may be categorized on a variety of bases such as similar function or use and similar appearance.

Categories and Verbal Context

The way an object is classified very much depends on how it is perceived and encoded. This fact was demonstrated in experiments by Labov (1973) who showed how the verbal context associated with an object can influence the way subjects classify the object. In these experiments Labov used cuplike objects, examples of which are shown in figure 8.3. All these drawings resemble cups, although some are a bit unusual. The cups along the left side of the figure (cups 5 through 9) show increasing elongation. The cups across the top (1 through 4) show an increase in the ratio of width to depth; as they become wider they begin to look more like bowls. Other differences

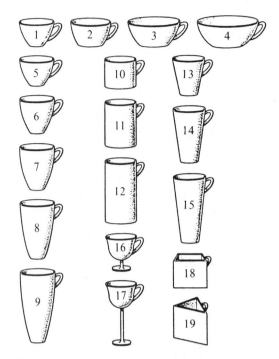

Figure 8.3 Series of cuplike objects for classification. (From "The Boundaries of Words and Their Meanings" by W. Labov, in C. J. N. Bailey and R. W. Shuy, Eds., *New Ways of Analyzing Variations in English.* Washington, D.C.: Georgetown University Press, 1973.)

are obvious. Cups 10 through 12 are cylindrical, cups 13 through 15 are conical, and cups 16 and 17 have stems. In Labov's experiments these drawings were presented one at a time, and subjects were simply asked to name them. This defined a *neutral* instructional condition. In other conditions subjects were asked to name the objects under different instructional sets. For example, subjects were asked to imagine the object sitting on a dinner table or filled with mashed potatoes or that someone was drinking coffee from it. After the various instructions, subjects were asked to identify the objects, one at a time, using a label or phrase.

The results are presented in figure 8.4, which shows the percentage of subjects giving a particular name as a function of width of the object and instructional set. The figure shows two important points. First, the frequency of "cup" responses decreases while the frequency of "bowl" responses increases as the width of the objects increases. The change is gradual, indicating that the boundary between cup and bowl is fuzzy. This, of course,

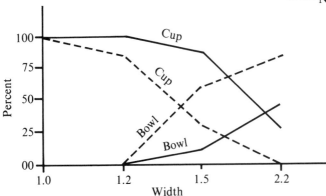

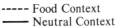

Figure 8.4 Percent of different name types applied to objects as the width increases and as a function of the verbal set. (From "The Boundaries of Words and Their Meanings" by W. Labov, in C. J. N. Bailey and R. W. Shuy, Eds., *New Ways of Analyzing Variations in English*. Washington, D.C.: Georgetown University Press, 1973.)

is not particularly surprising. The second point is that the frequency distributions of the *cup* label and the *bowl* label are influenced markedly by the verbal instructions or context. For example, an object is more likely to be called a bowl if it is thought of as filled with mashed potatoes as compared to the neutral context. These results show convincingly that a category is defined *both* by the *perceptual features* of the object (width) and by the prevailing *verbal-instructional context* under which the judgments are made.

The importance of verbal context in classifying objects is related to similar effects in human memory. Not only does verbal context affect how objects are classified and, hence, encoded, but also verbal context affects the discriminability and recognizability of objects (a fact long known). In a series of experiments, Ellis (1968, 1973) showed that the way visual shapes are verbally labeled affects memory for the shapes. Using random shapes, subjects were instructed to label them with verbal labels representative of the shapes. For example, a shape that looked something like a mountain was labeled "a mountain." Other subjects labeled the shapes with words having no relationship to the shape or with nonsense words. Under a variety of situations subjects' memory for the shapes was superior under the representative label condition, indicating that the label can influence how a shape is encoded and remembered. The effects of verbal context are important and operate in memory as well as in classification tasks.

Linguistic Context and Judgments

The role of *linguistic* context has been further demonstrated in a study by Roth and Shoben (1983). They presented subjects with the name of an exemplar embedded in a linguistic context; this was, in turn, followed by the names of exemplars. Specifically, the subjects were presented a category in different linguistic contexts and then asked to judge each example as to how well it fit the category. For instance, when animal was presented in a sentence about *milking,* cow and goat were judged as typical by the subjects. In contrast, when animal was presented in a sentence about *riding,* horse and mule were judged as more typical.

As Barsalou and Medin (1986) observed, these results demonstrate that the linguistic context in which people encounter a category can have an important impact on how they judge the category. Moreover, these results also indicate that a category is not necessarily represented by a static set of information in all situations. Instead, different information can represent the same category in different contexts.

Similarly, the point of view that a person adopts can readily influence how examples are placed or ordered in a category. Barsalou and Sewell (1984) had American undergraduate students adopt different perspectives or points of view while judging the typicality of example. Subjects were instructed, for example, to take various international viewpoints such as those of the average American, Chinese, or French citizen; or they were asked to take the viewpoint of an average U.S. housewife or businessman. As a general rule, the point of view that subjects adopted very much influenced how they classified exemplars as being typical.

Finally, people cannot only alter the representations of an existing category, as described above, but they can develop completely new categories with new knowledge and experiences. Barsalou (1983) has observed that people frequently construct new *ad hoc* categories as necessary to achieve some goal. For example, if someone is going camping for the first time, the person may construct *ad hoc* categories for places to go camping, things to take camping, times to go camping, and so forth. But with camping experience, new categories are formed and old ones altered.

Fuzzy Boundaries

Labov's studies also illustrate the point that many natural concepts have *fuzzy* or uncertain boundaries. Zadah, Fu, Tanaka, and Shimura (1975) have noted that many familiar concepts have uncertain boundaries which make precise categorization of events difficult. Consider the difference between a brook, stream, and river. For example, high in northern New Mexico are the headwaters of the Pecos River, which flows eventually into Texas and the Gulf of Mexico. But near the headwaters is a small (river, stream?) called the Holy Ghost. It is fast moving, but only a tributary to the Pecos River. It could be called one or the other, depending on one's perspective. If asked what it is, a person might reply by saying that the Holy Ghost is *essentially* a stream, qualifying and hedging in the response. And, in this fashion, the fuzzy or somewhat uncertain character of the concept is communicated. More generally, many natural concepts have what is called a *graded structure* (cf. Barsalou & Medin, 1986). Exemplars within a category can vary in how typical or good an example they are of the category.

Perceptual Categories

It is obvious that human beings have color concepts and that they learn to categorize colors in a reasonably consistent way. Are some colors better examples of color categories than are others? For example, are some reds more representative of the category *red* than others? Rosch argued that there are some colors that are best examples of a particular color category, just as there are some forms that best represent a particular form category. These best examples, as noted earlier, are called *prototypes*.

How are prototypes developed? In the case of color Rosch hypothesized that prototypicality might be based on certain properties of the nervous system. A best blue might be best, among all the blues, because the visual system is more sensitive to that particular blue. One can then speculate that, if this is the case, persons from different cultures might respond to the same color prototypes. Rosch was able to test this possibility by doing a series of color experiments with the Dani, a fairly primitive people in New Guinea. The Dani have no color-naming system as such; they differentiate colors only as dark and light. Since they have the same nervous system as persons of western cultures, Rosch argued that they should respond to the same prototypical values of color.

In one experiment, she found that the Dani subjects learned to associate names with color chips more rapidly when the colors were prototypical. For example, subjects learned to respond to a pure green more rapidly than to a color peripheral to the category such as yellow-green, even though they did not initially possess names for the colors. When the color chips were arranged in groups of three, say blue-green, pure green, and yellow-green, subjects learned the prototype more rapidly if it was made central in the category than when one of the other chips was made central. Similar findings were reported in studies of form categories. That is, there are prototypical squares and triangles as well as prototypical colors. The importance of Rosch's studies is that they establish the point that color concepts are internally structured, with some colors being more representative of a color category than others.

Table 8.1

Norms for Goodness-of-Example Rating for Two Semantic Categories

Member	Goodness of Example Rank	Member	Goodness of Example Rank
Furniture		*Vehicle*	
Chair	1.5	Automobile	1
Sofa	1.5	Station wagon	2
Couch	3.5	Truck	3
Table	3.5	Car	4
Easy chair	5	Bus	5.5
Dresser	6.5	Taxi	5.5
Rocking chair	6.5	Jeep	7
Coffee table	8	Ambulance	8
Rocker	9	Motorcycle	9
Love seat	10	Streetcar	10
Chest of drawers	11	Van	11
Desk	12	Honda	12
Bed	13	Cable car	13

From "Cognitive Representations of Semantic Categories," by E. Rosch, *Journal of Experimental Psychology: General*, 1975, *104*, 192–233. Copyright 1975 by the American Psychological Association. Reprinted by permission.

Semantic Categories

We have seen that perceptual categories such as color are organized such that prototypes for various colors exist. Does the same hold true for *semantic* categories? Semantic categories have no apparent perceptual basis as do color and form. So a different approach is required to answer this question and it was developed by Rosch (1975). She simply asked subjects to rate words which were members of categories, such as furniture and vehicles, as to how representative they were of the category. The results were strikingly clear; semantic-category prototypes do exist. For example, subjects agreed that *chair* is very representative of the category furniture whereas *desk* or *chest of drawers* is less representative. A *rocking chair* is regarded as intermediate in representativeness. Subjects also show a high degree of agreement in this task. Examples of norms for two categories, furniture and vehicles, are shown in table 8.1.

Rosch also showed that the time required for a subject to judge whether an item belongs to a given semantic category depends on the degree of category membership. Subjects were presented with statements of the form "A doll is a toy." In some cases the example was a good one, that is, very representative of the category, and in other cases the example was a poor one. Where the statement was *true,* subjects took longer to respond yes when the example was a poor member of the category.

Family Resemblances

Categories can be described in terms of common features or attributes and can also be described in terms of varying levels of generality. Now let us consider the issue of how instances within a category compare to each other. *Family resemblance* refers to how well members of a concept represent it (Rosch & Mervis, 1975). Returning to Table 8.1, we can see that people are in agreement that chairs, sofas, and tables are good examples of furniture. Although you may readily agree with this, the interesting issue is: Why are these good examples? Why, for instance, is a chair a good example and a love seat not as good? Rosch and Mervis (1975) propose that good members of a category are good because they share many attributes with other members of the category and few attributes with members of other categories. Thus a good example is one that has good generality.

Basic-Level Categories

The final issue in this section concerns the organization of categories. Rosch proposes that categories distinguish themselves best at what she calls the *basic level*. The basic level is the level at which a category has the clearest perceptual attributes *and* is most readily distinguished from other categories. A basic-level category is at the most general level and yet still corresponds to real-world objects. For example, consider the hierarchical sequence of categories: *evergreen, pine tree,* and *ponderosa pine tree. Evergreen* is the most inclusive or general of this category. An *evergreen* refers to a great variety of trees, shrubs, and so forth, that remain green year-round. But there are many different kinds of evergreens. A *pine tree* is a much clearer, distinctive category. *Pine trees* have needles, shed some but not all needles in the fall, and usually grow straight. In contrast, a *ponderosa pine,* while distinctive, is similar to other pines such as yellow pine, black pine, and so forth.

Rosch, Mervis, Gray, Johnson, and Boyers-Braem (1976) have noted that in taxonomies basic-level categories have special properties. These categories are present at the most inclusive level, a feature which can be illustrated by one of their studies. Subjects were given the names of several categories, each having varying levels within the category, and were instructed to list all features that applied to each item. For example, one category was furniture, which included such things as chairs. A chair, in turn, includes kitchen chairs, dining-room chairs, living-room chairs, and the like. In this grouping, furniture is the superordinate category, chair is the basic-level category, and kitchen chair is a subordinate. Furniture is a relatively abstract category which does not readily lead to a clear image, and subjects could list few attributes for furniture. In contrast, chair is an inclusive category which readily suggests many features and easily suggests an image.

The basic-level category is thus seen as an intermediate category. It is sufficiently distinctive to be easily distinguished from other categories, and yet it has sufficient number of features so as to be fairly concrete rather than abstract. Rosch argues that basic-level categories are the ones that human beings can most easily use and the ones that allow good, concrete images.

THEORIES OF CATEGORIZATION

In this section we shall examine three types of theories designed to explain how people develop and use categories. These are attribute, prototype, and exemplar theories. A major issue in the study of categorization concerns the kind of *mental representation* or code a person has for categories. Put simply, what kind of mental representation occurs when you think of a category such as tree, car, desk, or holiday?

Attribute Theory

One theory, the classical or definitional theory, contends that you think of a list of *defining attributes* or features. For example, fish swim and have gills. You could list the defining features of fish and then determine whether the particular example meets the criteria of possessing the defining features.

As Medin (1989) notes, "The classical view assumes that mental representations of categories consists of summary lists of features or properties that individually are necessary for category membership and collectively are sufficient to determine category membership" (p. 1470). Early versions of this theory proposed that words were simply abbreviated descriptions. Thus, in order to grasp a word's meaning, one had only to associate the word with its appropriate description or set of features (Devitt & Sterelny, 1989). As an example, the set of features associated with Picasso might be: famous Spanish artist, bald, painter of *Guernica,* the Spanish town that was severely bombed during the Spanish civil war.

Medin (1989) has pointed out some of the major deficiencies of the defining attributes model. First, he noted that it is not always possible to specify defining features. For example, a person may list "made of wood" as a necessary property of violins, and yet not all violins (contrary to popular opinion) are made of wood. Medin's second point was that the classical theory doesn't account for goodness-of-example effects. Some exemplars of a concept are more typical or representative than others, yet the classical view treats all exemplars as equally good because they possess the requisite defining features.

Prototype Theory

The difficulties noted above have led to the development of alternative models of categorization. One of these alternatives is *prototype theory.* Prototype theory states that when a person is presented a set of stimuli for purposes of learning, they abstract the commonalities among the stimulus set and the abstracted representation is stored in memory. This abstracted prototype is like a *schema,* described in the next chapter, and serves to help categorize new information.

A prototype is the best representation of a category. For example, a prototypical fish might be about the size of a trout (12 to 15 inches), have scales and fins, swim in an ocean, a lake, or river, and so forth. We have a general or abstract conception of fish which somehow is typical or representative of the variety of examples with which we are familiar. When given a particular example, we compare it to this abstract prototype of the category. If it is sufficiently similar to the prototype, we then judge it to be an instance of the category. If not, then we reject it as an instance of the category.

Priming Experiments and Prototypes

Attempts to differentiate these two views have been somewhat complex. One way of investigating this issue is to use a matching task in which subjects are required to determine whether two simultaneously presented words are the "same" or "different." The "same" judgment can mean physical identity, such as orange and orange, or categorical identity, such as apple or orange. When subjects are presented with a category label *before* seeing the two words (a procedure called *priming*) the effect of priming on how subjects make same-different judgments can be determined. This procedure is used to infer the kind of mental representation subjects have.

Here is the reasoning behind the procedure: If, as a result of priming, a person's representation of a category is like the list of attributes, then *same* responses to any pair of words should be faster, regardless of their degree of category membership. But if a person's representation of a category is more like that of the prototype, then reaction to the word pairs more typical of the prototype should be faster. The results were that priming facilitated the category matches, but that facilitation was greater for the good (more representative) examples of the category. These results, Rosch argues, favor the prototype interpretation over that of the defining attribute view.

Both Prototypes and Features?

Additional evidence in support of the prototype view comes from an experiment by Rosch and Mervis (1975). They examined the question of whether all members of a given category have features in common. Their experiment required two separate groups of subjects. One group was given a list of twenty instances each from six familiar categories (furniture, vehicles, fruit, weapons, vegetables, and clothing). They were asked to rate how typical or representative each instance was of its respective category. The second group of subjects was also given the same twenty instances and asked to identify the attributes (features) of each instance.

With these two sets of data, Rosch and Mervis then selected the five most typical and the five least typical instances of each category, and for these instances counted how many attributes were common to the most typical and least typical members. The results were strikingly clear. The most typical category members had several common attributes, ranging from three to thirty-six attributes, whereas the least typical category members had few or no common attributes, ranging from only zero to two.

The issue of what kind of representation a person has for a category continues, however, to be a source of active research and debate. Although we have just described evidence in support of a prototype viewpoint, there is still some evidence in support of the idea that a category consists of a list of features. For example, in his feature-list theory, Bourne (1982) describes a concept as a set of relations among a group of relevant features. For a given category, some features will be highly relevant. Thus a concept can be thought of as having a distribution of features, some being much more likely than others. In this theory, what is important in developing a concept is how many relevant, modal features are contained in a category. The more general implication of this argument is that *both* features and prototypes may be part of what a person learns when acquiring a concept. Instead of one or the other, both general categories or prototypes and lists of features may be part of a person's concept.

Exemplar Theory

The support for prototype theory is strong. Much evidence is in agreement with the idea that people do form categories by abstracting prototypes, matching new items to the prototypes, and forming categories that have graded, family resemblance structures. Nevertheless, one additional approach has been proposed, that of exemplar theory, discussed extensively in chapter 7, pages 193–196. The essential difference between exemplar and prototype theory is that exemplar theory does *not* assume the abstraction of a prototype, a best example, but instead assumes that in category learning all instances are stored in memory. New instances encountered are then compared with the set of exemplars stored in memory. Examples of this type of theory are seen in Medin and Schaffer (1978) and Medin and Shoben (1988).

There is some evidence in support of exemplar theories. For example, Medin and Schaffer (1978) conducted several experiments designed to evaluate their version of this theory. In one experiment subjects were shown a set of geometric forms varying in form, size, color, and position. Subjects first classified the patterns into categories and, following this training session, were shown new forms. The critical prediction was that the more similar the training forms, now stored as exemplars, were to the new test forms, the less likely the new forms would be called "new"; this prediction was confirmed. More recent studies by Nosofsky (1988; 1989) also support exemplar theory. For example, Nosofsky found that category decisions made by subjects were based on the similarity of test items to stored exemplars.

Summary of Theories

At present the evidence appears to best support a prototype theory; however, growing support for exemplar theory (Nosofsky, 1989) is also apparent. It is also possible that so-called mixed theories that combine some aspects of both approaches may become necessary (Homa, Sterling, & Trepel, 1981). Reed (1972) has offered the important suggestion that each theoretical approach may be representative of one aspect of categorization and that one approach may be better suited to a particular person or age group. Finally, the pervasive role of context, seen throughout cognitive psychology, has an important bearing on the categorization process (Barsalou, 1982; Barsalou & Medin, 1986). The importance of context in categorization has been noted and it calls attention to the importance of *inductive inferences*. For example, consider a thought experiment described by Murphy and Medin (1985). In this setting, imagine that you are at a party and you see a man jump into a swimming pool with all his clothes on. You would probably categorize the man as drunk, or at least having had too much to drink. However, this categorization is obviously not based on the similarity of the example to the prototype because your prototype for drunk is unlikely to include jumping into swimming pools clothed. Your prototype is most likely to include such things as slurred speech, walking with a stagger, and loud, sometimes aggressive behavior. Thus, the categorization is based on the particular context coupled with your making an inductive inference.

PRACTICAL PRINCIPLES IN FORMING CONCEPTS

It is appropriate to turn to some practical principles and to see how you can usefully apply the principles. In this section four practical points are discussed: (1) thinking of new examples, (2) using both positive and negative instances, (3) using a variety of examples, and (4) highlighting relevant features.

A moment's reflection may lead to the recognition that much of classroom instruction involves going from concepts to examples and from examples back to concepts. Frequently, instructors introduce a concept by briefly defining it and then proceed to illustrate the concept by giving one or two examples. After a few illustrations they proceed to refine and clarify the concept, developing it to the level required by its inherent complexity. Many textbooks also reveal this characteristic. In order that a concept be fully grasped and understood, *it is important that you think of additional examples beyond those presented by an instructor.* The instructor typically has time to present only one or two examples, perhaps a few more at best, and depends upon these examples to provide sufficient information for the essential features of the concept to be abstracted. Unfortunately, you may fail to understand the concept from only one or two examples, or at best you may achieve only a general idea of the concept. The instructor, however, may expect you to achieve a much more detailed and elaborate concept, one that cannot be obtained unless you continue to think of additional examples to aid in refining and enriching the concept.

Obviously, examples must be pertinent to the concept. If you are in doubt about the adequacy of your examples and hence about your full grasp of the concept, you must check by talking with other students or by continued reading in other sources, or by asking the instructor about the adequacy of your ideas. Generating new examples not only helps to sharpen and refine the particular concept, but also provides practice in retrieval of information, a process important for memory. Test questions frequently ask the student to produce new examples or illustrations as distinct from those given in a lecture. Thus, thinking of new examples not only sharpens, refines, and enriches the concept, but also provides practice in the important process of information retrieval.

The sharpness and precision of a concept develops as both positive and negative instances of a concept are processed. In learning a particular concept you must discriminate between instances of the concept and those instances which fail to fit the category. If you see only positive instances of the concept, you then have no opportunity to compare.

Consider teaching a young child the concept of *dog* in which all the examples are positive instances. Assume that the child is shown pictures of a collie, fox terrier, miniature poodle, and German shepherd. The child learns to say "dog" to each picture. But what are the relevant attributes of the concept? What features of these examples control the child's response? Obviously, we cannot be entirely sure in this situation. Moreover, if we show the child a picture of a cat or rabbit, we cannot be sure of the response unless we have additional information about the child's experience with these animals. Indeed, the child may well regard a picture of a cat as another instance of *dog*. It is for this reason that inclusion of carefully selected negative instances is helpful in developing a concept.

In order for a sharply delineated concept to be developed, negative instances must contain, toward a latter stage of training, irrelevant attributes that are likely to be found in the positive instances. Both dogs and cats are four-legged animals, so the property of "four-leggedness" is an irrelevant feature. Cats are frequently smaller than dogs, but obviously not always. Hence size is not a reliable feature. Nor is the presence of tails, paws, or coats of fur. It is clear that differences between cats and dogs are based on the presence and absence of several features in combination. Features like head shape and presence or absence of claws help to distinguish the two. Even with head shape there may be difficulty when a child is first shown a picture of a Pekingese. The more general point is that if concepts are taught only by the use of positive examples or if only positive examples are used for learning concepts, subjects may fail to respond to the *essential* features of a concept and respond instead to a superficial or unessential feature.

The use of a *variety* of examples is also important. The preceding discussion implicitly emphasized the importance of a variety of examples in learning concepts. When only one example is used, learners may easily attend to a nonessential feature of the concept and erroneously assume that they have learned the concept.

How many examples should be used? No simple answer can, of course, be given, because concepts vary in difficulty and complexity. Perhaps the best answer is that examples should be selected so that they encompass the *range* of the concept. Practical limitations will prevent consideration of all possibilities, but by sampling examples along a specific range, you are likely to include highly pertinent ones.

Finally, the highlighting of relevant features in order to make them distinctive is important. From the viewpoint of teaching, a major task is to highlight or emphasize the relevant features of concepts. One objective is to make the relevant aspect or essential parts of a concept more distinctive than the nonessential features. You can highlight the essential features of a concept by verbalizing these features to yourself. This effort can involve trying to define the concept in your own words, as distinct from memorizing a formal definition of the concept.

Relevant features of concepts can be made more distinctive by the *simultaneous presentation* of both positive and negative examples. This simply means that when a particular concept is taught, a positive instance as well as a negative instance should be presented to learners at the same time, allowing them to compare the instances. For example, when the concept *lake* is taught, show pictures of a lake, a stream, a river, and an ocean at the same time. Leaving all the pictures in view minimizes the burden on memory and makes discrimination between the relevant and irrelevant features easier. This superiority of simultaneous over successive presentation of stimulus examples holds for simple discrimination learning as well as for concept learning.

SUMMARY

Chapter 8 described some of the major characteristics of concepts and categories. We examined two major types of concepts, logical and natural concepts. We further saw that many concepts are prototypical and probabilistic.

Categories can be described in a variety of ways. Categories can be defined by perceptual features and appearance. Categories are also based on semantic properties. The mental representation of a category has been described in terms of defining attributes, prototypes and exemplars. How objects can be categorized also depends on the prevailing verbal context. Categories appear to be most easily used at the basic level.

Three important theories of categorization were described: attribute theory, prototype theory, and exemplar theory. There is some experimental evidence that supports (is consistent with) all of the theories. However, prototype theory seems best supported at present with growing support for exemplar theory.

The role of context was seen to play a pervasive role in categorization. Finally, some practical suggestions were made to aid the process of achieving and refining concepts.

MULTIPLE-CHOICE ITEMS

1. When a person has learned to classify a number of items such as apples, bananas, oranges, and so forth, as a member of the category *fruit,* we can say that a(n) _____ has been formed.
   a. hypothesis
   b. theme
   c. retrieval
   d. concept

2. Logical or artificial concepts are usually (but not necessarily) unambiguous, with all exemplars being either members of the concept or not members of the concept. In this case, the concepts are
   a. deterministic
   b. probabilistic

    c.   uncertain

    d.   fuzzy

3.   Labov's study, which required subjects to judge pictures of objects that looked like cups or bowls, showed the importance of _____ in judgmental tasks.

    a.   features

    b.   verbal context

    c.   color

    d.   size

4.   The best or most representative example of a category is called

    a.   a relevant dimension

    b.   a salient cue

    c.   a prototype

    d.   a category

5.   The strategy of focus gambling is one in which a person

    a.   changes only one attribute at a time

    b.   assumes that the first hypothesis is correct

    c.   is limited to only three hypotheses

    d.   varies two or more attributes at a time

6.   Attribute theory of categorization emphasizes

    a.   prototypes

    b.   features

    c.   rules

    d.   schemas

TRUE–FALSE ITEMS

1.   A deterministic concept is one in which an instance can be classified as either a member of the concept or not a member.

2.   A streetcar is likely to be a prototypical example of a vehicle.

3.   Labov's study showed the importance of verbal labels in classifying objects.

4.   A basic-level category does not correspond to or relate to real-world objects.

DISCUSSION ITEMS

1.   Distinguish between artificial and natural concepts.

2.   What makes a concept prototypical?

3. What are the various bases by which objects and events can be categorized?

4. Briefly note the essential features of three types of theories of categorization.

5. Think of two or three examples of how linguistic (verbal) context can influence your judgments in daily experiences.

ANSWERS TO MULTIPLE-CHOICE ITEMS

1. (d) The ability to classify objects properly is a major aspect of concept formation.
2. (a) A concept in which all the exemplars can be classified as a member or not a member of a concept is a deterministic concept.
3. (b) Labov's study showed that the verbal context or label assigned to the object influenced the way it was judged.
4. (c) A prototype is the best or most representative example.
5. (d) Focus gambling involves varying two or more attributes at a time.
6. (b) Features refer to the defining attributes of concepts.

ANSWERS TO TRUE–FALSE ITEMS

1. (True) Deterministic means that an instance is either a member of the category or not a member.
2. (False) A streetcar is not very representative of vehicles.
3. (True) Labov's study showed that the label influenced the kind of judgment subjects made.
4. (False) A basic-level category is general, yet is tied to or related to real-world objects.

9

COMPREHENSION AND KNOWLEDGE

I n this chapter attention is turned to the process of comprehension and how memory and comprehension are related. Consider the following story:

> Papa, as he was affectionately known to his close family, took his usual morning walk through the sleepy, southern town, dressed in his typical white suit, which somehow always looked rumpled. As October began to settle into the Shennandoah Valley, he increasingly found his thoughts turning to his beloved Mississippi and the old plantation. The chill in the air revived memories of warm, early autumn evenings on the veranda with wife and children. He missed Mississippi, and even more, he missed many of the lost values and traditions of the old south. This mountain town in which he now found himself was so different, the pace of life so incongruously rapid, compared to his earlier days in the deep south. These thoughts continued with him as he turned the block toward his large white clapboard house, where he would spend the rest of the day in essential solitude.

Reading, understanding, and remembering passages such as the preceding paragraph are such routine activities that they may appear trivially simple. But for the cognitive psychologist, an adequate description of these processes is a major challenge. To illustrate the complexity of this challenge, reflect for a moment on your comprehension and memory of the paragraph. Without referring to the passage, what do you remember about it? If your response is typical, it will reveal one of the important characteristics of memory for prose and discourse; namely, material is not normally recalled verbatim. When most of us are asked about a book or a movie, we do not launch into a word-by-word account. Rather, we tend to summarize the material, trying to capture the essential *meaning* or *gist* of what occurred.

One thing that is always included in memory of a passage is the central *theme*. The theme is the general topic or subject of the material. Themes are important because they guide both comprehension and memory for material. For example, based on the information given in the passage, you may develop the theme of "an old, unhappy, southerner forced to leave his former home." This theme then affects your interpretation of the entire passage. Given this theme, you reasonably assume that the last phrase about his returning home to solitude implies lack of opportunity to interact with other persons. You may also assume that the man is rather old-fashioned and unsophisticated. Actually, the passage is a semifictional account of the latter days of William Faulkner, who held a prestigious appointment at the University of Virginia. He, of course, was anything but unsophisticated, and his celebrity status forced him to seek solitude in order to work. Here can be seen the essential function of a theme, to guide the assumptions or inferences made in interpretation of material. In this example, if the passage had been entitled "William Faulkner in Charlottesville, Virginia" your interpretation and memory of the passage would have been different.

The process of inferring information is essential to comprehension in order to connect or organize the various ideas expressed in a passage. The inferences can be as simple as assuming that the "he" mentioned throughout the passage refers to "Papa." Such inferences serve to connect various sentences in the passage and are essential to establishing the coherence of the text. Other types of inferences are less directly tied to the text and consist of information derived from assertions in the text. For example, you probably inferred that the character in the passage was old, but reexamination of the material will show no direct reference to the man's age. As you may have inferred, this simple example illustrates the operation of two apparently opposing processes in comprehension. On the one hand, comprehension is the process of *extracting the general meaning* of a communication and discarding details. Memory is organized around the central theme such that the central idea is abstracted and little else is remembered. The effect of this process is to reduce the amount of information remembered while at the same time to ensure that what the material is about is also remembered. The other process *adds information* to the actual communication. An inference, for example, represents additional information not included in the original assertion. Thus, in one case the information is reduced, while in the other it is increased. There is a real parallel here with the concepts of organization and elaboration, which were discussed earlier. In both cases, abstractions from and additions to the presented material are integral aspects of encoding and memory. Let us now examine these processes as they apply to connected discourse.

INTEGRATION AND THEMES IN COMPREHENSION

As just stated, memory of information heard or read is rarely just a verbatim account of the information. Rather, the tendency is to summarize the content and integrate the discrete details into higher-order idea units. Integration of details involves combining related information, and this, of course, requires detecting one or more relationships. One of the important cues to detecting relationships is the theme or general idea of the passage or discourse. The guidance provided by the theme facilitates integration of information during comprehension but at the risk of distorting understanding and memory of the material. Just as with the perceptual processes discussed earlier, an increase in cognitive efficiency sometimes comes at the expense of complete accuracy.

Integration and the Loss of Verbatim Information

The phenomenon of integration can be demonstrated in a number of ways, some of which are familiar. The game of whispering a story to a person who in turn whispers it to another person until several persons have heard it can produce amusing results at final recall because of successive integration of the ideas. Indeed, the final version of the story as told to the last person can be dramatically different from the original version.

Controlled observations of the integration effect are possible in the laboratory, as illustrated by a classic experiment of Bransford and Franks (1971). They presented subjects with sentences which were derived from a complex sentence such as "The girl who lives next door broke the large window on the porch." This complex sentence expresses four propositions or ideas: (1) The girl lives next door, (2) The girl broke the window, (3) The window was large, and (4) The window was on the porch. The complex, four-idea sentence itself was not presented for study, but rather various combinations of one-, two-, and three-idea sentences were provided at input. For example, a subject might see the following sentences: "The girl who lives next door broke the window" (two-idea units), "The window was on the porch" (one-idea unit), and "The girl broke the large window on the porch" (three-idea units). When the ideas expressed by these separate sentences are integrated into a single, higher-order idea unit, the representation becomes a complex, four-idea sentence. To explore whether their subjects were actually integrating the input sentences, Bransford and Franks gave a recognition test for the input sentences.

Several types of sentences were available in the recognition test. Some of the sentences were *old;* these sentences were actually presented during study and from this example included, "The girl who lives next door broke the window." Some test sentences were *new;* these sentences were not presented at study but could be derived from a complex sentence such as, "The girl who lives next door broke the large window." Although this sentence sounds familiar, a look back shows that it was not one of the sample input sentences. Finally, a third type of sentence, *noncase,* was included in the recognition test. The *noncase* sentences were quite dissimilar in meaning from the input sentences, for example, "The boy broke a window in the house next door."

The results of Bransford and Franks's study are presented in figure 9.1. As shown in the figure, the outcome of interest was how confident the subjects were that a given test sentence was actually presented during study. Figure 9.1 illustrates three essential points bearing on the integration phenomenon. First, the subjects were incapable of discriminating *old* and *new* sentences. Since the *new* sentences were derived from the complex, four-idea sentences, this result suggests that the recognition judgments were made

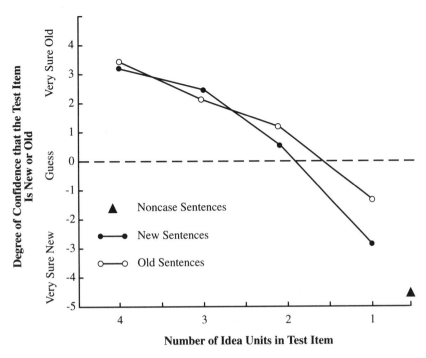

Figure 9.1 Degree of confidence in recognition judgment for *new* and *old* test sentences, depending upon the number of idea units in the sentence. Note that all 4-idea unit test items are new items. (From "The Abstraction of Linguistic Ideas" by J. D. Bransford and J. J. Franks, *Cognitive Psychology,* 1971, *2,* 331–350. Copyright 1971 by Academic Press. Used by permission.)

from memory of the complex sentences. If this assumption is true, integration must have occurred, because the complex sentences were never presented. Consistent with this interpretation is the second major point of the results: namely, as the number of idea units in the *old* and *new* sentences increased, subjects became more confident that all sentences were actually presented. Indeed, the subjects were most confident of the four-idea sentences, the ones which were never actually presented! If the subjects' memory was based on the complex sentences, the test sentences with more idea units would be most like their representation. Finally, the third point is that *noncase* sentences were well recognized as *not* being among the study sentences. Thus, if the meaning of a test sentence is quite discrepant from the study sentences, subjects can easily reject the sentence.

The conclusion from this experiment is that persons store as a unit different statements related to the same idea. Individual sentences are not always maintained in memory, but the *ideas expressed by the sentences are integrated into a single representation of the general idea expressed by a group of sentences.* The implication of this conclusion is that memory for individual sentences is quite poor, but memory for a general idea is good. *In other words, integration produces the gist of the message, and it is the gist, not the details, which is well remembered.*

Themes: The Central Idea

Among the major influences on how ideas are integrated is the theme or central idea of a passage or conversation. The theme may occur as the title of a passage or as the lead sentence of a paragraph, or the theme may be abstracted as the recurring, dominant idea of a passage or discussion. Regardless of the form in which it appears, the theme anchors the information in knowledge. Once the central idea is known, the various statements can be organized around that central idea. A good deal of evidence is now available indicating the importance of themes in comprehension and memory.

The theme of a passage is the most likely information to be remembered. This is simply to say that the central idea of a passage is remembered—not a terribly surprising fact. It is also the case, however, that the thematic information is less subject to forgetting over time. In short, memory for a passage will generally begin with the theme of the passage.

Once the theme is retrieved, it can then aid further reconstruction of the material. For example, a friend might say, "Do you remember the conversation we had this morning?" and you respond, "Oh, yes, we were talking about your party last night." From this theme you can then go on to reconstruct some of the details of the conversation. The influence of themes on the reconstruction of passages is illustrated in an experiment by Sulin and Dooling (1974). Subjects in this experiment read the following passage:

> *Carol Harris's Need for Professional Help*   Carol Harris was a problem child from birth. She was wild, stubborn, and violent. By the time Carol turned eight, she was still unmanageable. Her parents were very concerned about her mental health. There was no good institution for her problem in her state. Her parents finally decided to take some action. They hired a private teacher for Carol. (R. A. Sulin and D. J. Dooling, "Intrusions of a Thematic Idea in Retention of Prose," *Journal of Experimental Psychology,* 1974, *103,* 255–262.)

A second group of subjects read the same passage except *Helen Keller* was substituted for *Carol Harris.* A week later the subjects were given a recognition test which included the sentence "She was deaf, dumb, and blind." Only 5 percent of the subjects who read the *Carol Harris* passage claimed to have seen this sentence. Of the subjects reading the *Helen Keller* passage, over 50 percent of the subjects thought they had seen the sentence.

These kinds of data encourage the generalization that the theme is the focus of the memory representation and much of what is remembered is reconstructed from the theme.

The importance of themes to both comprehension and memory has been illustrated dramatically by Bransford and Johnson (1973). Consider the following passage:

> The procedure is quite simple. First, you arrange things into different groups. Of course, one pile may be sufficient, depending upon how much there is to do. If you have to go somewhere else due to lack of facilities, that is the next step; otherwise, you are pretty well set. It is important not to overdo things. That is, it is better to do too few things at once than too many. At first the whole procedure will seem complicated. Soon, however, it will become just another facet of life. After the procedure is completed, one arranges the materials into different groups again. Then they can be put into their appropriate places. Eventually they will be used once more, and the whole cycle will have to be repeated. (J. D. Bransford and M. K. Johnson, "Considerations of Some Problems of Comprehension," in *Visual Information Processing,* edited by W. G. Chase. New York: Academic Press, 1973.)

Although you can understand the individual sentences in this passage, the relationship among the sentences is unclear, and consequently integration of idea units is virtually impossible. This is because the passage is written such that the theme is quite obscure, and thus the passage is difficult to understand. Subjects in the Bransford and Johnson experiment had a very difficult time remembering this passage. However, if the title "Washing Clothes" is supplied, the passage becomes both more comprehensible and memorable.

Themes are central to comprehension and serve as the focus for organizing memory for discourse. Good use of this observation can be made in class by always extracting and understanding the theme of each subsection of the material. In brief, the first thing to do when trying to understand a lecture or reading assignment is to know what it is about. Actively construct a hierarchy of themes, relating each topic to its superordinate. For example, the general topic of memory was discussed, with the subordinate topic encoding processes and its subtopics organization and individual item processing. By setting up such a hierarchy of themes and understanding the relationship among them, you are in a much better position to appreciate details such as individual experiments and their implications. Indeed, as simple as this activity sounds, it is at the heart of what is called understanding, and if you will be aware of its importance, you can easily increase both comprehension and memory for all kinds of materials.

PRESUPPOSITIONS AND INFERENCES

When a communication is understood, the directly asserted information is usually elaborated such that what is understood goes far beyond what was said. For example, to understand most statements requires that other factors are *assumed* or *presupposed* to be true. The question "Have you finally stopped smoking?" obviously presupposes that you once smoked. Although the presupposition is not expressed explicitly, memory for some event is likely to include presupposed information. Furthermore, each assertion or statement implies further information, and given those implications, inferences which subsequently may be remembered are made. With both presuppositions and inferences *more* is remembered than was actually said.

Presuppositions and Eyewitness Testimony

Many statements can be understood only if other things are presupposed to be true. For example, when a professor says, "Congratulations, Smith, you have made the highest grade again," the professor is asserting that Smith made the highest grade this time, and the presupposition is that Smith had made the highest grade in the past. A presupposition must be made in order for an assertion to be understood fully. Either or both can be remembered and either or both may be true or false. Smith may or may not have made the highest grade this time, and Smith may or may not have made the highest grade in the past. Professors have been known to make these kinds of mistakes. In other situations, false presuppositions can have more serious consequences.

Consider the effect of eyewitness testimony upon a jury. If the jury must make a presupposition to comprehend the testimony of a witness, that presupposition may be remembered and later influence the decision. Thus, a clever attorney may try to discredit a witness by asking, "Do you still drink heavily?" The witness must deny not only the assertion, but also the presupposition. An indication of the subtlety and power of presuppositions on eyewitness accounts has been illustrated nicely by Loftus's research. For example, Loftus and Palmer (1974) showed subjects a film of an automobile accident and then questioned them about what they had seen. One of the questions was "About how fast were the cars going when they *(hit, smashed)* each other?" Some of the subjects saw the verb *hit* and others saw the verb *smashed*. The subjects who were asked in the context of *hit* gave lower estimates of the speed than those asked about *smashing* cars. Furthermore, the subjects who saw *smashed* remembered seeing broken glass in the scene; those who saw *hit* generally did not. No broken glass was actually depicted in the movie. The subjects in this experiment were influenced by presuppositions invoked by the verbs *hit* and *smashed*.

Table 9.1

Speed Estimates for Critical Questions with Various Verbs After Watching Film Strip of Car Accident.

Verb	Average Speed Estimate
Smashed	40.8 miles/hr.
Collided	39.3
Bumped	38.1
Hit	34.0
Contacted	31.8

(From "Reconstruction of automobile destruction: An example of the interaction between language and memory" by E. F. Loftus and J. C. Palmer, *Journal of Verbal Learning and Verbal Behavior, 1974 13,* 585–589. Reprinted by permission of the publisher and author.)

Smashed presupposes a more violent collision, a fact which influences both estimate of speed and amount of damage. This presupposition then appears to dramatically but subtly influence memory for the actual event.

The results of Loftus and Palmer's (1974) study are summarized in Table 9.1. The table shows the speed estimates depending on the verb used in the question.

There are several possible interpretations of these results and we shall consider two of them. One is simply a response bias interpretation which says that subjects really were uncertain of the speed of the car, but biased their estimates in the appropriate direction of the suggestive verb. A second possibility is that the verb actually changed the subjects' memory of the scenes in the film. In this case, the subjects truly remembered the severity of the accident. Both the *response bias* and *memory change* accounts have important implications for how we might regard the reliability of eyewitness testimony; however, Loftus and Palmer want to interpret the results as being due to an actual alteration in memory.

In a second phase of the experiment, Loftus and Palmer questioned their subjects a week later. Here they were asked more questions about the film but were not shown the film again. With the new questions, the critical item was the query "Did you see any broken glass?" No broken glass was shown in the film and 80% of the subjects answered "no" correctly. However, the majority of those who answered "yes" were in the "smashed" group. Loftus and Palmer conclude that what is being remembered is the *blended* or integrated memory of two events, memory for the original film plus memory for the additional information that is inherent in the question asked later. These two memories are thought to be blended over time so that they are not distinguishable as separate memories. All we have, then, is a single blended memory for the event.

The status of this interpretation continues to be controversial and open to question. On the one hand, Loftus and her colleagues have continued to argue for the blended, integrated memory interpretation (Loftus, Burns, & Miller, 1978; Loftus, Donders, Hoffman, & Schooler, 1989). In contrast, it has been argued that in such situations people may have both a blended memory as well as two separate memories of the events. Moreover, critics of Loftus's interpretation have argued that these findings do not necessarily reflect an integration process but are the result of response bias or other problems in the design of such experiments (e.g., Berkerian & Bowers, 1983; McCloskey & Zaragoza, 1985; Zaragoza & McCloskey, 1989).

McCloskey and Zaragoza (1985) argue that misleading post-event information doesn't really affect the original memory, but rather simply biases a person's tendency to respond in a particular way. They believe that, in these experiments, people tend to forget the original information over time, and that, by the time of testing the effects of post-event information, they are simply biased by the phrasing of the test question. Their argument has merit to the extent that it can be demonstrated that a control group of subjects has largely forgotten the original memory. On the other hand, it is possible that the post-event information can bias the original memory in certain situations. Arguments over the fate of the original information and the meaning of Loftus' results continue to be controversial. Whether it is actual memories, beliefs, or just reports that are being affected continues to be disputed. Regardless of the ultimate interpretations of these results, what is clear is that misleading information does change what a witness *reports,* regardless of how this is to be interpreted.

It should also be noted that Loftus and Palmer's (1974) findings are similar to those of Ellis and his colleagues (e.g., Ellis, 1968; Ellis, 1973; Ellis & Daniel, 1971; Daniel, 1972) in studies of perceptual memory. His studies have provided evidence that associating verbal labels with visual forms can influence both the perception and memory of such stimuli. More generally, his studies show that verbal labels can influence the interpretation of visual form stimuli and thus affect recognition memory. Moreover, in Ellis' studies the effects are not due to response bias because, in general, a forced-choice recognition procedure is used, that is, all subjects must make a recognition choice in the test so response bias is comparable in the various experimental conditions. With a forced-choice procedure, each subject *must* make a selection; thus, if response bias effects are present, they are equal across all experimental conditions. In these studies, a verbal label is typically presented *with* the visual form, the to-be-remembered event, whereas in Loftus's studies verbal context is presented *after* seeing a film or other target information. In both cases, the encoding effects of verbal context is present. We shall return to this issue again, in Chapter 11.

Inferences

Understanding a statement usually leads to certain conclusions or implications. If you say, "Jim does not own one single shirt with a polo pony on it," I may infer from this statement that it is important to you that a person own such a shirt and then go on to attribute to you a number of personality characteristics common to people who have such beliefs. Clearly, I have then gone far beyond your simple and rather straightforward statement. In fact, my inference may be totally wrong. You actually may have been expressing admiration for Jim, in which case a completely different set of inferences would be appropriate. In either case, this simple example illustrates the prevalence of inferences in comprehension and subsequent memory. Virtually every statement anyone utters or writes leads the listener or reader to certain inferences.

Notice the distinction between an inference and a presupposition. A presupposition is knowledge activated by an assertion in order to understand it. An inference is knowledge that is activated once the assertion is understood. Certain types of inferences, known as *logical inferences,* must follow from what was said. Logical inferences are, in a sense, demanded by the assertion. For example, the assertion that "John's actions forced Mr. Pettigrew to fire him" logically implies that John was fired. Unlike a presupposition, you do not have to think "John was fired" in order to understand the assertion, but the assertion does demand the inference because it would make little sense to conclude the assertion with "but Mr. Pettigrew did not fire John."

As an example of the effect of logical inference, consider the following experiment by Bransford, Barclay, and Franks (1972). Subjects saw sentences such as, "Three turtles rested on a floating log and a fish swam beneath it." Subjects were then given recognition memory tests for new, logically implied sentences such as, "Three turtles rested on a floating log and a fish swam beneath them." A large number of the subjects consistently claimed that they had seen the new sentences, which suggests that the logical inferences had been constructed and stored when the original sentences were presented.

Not all inferences, however, are logically demanded. Some, perhaps the majority, of the inferences are invited by the assertion. This second type of inference is known as *pragmatic inference.* A pragmatic inference does not have to follow from an assertion, but rather is reasonable based on world knowledge. For example, to say that "Bill and Mary were looking at engagement rings" in no way demands the inference that Bill and Mary are to be engaged; however, that inference is certainly reasonable given what is known about the world. A large number of experiments have been reported which demonstrate that pragmatic inferences are remembered as part of the original event.

As an example of these studies, Johnson, Bransford, and Solomon (1973) presented subjects with sentences such as, "John was trying to fix the birdhouse. He was pounding the nail when his father came out to watch him and to help him do the work." This passage clearly implies, although it does not logically demand, that John was using a hammer. Subjects later falsely recognized the sentence "John was using a hammer to fix the birdhouse when his father came out to watch him and help him do the work." As with the logical inference, the pragmatic inference is remembered as if it had actually occurred.

Recognition of the prevalence and power of inferential processing is extremely important in understanding communication. Much of what is communicated is in fact left unsaid. Speakers rely on listeners to draw appropriate inferences and listeners generally trust the inferences drawn from speakers' statements. The ability to communicate without explicitly saying everything we are trying to convey enormously enhances efficiency in communication. As with other cognitive processes, increased efficiency comes at the cost of increased error. Again, the error and the efficiency result from the diametrically opposed processes of abstraction and integration on the one hand and elaboration through inference on the other hand.

Miscommunication in Advertising: Inferences in Action

Surely all of us occasionally say things in such a way that the listener is in a position of inferring information which may not be entirely accurate. Interestingly, we do not consider this a case of blatant lying, but simply claim that the listener is misled. To establish whether a speaker was indeed dishonest, the speaker's intentions must be discovered, a very hard thing to do if the actual assertion is in fact accurate. Consequently, it is easy to mislead either when sufficient information to evaluate an assertion is intentionally withheld or when vigilance about drawing inferences is not observed. Good advertising copy provides an interesting case in point.

Among our favorites is a classic running television commercial for a pain reliever. The script asserts, "This product contains more of the pain reliever that doctors recommend. You can't buy a more effective pain reliever without a prescription." The last sentence encourages the inference that this product is the most effective pain reliever to be bought without a prescription, but this clearly is not what the sentence asserts. Further, the pain reliever that doctors recommend most is aspirin, and beyond some maximum dosage, which can be obtained from two or three tablets of any brand, additional aspirin has little effect. By not mentioning that the pain reliever in question is aspirin, the advertisement sets us up to infer that the product contains some esoteric drug and lots of it. Successfully competing in the aspirin business is difficult, since all of the brands are very much alike, and thus any competitive edge provided by advertising is helpful, including misleading information. Are we really susceptible to such techniques?

Harris (1977) reported an experiment which indicates that persons are quite susceptible to the inferences created by advertising assertions. Harris used the following text from a Listerine commercial:

> "Wouldn't it be great," asks the mother, "if you could make him cold proof? Well, you can't. Nothing can do that. [Boy sneezes.] But there is something that you can do that may help. Have him gargle with Listerine Antiseptic. Listerine can't promise to keep him cold free, but it may help him fight off colds. During the cold-catching season, have him gargle twice a day with full-strength Listerine. Watch his diet, see he gets plenty of sleep, and there's a good chance he'll have fewer colds, milder colds this year."

Harris substituted "Gargoil" for "Listerine" in the text, but otherwise the advertisement was heard verbatim. Although the advertisement never asserts that "Gargoil" prevents colds, every subject in the experiment responded yes to the question "Does gargling with Gargoil prevent colds?" Does this commercial perpetuate a falsehood?

Regardless of the source of the information, the point of this discussion is that the elaborative nature of comprehension can be and is used to imply potentially inaccurate information. Based on what you now know about comprehension and memory, you are in the position of protecting yourself against this possibility by directly questioning assertions and carefully analyzing your own inferences.

THE LOCUS OF CONSTRUCTIVE PROCESSES

A question of some interest is: Do inferences actually occur at encoding or at retrieval? For example, you know that a friend has an examination in a particular class and you later see the person leaving the class in an obvious state of pleasure. Do you immediately infer that the examination went well and remember the inference, or do you later remember what you actually saw and based on that memory infer that the examination went well? Beginning with Bartlett's (1932) early work, retrieval has been assumed to be reconstructive; that is, inference is assumed to occur during retrieval. More recent research suggests that constructive processes also occur during encoding.

Constructive Processes at Encoding

In the previously mentioned work of Bransford and Johnson, paragraphs that were very difficult to comprehend in the absence of a title or theme were presented either with or without the title. Further, the title was given either during the study period or at the time of the memory test. Persons were better able to remember the paragraph when the title was given during the study period than at the time of the memory test. Since the title facilitates making inferences which render the paragraph more comprehensible and memorable, this result suggests that inferences occur during the study phase itself, that is, at encoding.

Another line of evidence for constructive processes at input comes from the work of Kintsch and students (Kintsch, 1974). Consider an experiment by Baggett (1975) which is representative of this research. Subjects saw a series of picture frames which told a story, much like a newspaper cartoon. One story showed a rather long-haired man entering a barbershop, then sitting in a barber chair, and finally leaving the barbershop. The sequence is depicted in figure 9.2. In a subsequent recognition test, subjects also saw a frame depicting the actual haircut, which had not been presented originally. Persons were reasonably good at remembering that this frame was not present at input *if* they were given the test immediately after study. But if the test occurred a week after the initial presentation, most persons claimed that they had seen the haircutting picture. Baggett suggests that when they are tested immediately, subjects are able to discriminate the old pictures from a plausible inference scene because they still have some of the surface information about the pictures in memory. After a week, however, the surface information decays, and the discrimination between what actually occurred and the inferences drawn from what occurred can no longer reliably be made. This interpretation, then, emphasizes the storage of inferences during input or encoding. Similar results and interpretations from stories presented verbally were also described by Kintsch (1974).

Reconstructive Processes at Retrieval

Equally clear, however, is that inferences and presuppositions can be induced at retrieval. In recounting an event, memory for what actually happened may lead to enrichment of the account with plausible inferences. For example, we may remember that Bill and Mary were seen looking at engagement rings and, on the basis of this memory, tell someone that they are to be married. In this case, information is reconstructed from what was remembered about the actual event. Inferences which occur during this type of reconstructive retrieval begin with memory for a specific aspect of the actual event.

Study Sequence   Test

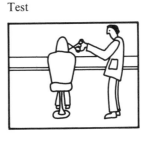

Figure 9.2 Sequence of pictures used by Baggett to examine inferences. Note that the test picture is not present in the study sequence, but can be inferred to have occurred between the third and fourth frames. (From "Memory for Explicit and Implicit Information in Picture Stories" by P. Baggett, *Journal of Verbal Learning and Verbal Behavior,* 1975, *14,* 538–548. Copyright 1975 by Academic Press. Used by permission.)

Other cases in which inference clearly occurs at output are the situations represented by the Loftus and Palmer (1974) experiment discussed earlier. In some instances, the way in which memory is probed leads to responses which are inconsistent with the original event. For example, as we noted, Loftus and Palmer were able to influence memory for speed of the automobiles by changing the verb in their question from *hit* to *smash*. Actually, it is not so clear that the question distorted the subjects' "memory of the speed"; the subjects may not have stored such information directly. For example, McEwan and Yuille (1981) have shown that subjects are not influenced by presuppositions if they have clear memory for an event. If subjects can remember only that an accident occurred and are forced to answer the question, their estimate of speed is really a guess which is heavily influenced by the presuppositions demanded by the verb. The point here is that some aspect of an event which was not clearly attended and stored may subsequently be reported incorrectly, and the magnitude and direction of the inaccuracy can be influenced by the questions asked of memory.

It would seem, then, that *inferences and presuppositions occur during both input and output. Memory is constructive in that events are elaborated with inferences and presuppositions in order to comprehend. Memory is also reconstructive in that inferences are added to what is retrieved about the original event.* This conclusion suggests that real-world memory is always potentially suspect, is at the mercy of the comprehension process, and is likely to be distorted. Such a conclusion appears different from the impression gained from the previous discussion of studies based on lists of words. Are the differences between these two situations so great that the concepts derived from list studies cannot be applied to memory based on comprehension of higher-order discourse? Let us examine this issue.

CONCEPTS FROM DISCOURSE AND LIST MEMORY

The most striking difference between research using connected discourse and research using a list of discrete items, such as words, is the level of verbatim memory in the two tasks. As would be expected from experiences in retelling stories, the research on memory of stories or passages shows clearly that the account is not usually recalled verbatim, but rather major themes are selected, related ideas are integrated, and the actual event is elaborated with inferences and presuppositions. Is this not considerably different from studies in which persons appear either to remember a word or not remember it? The answer is yes and no.

The complexity of connected discourse, either prose or conversation, far exceeds that of a simple word list. Hence, studies of comprehension and memory for connected discourse allow important observations and insights into the complex psychological processes brought to bear in interpreting normally encountered information. For example, list studies have never produced the dramatic evidence for elaboration and addition of self-generated information that was evident from the outset in studies of connected discourse. On the other hand, some concepts derived from studies of list memory have been at the heart of the analysis of prose memory.

The general view of comprehension as an active process of transforming the surface material into a meaningful psychological representation is, in principle, the same as the encoding of single words into their conceptual representation. In both cases, the information is actively transformed and retained in an abstract, semantic code. Furthermore, in both cases the abstract semantic code is assumed to be elaborated upon and organized in accord with the existing knowledge structure. The work from levels of processing on elaboration of individual words leads to the same sort of idea about memory as does the work on inferences in prose memory. The organization of word lists and abstraction of a superordinate category is similar conceptually to the integration of idea units and the abstraction of themes. In summary, it is reassuring to understand that theoretical descriptions of memory for words and for connected discourse converge on the same basic ideas about human memory.

SCHEMAS IN COMPREHENSION AND MEMORY

Much of what we have just said leads to a discussion of the role of schemas in comprehension and memory. A *schema* refers to a large body of organized information people have about various concepts, events, or knowledge domains. For example, we can be said to have a schema for vacations, for basketball games, or going on a picnic, to mention a few instances. Our schema for a vacation might include a series of events such as: plan travel with wife (or friend), talk to travel agent, decide where to travel, buy tickets, pack luggage, fly to specific vacation spot, all the activities during vacation, pack, and return home. Since a schema represents an organized body of knowledge about something, a schema can serve to facilitate the encoding of new information, to aid in making inferences about material being processed, and to affect the retrieval of information which is pertinent to the schema (cf. Ellis, 1987; Mandler, 1984; Alba & Hasher, 1983). More generally, we will see that schemas play an important role in the process of comprehension.

The structure of a schema is not necessarily hierarchical, as say in a hierarchical model of semantic memory such as the TLC model, discussed in chapter 7. There we noted that information was organized in terms of a superordinate-subordinate hierarchy. A schema is frequently organized *temporally* or *spatially* (Mandler, 1984; Rabinowitz & Mandler, 1983). For example, *event* sequences such as taking a vacation or going to a baseball game can be organized into temporally ordered sequences of events, as noted in the above illustration. Such schemas have been labeled *scripts* by Schank and Abelson (1977) and a typical example is a restaurant script that describes the temporal sequence of activities we expect to occur when going to a restaurant. *Scene* schemas refer to the physical or spatial relations among objects in space (Mandler, 1984) such as the relations among a sofa, chairs, and coffee table in a typical living room. Similarly, a football stadium has a playing field surrounded by seats, refreshment booths, and areas for newswriters. As Maki (1990) has shown, the relevance of script actions is an important factor in influencing what we remember.

Scene Schemas

The role of a schema in memory is illustrated nicely in an experiment by Brewer and Treyens (1981). Their subjects were brought into a small room and told that it was the office of the experimenter where they were to wait until called upon to participate in the experiment. The experimenter indicated that he or she would check in the laboratory to see if the previous subject had finished. After 35 seconds the experimenter returned and took the waiting subject to a nearby room. The subject was then asked to write down everything that could be remembered about the room. The important question was: What would be remembered? Brewer and Treyens reasoned that subjects would be influenced by their schema of what a typical office contains. It was therefore expected that subjects would do well at recalling items in the office that were consistent with the schema of an office. In contrast, it was expected that subjects would be poorer in recalling items that were not consistent with the schema. And this is just what they found. All but one of the subjects recalled that the office had a desk, or walls, or a chair. In contrast, only eight of the thirty subjects accurately recalled that it contained a skull, an item not typical of most offices. And a third of the subjects said the office contained books, which it did not. Thus a schema can facilitate accurate recall, but can also lead to incorrect recall of items that are consistent with the schema.

Event Schemas

We have just noted that events, scenarios, or action sequences, such as going on a vacation, can be represented as schemas. For instance, a going-to-Hawaii schema involves a list of events which involve planning the trip, flying to Hawaii, going to a hotel, activities in Hawaii, preparing to return, and returning home. The list below indicates a possible sequence of items:

> Visit travel agent
> Discuss a Hawaiian vacation
> Read travel brochures
> Select vacation package
> Buy tickets and hotel package

Pack for trip
Leave for airport
Board plane
Watch in-flight movie
Arrive in Honolulu

Receive lei greeting
Take taxi to hotel
Register at hotel
Go to room
Unpack luggage

Put on swimsuit
Go to beach
Swim in ocean
Try to surfboard
Walk on beach

Go to luau
Dine on festive foods
Watch show and dances
Drink Mai-Tais
Join in dances

Rent car
Drive around island
Go to Polynesian Cultural Center
Watch surfers at Makapu
Look at fields of pineapple
And so on . . .

Jean Mandler and her colleagues have made extensive studies of memory and comprehension of event schemas (cf. Mandler, 1984). In one study, Rabinowitz and Mandler (1983) examined the memory of event scenarios that were presented to subjects as either organized sequences of phrases or as randomly presented phrases. In the first condition, subjects were presented a series of phrases that were schematically organized in accordance with a particular schema. Five phrases were presented for each of five schemas without the schema title. Below are shown two examples of the five schemas:

Going Skiing
Go to mountains
Put on down jackets
Buy lift tickets
Ski down slopes
Drink hot chocolate

Going to a Baseball Game
Put on Padres' cap
Go to stadium
Buy admission ticket
Watch baseball game
Eat peanuts

In the second condition subjects heard the same twenty-five phrases, but they were randomly presented so that subjects were without benefit of the schematic organization present in the first condition. Following presentation of the phrases, subjects in both groups were asked to recall as many of the phrases as possible. In this fashion, Rabinowitz and Mandler could observe the benefits to memory from schematic organization, should it occur.

The results were quite clear. From a possible recall of 25 phrases, subjects who were given the schematic organization recalled 19.2 phrases whereas the random group recalled only 12.5 items. This same magnitude of difference was apparent whether verbatim (exact) recall was measured or whether paraphrases were allowed. In addition, the two groups differed in the amount of schematic clustering in recall, which is a measure of whether they tended to recall the phrases of a given schema, as a group, before recalling another schema. Where perfect clustering would yield an index of 1.00, subjects in the schematic group showed a clustering index of .97 whereas subjects in the random group showed a clustering index of only .27.

The effect of schematic organization, as just described, is present regardless of whether the schema represents pleasant or unpleasant activities. Using both pleasant and unpleasant schemas, Ellis et al. (1987) found that the schematic organization effect appeared with unpleasant phrases as well. Examples of the unpleasant phrases are shown below:

Going to Dentist	*Getting Traffic Ticket*
Go to appointment	Run stoplight
Sit in dentist chair	Hear loud siren
Get novocaine shot	See angry officer
Have tooth drilled	Hand over license
Pay bill	Get heavy fine

Again, a total of five schemas were employed with five phrases in each schema, for a total possible correct of 25 phrases. Subjects in the schematic organization condition recalled a total of 12.7 phrases, while those in the random group recalled only 7.1 phrases. This difference was preserved regardless of whether verbatim or paraphrase scoring was used. One interesting additional point is that subjects recalled only 50 percent of the unpleasant phrases whereas they recalled about 75 percent of the pleasant phrases, indicating that the affective character of the material was also important in influencing recall. The role of emotional factors in memory and cognition is described in chapter 12, but we note that in this setting subjects recall more of the pleasant or happy phrases than the unpleasant phrases.

SCHEMA THEORY

Let us return to the idea of a schema. Schema theory assumes that what is encoded in memory is strongly influenced by schemas (knowledge frameworks) that help select and interpret new incoming information so that it is reasonably consistent with one's schema. Because schema theory emphasizes selectivity in encoding, it is able to account for memory distortions and inaccuracies.

In the classic work of Frederick Bartlett (1932), the schematic nature of the recall of stories and folktales was demonstrated. In his studies, subjects were presented with a story and they were later asked to recall the story over several sessions. In other experiments, Bartlett had subjects tell the story to another person who, in turn, told it to another, and so forth. This procedure is sometimes used in dinner party games where one person passes on a story to the adjacent person and the story is repeated in this fashion around the dinner table until it returns to the originator of the story. The original story is then compared with the final recall, usually accompanied by laughter because the final story is sometimes quite different and distorted from the original story. Indeed, its meaning and intent can be completely changed.

In one study, Bartlett examined how people recall a legend entitled "The War of the Ghosts," which is a story about a tribe of North American Indians. What Bartlett found was that the recall of the story differed in several substantial ways from the original story. The story became more compact, more organized or sharpened during recall. Many details were dropped out, and distortions in recall occurred. Bartlett interpreted his findings by concluding that subjects form a schema when reading the story which they try to relate to their existing store of knowledge. The schema becomes assimilated into the person's knowledge structure, and thus becomes part of what is remembered.

Four Processes in Schema Theory

The schema concept has been used in a variety of ways since the time of Bartlett. There is no generally agreed upon formal definition of a schema; however, there are four basic processes that are evident in all schema theories according to Alba and Hasher (1983). They note that, typically, schema theories are characterized by the four processes of (1) *selection,* (2) *abstraction,* (3) *interpretation,* and (4) *integration.* A brief description of these four processes will help make the concept of a schema more explicit.

The first process, *selection,* emphasizes that information is encoded selectively in accordance with an existing schema. Whether or not a particular piece of information will be selected for encoding depends upon the existence of a relevant schema, the activation of that schema, and the importance or perceived relevance of the incoming information with respect to the schema (Alba & Hasher, 1983). A considerable amount of evidence supports this process and some of the evidence has already been discussed in this chapter. The research on themes and prior knowledge (e.g., Bransford & Johnson, 1973; Sulin & Dooling, 1974) is quite supportive of and consistent with the idea of a schema.

Once information is selected for encoding, it is processed further by way of *abstraction* in which the gist or meaning is coded and many nonessential details are dropped out of memory. The central issue here is: Just how abstractive is memory? Although there are a number of experiments which demonstrate the abstractive character of memory (e.g., Sachs, 1967; Kintsch, 1974), there also are experiments which show that humans can retain detail as well as the schema. In short, memory is not completely abstractive in all situations. For example, most of us still retain the details of overlearned messages such as the Pledge of Allegiance or the Lord's Prayer and they may persist for years (Rubin, 1977). Other examples from Rubin's studies of long-term memory for details of rhymes and songs were discussed in Chapter 5.

It is widely recognized that humans *interpret* and elaborate upon information during encoding and even after the information is stored. We have already seen how interpretations work because they are typically inferences, which were described earlier. With respect to schema theory the issue can be stated as follows: To what extent do humans make inferences and is inference making an obligatory process? There are a number of studies that show that humans do make inferences during comprehension (e.g., Johnson et al., 1973). Also, schema theories assume the process of *integration* in which information that remains after encoding will be somehow integrated with previously acquired relevant information (e.g., Bransford & Franks, 1971; Loftus, Miller & Burns, 1978). Finally, it should be pointed out that Alba and Hasher are actually critics of schema theory; their concern is with schema theory's lack of precision and with the evidence for good verbatim recall in some situations. Despite this, their review of the four processes in schema theory is quite useful.

Some critics of schema theory claim that the schema concept is mentalistic. This can be true *if* the concept is used in an uncritical fashion. However, properly used, the schema concept is no more mentalistic than other concepts in psychology. A schema is simply an *inference* from behavior. In short, a schema is like other concepts in psychology such as habits, expectancies, drives, motives, learning, and so forth, in that it is an abstract concept used to help summarize experimental findings.

Let us summarize up to this point. The concept of schema has been and continues to be a valuable, integrating idea in understanding memory and comprehension. Schema theory has had a strong impact on our understanding of memory and comprehension and has raised a host of new and important questions. Schema theory has nevertheless been less precise than desirable and lacks a formal structure that would permit more careful evaluation. In brief, schema theory provides a useful though imprecise picture of how memory and comprehension operate.

Brewer & McNamara's Taxonomy

Brewer and McNamara (1984) have offered a taxonomy of memory processes similar to the four processes described by Alba and Hasher. They propose *five* such processes or mechanisms which lead to the various effects of schemas just described. Their taxonomy of processes consists of (1) *selective attention*, (2) *integration*, (3) *framework effects*, (4) *guiding retrieval*, and (5) *output editing*. We note that (1) selective attention and (2) integration processes are like those described by Alba and Hasher (1983) so we will comment on only the three remaining processes. Brewer and McNamara point out that a (3) schema can act as a scaffolding framework in memory that better preserves incoming information in memory. For instance, if you have read a good deal about the new model cars this year, in preparation for buying a new car, then you can better understand and remember what a salesperson tells you when you go to the car showroom. In addition (4) schemas can better guide the retrieval process in order to locate information in memory. In the above example, you would be better able to recall specific information about a car with a well-developed schema; moreover, you would be better able to ask the salesperson good questions. And finally, (5) schemas can influence what you say when talking or trying to decide what to say (output editing) once you have recalled information. In this case, the course of the discussion you have with the car salesperson can be readily influenced by what kind of schema you have about cars in general and about the specific cars at a particular dealership.

Schema Pointer Plus Tag: Graesser's Model

In recent years Arthur Graesser and his colleagues have developed a model of schemas designed to account for the processing of prose materials. This model is somewhat complex so we will deal only with its general features. *What is fundamental about Graesser's model is that it deals with the way humans incorporate both typical information consistent with an existing schema and atypical information that is unique and unrelated to the schema.* This model was first described by Graesser (1981) and then developed in a number of subsequent reports (e.g., Graesser & Bower, 1990; Nakamara & Graesser, 1985).

The schema pointer plus tag (SP+T) model makes several assumptions, beginning with the idea that people have a large number of content schemas in memory which correspond to different domains of knowledge. It is further assumed that each specific memory representation contains a *pointer* to the specific schema or script and *tagged actions* that are unrelated or irrelevant to the script. When new information is being processed, the SP+T model assumes three kinds of processes can occur in incorporating this information into memory. (1) First, it is assumed that when this information enters the memory system, that a *pointer* specifies which of the existing schemas best fits the incoming information. This process then accounts for the assimilation of information into a schema. (2) The second process deals with recognizing that some of the incoming information is only moderately typical of the schema but not very typical. This information is then linked to the schema but with a "unique tag" so as to indicate that this new information is "a little different." (3) Finally, some new incoming information may be unrelated or atypical of the schema, and it is *tagged* as being *atypical*. Any tagged information is encoded as different from or as a *deviation from the schema*. Thus, in summary, *information may be represented in basically three ways: as part of the schema, related to the schema but a little different, and as really different from the schema*.

The SP+T model makes a number of predictions and we shall examine just one of these. This prediction is that accuracy in memory discrimination for actions in passages is better for atypical than typical actions, and this is the case for both recognition and recall tasks for *immediate* tests of memory. However, as the retention interval increases, the tagged items in the memory trace become less accessible and retrieval becomes more dependent upon the schema. Thus, although there is initially better memory for atypical actions, atypical events are forgotten faster than typical ones. Smith and Graesser (1981) found that by increasing the retention interval up to three weeks, atypical items became less available and retrieval became more dependent on the general schema, providing clear support for the model.

Summary of Schema Theory: Assumptions

It is useful at this point to summarize the major assumptions of schema theory. We can identify eight assumptions as noted by Eckhardt (1990).

1. *Prior Knowledge*. Schema theory assumes that people have prior knowledge which is stored in long-term memory and then activated and used when appropriate as new events, information, etc., are encountered. The assimilation of new information is a function of the amount of relevant prior knowledge. However, without this knowledge

there is no available schema into which new information can be integrated so it is quickly lost. Mere possession of prior knowledge is insufficient; it must be *activated* at the time of encoding new information. Finally, an existing schema that is activated during encoding will enable selection of some of the information for encoding, that is, a person stores only a selective subset of information encountered.

2. *Important Ideas.* The ideas that are most important, that is, have meaning or relevance to the theme of the information will be remembered best. Both Eckhardt (1991) and Wood (1990) found that central events or themes were better recalled than peripheral details in both immediate and delayed retention of television stories. Since different people may have different schemas during encoding, this can result in the same information being encoded differently by different people.

3. *Reconstructive Memory.* Recall is more than the passive reproduction of stored memories. Memories do not necessarily exist in the original form but are altered by way of reconstructive processes described earlier (e.g., Loftus & Palmer, 1974; McEwan & Yuille, 1981).

4. *Development of Schemas.* Mental structures such as schemas develop over time from encounters with many instances of events, information, scenes, etc.

5. *Active Process.* Schemas represent an active process and can change over time as a result of new experiences and learnings.

6. *Culture Specific.* Schemas are culture specific. For example, what constitutes one's schema for *gourmet dining* can vary from different parts of the world, countries, or even regions within a given country.

7. *Large Units.* Schemas are large units. Schema theory is not an elemental, molecular theory, but adopts a molar, large-unit viewpoint.

8. *Verbatim Memory.* Contrary to some critics, schema theory does not imply that people fail to recall specific details or verbatim information which is unrelated to the schema. Certainly we recall details and verbatim information. Thus *all* memory is not reconstructive.

PRIOR KNOWLEDGE, CAPACITY ALLOCATION, AND TEXT PROCESSING

In the summary of schema theory just described we listed eight general assumptions, one of which concerned the role of prior knowledge. Our description of the effects of themes on the comprehension of passages also illustrated the more general role of prior knowledge in comprehension. It is clearly the case that a person's knowledge of some topic or skill will influence comprehension of new information in that area. This point was illustrated by the descriptive story of an old man presented at the beginning of this chapter, and by studies of the role of themes in text processing (Bransford & Johnson, 1973; Sulin & Dooling, 1974).

A second issue in the study of comprehension focuses on the role of prior knowledge in the momentary demands on cognitive capacity, or cognitive effort, during the reading and processing of textual material. Two different views have been advanced with respect to capacity allocation during the processing of textual material. The first position, which is derived from the work of Kintsch and van Dijk (1978), van Dijk and Kintsch (1983), and Graesser and Riha (1984), contends that the possession of relevant prior knowledge during text processing increases the comprehension of text materials. This is reflected in the enhanced recall of text materials, but also in the reduction of cognitive demands placed on the reader, that is, the amount of cognitive effort necessary to comprehend the text. Our interest in this section is on the issue of effort or capacity allocation during reading.

It has been pointed out that the availability of relevant prior knowledge about a topic can reduce the amount of effort required to understand text in two ways (McFarland, 1986). First, topic knowledge allows a reader to establish the meaning of text more readily (Sanford & Garrod, 1981), and does so because it narrows the range of possible interpretations of the text, that is, the text becomes more "predictable" to the reader. With the range of possible interpretations narrowed, the reader has to keep less topical information available in working memory, and thus allocates less cognitive effort as a result of having relevant prior knowledge. Second, the possession of prior knowledge about material being read can reduce the number of reinstatement searches of long-term memory for information required to maintain a coherent understanding of the text (Lesgold, Roth, & Curtis, 1979). A number of experiments have supported this assumption by showing that the time required to read a text passage, used as a measure of cognitive capacity, is reduced with subjects who possess greater knowledge about the passage (e.g., Miller & Kintsch, 1980; Just & Carpenter, 1984; van Dijk & Kintsch, 1983).

The second position regarding the role of prior knowledge on the allocation of cognitive capacity contends that while prior knowledge does increase the comprehension of material, as held by the first position, prior knowledge also serves to *increase* the amount of capacity allocated during reading rather than decrease it. A reader with more pertinent knowledge about the text might activate and maintain more information to assist in interpretation of the text, thereby making it more memorable but also using more capacity in the process. Thus, two positions have been proposed which make opposite predictions regarding capacity allocation. The second position has been advanced by Britton and his colleagues (e.g., Britton & Tesser, 1982; Britton, Westbrook, & Holdredge, 1978; Britton, Glynn, Meyer, & Penland, 1982).

In this section we shall examine some experiments that manipulate the amount of prior knowledge people have about certain topics and see how this influences their comprehension of new information. Such experiments provide one way of studying the role of schemas in comprehension.

Britton and Tesser's Experiments

Three experiments by Britton and Tesser (1982) serve to illustrate the second position described above. In all experiments, subjects were assigned to one of two groups consisting of high or low prior knowledge conditions. The studies differed in several ways but only one study is described because they were all quite similar in design. In the low prior knowledge condition, subjects read two pages from one story and then read one page from a new story which was the target or criterion passage. The two preliminary pages of text were irrelevant to the target passage, hence this condition was designated as the low prior knowledge condition. In the high prior knowledge condition subjects read three consecutive pages of material from the same novel, where the first two pages consisted of relevant prior knowledge. The target (criterion) page was the same for both groups. In the course of reading the target page, subjects were presented a signal, at unpredictable times, and asked to respond as quickly as possible. Thus a secondary task procedure, as described in chapter 3, was used. The assumption is that longer reaction times to the signal reflect greater allocation of capacity to the text (cf., Kerr, 1973; Tyler et al., 1979).

Britton and Tesser's (1982) results were quite clear. They found that subjects in the high prior knowledge condition showed longer reaction times to the probe signal than did subjects in the low prior knowledge condition. They concluded that the availability of prior knowledge led to greater, not less, allocation of capacity during reading and thus provided support for the second viewpoint described above.

There is, however, a potential problem with their experiment concerning the way prior knowledge was manipulated. It was not the case that the low prior knowledge received little or no relevant information. Rather, they were presented an *unrelated* passage, that is, two pages of a different story. Thus the shift to a target page of quite new material could have been a somewhat strange and disruptive experience to the readers. They may well have experienced a violation of their expectancies when shifted to a new topic and, therefore, allocated less capacity to this task. The significance of this interpretation is that the low prior knowledge condition may not have functioned as an appropriate control condition for studying the effects of prior knowledge. In this case, the longer reaction times in the high prior knowledge condition may have been spuriously inflated if subjects responded quickly to the low prior knowledge condition. A more appropriate control condition might have been, for example, a condition in which the low prior knowledge group read only one page of material or even had no prior reading. The point is that the control condition read *irrelevant* pages that may have created some cognitive discrepancy for the reader when reading the target passage, and thus may not have been an adequate control.

McFarland's Experiments

In a reevaluation of this issue, McFarland (1986) conducted two experiments. In the first, he established that reading times were shorter for subjects who were given contextual (background) information about the passage they were reading. Subjects were given four different descriptive passages to read with presentation order of the passages counterbalanced. In order to vary knowledge about the passages, subjects were assigned to either a context or a no-context condition. In the context condition, subjects were presented a topic phrase such as "Washing Clothes," "Making and Flying Kites," "The First Trip to the Moon," and "Voyage of Christopher Columbus." In this fashion subjects were informed about the material they were about to read. In the control condition subjects received no topic phrases and were thus uninformed about the context of the passages. McFarland's findings clearly supported the general idea that prior knowledge about a topic makes its comprehension easier, as reflected in shorter reading times.

McFarland's (1986) second experiment more directly addressed the issue raised earlier regarding the interpretation of Britton and Tesser's (1982) findings, the issue concerning the adequacy of their control condition. In this experiment, he manipulated context as in his first experiment and used three rather than four passages. The essential feature of this manipulation of prior knowledge (context titles versus no titles) is that subjects either received relevant prior knowledge or no prior knowledge. No *irrelevant* or potentially disruptive prior knowledge was presented to subjects. He also used a secondary task procedure in which he presented auditory signals (probes) during subjects' reading which enabled a measure of capacity allocation during reading of the passages. Following the reasoning described previously, we would expect longer reaction times (hence, more capacity allocation) in the context-provided condition if Britton's position is to be supported. But if the critique of Britton and Tesser (1982) is supported, then we would expect shorter reaction times to the probe stimulus. Subjects were given a total of four probe signals during reading, with the first probe being used as a warm-up probe. The remaining three probes were placed in different locations during passage presentation.

Table 9.2
Reaction Times During Reading of Text Passages

Location of Reaction Time Probe	Context Present (Prior Knowledge)	No Context (No Prior Knowledge)
Sentence Beginning	421 msec.	486 msec.
Sentence End	392 msec.	491 msec.
Within Clause	378 msec.	450 msec.

From A. O. McFarland. "Cognitive effort during reading: Effects of topic knowledge." Unpublished doctoral dissertation, University of New Mexico, 1986. Reprinted by permission of the author.

The results are shown in table 9.2 which indicate that, regardless of the location of the probe, subjects who were given knowledge of the passage (context) showed reliably shorter reaction times to the probe than did the non-context group. These results indicate that subjects with high prior knowledge were allocating *fewer* resources or capacity during reading, not more, a finding in accord with van Dijk and Kintsch (1983) and others.

A Proposed Resolution

The presence of seemingly conflicting findings presents us with a puzzle. The results of McFarland's (1986) second experiment are clearly at odds with those of Britton and Tesser (1982). Using relevant descriptive titles of passages as a way of varying prior knowledge, McFarland found that those subjects receiving the title allocated fewer resources than those who did not receive the title. But Britton and Tesser (1982) found the reverse effect when comparing groups differing in prior knowledge using a quite different manipulation of prior knowledge. Since McFarland did not employ a manipulation identical to that of Britton and Tesser, his study does not automatically refute Britton and Tesser's results. To have done so would have required an experiment using their manipulation of prior knowledge in which a control involving no prior passages, or only relevant prior passages, were used. Thus a direct test of the appropriate control for their particular study, described earlier, is yet to be conducted. Therefore, despite McFarland's results, it is also possible that under some circumstances relevant prior knowledge might also lead to an increase in the allocation of resources. In summary, both sets of results may occur.

One conceivable resolution is that, depending upon various circumstances, prior knowledge about some topic might lead to either a decrease or an increase in the allocation of capacity during text processing. How might this occur? Our comments here are speculative, but we outline one possible scenario. We recognize that text passages can vary considerably in their difficulty, familiarity, organization, and general ease of comprehension. If the text passage is generally high in these features, that is, easy to comprehend, then we might expect that having some prior knowledge about a relatively easy-to-comprehend passage could lead to reduced capacity allocation. Such a finding would be consistent with McFarland's (1986) results. In contrast, if the text passage were very difficult or obscure, subjects with prior knowledge might actually allocate greater resources in an effort to comprehend the passage. And this finding would be consistent with Britton and Tesser (1982). Experiments to test this possibility are yet to be conducted. In summary, we propose that either a reduction or an increase in capacity allocation during reading is a reasonable possibility depending upon some range of task features, one of which may be task difficulty. Instead of the issue being an either-or (increase-decrease) one, we raise the possibility that both options are reasonable outcomes.

A GENERAL THEORY OF COMPREHENSION AND MEMORY: KINTSCH AND VAN DIJK

First, it should be realized that all of the theories of semantic memory discussed in chapter 7 are designed to explain comprehension. Although any of the theories can explain at least some aspect of the comprehension process, the ideas which seem most applicable to connected discourse are those which rely on a knowledge representation larger than a single word, namely, the propositional theories. Propositional theory is particularly useful because the knowledge extracted and remembered from connected discourse encompasses units larger than individual words. We shall outline a general overview of one such theory which was explicitly designed to describe memory performance following comprehension.

The general idea, proposed by Kintsch and van Dijk (1978), is that comprehension begins with the extraction of propositions from the textual material. These propositions follow the rudimentary organization of the text, but further organizational processes are imposed, as part of comprehension. For example, related propositions are grouped, although much of the grouping occurs through organization of the text itself. Further, the propositions are organized around the goals of the reader.

The goals may simply be to understand and interpret the material, as, for example, in reading a novel for entertainment. Here the rules about stories guide organization of the propositions; good stories begin with a setting, proceed through a series of events, and end with a resolution. Propositions can be organized around these segments such that ultimate comprehension and memory for the story is highly ordered. With other types of materials, the purposes or goals may be different, as in reading an academic text. You may have a specific goal, such as finding evidence for feature theories of pattern recognition, or a general goal of understanding and remembering the material on comprehension and knowledge. In the latter case, the text structure should help you organize materials, in that section headings provide a theme around which to group ensuing propositions.

Additions to and deletions from the material occur in accord with the purposes and goals of the reader. For example, when the search is for a specific bit of information that cannot be found, an inference to fill the gap may be made. The text may provide information which is unnecessary for the purpose, and those propositions are deleted from memory. Suppose you are interested in determining the inflation rate in Germany following World War I, and the material you read mentions that a loaf of bread cost two bags of money. Although this is not yet specific information about the inflation rate, you are able to make a clear inference. The material might also mention that the physical size of the money was quite large, but since size has nothing to do with your purpose, you delete this proposition.

The view emerging from Kintsch and van Dijk's theory is of an active process of comprehension in which propositional representations are extracted and organized around themes. The organization may involve integration of separate propositions and almost certainly will include inferences. Although theories of comprehension and memory are in their infancy and will undoubtly undergo dramatic revision, the ideas of Kintsch and van Dijk provide a useful description of the processes involved including integration, thematic organization, and inference.

SUMMARY

Comprehension is a very active process of organizing and elaborating the material that is heard and read. Memory is, then, a product of the organization and elaboration. As with simple pattern recognition, much of what is remembered was not contained in the original message, but is inferred from knowledge of the world. The processes which elaborate the original event seem to occur at both input and output and can be viewed as analogous to the same types of processes operating in studies of list memory.

This chapter described the importance of integration and the loss of verbatim information in memory, the role of themes, the operation of presuppositions in memory, and the importance of inferences in everyday memory. Attention was given to the role of presuppositions in eyewitness testimony as illustrated in Loftus's research. The interpretation of the role of presuppositions in eyewitness testimony, with respect to the issue of blending of memories, is still controversial. Both response bias and actual memory change interpretations have been proposed.

The concept of schema is important and useful in our understanding of memory and comprehension. Schemas can consist of events and scenes and are temporally or spatially organized. Schemas serve to facilitate both the encoding and retrieval of information. Contemporary schema theories all involve four basic processes: selection, abstraction, interpretation, and integration.

Brewer and McNamara (1984) point out, in addition to (1) selection and (2) integration processes, the importance of schemas (3) as a framework for preserving information in memory, (4) in guiding the retrieval process, and (5) in output editing. An important model of how schemas operate is Graesser's (1981) schema pointer plus tag model. Finally, in summarizing schema theory, eight important assumptions were identified: (1) prior knowledge, (2) important ideas, (3) reconstructive memory, (4) development of schemas, (5) schemas as an active process, (6) culture specific nature of schemas, (7) schemas as large units, and (8) verbatim memory, that is, not all memory is reconstructive.

An important line of research has examined the allocation of capacity during text processing. One important issue is the role of prior knowledge in processing textual material, and it is clear that prior knowledge helps a reader in comprehending the text. A second issue concerns the role of allocating capacity during reading, and here two different sets of results have occurred. Prior knowledge has been found either to increase or to decrease the allocation of capacity during text processing, and it is possible that both processes can occur depending upon the conditions of the experiments.

Most theories of comprehension rest on the propositional representation of knowledge and assume that text is analyzed and remembered in propositional form. An understanding of comprehension and memory can enable you to communicate more precisely as well as to understand precisely what is said and what is left unsaid.

MULTIPLE-CHOICE ITEMS

1. When material is integrated in comprehension, memory for that material is likely to be
   a. verbatim
   b. highly detailed
   c. gist
   d. inference

2. Which of the following did *not* occur as a result of Bransford and Franks's experiment?
   a. old sentences were better remembered than *new*
   b. *new* sentences were frequently called *old*
   c. *noncase* sentences were frequently called *new*
   d. sentences never presented were recognized as *old*

3. Themes do all of the following except
    a. guide organization of text
    b. influence the type of inferences drawn
    c. facilitate comprehension
    d. prohibit presuppositions from occurring

4. If the possession of a good deal of knowledge about a topic leads a reader to allocate greater capacity when processing textual materials then probe reaction time (RT) latencies should be
    a. shorter than a control group's RTs
    b. longer than a control group's RTs
    c. same as a control group's RTs
    d. unknown

5. Inferences seem to occur
    a. at neither input or output
    b. at both input and output
    c. only at input
    d. only at output

6. According to the Kintsch and van Dijk model of comprehension, what is remembered is
    a. primarily due to retrieval processes
    b. not really influenced by the structure of the text
    c. influenced by the purpose for reading the material
    d. not influenced by the theme

TRUE–FALSE ITEMS

1. Without inferences, we would have to say a lot more to communicate with others.

2. Bransford and Franks's study showed that persons are very good at remembering the wording of a sentence.

3. If I say, "Tom is smarter than Bob, and Bob is smarter than Sam" and you then think, "Tom is smarter than Sam," you have made a logical inference.

4. Research has clearly shown that eyewitness testimony is quite reliable and accurate.

5. Persons do not make inferences with visual stimuli as they do with verbal materials.

6. The discussion suggests that the processes involved in memory for lists of words are drastically different from the processes involved in memory for connected discourse.

DISCUSSION ITEMS

1.   Describe Bransford and Franks's experiment and results, explicitly discussing the points which provide evidence for integration.

2.   Discuss the relationship between themes and inferences. What effects do each have on comprehension and on memory?

3.   Discuss how inferences can be made from advertisements on television.

4.   What roles do schemas play in memory and comprehension?

5.   Compare the response bias and memory change interpretations of Loftus and Palmer's (1974) study.

6.   Distinguish between event and scene schemas.

7.   Identify the *four* important processes that are part of schema theory as identified by Alba and Hasher (1983).

8.   Identify the *five* processes in schema theory as outlined by Brewer and McNamara.

9.   Explain the essential features of the schema pointer plus tag model.

10.   Summarize the eight basic assumptions of schema theory.

ANSWERS TO MULTIPLE-CHOICE ITEMS

1.   (c)   Integration is the process of discarding detailed surface information and remembering a semantic unit or gist.

2.   (a)   The *new* sentences were called *old* with just as much confidence as the *old* sentences were called *old*.

3.   (d)   There is no reason to assume that themes preclude presuppositions.

4.   (b)   Longer reactions will be obtained because readers are allocating greater capacity due to their prior knowledge.

5.   (b)   Inferences can be drawn at input during comprehension and can be based also upon what is retrieved at output.

6.   (c)   Purposes and goals have a lot to do with what is remembered from the text.

ANSWERS TO TRUE–FALSE ITEMS

1.   (True)   Much of what is communicated is implied, not directly stated.

2.   (False)   Bransford and Franks found that people cannot discriminate between *new* and *old* sentences on the basis of wording.

3. (True) Logic dictates the inference that is drawn in this case.

4. (False) Research has shown that eyewitness testimony is quite subject to distortion about the actual event.

5. (False) Baggett's study using pictures showed a clear tendency to make inferences.

6. (False) While discourse is more complex and may involve somewhat more complicated processing, many of the same processes seem to be operating in the two situations.

10

PROBLEM SOLVING
AND REASONING

Human beings face and solve problems everyday. Problems vary in complexity from the simple problem of locating a car in a large parking lot, to the more complex one of deciding on priorities in paying bills, to the very complex one of planning one's life work. Some problems are solved with little effort. For example, it is easy to decide which television channel to select for watching the evening news. But other problems require considerable effort and may never be completely resolved. For example, weighing the pros and cons of a midlife career change may preoccupy a person for an extended period of time. And the same problem may vary in complexity from person to person. In buying a new house, for example, one person may be able to decide quickly after inspection of two or three choices, whereas another may agonize over alternatives for months.

Psychologists have preferred to concentrate their research efforts on problems of roughly intermediate difficulty. With this type of problem the solution is not immediately obvious (and thus trivial), and the task and solution options are fairly well-defined. Interest is focused on how a person arrives at a solution to a problem. Problem-solving tasks are usually structured so that many response alternatives are possible, although only one solution may be correct. Some tasks are artificial, but many are borrowed from everyday life. Tasks can include such situations as chess problems, anagrams, verbal problems, mathematical problems, cryptarithmetic problems, analogy problems, logical problems, and puzzles such as the famous Rubik's cube.

Not all problems are well-defined and they can range from well-defined to poorly defined tasks (e.g., Simon, 1973). In well-defined problems the features or aspects of the task are all identified. For example, if instructed to calculate your current bank balance, in which all outstanding checks are known, then the task is a straightforward one of subtracting the sum of the outstanding checks from the prior balance in order to obtain a current balance. In contrast, with ill-defined problems a person has considerable uncertainty about one or more features of the problem. For instance, one may have uncertainty about the information given, appropriate procedures, or even the final outcome. In the latter case, one may be uncertain as to what a good or acceptable solution will be. For example, a beginning graduate student may have difficulty in proposing a thesis problem because of uncertainty about what constitutes an acceptable thesis problem. For some students this may be a fairly well-defined problem, but for others it is the beginning of a period of unproductive floundering, confusion, and anxiety.

REPRESENTATIVE PROBLEMS: IMPORTANCE
OF MENTAL REPRESENTATION

The following examples are typical of problem-solving situations used in the laboratory. They are all characterized by presenting subjects with an initial state, including assumptions and constraints, and asking the subjects how they would go about achieving a specific goal state. The first is the bird-train problem. Critically important to the solution of the problem is how it is interpreted. Obviously, if it is misinterpreted, there is little chance of solving it.

> Two train stations are fifty miles apart. At 2 P.M. one Saturday afternoon two trains start toward each other, one from each station. Just as the trains pull out of the stations, a bird springs into the air in front of the first train and flies to the front of the second train. When the bird reaches the second train, it turns back and flies toward the first train. The bird continues to do this until the trains meet. If both trains travel at the rate of twenty-five miles per hour, and the bird flies at one hundred miles per hour, how many miles will the bird have flown before the trains meet? (M. I. Posner, *Cognition: An Introduction.* Glenview, Ill.: Scott, Foresman, 1973.)

Posner points out that if this problem is interpreted in terms of the bird's flight pattern, the solution might be very difficult to achieve. For example, one method is to calculate how far the bird flies on its first trip, add that amount to how far it flies on its second trip, and so on. But if a less obvious or less direct representation of the problem—how much time does the bird spend in flight?—is selected, the problem then becomes solvable. Since the two trains are 50 miles apart and travel at 25 miles per hour, it will take only one hour for the two trains to converge. And since the bird flies at 100 miles per hour, it will cover 100 miles during that hour.

Consider another example of how the mental representation of a problem can affect the ease of its solution. This problem is the Buddhist monk problem and originated with the psychologist Karl Duncker.

> One morning, exactly at sunrise, a Buddhist monk began to climb a tall mountain. A narrow path, no more than a foot or two wide, spiraled around the mountain to a glittering temple at the summit. The monk ascended at varying rates of speed, stopping many times along the way to rest and eat dried fruit he carried with him. He reached the temple shortly before sunset. After several days of fasting and meditation, he began his

journey back along the same path, starting at sunrise and again walking at variable speeds with many pauses along the way. His average speed descending was, of course, greater than his average climbing speed. Show that there is a spot along the path that the monk will occupy on both trips at precisely the same time of day. (Karl Duncker, "On Problem Solving," *Psychological Monographs,* No. 270, *58,* 1945.)

Again, how this problem is represented determines its ease of solution. A mathematical-type solution, as in the bird-train problem just discussed, might be tried, but would not produce the accurate solution. Further thought might produce the decision that there is *no* such spot, or that it is most unlikely that the monk would find himself at the same spot on two different days. This decision is also incorrect. However, when a mental picture of the monk climbing to the temple and then descending is visualized, the solution becomes clear. Plotting the monk's travels in the mind will easily show that the two paths must meet at some point. That is, the monk must climb from the bottom of the mountain to the top and then return, and this activity occurs each trip within the time period of one day. No matter how fast or how slowly the monk goes, there must be a meeting point, given the manner in which the problem is structured. If you have trouble with this, consider this solution: It can be easily solved if you think of one monk starting up the mountain at the same time another monk is starting down. They must cross one spot at the same time.

Finally, consider one more problem. This is the Christmas tree problem described by Hayes (1981). The problem is this: Arrange ten Christmas trees in five straight rows of four trees each. When I (HCE) first encountered this problem, I found it very difficult. I drew several arrangements of trees, none of which provided the solution. Only after I realized that the trees must be arranged in more than one row was I able to solve the problem. The solution is, of course, obvious once it is seen. The problem is solved when the trees (represented as dots) are arranged in a star pattern. Prove this by arranging ten dots so that when they are connected a five-pointed star is formed.

A CLASSIFICATION OF TYPES OF PROBLEMS

Psychologists have studied a variety of problem-solving situations ranging from laboratory tasks to classroom problem solving to everyday problems in familiar settings. In a review of problem-solving research, Greeno (1978) has classified problems into three basic types based upon the cognitive processes involved in reaching a solution. The three problem types are those of (1) inducing structure, (2) transformation, and (3) arrangement. A problem can, of course, involve a mixture of these processes and not just a single process.

Problems that involve *inducing structure* require a person to discover a pattern that will relate elements of the problem to each other. One example is that of verbal analogies such as: Chimney is to house as ___?___ is to ship. A person solving this problem must understand that a chimney is a structure designed to allow smoke to escape safely from a fireplace in a house. With this knowledge, a person can properly produce *smokestack* as the analogous structure for a ship. With this understanding, a person will reject other responses, such as *door,* which do not serve this function.

Consider another analogy: Toulouse is to Lautrec as Rimsky is to ___?___, a more difficult analogy. Here a person must recognize that Toulouse-Lautrec is the joint name of a famous French painter, and thus seek a solution which involves a double name beginning with Rimsky-_____. Since Rimsky-Korsakov is the name of a Russian musician, Korsakov fits the analogy. Usually, a person is given a set of choices such as *Cezanne, Korsakov, Pushkin, Romanov,* and *Tchaikovsky.* The problem solver must recognize that Cezanne, a French painter, does not satisfy the analogy because it does not make a double name. The remaining four names are Russian: Pushkin was a writer, Romanov the name of a Russian royal family, and Tchaikovsky was a composer. None of these are double names, so they cannot satisfy the analogy. Recognition of Rimsky-Korsakov as a name will then lead to the correct solution.

A second type of problem is one of *transformation.* With this type of problem a person must manipulate objects or symbols in accord with certain rules in order to obtain a solution. A good example is the Luchins (1942) water-jar problem, described in this chapter under the section entitled "Persistence of Set." The basic problem requires that a person determine how to fill a jar of water in order to obtain a specified amount, using three jars, each containing a different amount of water. Similarly, word problems that require one to transform the information in sentences to algebraic equations represent another example. In general, this second class of problem requires that objects or information be transformed from one state to another (e.g., sentences to equations) in order for a solution to occur.

The third type of problem involves *rearrangement of elements* of a task in order to solve a problem. All of the elements of the task are given and the person must rearrange the elements in some way that solves the problem. A good example is rearranging the letters in an anagram to make a word. Mayer (1983) describes the following example in which college students are asked to form a word from the anagram *GANRE.* There are two apparent solutions to this anagram and most college students give the answer *RANGE* with an average response time of about 8 seconds. A less frequent answer is *ANGER,* which takes an average of about 114 seconds. Here's another to try before you read further: *TARIL.* This also has two solutions. Try to come up with an answer before you read on. The answers are given at the end of this chapter.

Another example of problems involving rearrangement are cryptarithmetic problems. These are puzzles in which a solution requires you to substitute digits for letters to solve a problem. A detailed example is given later on in this chapter in the section entitled "Means-Ends Analysis."

With these examples in mind, we now describe some of the features of problem-solving activity.

STAGES IN PROBLEM SOLVING

Typically there are several stages in the process of solving problems. Sometimes progress through these stages is done in a matter of minutes. Other situations may require days, weeks, or longer periods for solution. Psychologists have described several stages in problem solving, but all can be reduced to a basic few: (1) understanding the problem, (2) generating hypotheses about solutions and selecting among the alternative hypotheses, and (3) testing and evaluating the solutions. Although a person logically goes through the three stages in the order mentioned, *understanding, generating,* and *evaluating,* much problem-solving activity involves recycling through the stages. For example, when a solution is found to be worthless, a person may return to the first stage in an attempt to better understand the problem. In a general book on problem solving, Polya (1957) outlined a similar series of four steps in problem solving based on his experience in teaching mathematics. Polya's four steps are: (1) understanding the problem, (2) devising a plan, (3) carrying out the plan, and (4) looking back, which is checking the results using another solution.

Understanding the Problem

Before a problem can be solved, it must first be understood. Unless you have a clear, accurate picture of the problem you will most likely fail to reach an accurate solution. Individuals vary in the amount of time spent in trying to understand the problem. Regardless of the nature of the problem, the key to a successful solution lies in how the problem is *represented,* that is, how a person comes to interpret the problem. And in interpreting the problem a variety of factors may need to be identified including what is known or given about the problem, criteria for solution, constraints placed on solutions, and various solution options.

Return for the moment to the Buddhist monk problem. It was shown that a visual representation of a problem will allow it to be solved. In that case, visual representation of the monk climbing and descending within the same time frame clearly showed that there was one place on the path which the monk would occupy on both days.

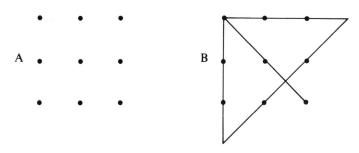

Figure 10.1 Example of a problem whose solution depends on appropriate representation. *A*, The nine-dot problem. *B*, The solution to the nine-dot problem.

Another example of a problem whose successful solution depends on the appropriate representation is presented in figure 10.1. This is the nine-dot problem. The problem is to draw four straight lines through all of the nine dots without lifting the pencil. The problem can prove difficult when subjects have an inadequate representation of it. Subjects frequently assume, incorrectly, that the solution requires that all lines intersect at one of the dots. This tends to prevent them from seeing the solution, which requires that the lines be extended past the dots. As a general rule, if you are not making good progress in solving a problem, back up and take another look at it. You may discover that you misinterpreted the problem in the first place and that a second look will correct the situation.

Generating Solutions

The next stage in solving a problem involves generating one or more solutions. Human beings generate possible solutions to a problem in several ways. At one extreme the attempt at a solution is haphazard and unsystematic, and at another level the approach is organized and systematic (cf. Cohen, 1971; Newell & Simon, 1972; Simon, 1978). As a general rule, persons attempt to solve problems by using some kind of *strategy,* which represents the systematic attack of a problem.

Algorithms and Heuristics

Psychologists distinguish between two general kinds of strategies, algorithms and heuristics. An *algorithm* is a set of rules or procedures which ensures the solution. A *heuristic* strategy, by contrast, is a rule of thumb or approximation which may or may not ensure the solution. A simple example makes the distinction clear. Suppose you are trying to locate the address of a friend, J. Smith, in the telephone book of a large, unfamiliar city. Inspection of the directory shows that there are forty-one persons named Smith having the initial *J*. One solution is to simply phone, one by one, all the J. Smiths in the directory until you find your friend. This strategy is guaranteed to work (assuming your friend is listed and is at home when you call). The strategy, however, is quite cumbersome and time-consuming. By contrast, if you assume that your friend lives in one section of the city, say the northeast area, you can phone only the J. Smiths listed in that area first. This general rule of thumb or heuristic has a reasonably good chance of working, but it cannot guarantee that you will locate your friend. It is a shortcut method that is worth trying but is not perfect.

Why would a person use a heuristic rule of thumb when an algorithm is guaranteed to solve the problem? Many problems simply do not have an algorithm, and even when it exists, an algorithm may be cumbersome or time-consuming. In the example just given, making forty-one phone calls would be time-consuming and also expensive.

Generate-Test Method   One type of heuristic is the *generate-test method* (Newell & Simon, 1972). As a process it is similar to the generation-recognition models of retrieval described in chapter 6. The basic idea is a two-step process in which, first, a possible solution is generated and then tested to see whether it works. This is something like the old trial-and-error process in which solutions are tried and discarded until one that works is discovered. But there are problems with this type of heuristic. One problem is that there may be a large number of alternative solutions to consider. This is simply to say that the *problem space* may be very large. Consider this question: What is the best place in town to eat? If there are a hundred restaurants, then it is not practical to test all the alternatives; it is especially not practical to test the alternatives if you are a visitor in town and plan to dine out only once.

Newell and Simon have labeled a person's representation of a problem as the *problem space*. When a person attempts to solve a problem, he or she does not usually have full understanding of the task. Thus, when faced with an unfamiliar problem, the person must encode the appropriate features and construct some kind of mental representation of the problem. Conceptually, Newell and Simon regard the problem space as a collection of nodes in memory like those described by models of semantic memory, discussed in chapter 7.

Means-Ends Analysis   Another heuristic that is useful is called *means-ends analysis*. In studying problem solving, Newell and Simon (1972) observed that subjects frequently attempted to change (by various means) from one state of knowledge about a problem to another (an end). As a general rule, the effort of subjects can be described as the attempt to change from the initial problem state to a desired solution or end state. This process requires that they determine the *ends* they wish to achieve and the *means* by which they will reach these ends. For complex problems the desired end cannot be accomplished in one stroke. Subjects must establish subgoals which gradually lead toward the final desired goal.

To study problem-solving behavior Newell and Simon used several problems including "cryptarithmetic problems." These problems are puzzles in which it is necessary to substitute digits for letters to solve a problem. Each letter in a problem represents a unique digit. A typical problem is as follows:

$$\begin{array}{l} \text{D O N A L D} \\ + \ \text{G E R A L D} \\ \hline \text{R O B E R T} \end{array} \qquad \text{D} = 5$$

The problem is correctly solved when the digits are substituted for the letters in an arithmetically correct sum. The difficulty is in finding a complete solution in which all specific digits can be substituted for the letters. All this cannot be accomplished at once, so the problem must be broken into steps. How this works can be seen by examining a few steps.

Step 1

$$\begin{array}{l} \text{D O N A L D} \\ + \ \text{G E R A L D} \\ \hline \text{R O B E R T} \end{array} \qquad \text{D} = 5$$

Now substitute 5 for D, to give

Step 2

$$\begin{array}{l} \text{5 O N A L 5} \\ + \ \text{G E R A L 5} \\ \hline \text{R O B E R T} \end{array}$$

Since D = 5 and T = D + D, then T must be equal to 1∅ (the slashed zero distinguishes it from the letter O) and carry 1.

Step 3

$$\begin{array}{l} \quad \ \ 1 \\ \text{5 O N A L 5} \\ + \ \text{G E R A L 5} \\ \hline \text{R O B E R ∅} \end{array}$$

What next? Note that R = 2L + 1. Since two times any number is always an even number, the carried 1 means that R must be an odd number. But as also can be seen from the first column, R = 5 + G, R must be at least 5, because G must be at least ∅. Since R = 2L + 1, R must be 5, 7, or 9, and L must be 2, 3, or 4. Since each letter has its own unique number, and D is 5, then R must be 7 or 9 and L 3 or 4. Try R = 7, L = 3 which gives, as a preliminary partial solution,

Step 4

```
    5 O N A 3 5
+   G E 7 A 3 5
    7 O B E 7 Ø
```

From this start it should be possible to carry the problem to the complete solution. Again, the important point is to note that means-end analysis involves the setting of successive subgoals that eventually allow the final goal to be reached.

The final solution of this problem is as follows:

```
    D O N A L D              526485
+   G E R A L D        =  +  197485
    R O B E R T              723970
                         ROBERT
```

Note that to reach this state from Step 4, L must equal 8 (not 3), and the values for the remaining unknown letters must be solved.

Working Backward As you can see, means-ends analysis is a step-by-step process in which the process is in a forward direction toward the solution. It is also possible to *work backward* toward the solution. This amounts to seeing what the solution ought to look like and then working backward from the solution to the current problem state. Consider an example used by Ellis, Bennett, Daniel, and Rickert in which the problem is stated: "How can I spend the spring vacation in Mazatlan?" (Mazatlan is a popular beach resort on the west coast of Mexico.) They note:

> Working backward from the goal, it will be noted that an essential step is to get to Mazatlan. Thus, some means of transportation will be required. Transportation costs money, so the next step backward is to determine how to accumulate the needed funds. Eventually, the working-backward strategy may lead you to forego a planned ski trip so as to have money to purchase transportation to go to Mazatlan to enjoy your spring break. (H. Ellis et al., *Psychology of Learning and Memory.* Monterey, Calif.: Brooks/Cole, 1979.)

Note that in either case, working backward or forward, a large, complex problem is divided into a set of subgoals. Each subgoal is then solved one at a time while the complete solution is gradually worked toward. A subgoal is simply a step necessary to achieve on the way to the final goal. For example, in the cryptarithmetic problem described above, each step solved is a subgoal which directs the person to the final goal.

Evaluating Solutions

The final stage in problem solving is to evaluate the proposed solution. Some kind of judgment regarding the effectiveness of the solution being considered must be made. As long as the criteria are clear, this is a relatively easy step. For example, in the cryptarithmetic problem just discussed, a solution is correct if the addition works. When a vacation to Mazatlan is planned, the important thing is to be able to obtain sufficient funds. Of course, "sufficient" must be carefully defined since it depends on how elaborate the vacation is to be. For instance, do you plan to camp on the beach, stay in an inexpensive small hotel, or stay in one of the luxury resorts on the north beach? Therefore, an effective solution will depend upon the willingness and ability to spell out the criteria clearly.

Evaluating solutions can be much more complex when the criteria are vague or unspecified. Under these circumstances it is desirable to identify the important features of a solution as clearly as possible.

Incubation in Problem Solving

Problem solving typically involves the three stages just described. Some psychologists have pointed out, however, that an additional process sometimes occurs. When all the possible hypotheses are thought of and tried and none is a suitable solution, a person may temporarily withdraw from the problem and engage in other activities. The French mathematician Henri Poincaré (1929) described this process that led to one of his important discoveries. During a period in which he was trying unsuccessfully to solve a certain mathematical question, he temporarily abandoned his work to take a beach vacation. One morning during a walk, the solution to the mathematical question came to him almost spontaneously as he was thinking about other things. Poincaré's example raises the question of the occurrence of unconscious mental activities during the period in which a person turns away from the immediate problem. This rest period is called the *incubation stage* in which problem-solving activity continues, but without conscious attention to the problem. Most of the evidence about incubation comes from introspective reports of mathematicians, artists, scientists, and other persons who report the sudden solution to a problem after a period of preoccupation with unrelated issues.

Why an incubation period seems to help in the effective solution of problems may be for several reasons. First, it may be simply a matter of rest which allows fatigue to dissipate. It might also be that incubation allows for forgetting of inappropriate sets and approaches to the problem and thus permits new approaches to be more easily perceived. Also, additional practice may occur during incubation, even though many persons report that they do not practice. For whatever reason or reasons, incubation appears sufficiently useful that it is recommended when you are stalled in the effort to solve a problem.

It should be cautioned, however, that most of the evidence for incubation is anecdotal. While we may regard incubation as "the pause that refreshes," Wickelgren (1974) has noted that there is very little experimental evidence to consistently support the concept. Our recommendation, which is reasonable, is nevertheless based on anecdotal reports rather than on laboratory evidence.

An Everyday Illustration of the Stages in Problem Solving

As we have seen, people typically go through three stages in solving problems. Now let us illustrate these stages in an everyday setting.

Suppose that you are trying to select a major area in your college career. Your problem is that you cannot decide on an appropriate major, and you therefore flounder around taking general courses in the hope that a solution will appear. How will you select an appropriate major? How will you solve this problem? The first step is simply to recognize that the problem exists. You decide that you must select a major, and normally you must do this no later than the beginning of the junior year in college. In order to interpret this problem, you must collect information about yourself; you need information about your abilities, aptitudes, interests, and goals. You need to decide what kinds of things you like as well as the kinds of things you dislike. You might also wish to be informed about the realities of the job market and the predicted future needs in various job areas. With this basic information you proceed to the next stage, which is to generate hypotheses. You may have decided that the health sciences represent one of your major areas of interest and ability, and that an undergraduate major with emphasis on premedical studies is appropriate for entering a professional program such as medicine or dentistry or a graduate program such as clinical psychology. If more than one alternative is plausible (such as a premedical course versus a pharmacy course or a premedical course versus a course in medical technology), you must then decide among the plausible alternatives. Once you choose a particular plan, you must test the reasonableness of your choice. In other words, you must evaluate your choice, which may take several semesters. You will pursue your program of, say, a premedical course as long as you do excellent academic work. However, a few instances of poor grades in biology and chemistry should lead you to reevaluate your decision and to consider other alternatives.

This example illustrates the stages of problem solving in choosing a career goal, a problem which is usually not solved quickly and which indeed many persons may take years to solve. The same sequence of stages generally occurs even for problems which can be solved in a shorter time. For instance, to solve problems such as where to live, where to obtain an undergraduate education, and what topic is suitable for a term paper, persons tend to go through the three stages of problem solving, although decisions about where to live are usually reached more quickly than decisions about choosing an undergraduate major.

PROCESSES IN PROBLEM SOLVING

In the discussion thus far we have already referred to a number of processes in problem solving. We have emphasized the importance of problem representation, noting that the way a problem is represented will influence the ease in achieving an effective solution. Indeed, appropriate representation of the problem is critical to a successful outcome, although it does not guarantee one. We also discussed some of the problem-solving strategies that a person can develop. In this section we shall examine some additional processes in problem solving.

Persistence of Set

When a person repeats a mental activity, there is some tendency for it to persist in a new situation. But the persistence of an old strategy or mode of attack in a new situation may be inappropriate. This type of process was extensively studied by Luchins (1942) in what is called "the water-jar problem" and provides a clear demonstration of the *persistence of set* in problem solving. The task requires a person to determine how to fill a jar of water in order to obtain a specified amount. All problems follow this general form: "You will be given three empty containers, A, B, and C, and your task is to describe how to obtain a specific quantity of water, Y."

Table 10.1 illustrates a typical problem sequence. Problem 1 is an illustrative problem. Here the solution is to fill jar A, then remove 9 quarts from it by filling jar B three times. Problems 2 through 6 are training problems in which the solution is always to fill jar B first, and then from that jar fill jar A once and jar C twice, which leaves the exact quantity specified. All problems, therefore, have the general solution of the form Y (the quantity specified) $= B - A - 2C$. Problems 7 and 8 can also be solved this way. However, for problem 7, there is a much simpler and direct solution in which jar A is filled first, then poured into jar C once, leaving the exact amount required for problem 7. For problem 8, the amounts in A and C are added. Problem 9 requires a simple solution. Go through the sequence of problems in table 10.1 and actually solve the problems so that you experience the task.

Table 10.1

An Example of the Water-Jar Problem

Problem		Size of Jars (in quarts)			Quarts of Water Desired
		A	B	C	Y
Example ⟶ 1		29	3	—	20
	2	21	127	3	100
Training	3	14	163	25	99
Problems ⟶	4	18	43	10	5
	5	9	42	6	21
	6	20	59	4	31
	7	23	49	3	20
Test ⟶	8	15	39	3	18
Problems	9	28	76	3	25

From *Fundamentals of Human Learning, Memory, and Cognition,* 2nd ed., by Henry C. Ellis. Dubuque, Iowa: Wm. C. Brown Company Publishers, 1978.

If human beings receive no instructions about the change in problems 7 and 8, they tend to persist in solving these problems like problem sequences 2 through 6. It is as if the repeated use of one successful strategy makes it difficult to discover alternative approaches. This simply illustrates the more general principle, namely, that most human beings have a strong tendency toward *persistence of set. Once you have learned a rule that works, you may tend to continue applying that rule even when a simpler solution is possible.* Old strategies continue to be used even when they are less efficient if we *fail to perceive* that the situation has changed.

Another example of persistence of set can be seen in anagram problems. The anagram has been a popular task in studies of problem solving and reasoning (Dominowski, 1972, 1977). The anagram is a scrambled series of letters such as *BOLREMP,* which when rearranged makes a word such as *PROBLEM.* The subject may be asked to form only one word or may be given an anagram which allows several possible solutions and asked to produce as many words as possible. Usually the first procedure is used. Either the number of correct solutions achieved in a fixed time period or the time to obtain a solution is measured.

Anagram problems can be used in a fashion directly analogous to the water-jar problem. Subjects can be given a series of anagrams such as the following:

Training Problems	**APMR**
	OSYB
	AEVH
	OTAG
	AFIW
Test Problems	**LCAM**
	OFRT

The first five anagrams can be solved by the formula 4–1–3–2, where 1–2–3–4 is the presented order of the letters. For example, unscrambling *OTAG* yields *GOAT.* During training, subjects learn a particular rule, although it may not be verbalized. During the next part of the sequence, the subjects are given test anagrams which require a new rule for solution. The problems are presented in a continuous series so that subjects do not know, of course, that the rule has changed. Under this circumstance, subjects have a strong tendency to persist in trying to use the old rule, taking longer to discover the new rule than do control subjects who did not undergo the initial training.

Many instances of the persistence of set can be seen in everyday life. For example, you may continue to try to solve mathematics problems using a rule no longer appropriate to the situation. The mathematics problem may require a combination of two rules or principles, whereas you may be using only one of the rules. Similarly, inexperienced chess players may continue to make the same types of moves even when the moves are no longer strategic or efficient. Only when they can "break their set" will they have the opportunity to consider a new mode of attack.

Functional Fixedness

Another kind of interference in effective problem-solving strategy occurs in tests of functional fixedness. *Functional fixedness* refers to the tendency to think of objects as functioning in one certain way and to ignore other less obvious ways in which they might be used.

A typical problem is one developed by Duncker (1945). The subject is given a set of objects and asked to arrange them as a stand capable, say, of supporting a vase of flowers. Some of the objects are appropriate to solving the problem, while others are inappropriate or irrelevant. The point of such a task is to require one to use a familiar object in a novel fashion. In this example, the objects consist of a rectangular piece of plywood which has a wooden bar wired to it, pliers, and two L-shaped metal brackets. The first step is to use the pliers to loosen the wire and detach the wooden bar. The wooden bar can be used as a support for the plywood board, but this in itself is not sufficient. Use of the L-shaped metal brackets appears reasonable to many subjects, but the brackets will not support the board. In order to solve the problem, the subject must use the pliers in an unusual way as legs for the plywood stand. This is accomplished by opening the pliers and placing them under the stand. The weight of the stand keeps the pliers steady at one end, while the wooden bar supports the stand at the other end.

As emphasized, the principal interest in this kind of task is to see whether a subject uses a familiar object in a novel and unusual way to solve a problem. The ability of human beings to solve this kind of problem is hampered to the extent that they tend to think of the pliers in terms of typical function. One must be able to break an established set in order to deal with this type of problem.

Another demonstration of functional fixedness introduced by Duncker involves the candle problem. A subject is presented a box of tacks, some matches, and a candle, all placed on a table. The task is to mount the candle on a wall in such a way that it will burn without dripping wax on the table. The solution requires that the subject empty the box of tacks, tack the empty box to the wall, and place the candle on the box. Duncker found that many subjects could not solve the problem. And it is a difficult task because the box is seen as a container for tacks, not as a support for the candle.

Solution effectiveness also depends on how the objects are verbally labeled by the experimenter. Glucksberg and colleagues (Glucksberg & Weisberg, 1966; Glucksberg & Danks, 1968) found that when the experimenter named the box while instructing the subjects, more solutions were obtained. In contrast, when they labeled the tacks "tacks," fewer solutions were obtained. A reasonable interpretation of these results is that when a subject hears the word *box,* the various possible encodings of *box* may be activated and hence a solution is more likely. But when a subject hears the word *tacks* a memory representation of *box* as such is less likely to be activated. More than just labeling is involved in functional fixedness. Functional fixedness is dependent not only on the resultant encoding or memory representation based on the labels used, but also on how an object is presented, such as the box with or without the tacks in it, and whether or not the subject has used the object. For instance, if a person has never used pliers for their usual purposes, they may be less subject to functional fixedness.

The studies of functional fixedness again attest to the importance of attaining the correct representation of a problem. Unless subjects perceive and represent the pliers as "legs" for the plywood stand, no reasonable solution will occur; similarly, unless subjects perceive and represent the box as a support for the candle, no reasonable solution can occur.

Memory and Problem Solving

The importance of memory can vary in different problem-solving situations. In some cases long-term memory plays a rather limited role, whereas in other cases the ability to draw on information stored in long-term memory is very important. Consider the cryptarithmetic problems discussed earlier. How would memory play a role in solving this class of problems? Certain information, such as the rules of subtraction, must be retrieved from long-term memory. Knowledge of the alphabet and the number system is also assumed. But once a person understands the task, the problem can be solved by application of means-ends analysis. In contrast, in the nine-dot problem presented at the beginning of chapter 10, once the problem is understood, a solution can be achieved which depends very little on long-term memory. As a general rule, it is reasonable to assume that, as a problem increases in complexity, more demands on memory will be made.

We noted in chapter 7 on semantic memory that people differ in knowledge and that high-knowledge people are better at remembering and comprehending new, related information than are low-knowledge people. As was seen, experts in a given task are better at encoding and remembering new events because of their organized knowledge base. What do these findings suggest for the role of memory in problem solving? One reasonable expectation is that good memory of *relevant* information is related to efficient problem solving, and this expectation has been shown to be valid. A study of chess performance has provided a useful vehicle for examining this question. The role of expertise is obvious in chess, because it takes years of practice to become a master player.

The classic work on the role of memory in chess performance was conducted by DeGroot (1965, 1966). The principal interest was in the difference between expert or master chess players and novices. In order to examine this issue, DeGroot observed the way masters and weaker players performed. Interestingly enough, almost no difference between the master players and the novices was found, except the expected result that master players make better moves. The one exception was that master players can reproduce a chessboard arrangement much more accurately than can novices.

This finding was pursued in a fascinating study by Chase and Simon (1973). In their study subjects were shown a chessboard with various pieces for only five seconds and then required to reproduce the board arrangement. Subjects could not "look back" at the board, but were required to

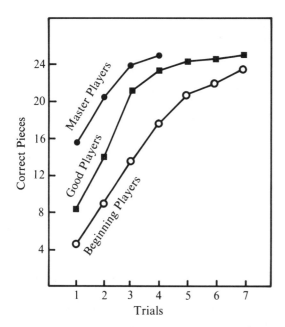

Figure 10.2 Recall of correct chess pieces for three categories of players. (From "The Mind's Eye in Chess" by W. G. Chase and H. A. Simon, in W. G. Chase, Ed., *Visual Information Processing*. New York: Academic Press, 1973.)

reproduce it from memory. They used three types of subjects in their experiment: master players, very good players, and beginning players. They were given seven trials to reproduce the chessboard. The results are shown in figure 10.2. The figure is a plot of the number of correct reproductions made by each player. It shows that the subjects' memory for the chess pieces is nicely ordered as a function of skill level. Master players show the best recall, very good players are next, and beginning players have the poorest recall.

Does this mean that master chess players have better memories in general? To test this possibility, Chase and Simon showed the players *random* arrangements of pieces on a chessboard, positions that would not normally occur. In this case, reproduction of the positions was the same for both very good and beginning players, and master players were poorest. So it is not the case that master players have better memories in general; they simply are good at encoding and remembering the positions of pieces in chess. Moreover, Chase and Simon argued that the reason master players perform so well is because they can recognize larger groupings of positions (meaningful units) than can poorer players. They contend that the expert chess player, as a result of years of practice, acquires a very large number of recognizable groupings or patterns, with reasonable moves associated with each grouping. Thus what the expert is capable of doing is recognizing particular groupings and recalling moves associated with each grouping.

Plausible as this view appears, it has been questioned by Holding and Reynolds (1982). They found that experts still selected better moves than novices even when expert-novice differences in memory for arrangements of chess pieces did not exist. Charness (1981) has also questioned the Chase and Simon explanation of chess experts' performance by studying chess playing with subjects of varying age ranging from sixteen to sixty-four years. Charness found that although the older players showed poorer performance on memory for arrangement of chess pieces, they showed no decrement in selecting good moves. This finding suggests that chess performance, in the sense of making good moves, is not necessarily dependent upon recognizing patterns and their associated moves. Instead, the results of these two studies suggest that chess experts are better at evaluating alternative choices because they have better criteria for making judgments, not because they are better at recognizing patterns.

Creative Problem Solving

Most of us seem to recognize that there are vast differences in creativity among individuals. If asked to identify highly creative individuals we can easily point to brilliant scientists such as Einstein or renowned artists and musicians such as Rembrandt and Beethoven. But this does not say anything about the creative process itself.

Creative problem solving usually involves the production of original ideas which are practical or relevant to the solution of a problem. Original ideas are uncommon, and frequently it is the juxtaposition of old ideas in a novel way that makes them creative. But having unusual or rare qualities is insufficient for an idea to be called creative. After all, a severely disturbed psychotic person might produce some unusual ideas due to disturbed thought processes. The ideas must also be useful, that is, have some value.

Studies of creative persons have shown that they tend to have a number of distinctive personality characteristics shared in common. As a general rule, persons characterized as creative tend to be highly individualistic and independent, somewhat introverted, low in conformity, intuitive, and self-accepting. They are not necessarily popular and are sometimes self-centered.

Research in creative problem solving has focused on how original and practical ideas are generated. While it is not too difficult to produce original ideas, it is much harder to produce ideas that are both original and practical. Many original ideas are simply not practical, and thus fail to meet the criteria of creativity. There have been attempts to enhance creativity by using originality training. In originality training subjects are given practice and reinforcement for generating unusual ideas. Such practice is effective in increasing the number of original ideas produced; unfortunately, it has no effect on the number of creative ideas produced.

There appears to be a clear relation between age and creativity. Studies show that in most fields creative persons produce their best work at a relatively early age. Usually, the most creative period is between the ages of thirty and forty years; however this age varies with a particular field. Mathematicians and physicists show their greatest creativity between thirty and thirty-five years of age and biologists and psychologists between the ages of thirty and forty years, whereas musicians and painters continue typically to be productive for a longer period of time. Not only do scientists do their best work between the ages of thirty and forty years, but they also are most productive during these years. One way to interpret these age differences is simply to credit it to sheer energy. It seems reasonable that a young person's greater productivity may be related to a high level of energy. And the more productive persons may have a greater likelihood of being more creative simply because they are making more contributions. There is some evidence for this line of reasoning in that in most scientific fields the more distinguished researchers tend to produce more works than their less distinguished colleagues. Another possibility is that senior scientists are more reluctant to publish their work.

Finally, let us consider the relation between creativity and intelligence. It is certainly reasonable to believe that some minimum level of intelligence must be present for creative thinking to occur. While there is a positive correlation between intelligence and creativity, the relation is not a perfect one. In short, creativity is more likely to be observed in more intelligent individuals, but intelligence is not a guarantee of creativity.

Guilford's Approach to Creativity

In his research on intelligence, Guilford (1959, 1967) described creative thinking as a trait related to three important factors: fluency, flexibility, and originality. Fluency is the ability to generate several (or many) alternative solutions to a problem, all of which fit a set of requirements. An example would be listing as many synonyms or antonyms to a word as possible in a specified time period. Flexibility is the ability to change approaches to solving a problem. This, for example, is represented in your ability to shift gears in solving a series of math problems each of which requires a different strategy. Originality refers to the ability to generate novel or special solutions.

In addition, Guilford made an important distinction between two types of thinking. *Convergent* thinking is thinking that moves in a straightforward fashion toward a single, specific answer. For example, calculating the interest payments on a car loan of $16,000 at 2.9 percent yields only one correct answer. In contrast, *divergent* thinking differs in that it moves outward from the problem in a variety of directions. For example, if you were asked to list in a one-minute period all the possible uses of a tennis racquet, you would have to think broadly in order to come up with alternative uses. Guilford noted that creative problem solving is most clearly related to divergent thinking. Therefore, creativity is usually measured by testing divergent thinking (e.g., Torrance, 1968). As Torrance notes, such a test typically measures at least three aspects of performance: quantity, originality, and importance. Quantity is measured by the number of different answers. Originality can be measured by counting how many people give the same answer, or by calling on experts to rate the originality of the solution. Finally, the solution must be judged a useful one, again, by experts or by those sufficiently familiar with the problem to make an informed judgment.

Creativity and Expected Evaluation

If a person expects his or her work to be evaluated, what effect does this have on their creativity? In a view of research on creativity, Amabile (1983) describes some interesting findings. In one study, college students were instructed to write a poem. Half of the students were told that the experimenter was interested in their handwriting and so they presumably did not expect to have the content of their poem evaluated. The other half were informed that the experimenter was interested in the poem's content, that the poem would be evaluated by judges, and that they would receive a copy of the evaluations of their poems. In addition, half of the students worked alone and half worked in groups.

The poems were judged by experts in the field using an agreed-upon procedure for rating the creativity of the poems. The results showed that having an expected evaluation clearly impaired the judged creativity of the poems, and this was true whether the students worked alone or in groups.

Does this mean that people should not be evaluated? Obviously not, for the simple reason that the creative works of artists and others are usually judged and evaluated in some kind of context. What Amabile's (1983) results indicate is that the expectation of evaluation can inhibit the creativity of novices but not necessarily experts in writing poems.

Brainstorming and Creativity

A popular idea designed to stimulate creative solutions to problems has been brainstorming. Brainstorming involves people working in groups in which as many ideas as possible are put forward with no evaluation until later. Thus criticism of the ideas is initially withheld. Wild, far out ideas are encouraged, ideas can be combined, and everyone is instructed to speak freely. Recently, Weisberg (1986) has questioned some of the assumptions of this technique. He reports that people may be more creative working alone than in groups. In addition, brainstorming may produce more ideas, but he believes they are frequently of lower quality. The general conclusion is that brainstorming may be useful in some settings but that it is not a substitute for the individual production of ideas.

Expertise

An important area of investigation in recent years has been the effort to describe the differences between experts and novices. We recognize that experts in a specialty such as physics or medicine have more education and experience than do novices, but the interesting issue is how experts use their superior knowledge in solving problems and what general characteristics with respect to problem-solving strategies experts display.

Studies of experts have investigated how expertise relates to performance in chess, physics and mathematics, social studies, medical diagnosis, and several other areas. We have already discussed some of the research on chess expertise (Chase & Simon, 1973). This research also points to some of the main characteristics of chess experts. They generally have many years of practice and an excellent memory for regular chess positions. Their expertise is not a matter of considering many moves, but they develop the ability to make rapid moves if speed is part of what is practiced. Finally, high intelligence is not essential to becoming a chess expert.

Similarly, extensive studies of expertise in physics have been conducted. For example, Larkin (1981) has compared performance of first-year college students in physics (novices) with that of physics teachers. In terms of experience, this involves about 200 hours of exposure to physics as contrasted to about 10,000 hours. Larkin investigated the way in which experts and novices solved problems in which a block is sliding down an inclined plane. The person's task was to find the velocity of the block when it reaches the bottom of the plane. What Larkin found was that the novices frequently worked backward to solve the problem. They would start with the unknown, v (velocity), then find an equation to calculate v, and then calculate a, the acceleration. Experts used similar equations but worked forward. They tended to start with quantities which could be directly computed, such as gravitational force, and then worked toward the desired velocity.

Another interesting area for research has been the study of expertise in medical diagnosis by radiologists (Lesgold, 1984). Radiological diagnosis requires careful and detailed examination of the *pattern* of information contained in X-rays. Achieving skill in this area requires considerable training and is a skill not easily learned. Part of the difficulty lies in the fact that the radiologist must interpret a complex configuration of information involving shading, depth, location, and other features. It involves making a complex relational judgment while weighing a good deal of information in the picture. What Lesgold notes is that experts have acquired the skill to *abstract* information from the complex pattern in the X-ray, whereas novices tend to look for specific, discrete features.

Are there any general conclusions about experts? Chi and Glaser (1985), Hayes (1981), Chi, Glaser, and Rees (1982), and others have suggested several general characteristics about experts. Some of these tentative generalizations include: (1) Experts differ from novices in their representation of a problem. Experts learn to represent the problem in terms of more abstract features, features that are more likely to be predictive of reaching a problem solution. In contrast, novices more frequently use surface features of a problem task. (2) Experts are better able to reorganize their approaches to a problem, that is, they show greater flexibility in their approach to solving problems. (3) Experts tend to develop better memories specific to the task. (4) Experts tend to approach problems with a more deliberate style and are much less likely to be impulsive. In this respect, they are more reflective and sometimes slower to respond with proposed solutions.

Ill-Defined Problems: Experts and Novices

As we noted at the beginning of this chaper, problems can range from well-defined to poorly-defined tasks (e.g., Simon, 1973; Reitman, 1964; 1965). In well-defined problems the critical or important features of the task are identified; in brief, the original state, the goal state, and the rules are identified. With an ill-defined problem, the original state (the conditions present at the beginning), the goal state (what the objectives are), and the rules are unspecified or only partly described. And what is an ill-defined problem for one person may be relatively clearly defined for another. For example, in assigning a term paper an instructor may note that many students understand the goal of the project whereas a few students may be confused until they receive more information.

Some examples of ill-defined problems noted by Halpern (1984) include such things as saving money for college tuition, building a better mousetrap, and slowing down the nuclear arms race.

Jim Voss and his colleagues have studied the role of knowledge levels of people in solving ill-defined problems (e.g., Voss, Greene, Post, & Penner, 1983; Voss, Tyler, & Yengo, 1983). The problem posed involved solving production problems in agriculture in the Soviet Union which was presented to three different groups of people with differing levels of expertise. One group, the experts, consisted of political scientists whose speciality was the Soviet Union. A second group consisted of chemistry professors, experts in their speciality, but who were beginners with respect to knowledge about Soviet affairs. A third group consisted of students enrolled in a course in Soviet domestic policy.

All groups of subjects were given this same core problem: Imagine that you are the Minister of Agriculture for the Soviet Union. Crop productivity has been too low for the past several years. What plan would you devise to increase it? As you can see, this is truly an ill-defined problem because much information is lacking. We don't know the initial state or conditions, the precise goal constraints, or any rules. Granted that your task as Minister of Agriculture is to increase productivity, the question is: What constitutes an appropriate level of increase? 50%, 100%, or what?

Experts differed from novices in the way they approached the problem. For the Soviet experts, 24% of their verbal reports dealt with some elaboration of the initial state of the problem whereas only 1% of the reports of the novices dealt with this issue. In addition, the experts tended to identify possible constraints in the problem whereas the novices did not. In both cases the experts and novices attempted to define the problem; however, the experts were better at defining assumptions, constraints and boundary conditions.

Analogical Problem Solving

Earlier in this chapter we examined one type of problem that involved inducing structure, verbal analogies. Analogies require that a person discover a pattern or rule in one setting and then transfer or apply it to another setting. When we have little or no knowledge about the transfer task, that is, the new setting, then the ability to solve the task by way of analogical problem solving is certainly a form of creative problem solving.

Researchers who have studied analogical problem solving (e.g., Gick & Holyoak, 1983; Holyoak, 1985; Holyoak & Koh, 1987) describe the solution of analogies as one that involves the mapping of a conceptual structure of one set of rules or ideas (called the base domain) into another set of rules or ideas (called the target or transfer domain). For example, consider the analogy problem described earlier in this chapter: Toulouse is to Lautrec as Rimsky is to ___?___; Toulouse is to Lautrec is the base domain and Rimsky is to ___?___ is the target or transfer domain. The ability to solve this analogy is called analogical mapping, going from a base to a target domain. Holyoak (1985) points out that in analogical mapping a person notices that there are patterns or relationships that are similar in the two settings; in this example Toulouse-Lautrec is a joint name and a double name beginning with Rimsky will satisfy the analogy. A correct solution thus requires that certain aspects of the base domain be transferred to the target domain.

In order to study analogical mapping, Gick and Holyoak (1980; 1983) had subjects solve analogies in problem-solving tasks. They gave subjects analogy problems taken from Karl Duncker's (1945) radiation problem. In the radiation problem a physician attempts to destroy a malignant tumor using radiation. High intensity radiation is needed to destroy the tumor but such radiation will also destroy healthy tissue. In contrast, if low intensity radiation is used the healthy tissue will be saved but the tumor will not be treated. This problem can be solved if the physician sends radiation from a number of different directions so that it converges on the tumor and destroys it. Few subjects solve this problem as such. However, if subjects are given a story about a general attacking a fortress prior to the radiation problem, many more are able to solve the problem. In the military attack story, the general was prevented from using his entire army to take the fortress because the roads leading to it were mined so as to explode if large units of men traversed the road; small groups could pass. The general divided his army into small groups and dispatched them along different roads to the fortress so that they eventually converged on it. When subjects were given this story, almost 80% were then able to solve the radiation problem. This provides good evidence that they were solving the problem by analogy; that is, they are able to match various features of the base story to the transfer task. Once a person has acquired a "convergence" schema for solving the problem it will become easier for them to recognize the usefulness of this schema in similar settings.

You might also suspect that the ability of subjects to use information in the base domain (the initial story) also depends on the surface similarity of the base and target domains. Holyoak and Koh (1987) found that subjects given a similar story (a surgeon using rays on cancer) were much better able to transfer their knowledge than those given a dissimilar story (the general story) when tested several days after receiving the base story. Many of the subjects recalled the similar story (88%) whereas few (12%) recalled the dissimilar story.

Problem Solving in the Classroom

One of the important contributions of cognitive psychology is the awareness that errors that students make in math may be systematic, that is, may be based on the application of faulty rules. Consider the following subtraction problem $384 - 129 = ?$ in which a student's answer is 265. Doing the arithmetic you realize that the answer is 255, not 265. You might think that the student is way off; however, another look at the problem would suggest that the student knows some of the procedures for subtraction, but has failed to grasp the procedures for borrowing (Ashcraft, 1987).

Brown and Burton (1978) have made extensive analyses of children's errors in math and found that many errors are systematic, not simply random, casual mistakes. What is the case is that some children have learned some procedure or a part of it incorrectly, but that other related procedures have been correctly learned. From the viewpoint of diagnosis and correction, what is important in instruction is to be able to diagnose the basis of errors in math so that the students' faulty procedures can be corrected. Ashcraft (1989) has pointed out that one advantage of this approach is that educators are likely to become more aware of the systematic, as distinct from random bases of errors. If teachers incorporate this view, then their approach to teaching will place emphasis on understanding the rule-based or faulty procedures underlying errors, an approach which in turn leads to helping students learn correct procedures.

TIPS ON PROBLEM SOLVING

What can be summarized about problem solving that can be useful in everyday situations? Ellis (1978) identified five rules of thumb which are useful in virtually all problem-solving situations. They include the following: understand the problem, remember the problem, identify alternative hypotheses, acquire coping strategies, and evaluate the final hypothesis. These rules are reviewed in the following discussion. Additional suggestions are outlined in several texts such as Davis (1973), Wickelgren (1974), and Hayes (1981).

1. *Understand the problem.* Before you can solve a problem, you must first be sure you *understand* it. Perhaps this suggestion appears so obvious as to sound trite. Yet all too frequently the basic difficulty in solving a problem is the failure to have a clear conception of its components. One of the frequent reasons that students do poorly on examinations is that in their haste to answer a question they fail to analyze and reexamine the question itself. An all-too-familiar experience of students is to discover that they have written an answer to a question other than the one asked. Thus, not until you understand a problem can you attempt to solve it effectively. Moreover, once you have clarified a problem, it is good practice to check again to see whether your initial understanding is still correct.

2. *Remember the problem.* Another source of difficulty arises when you *fail to remember* the problem accurately. On occasion students produce incorrect answers on an essay examination because they fail to remember the problem as it is formulated. Somewhere in the course of writing an answer students may veer away from the central issue and deal with irrelevant issues. They may, so to speak, shift in midstream from the main thesis to trivial, secondary, or utterly unrelated topics if they fail to keep the problem in mind. Therefore, periodically recheck your memory of the problem to ensure that you stay with the issue.

3. *Identify alternative hypotheses.* Problem solving requires, of course, that you produce hypotheses. Rather than fixate on one or two hypotheses, *try to identify and classify several hypotheses* that appear reasonable. It is generally advantageous to try the easier or simpler hypotheses first, and if these fail, then to shift to more complex hypotheses. Finally, avoid the premature selection of a particular hypothesis until you have had opportunity to evaluate reasonable alternatives, that is, generate a list of hypotheses.

4. *Acquire coping strategies.* Coping strategies refer to ways of dealing with the difficulty, failure, and frustration encountered in problem situations. Frustration and difficulty are inevitable accompaniments of problem solving. Since frustration cannot in the long run be avoided under all circumstances, a major task is to learn how to *cope* with such difficulty. Blind persistence in using old rules and excessive motivation, particularly in the form of frustration, are seen as barriers to successful problem solving. Therefore, you should attempt to recognize rigidity in yourself and to avoid inflexibility when solving problems. One way of doing this is to cultivate a general plan of using variable modes of attack as the situation demands. The colloquial expression *hang loose* captures much of the meaning of what is required for effective problem solving. Thus, it is important to remain open for new options, alternatives, and approaches.

5. *Evaluate the final hypothesis.* Once you have decided on a final hypothesis, *reevaluate your choice.* Consider the issue of implementing your choice. Even though it may be a good one on rational and logical grounds, is it practical and feasible? In summary, take one final look before you commit yourself to a particular sequence of action.

Two additional tips noted by Moates and Schumacher (1980) are relevant.

6. *Explain the problem to someone.* Talking about the problem to someone else may help you gain a better perspective.

7. *Put the problem aside.* Incubation appears to work for some persons some of the time, at least according to anecdotal reports. But do not use the waiting period as a way of regularly avoiding problems.

THEORETICAL APPROACHES

Current theoretical work in problem solving is dominated by the information-processing approach. This stands in contrast to earlier, traditional approaches stemming from behavioristic or associative theories and Gestalt psychology. In this section these approaches are briefly characterized.

Traditional Approaches

One traditional approach attempted to explain problem solving using principles of stimulus-response (habit) formation derived from studies of conditioning and learning. It is assumed that in any problem situation a learner brings to the task a number of possible habits. These habits are assumed to be readily available in the sense of being already formed at some level of strength. These habit tendencies vary in strength and are arranged in habit-family hierarchy. The stimulus-response associative approach contends that the problem situation is more likely to produce some of these habits than other habits. In problem solving, these habits are run off covertly, and when one is successful the habit is strengthened, whereas the unsuccessful habits are weakened. In general, this approach assumes that problem solving can be explained from principles derived from associative learning.

A different approach to problem solving was outlined by the Gestalt psychologists. How persons solve problems depends on how they perceive and structure their problem environment. The characteristic approach of Gestalt psychologists has been to place subjects in a problem-solving setting and observe the way they go about solving a problem. A typical problem is the *detour* task in which a barrier is placed between subjects and the goal object; the barrier is constructed so as to prevent subjects from directly obtaining the object. The subjects, sometimes children, must detour by going around the barrier to obtain the goal object. Other problem settings have required animals to use two sticks, which are joined so as to form a rake for obtaining food. Descriptions of the behavior of animals solving problems emphasize such features as their observing the objects for a period of time, which is followed by a rapid (insightful) solution of the problem. The Gestalt psychologists contend that this rapid problem-solving activity indicates that subjects are able to reorganize their perception of the problem environment and thus achieve insight into the problem.

A number of experiments have been conducted to test these traditional approaches. Although the data and generalizations resulting from these experiments have been useful, these two approaches have been inadequate as general models of problem-solving activity. They lack the comprehensiveness necessary for a good theory. As an alternative, the information-processing approach, emerging around 1960, now provides the most comprehensive theoretical approach to problem solving. And in some cases, the ideas from the traditional approaches were integrated within the information-processing approach.

Information-Processing Approaches: Newell and Simon

Information-processing approaches to theorizing about psychological events have received considerable attention since about 1960. Just as there are information-processing approaches to perception, attention, memory, and concept formation, as noted in earlier chapters, there are also information-processing approaches to problem solving.

It is useful at this point to characterize again some of the general features of this approach. Information-processing approaches to psychological events attempt to formulate a flowchart, or sequence of events, using the format of a computer program. A computer program consists of a series of steps or rules that tell a computer what to do. In a similar vein, the basic idea of information processing is to identify the steps involved in a specific psychological activity, list these steps in proper sequence, and then see whether the computer can simulate these activities. To the extent that the computer can simulate the actions of a human being, the psychologist may gain some understanding of what must go into a theory designed to explain such actions.

Clearly, of course, a human being is much more than a computer. Basically, all that is implied by information-processing approaches to behavior is that a program which can simulate some psychological process can, in turn, serve as a highly abstract model of the kinds of events that must make up the process. Thus, the theory of a process becomes essentially a statement of the rules of operations, of restrictions placed on the rules, of how the rules combine, and of how much information the program must contain.

Several kinds of programs for problem-solving activities have been developed. An example of an early type is the letter-series completion tasks used by Simon and Kotovsky (1963). These problems contain a series of letters and require that the subject fill in the missing letter. A simple example is as follows:

B D F H _

Here the rule is very simple and can be solved by children seven or eight years old. Another series takes this form:

B T C T D T _

And a more difficult series takes this form:

P X A X O Y B Y N Z _

This type of task can be made even more difficult, so that most college students are unable to solve the problem.

A problem-solving program of this type must contain a number of features. It must be able to recognize and distinguish letters. It must be able to detect regularities in the pattern by looking for repeatable periodicities in the sequence. More generally, it must be programmed to discover whatever regularity is intrinsically built into a particular letter series. Finally, if the program can successfully solve a given class of problems, the psychologist then gains some conception of the kind of rules that must be present in any theory of problem-solving activity.

In discussing a number of experiments on problem solving we have implicitly described some of the general features of the information-processing approach. For example, in the discussion of cryptarithmetic problems, many of the features of the information-processing approach were used. Let us now formalize some of these features.

The general features of information-processing systems were outlined in chapter 1. In addition, as applied to problem solving, these features have been extensively described by Newell and Simon (1972). As a general rule, three characteristics have been noted: these are aspects of the task environment, mental representation of the problem as a problem space, and selection of an appropriate operator.

Task environment refers to the description of the problem as presented to the subject and includes the information, assumptions, and constraints presented as well as the context in which the problem is presented. We saw earlier, for example, that mere verbal labeling of a "box" can influence the ease of solving the candle problem. Similarly, being told that D = 5 in the cryptarithmetic problem points out the reasonable place to begin solving this problem.

Problem space refers to a subject's mental representation of the problem, as well as the various solutions that may be attempted. Problem spaces are the various ideas or hypotheses that a person might develop about a problem. We have already noted that a critical feature of effective problem solving is the development of an appropriate representation of the problem. The problem space will, of course, change in the course of trying to solve the problem.

Finally, to get from one problem state to another an *operator* must be selected and applied to the problem. An *operator* refers to a sequence of operations that takes the problem solver from the initial state to the goal state.

REASONING

The study of reasoning deals with how humans reach certain conclusions from either explicit or implicit premises. Reasoning and problem solving are closely related topics in that both are concerned with aspects of what is normally called thinking. The focus of reasoning, however, is on how a person goes about reaching a conclusion and evaluating whether a conclusion is valid or invalid. Reasoning is involved in problem solving in that some form of reasoning is usually part of solving problems.

The study of reasoning was historically related to the study of logic. The study of logic, which is part of philosophy and mathematics, attempts to specify the characteristics of good and bad arguments, that is logically valid and invalid arguments. Logic is a formal system for deriving valid conclusions, that is, logic is the set of rules by which we can reach a valid conclusion about events or things. For instance, if you are informed that *All Toyotas* (A) are *Japanese Cars* (B) and that *All Japanese Cars* (B) are *Good Buys* (C), then it follows that *All Toyotas* (A) are *Good Buys* (C). It follows from formal logic that all As are Cs, given that the two assumptions are valid. Formal logic is not concerned with the empirical validity of the assumptions themselves, but is concerned with the validity of the deductions that are derived. Thus the empirical truth of *All Bs are Cs* is not an issue for logic, but is an issue of fact to be determined by means other than formal logic. As an instance of invalid reasoning in this example, the deduction that *Some As are not Cs* is not valid given the stated premises.

What is important for our purposes is that formal logic specifies a prescription for correct reasoning. It does not, however, accurately describe how most people reason in everyday affairs. Thus the study of reasoning is not restricted to logic because people do not always operate according to the rules of logic. Indeed, many thinkers have pointed out that humans are frequently illogical in their reasoning.

Types of Reasoning

There are two basic kinds of reasoning: deduction and induction. Deductive reasoning involves reaching a conclusion based upon assumptions that are known to be true. For example, consider the following argument, which is an instance of a linear-order problem, a type of problem based on relations among items:

> John is taller than Diane.
> Diane is taller than Joan.
> Therefore, John is taller than Joan.

If we assume that the first two statements are true, then the conclusion must follow. Deduction thus involves reasoning and reaching a conclusion based upon general assumptions (premises) which are valid. If the rules of logic are followed, then the deduction *must* be valid. In contrast, inductive reasoning is the process by which we draw a conclusion based upon specific happenings. An induction is something that is likely to be true on the basis of past experience, but there is no guarantee that it will be absolutely true

(Pellegrino, 1985). For example, if you are a straight-A student in your junior year in college, you might draw the conclusion that you will be an A student in your course in Cognitive Psychology taken in your senior year. In this case, you are very likely to be correct in your inference, but it is possible that you could get a different grade. Similarly, if you are visiting in Hawaii where the daily temperature is very stable, you could conclude that the daily high temperature for April might be 86° F (± 4° F). You are likely to be correct, but you could be wrong in the event of an unusual storm or some other event that could lower the temperature well below normal.

Deductive Reasoning

Psychologists have studied several types of deductive-reasoning problems. Three frequently used types are propositional reasoning, syllogistic reasoning, and linear-order problems. We are familiar with propositional reasoning because we use it frequently in daily affairs. Here is an example that may be familiar to some of you:

> Unless the dealer lowers the price of the car by two thousand dollars, I won't be able to buy it.
> The dealer will lower the price by only six hundred dollars.
> Therefore, I won't be able to buy the car.

One type of reasoning that has been studied fairly extensively involves what is called propositional reasoning (Marcus & Rips, 1979; Rips, 1983). In this situation, statements or propositions are represented by the symbols p and q, and by $\supset$ which means *implies*. For example, if we let p stand for the first part of the proposition, *If I win the next three cases for my law firm, I will receive a salary raise,* and q for the proposition, *I win the next three cases for my law firm,* then we can by the rules of logic draw the conclusion, *Therefore, I will receive a salary raise.* This type of argument is called, from Latin, *modus ponens,* which is a rule of inference that states if we are given p *implies* q and p, then we can infer q.

If I win the next three cases for my law firm, I will receive a salary raise.	$p \supset q$
I win the next three cases.	p
Therefore, I will receive a salary raise.	$\therefore q$

Table 10.2

Arguments in Propositional Reasoning

Example	Name	Form	Validity
1. If John is intelligent, then he is rich. John is intelligent.	Modus Ponens	$p \supset q$ p	Valid
Therefore, John is rich.		$\therefore q$	
2. If John is intelligent, then he is rich. John is not rich.	Modus Tollens	$p \supset q$ $\overline{q}$	Valid
Therefore, John is not intelligent.		$\therefore \overline{p}$	
3. If John is intelligent, then he is rich. John is rich.	Affirming the Consequent	$p \supset q$ q	Invalid
Therefore, John is intelligent.		$\therefore p$	
4. If John is intelligent, then he is rich. John is not intelligent.	Denying the Antecedent	$p \supset q$ $\overline{p}$	Invalid
Therefore, John is not rich.		$\therefore \overline{q}$	

There are four basic types of propositional arguments, which are shown in table 10.2. The first two arguments are examples of valid inferences and the second two are examples of invalid inferences. The third argument is a particularly interesting case because it is a common logical fallacy that is made both in everyday reasoning and in scientific affairs (Johnson-Laird & Steedman, 1978).

Consider how the fallacy in the third argument appears in scientific reasoning. Much of scientific reasoning involves deriving predictions from a theory, testing the predictions, and determining if the results support the theory. This sequence of events readily allows for invalid reasoning of the form outlined in the third argument, as illustrated in the following example:

If theory X is true, then behavior Y will occur.	$p \supset q$
Behavior Y occurs.	q
Therefore, theory X is true.	$\therefore p$

The fallacy in this argument is that the occurrence of behavior Y does not prove that theory X is true. The behavior, Y, could have occurred for any number of reasons and does not necessarily mean that theory X is the explanation for that behavior. All that can be said is that the observed behavior is *consistent* with the theory, but does not prove that the theory is correct. In their book on reasoning, Wason and Johnson-Laird (1972) point out a number of good examples of how invalid reasoning occurs.

Another type of reasoning task that has been widely used in studies of deductive reasoning is the categorical syllogism. The syllogism is a set of propositions that refer to the quantity of something such as some, all, none, or some not. Consider the following example:

All rich people are Republicans.	All As are Bs.
All Republicans live in mansions.	All Bs are Cs.
Therefore, all rich people live in mansions . . .	All As are Cs.

Most readers will recognize this as a valid deduction even though you may doubt the truth of the premises. But given the premises, you recognize that the deduction is correct.
Now consider the argument:

Some rich people are Republicans.	Some As are Bs.
Some Republicans live in mansions.	Some Bs are Cs.
Therefore, some rich people live in mansions.	Some As are Cs.

This type of argument is invalid although many people tend to accept it as correct. It is true that *some rich people live in mansions,* but the conclusion is not warranted by logic.

If you fail to see how this argument is invalid, consider it in this context:

Some women are Chinese.
Some Chinese are men.

Therefore, some women are men.

The third type of deductive reasoning task, the linear-order problem, was described at the beginning of this chapter. A linear-order problem sets up a relation among propositions and requires that a person draw a conclusion about how items are related.

Reasoning Errors

Why do people make errors in reasoning? Another way of addressing this question is to ask: What cognitive processes do people use when they make invalid conclusions and what factors are likely to encourage such errors? A number of processes and factors have been examined and one of these is the classic *atmosphere effect* account proposed by Woodworth and Sells (1935). According to their explanation, the way the premises were stated would predispose a person to accept a particular conclusion. For example, if the premises and the conclusions were stated using the same modifiers (some, all), then a person would be more likely to accept the conclusion. Thus, in the example given in the previous section, the use of some in both the premises and the conclusion would lead a person to more readily agree with the statement.

Consider the phrase "If it's Tuesday we must be in Belgium," the expression uttered by a tired tourist on an extended European tour. Now, turn the phrase around to say "We're in Belgium, so it must be Tuesday." This may be true; however, if the tour is in Belgium for two days, Tuesday and Wednesday, the reverse statement has only a 50% chance of being true. This type of invalid reasoning occurs frequently.

Another factor in producing errors in reasoning lies in the finding that when people arrive at a generalization, they are reluctant to try to reexamine it and prove it incorrect. Wason and Laird-Johnson (1972) point out that people tend to have some investment in their generalizations and feel the need to convince themselves of their truth. In this situation, people tend to be unwilling to propose ideas that would be inconsistent with their generalization, and in doing so, may fail to see the error in their generalization. This type of error is the direct result of a cognitive bias that many people have, namely, an unwillingness to rethink an idea or to test evidence that may contradict their idea.

Inductive Reasoning

The process of inductive reasoning is important because it is frequently part of our daily activities. All of us reason in situations based on our knowledge of what is likely to be the case. For example, when planning a beach vacation to Acapulco, we know that the weather is typically warm and that we should pack appropriate clothing for the tropics. Because of Acapulco's location, we are likely to be correct in our judgment of the weather most of the time, and thus our reasoning is going to be valid. But consider a beach vacation in Mexico at Mazatlan, a beach resort farther north and located on the Tropic of Cancer. Here the weather is typically warm; however, Pacific storms can blow in and the weather can be cool during the winter. In this case, we have more uncertainty in the weather and may reach an invalid conclusion if we reason that Mazatlan is always going to be warm and balmy because of its location.

The example just presented illustrates the difficulty of inductive reasoning in that we cannot be absolutely certain of our reasoning. Consider another situation in which a student is trying to evaluate the way he is perceived by the instructor:

> On occasion, the instructor fails to call on the student when
> he raises his hand in class.
> The student goes to the instructor's office, but the instructor
> is too busy to see him.
> The student receives an F on his first quiz.
> _____
> Therefore, the instructor does not like the student.

The difficulty with this reasoning is that there are other explanations for the instructor's behavior, none of which involve the instructor's attitudes toward the student. Each one of these situations can be explained by other factors and thus may have no bearing on what the instructor thinks about the student. Indeed, the instructor may not even know the student and thus has no opinion about him. It is also possible that the conclusion is correct; however, until alternative explanations are considered, there is no way of being sure that your reasoning is valid.

Teaching Reasoning and Thinking Skills

In this section we shall briefly comment on the issue of teaching reasoning skills. More generally, this is presented as one of teaching thinking skills, of which reasoning is one component. There is now substantial evidence that skills in reasoning and thinking can be taught, although this is not an easy process. In an interesting book, Baron and Sternberg (1987) have assembled a number of papers that address the teaching of thinking skills. This is a useful summary of what we know about teaching thinking by educators. Similarly, Nickerson, Perkins, and Smith (1985) have provided an excellent review of the issues in teaching thinking.

One issue that is usually raised is whether it is necessary to teach thinking. Nickerson (1987) has provided a good discussion of why it is. Your immediate reaction might be that such teaching is unnecessary, because certainly everyone thinks. It is the case that we do think without always being prodded and without the benefit of formal training in thinking.

As Nickerson suggests, we can no more avoid thinking than we can avoid breathing. But what *can* be done is to teach people how to think more effectively, more coherently, more creatively, or more deeply than is normally the case. The fact that thinking occurs spontaneously does not protect us from poor and unclear thinking, nor does it protect us from the persuasiveness of advertisers or anyone else who would convince us of the correctness of their views. However, there appears to be little evidence that students will acquire good thinking skills simply from taking conventional courses. Indeed, Glaser (1985) has argued that good thinking skills are unlikely to be the by-product of the study of any conventional subject matter. And Nickerson points out that to acquire good thinking skills in the classroom or elsewhere, explicit attention will have to be given to these skills and ways to develop them.

What are the characteristics of good thinking? Nickerson (1987) proposes a list of twenty-three characteristics he would consider important, including the following ten:

1. Skillful and impartial use of evidence
2. Organized thoughts articulated concisely and coherently
3. Ability to distinguish between logically valid and invalid inferences
4. Ability to comprehend the idea of degrees of belief
5. Ability to see similarities and analogies that are not superficially apparent
6. An understanding of the difference between winning an argument and being right
7. Recognition that most real-world problems have more than one possible solution and that those solutions may differ in numerous respects and may be difficult to compare in terms of a single figure of merit
8. An understanding of the differences among conclusions, assumptions and hypotheses
9. Sensitivity toward the difference between the validity of a belief and the intensity with which it is held
10. Ability to represent differing viewpoints without distortion, exaggeration, or characterization

The teaching of reasoning and thinking skills must be seen as a lifelong process and not something that is taught in a specific course and thence forgotten. One way that such skills can be learned is through the use of self-help books that have the objective of teaching skills in reasoning, judgment, problem solving, decision making, and creative thinking (e.g., Levine, 1987). One of the best such volumes available is entitled *Thought and Knowledge* (1984) by Diane Halpern. Halpern provides for a variety of examples and exercises designed to sharpen one's thinking skills, to recognize muddy thinking, and to clarify one's thinking about a variety of topics. She applies principles of cognitive psychology to numerous everyday situations. For example, consider the following illustration:

> If you pay careful attention to bumper stickers, you'll probably be surprised to find that many are simple reasoning problems. Consider the bumper sticker I recently saw on a pickup truck:
>
> > Off-Road users
> > are not abusers
>
> The off-road users that this bumper sticker refers to are dirt bike riders who enjoy racing through open land (unpaved areas). Many people are concerned that this sport is destroying our natural resources by tearing up the vegetation. This bumper sticker is designed to present the opposite view. Notice how this is accomplished. The term "all" is implied in the first premise, when in fact "some" is true. You should recognize this as a syllogism with an implied conclusion that is invalid.
>
> Another popular bumper sticker is:
>
> > If guns are outlawed,
> > only outlaws will have guns.
>
> This is a standard "if, then" statement. The implied conclusion is "don't outlaw guns." What do you think about this statement? Some questions to ask yourself when evaluating claims of this sort are: (1) Are the premises true? (2) Does the implied conclusion logically follow? (3) Are there other relevant arguments (e.g., police would still have guns)? (p. 82)

Another way that thinking skills can be taught is through formal instruction and schooling. A number of illustrations of this approach are noted in Baron and Sternberg (1987), which is a collection of essays primarily by educators. Many of these papers describe programmatic approaches to the teaching of thinking skills. What they have in common is a description of a variety of task settings that require problem solving, reasoning, decision making, judgment, and the like. What is built into the curriculum is not just the teaching of factual information, but the teaching of thinking skills that are supported by a variety of exercises that require a student to think in many different settings.

In summary, an important development is occurring, which is the application of principles of cognitive psychology to instructional situations. This activity has burgeoned in the last fifteen years and we can only touch on a few of the kinds of applications that have been made. The interested reader should explore Chipman, Segal, and Glaser (1985), Nickerson et al. (1985), and Segal, Chipman, and Glaser (1985) for excellent summaries.

SUMMARY

Chapter 10 outlined some of the major features of and issues in problem solving and reasoning. The importance of appropriate mental representation of the problem was noted early in the chapter. Problem solving consists of three basic stages: understanding the problem, generating solutions for the problem, and evaluating the solution. Sometimes incubation is included in this list. Understanding the problem is critical to a good beginning. In generating solutions humans use a variety of heuristics or rules of thumb. These include the generate-test method, means-ends analysis, and working backward. Evaluating a solution can be easy or difficult, depending on a number of factors, including the complexity of the problem. Three types of problems were described: problems of inducing structure, transformation problems, and arrangement problems.

We examined several processes in problem solving, including persistence of set, functional fixedness, memory and problem solving, and creative problem solving. We also identified several practical rules of problem solving. We briefly examined two traditional approaches to problem solving and the contemporary information-processing approach. Current theoretical efforts are dominated by the information-processing approach. A distinction between convergent thinking and divergent thinking was presented. In the important area of the study of expertise, research has begun to describe characteristics of experts.

The study of reasoning has distinguished between deductive and inductive reasoning. Humans are not always logical and are prone to make errors in reasoning. Research indicates that skills in reasoning and thinking can be deliberately taught in explicit ways.

MULTIPLE-CHOICE ITEMS

1. In the discussion of problem solving several stages were described. Which stage was *not* described?
    a. interpreting the problem
    b. associating old ideas
    c. generating hypotheses
    d. testing hypotheses

2. The idea of incubation in problem solving comes from situations in which the problem solver
    a. shows immediate insight
    b. solves the problem in systematic steps
    c. adopts clever strategies
    d. withdraws from the problem for a period and then discovers a solution

3. The water-jar problem is designed to study the persistence of set in problem solving. Another way of describing this is
   a. flexibility
   b. accommodation
   c. rigidity
   d. retrieval

4. An important aspect of problem solving is learning how to handle frustration and difficulty. This process was described as acquiring
   a. insight
   b. perceptual reorganization
   c. flexibility
   d. coping strategies

5. A critically important feature of successful problem solving is how the problem is
   a. retrieved
   b. represented
   c. incubated
   d. fixated

6. A rule or procedure which ensures the solution to a problem is called
   a. generate-test method
   b. algorithm
   c. successive approximations
   d. heuristic

TRUE–FALSE ITEMS

1. Persistence of set refers to the fact that humans may tend to apply old rules or principles when they are no longer appropriate.

2. Information-processing approaches to problem solving attempt to state the rules of operations (or steps) involved in a process.

3. Accurate mental representation is important only in the latter stages of problem solving.

4. Functional fixedness refers to the difficulty in visualizing new ways of using familiar objects.

5. Means-ends analysis refers to a typical algorithm in problem solving.

6. An important aspect of problem solving is being able to identify alternative hypotheses if more than one exists.

DISCUSSION ITEMS

1. Select a particular problem and outline the stages of problem solving you might use.

2. Since persistence of an inappropriate set is an obstacle to problem solving, how might you teach yourself (or someone else) to become more *flexible* in your (or his or her) approach to problems?

3. Give a concrete example describing how you could apply the practical principles of problem solving identified in the text.

4. Speculate on how the levels-of-processing idea in memory might be related to efficient problem solving.

5. Explain the concept of analogical mapping in reasoning problems.

6. Why is it difficult to be perfectly sure of your conclusion when you reason inductively?

7. What are the general characteristics of thinking by experts? How would they apply in a specific situation?

8. What are some of the main features of creative problem solving?

ANSWERS TO MULTIPLE-CHOICE ITEMS

1. (b) Nothing was said about associating old ideas, although this process could occur as a part of the stage of generating hypotheses.

2. (d) Incubation is basically a rest period in which the problem is set aside and you go about other affairs. A solution appears subsequently after you have withdrawn from the task.

3. (c) The persistence of set in water-jar problems can be described as a form of rigidity, which is resistance to change or unwillingness to try new approaches or ideas.

4. (d) Learning how to handle frustration is a matter of acquiring appropriate coping skills and strategies.

5. (b) The initial representation of a problem is quite important in determining how readily and effectively a problem will be solved.

6. (b) Algorithms guarantee a solution; heuristics do not.

ANSWERS TO TRUE–FALSE ITEMS

1.   (True)   The carry-over of old rules, habits, or strategies is called persistence of set.

2.   (True)   Information-processing conceptions formulate some kind of sequence of rules, usually in the format of a flowchart showing each step in the process.

3.   (False)   Accurate mental representation is important at the earliest stage of problem solving.

4.   (True)   The persistence of "seeing" old objects in their typical function is another type of rigidity or persistence of set. In this case it is called functional fixedness.

5.   (False)   Means-ends analysis is a typical heuristic.

6.   (True)   This is an important part of problem solving, especially if there are disadvantages to some of the alternatives which must be weighed.

ANSWERS TO ANAGRAM

The answers to the anagram *TARIL are TRAIL* and *TRIAL*.

11
LANGUAGE

The one kind of activity that appears to distinguish most clearly human beings from other organisms is their facility with language. Although it can be demonstrated in controlled laboratory situations that lower animals can think, remember, learn concepts, and solve problems, language is frequently said to be a distinguishing human feature. Recent investigations of language behavior in chimpanzees suggest, however, that the human species may not be the sole possessor of language. Even these animals have been shown capable of using language at a simple level. But we shall see that the issue of language in animals depends upon what features of human languages can be said to be truly shared by animals.

Language is our principal means of communication with other persons. Yet we frequently take this complex ability for granted. Perhaps this is because, as adults, we have little memory of the long process of language acquisition. For many of us language is a natural and simple process until, as adults, we attempt to learn a second language. This is not to say that learning a foreign language is the same as learning a first language. Indeed, early language learning appears relatively effortless compared to learning a foreign language as a college student.

One theory of the relation between language and thought is that language is "the tool of thought." Jean Piaget, a distinguished Swiss psychologist, made an interesting analogy in pointing out that language is to thought as mathematics is to physics. Just as mathematics is used as the language of physics, ordinary language bears a similar relationship to thought.

Language is composed of linguistic units combined according to rules operating at several levels. For example, words are composed of basic vowel and consonant sounds, or *phonemes,* phrases are composed of words, sentences of phrases, and so on. The characteristic or *design feature* of language whereby units can be rearranged and combined at successively higher levels (e.g., *a, t,* and *p* into *pat* or *tap*) is referred to as *duality of patterning,* and accounts for the infinite *productivity* or creativity of language (Hockett, 1963). The phoneme is often considered the basic linguistic unit of language but, as we shall see, it appears more likely that either syllables or words are the basic psychological units involved in the perception and comprehension of language (Johnson, 1986; Paivio & Begg, 1981).

At a general level, spoken language represents the major system available to the human being for communication, although *signs* also can be used to communicate. Technically, "sign" is a broad term including any conventionally agreed upon symbol (or string of symbols) that designate some referent. Beyond the linguistic signs of words, there are road signs that convey information relevant to motorists, mathematical formulas that convey abstract relationships and operations, bodily signs that convey emotional feelings, and *manual signs* that convey information using the hands either *iconically* or *arbitrarily,* the way that letter patterns arbitrarily stand for their referents. Manual signs include the several distinct forms of sign language used by deaf individuals (e.g., Ameslan, Signed English), as well as conventional symbolic gestures (like the "Shhh!" gesture), novel gestures, and pantomime (McNeill, 1985; see Marschark, Everhart, Martin, & West, 1987, for descriptions and related research). All of these signs are symbols in the sense that they convey meaning. They provide some kind of information which in turn allows some kind of response by other human beings.

In this chapter we examine some of the basic features of language. In particular, we discuss the functions of language, the structure of language, the processes in language, and a range of selected issues in language.

FUNCTIONS OF LANGUAGE

Language serves several functions which are all related to the fundamental process of communication. Perhaps most important is that language conveys meaning and is part of almost all kinds of social interaction. Language conveys intentions, motives, feelings, and beliefs. Language is used to issue requests and commands such as, "Get me a glass of water." Language is also used to teach and to convey information. Indeed, due to duality of patterning and productivity, an infinite range of knowledge and beliefs can be conveyed via language.

Language is useful because it can represent ideas and events that are not tied to the here and now. Hockett (1963) identified this as another of the design features of language, and referred to it as *displacement.* He pointed out that through language, unlike other forms of animal communication, we can communicate about the past as well as convey plans for the future. You can describe abstract ideas such as beauty and justice as well as concrete objects of everyday experience. Thus language is *symbolic,* in that speech sounds and utterances stand for or represent various objects, ideas, and events.

In any language communication system, there consists a speaker or producer, a listener or receiver, and a system for communication, such as the English language or American Sign Language (Ameslan). Communication begins with "speakers" who decide to convey information. They select a medium of communication, such as English, and produce sentences (or approximations to them). "Listeners" receive the signals being presented (speech sounds or signs) and represent them in memory. There are three elements of human communication that have been identified as operating in this speaker-listener situation, regardless of whether we are considering spoken language, written language, or sign language: *speech acts* (Searle, 1969, 1975), *propositional content,* and *thematic structure.* We will examine these elements in the following section, and the description follows the analysis outlined by Clark and Clark (1977).

Speech Acts

Speakers normally intend to have some influence on their listeners and, to do so, must get them to recognize their intentions. Indeed, failure to recognize these intentions can result in awkward situations. For example, consider the following short-circuited phone exchange:

> Person A: "Hello, is John home?"
> Person B: "Yes."
> (lengthy pause)
> Person A: "May I speak with him, please?"
> Person B: "Oh, you want to talk to him? . . . I'll get him."

Person A had two intentions that needed to be recognized by Person B: to find out John's whereabouts and to talk to John. While Person B recognized the former, the latter was clearly missed. Utterances such as "Hello, is John home?" are called *speech acts*. Speech-act theory holds that all utterances can be classified as to the type of speech act they represent. For example, speech acts may make assertions, make verbal commitments, convey thanks, give a warning, or issue a command. Typical examples of speech acts include the following: "I insist that you turn down the volume on the stereo" (a command); "What are your plans for Saturday night?" (a question); "I promise to pay you tomorrow" (a verbal commitment); and "I know that Professor Jones is the best instructor in the psychology department" (an assertion). In these examples, we see the acts of ordering, questioning, committing, and telling, which are common *direct* speech acts.

Searle (1969) also pointed out that some speech acts are *indirect*. When your mother asks if you live in a barn, a guest in your house asks if you are chilly, or someone in a bar asks if you would like to see his or her etchings, they are conveying information about their desires, but in a rather indirect, nonliteral way. Some indirect speech acts, like these, have gained well-recognized meanings through their repeated use. For example, consider the utterance, "Can you pass the salt?", where the intended meaning involves a request to pass the salt rather than an inquiry into one's ability to do so. The meaning of any particular speech act, however, including whether it is direct or indirect, will depend on the *context* in which it is uttered (Gibbs, 1986), as well as its content.

Recent evidence has uncovered how systematic the effects of context can be in certain types of conversations. For example, indirect requests appear to be tailored to assure that speaker does not overly offend or impose upon the listener. Rather, the form of the request is devised to overcome speaker perceived obstacles to the listener's carrying out the request (Francik & Clark, 1985; Gibbs, 1985, 1986). For example, Gibbs (1986) found that when a speaker perceives that the listener is not *able* to carry out the request the speaker is more likely to frame the request as "Can you . . . ?" than "Would you mind . . . ?" or "Will you . . . ?"

Propositional Content

The second element of communication concerns the *propositional content* of a sentence. In communication, speakers want to convey certain ideas and to do this, they must be sure that they are understood. Thus the content around a speech act is very important. As a general rule the propositional content of a sentence is used to describe certain states or events; it can also describe certain facts about the states or events, or it can be part of other propositions. For example, the sentence "The bright student received an A in calculus" expresses two separate propositions, "The student is bright" and "The student received an A in calculus." Combined into a single sentence, the propositions convey what the speaker intends to convey. Note that the statement *You weren't raised in a barn!* contains propositional content at two different levels: the superficial, literal statement of fact concerning the residence of your childhood, and the nonliteral, intended reference to your having left a door open. There is experimental evidence that we represent sentences as propositions. For example, the more propositions contained in a sentence, the longer the time required to read the sentence (see van Dijk & Kintsch, 1983).

Thematic Structure

Finally, the third component in communication is *thematic structure*. To communicate effectively, good speakers pay careful attention to their listeners. Good speakers have to judge what listeners do and do not know, keep track of where they are leading their listeners, and regularly examine any assumptions about the listeners' knowledge of the topic being discussed. In short, the speaker must be able to make reasonably accurate judgments of the listener's current level of understanding.

All of these features are present in good teachers, entertaining and effective storytellers, and interesting conversationalists. Unfortunately, all of us at one time have probably experienced a talk, lecture, or presentation in which the speaker droned on without any apparent interest in our level of understanding. Sometimes we are victims of eager monologists who are so anxious to relay their views of the world that they forget to check our understanding of what's being said. Similarly, there is the occasional teacher who lectures "in a trance," following a rigid format and without pausing to check on audience comprehension. Indeed, this inability to be sensitive to the listener is a major problem in communication.

One function of thematic consideration is to convey both given (understood) and new information. (See also chapter 9 for a related discussion.) Good speakers attempt to tailor their sentences to fit what they think their listeners already know. For example, the sentence "It was your *son* who scored the touchdown" assumes that the listeners (parents) know that a touchdown was scored, but not that their son scored the touchdown. Thus the given information in the sentence is that a touchdown was made, and the new information is that their son made the touchdown. The emphasis or stress in the sentence is on *son,* not on the fact that a touchdown was made. Similarly, semantic (conceptual) and syntactic (grammatical) structures can signal differences between given and new information across as well as within sentences (Conrad & Rips, 1986).

Sometimes a speaker emphasizes a particular phrase in a sentence by placing it at the beginning. In this fashion the speaker focuses attention on the particular context in which the event occurred. For example, "At her cocktail party Mrs. Jones was very gracious" makes it clear that Mrs. Jones was gracious in a particular context. The reader is thus implicitly cautioned that Mrs. Jones may or may not be gracious in other settings, without this specifically being mentioned.

To summarize, the functions of language are seen in speech acts, propositional content, and thematic structure. Speakers signal their intent by the choice of a speech act which includes telling, asking, or commanding someone. The propositional content of a sentence is the particular information that is conveyed. And the thematic structure involves making judgments about the listener's knowledge, often by stressing new information in the context of known or given information. Now we turn our attention to certain structural properties of language.

STRUCTURE OF LANGUAGE

As should be evident by now, language can be divided into three basic parts, each with its own structure and rules: phonology, syntax or grammar, and semantics. The first of these, *phonology,* concerns the rules for pronunciation of speech sounds. The second aspect of language, *syntax,* deals with the way words combine to form sentences. And *semantics* focuses on the meaning of words and sentences. In this section we examine certain aspects of the structure of language.

Basic Units of Language: Phonemes and Morphemes

All languages are made of basic sounds called *phonemes.* Adult human beings can produce approximately 100 phonemes, and the English language is made up of about 45 phonemes. Languages vary in the number of phonemes, ranging from as few as 15 to as many as 85. One reason why it is difficult for many Americans to learn foreign languages is that different phonemes are used. For instance, Germanic and Slavic languages contain phonemes never used in the English language.

Phonemes are in turn composed of about twelve *distinctive features.* The linguist Roman Jakobson (Jakobson & Halle, 1956) constructed a classification of distinctive features by which phonemes differ. For example, a given phoneme (speech sound) may be sounded nasally or orally. Another feature is the explosive or tense character of some sounds as seen when /p/ or /f/ (phonemes for the letters *p* and *f*) are pronounced.

A *phoneme* can be defined as any single change in the sound of a word that also makes a difference in meaning: *pin* versus *bin,* for example. Furthermore, contrasts that make a meaningful difference in one language may not make a difference in another language. English speakers do not, for example, distinguish between the aspirated and unaspirated forms of /p/: *pin* (aspirated /p/) versus *spin* (unaspirated /p/). To demonstrate that the /p/ in *pin* is aspirated, hold a match in front of your mouth while saying the word and note that the flame flickers. However, this does not happen when *spin* is said.

Another unit of language is the *morpheme,* which is the smallest meaningful unit in a language. Morphemes usually consist of combinations of two or more phonemes and roughly correspond to the most elementary words. The words *good, put,* and *go* are single morphemes. *Goodness, putting,* and *going* consist of two morphemes. Thus, single morphemes may be root words of a language; they may also consist of prefixes or suffixes.

Higher Levels of Linguistic Analysis

We have just considered the most basic analyses possible of language. The study of the speech sounds which make up a language is called *phonology,* and the study of how these sounds combine to produce morphemes is called *morphology.* However, psychologists are frequently interested in a more global analysis of language than is provided by phonology and morphology. Psychological investigations of language typically adopt words, phrases, sentences, or prose as the most fundamental unit of analysis, rather than more elementary speech sounds.

There are several levels at which these higher-order analyses can be made. First, one could analyze the *lexical content* of a sentence or of some other unit of language production. When a lexical analysis is performed, the question is simply: What words are used in this sample of language? This was the basic approach of Thorndike and Lorge who tabulated the frequency with which different English words occurred in large samples of printed material. For example, these investigators reported the average frequency of occurrence per million words of text for each of a large number of common words such as *kitchen* (over 100 times per million) and rare words such as *rostrum* (only 1 time per million). Information gained from lexical analyses of language such as that by Thorndike and Lorge has proved to be very useful in predicting the ease with which different words can be learned in laboratory situations.

At another level of linguistic analysis, the *syntactic content* of language text may be investigated. In the study of syntax, interest is focused on the arrangement or ordering of words to form phrases and sentences. The question asked in this type of analysis is: How is this phrase (or sentence) structured? Psychologists and linguists interested in syntactic theory have attempted to specify rules that will generate an infinite number of grammatically correct sentences and no incorrect sentences, that is, the rules that account for the productivity of language, its most important characteristic (Chomsky, 1985). The set of rules indicating how the elements of the language may be combined to make intelligible sentences is referred to as a *grammar*. Although a large number of different grammars have been proposed, linguists have not been able to write down the extremely complex system of rules which generates all the syntactically correct sentences of the English language, or of any other natural language. At present, there is little agreement about the necessary features of an adequate grammar. However, an important part of many of the proposed grammars is the rules for phrase structure, which we consider in the next section.

Perhaps the most important level of analysis of language is the one which considers the *semantic content* or meaning of a passage. This perspective on language results in the asking of questions such as: What does the passage communicate? What is the meaning of this particular sentence? Unfortunately, psychologists and linguists know less about the rules for determining the meanings of words and combinations of words than they do about the rules of syntax or morphology. For example, for many years, it was thought that word meanings were represented as a set of fixed properties or features (see Bierwisch, 1970; Clark & Clark, 1977; Katz, 1972). These features were "semantic primitives" from which the meanings of all words were composed. For example, the word *short* was considered to represent in our "mental dictionary" as **NOT (TALL)** and the verb *kill* was represented as **CAUSE (TO DIE)**. However, it has since been found that it is difficult to specify what this set of features should be (see Lakoff, 1987; Medin, 1989). Further, there is also evidence that people do not always need to use these features to understand words (van Dijk & Kintsch, 1983; Fodor, Garrett, Walker, & Parkes, 1980). Lastly, words exhibit different meanings (i.e., are polysemous) in different contexts, something that shouldn't happen if a set number and collection of features are always conveyed by their use (Lakoff, 1987). A current, alternative, view of word meaning is based on the *categorization theories* discussed in chapter 8, where instances belong to categories that are represented as a collection of features having "fuzzy boundaries" (see Medin, 1989). In this view, word meaning is a function of the interaction between word features and the extent to which they match those belonging to certain prototypical and nonprototypical contexts (Lakoff, 1987). Here, both feature theory and prototype theory are seen as important.

The critical role of semantics is not under question, and has been clearly demonstrated in a number of psychological investigations. For example, when subjects listen to passages of connected discourse, their recognition memory for sentences after a short delay is much more sensitive to changes in semantic (e.g., subject-object reversal) than to changes in syntactic content (e.g., switching from active to passive voice) (Sachs, 1967). Current views of semantics and comprehension in general view the listener (or reader) as an *active participant* who formulates hypotheses about subsequent input based on context (both verbal and situational), knowledge of constraints in the language, and knowledge of the world. This is in contrast to the more passive view of the comprehender as someone who waits for the input before acting upon it.

Although theories of semantics cannot here be considered in further detail, it is appropriate to point out the dramatic differences in approaches to theorizing in this area. On one hand, associationistic theories have been proposed in which meaning is viewed simply as a conditioned response. Thus the responses made to a word are thought to be modifications of the unconditioned response once made to the object referred to by that word. In contrast to this approach, more recent theories have suggested possible structures of the semantic memory necessary for the use of language. This newer approach has considered the human being as an information-processing system rather than as an association learner and has resulted in a number of computer programs which attempt to model human ability to deal with semantics. Certain of these computer programs provide persuasive demonstrations of their understanding of portions of the English language. For example, computer programs have been written which can respond in ordinary English to questions concerning the properties of objects or events which the computer has stored in its memory after being presented with a series of sentences describing those objects or events. These issues were discussed in chapters 7 and 9. The collaboration among computer scientists, psychologists, and linguists offers one of the most promising approaches to the study of how human beings acquire knowledge of semantics.

Phrase Structure in Sentences

In order to understand language in the adult, it is necessary to examine the structure of sentences. At one level of analysis a sentence can be regarded simply as a string of phonemes. The single phoneme, however, is not a particularly useful way of analyzing sentences since this would be looking at a sentence as a series of isolated speech sounds. At another level, a sentence can be regarded as a series of morphemes, which are groupings of phonemes. From this viewpoint, however, the sentence is viewed as a string of words. Linguists have found it more useful to describe a sentence in terms of *phrases*, which are groupings of words.

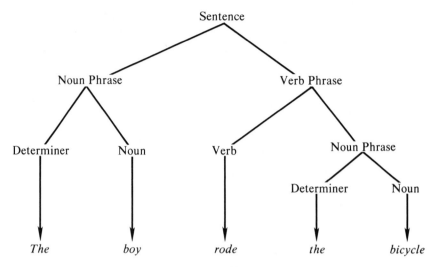

Figure 11.1 Phrase structure in a sentence, The boy rode the bicycle, represented by a tree diagram. (From *Fundamentals of Human Learning, Memory, and Cognition*, 2nd ed., by H. C. Ellis. Dubuque, Iowa: Wm. C. Brown Company, 1978.)

Analysis of a sentence into its various phrases describes the *phrase structure* of a sentence. A sentence is viewed as composed of two basic phrases, a *noun phrase* and a *verb phrase,* which are in turn composed of subcomponents. Figure 11.1 shows the phrase structure of a simple sentence, "The boy rode the bicycle." The noun phrase is composed of a *determiner* and a *noun,* and the verb phrase is composed of a *verb* and *noun phrase;* the latter noun phrase is also composed of a determiner and a noun. The relationship between the two phrases is portrayed in the tree diagram of figure 11.1. Pauses in speech usually reflect underlying phrase structure (see e.g., Gee & Grosjean, 1983). For example, we are most likely to say, "The boy . . . rode . . . the bicycle," pausing ever so briefly after *boy* and *rode.* We are not likely to say, "The . . . boy rode . . . the bicycle," grouping *boy* and *rode,* or "The . . . boy rode the . . . bicycle," grouping *boy, rode,* and *the.* While in normal speech a speaker may search and grope for a particular word, and thus alter the pauses, the listener still tends to understand the message.

Surface and Deep Structure in Sentences

Linguists distinguish between surface structure and deep structure of sentences. The *surface structure* is the organization that describes the sequences of phrases in a sentence as it is actually spoken (or read) and reflects the phonological realization of the complex, underlying linguistic structure.

Deep structure, in contrast, refers to this underlying structure that includes the relevant string of linguistic units, the grammatical requirements for lexical (word) selection, and grammatical relations between words in sentences. The deep structure of a sentence thus specifies the derivations of both its surface structure and its meaning.

Consider the sentences "John threw the ball" and "The ball was thrown by John." Both sentences convey the same meaning despite the fact that they sound different. Hence their deep structure is the same. But consider the sentence "The lamb is ready to eat" which can have two meanings. The lamb may serve as food to be eaten, or as an animal, the lamb is prepared to eat food. Thus, the deep structure can vary with the same sentence, depending on what meaning the speaker wishes to convey. Consider the following ambiguous sentences, "Visiting relatives can be a nuisance," "Bill shot the man with a gun," and "The corrupt police can't stop drinking" and evaluate their meanings.

These illustrations indicate the necessity of distinguishing between surface and deep structures. Sentences with essentially a single deep structure and two or more surface structures are *synonymous.* Sentences with different deep structures and the same surface structure are *ambiguous.* The important problem remaining thus concerns the theoretical rules by which the deep structure of a sentence comes to be realized in a particular surface structure. Rules for the specification of this linkage process, called *transformational rules,* have been developed by Noam Chomsky (Chomsky, 1965, 1975) and other linguists.

Transformational rules have clear implications about what features of sentences human beings do store in memory. If the sentence is very simple, so that its deep structure approximates its surface structure, then features of the surface structure may be stored. As sentences become more complex, what is thought to be stored is some underlying base structure or *schema,* plus one or more "footnotes" that serve as rules necessary to regenerate the sentence in its original surface form. This is simply to say that what is stored is some coded representation of the complex sentence.

Transformational Grammar

Information contained in a linguistic message tends to be comprehended, and sometimes is remembered, in syntactically defined chunks, although semantically based chunking also may be used, depending on the demands placed upon the listener and the nature of the material (Aaronson & Scarborough, 1976; Marschark, 1979). The phrase structure of a sentence thus appears to play an important organizational role in language processing at a very basic level (Ferreira & Clifton, 1986). Some linguists such as Chomsky point out that the phrase structure analysis of language is nevertheless incomplete and that the complete analysis of language must have a transformational component. By making a distinction between the underlying structure of a sentence and the surface form of the sentence, transformational grammar provides a way to represent relationships among sentences which on the surface take quite different forms. Transformations are based upon rules which apply to sentences, and the transformation allows the same idea to be expressed in, say, either an active or a passive sentence. For example, "The dog chased the cat" and "The cat was chased by the dog" have quite different phrase structures as sentences, but both share a common underlying or deep structure.

The surface structure of a sentence is produced by the application of various transformational rules to the deep structure. For instance, the first sentence, "The dog chased the cat," is an active-declarative transformation of the deep structure, and the second sentence, "The cat was chased by the dog," is a passive-declarative transformation. A variety of different surface structures thus may be derived from essentially the same deep structure. The basic relationships expressed by a simple sentence are those among the subject, verb, and object; and these are contained in the *base string,* which then undergoes transformation. The base string having to do with the description of the dog chasing the cat can be transformed into various forms (such as, "The cat was chased by the dog" and "Did the dog chase the cat?"). While the surface structures may be different, they all relate to a common base string.

PROCESSES IN LANGUAGE

In this section we will examine some basic processes in language. The focus is on three processes: production of language, speech perception and comprehension, and language development.

Production of Language

The beginning of a dialogue is usually the production of speech by one of the participants, although a gesture or other sign may initiate such an interaction and have its origins in a similar verbal plan (McNeill, 1985). But before uttering a sentence or manually expressing any information, the speaker must do some planning based on the intended effect the utterance is to have on the listener; the speaker's knowledge of the listener's scope of understanding (e.g., Is the listener familiar with the topic?); and the syntactic, semantic, and *pragmatic* or social form that the production and its desired effect requires. Thus, speaking is very much an *instrumental act,* which is to say that speakers talk in order to produce an effect of some kind.

The process of speaking is basically concerned with planning and execution. But just how is speech planned and executed? Clark and Clark (1977) described a rough outline of this process which involves five steps.

The first step for speakers is to decide on the kind of discourse to be initiated, which is the issue of *discourse plans*. Do they want to engage in a conversation, or describe an event, or give instructions, or regale a friend with a humorous story? Each type of discourse has a particular structure, and speakers must plan their utterances to fit that structure. For example, if you are telling a joke, you first describe the setting or context, then describe the sequence of events, and end with the punch line. If you fail to follow this structure, you obviously will not be an effective joke teller. For example, if you give away the joke by accidentally telling the punch line before the appropriate time, you will defeat your purpose. Similarly, instructions and conversations have an orderly structure.

One set of guidelines that speakers and listeners seem to follow to foster good communication during a conversation has been described by Grice (1975) and others (e.g., Levelt, 1989). These "Gricean Maxims" are:

(1) *Quantity:* Avoid running off at the mouth.

(2) *Quality:* Don't lie or stretch the truth.

(3) *Relation:* Avoid making statements irrelevant to the topic of conversation.

(4) *Manner:* Avoid vague or ambiguous statements.

Failure to follow these maxims often results in a *conversational implicature.* For example, imagine that you are reviewing an applicant's letter of recommendation for a highly technical job, and the letter reads:

> *I am writing a letter on behalf of John Smith. John dresses very well and has a charming wife. He also drives a nice automobile and sings in his church's choir. Thank you.*

Would you hire John based on this letter? Probably not. Clearly, the content of this letter violates the Relation Maxim. Because of this, the letter writer has conversationally implied that John is not the person for the job. Speakers (and letter writers) usually adhere to these Gricean Maxims; but as this example demonstrates, it is quite informative when they don't.

Planning discourse is planning at the global level. The second stage involves *planning of sentences*, the components of discourse. Once the nature of the discourse is decided, specific sentences that will accomplish the objective must then be selected. The speech act, the propositional content, and the thematic structure need to be determined. The order in which sentences are produced and the type of information to be conveyed must be thought about. For example, suppose you are describing your new house. You might first describe the location: "We're ten miles outside of town near the mountains—in South Sandia Heights." Next, you might describe the overall type of house: "It's a two-story contemporary house made of redwood, stucco, and stone." Then you might proceed to describe the floor plan and arrangement of rooms and finally give specifics of each room. Notice that there is a structure present which involves going from global or general information to progressively more specific details.

The third phase deals with *constituent plans* of the sentence. Once a sentence is decided on, its components must then be planned. The appropriate words, phrases, and so forth, must be picked out and put in the right order. These first three phases describe three levels of planning. At the most general level, planning is directed toward the type of discourse. At the next level, planning concerns the type of sentence to be uttered, and finally planning deals with specific components of the sentence.

An interesting feature of slips of the tongue is that they point out regularities in the planning stages of productions. For example, slips are seldom "illegal" combinations of sounds for the language; morphemes tend to slip as entire units (Clark & Clark, 1977). Some classic slips are known as "bloopers" in the world of radio and television. Some bloopers are fairly obvious. For example, an announcer for the *Friendly Homemaker Program* said, "And now we present our homely friendmaker." Another example is a remark of the commentator covering a visit of the king and queen of England: "When they arrive, you will hear a twenty-one son galute." And from the commercial world comes this classic: "And Dad will love Wonder Bread's delicious flavor, too. Remember it's Wonder Bread for the breast in bed."

The fourth phase deals with what is called the *articulatory program.* This concerns the plans for the execution of speech, which is a coordinated sequence of muscular contractions in and about the mouth. And the final phase is *articulation* itself. This is the actual output of speech. Interested readers are referred to Clark and Clark (1977) and Levelt (1989) for a detailed discussion of planning and execution of speech.

Speech Perception and Comprehension

The comprehension of speech begins with the perception of raw speech sounds. Comprehension starts where speech production ends. Speakers produce a stream of sounds that arrive at the listeners' ears. And listeners are able to analyze sound patterns and to comprehend them. Speech perception is not, however, the simple identification of sounds. It involves the complex processes of encoding and comprehension discussed in earlier chapters. In other words, interpretative processes, meaning, contextual influences, and the like, play important roles in speech perception. Thus the transformation from raw speech sounds to propositions in memory is a complex process. The physical signal that reaches the ear consists of rapid vibrations of air. While the sounds of speech correlate with particular component frequencies, there is no direct one-to-one correspondence between the sounds of speech and the perceptions of listeners.

Recognition of words is very much dependent on context, expectations, and knowledge. For example, a hungry child can interpret the question "Have you washed your hands for dinner?" as a call to come directly to dinner (i.e., as an indirect speech act rather than a direct question). The role of context also can be easily seen in incomplete sentences where context allows words to be inferred quite easily. For example, the sentence "The young girl was awakened by her frightening d . . . " allows listeners to infer readily *dream*. There is no need to think about what the word might be; it just seems to pop out automatically. A similar context effect was studied in the laboratory by Warren (Warren & Obusek, 1971) using phonemes. Subjects were read sentences that had a single speech sound obscured. For example, the sentence "The state governors met with their respective legislatures convening in the capital city" had the first *s* in *legislatures* masked by a coughing sound. The experimenter then asked the subjects to identify where the cough had occurred. The results indicated that subjects somehow "restored" the missing *s* sound and were unable to locate the interjected cough. This phenomenon, appropriately called *phonemic restoration,* has been shown to be even more likely when more than a single word can result from the restoration (e.g., "_egion" can become either "legion" or "region"), indicating an active word-searching process in speech perception (Samuel, 1987).

Many persons have the impression that the words they hear are distinct, separate combinations of sounds. But this impression is not correct. Cole (1979, 1980) and other speech researchers have demonstrated that words usually run together as sound patterns. This is seen by use of a spectograph, which is an electronic device for measuring the variations in energy expended when a person talks. Moreover, it is often the case that a single word cannot be recognized correctly when it is taken out of its sentence context. This was shown some years ago by Pollack and Pickett (1963) who played different segments of a normal conversation for subjects. But when the subjects heard just one word from the conversation, it was often incomprehensible. Without the context of the meaningful sentence, the single word could not be understood.

More generally, an important feature of speech perception is that speech is not comprehended simply on the basis of the sounds per se. Rather, speech is comprehended on the basis of many additional factors which include intentions, context, and expectations, from which an interpretation of what the speaker says is constructed. (Tyler & Marslen-Wilson, 1986; see Paivio & Begg, 1981, for a review.)

Language Development

Language development follows a fairly orderly course. The beginning of language is evidenced in babbling, which is an elementary type of vocalization. Children do produce sounds earlier than six months of age, but babbling, which is the repetition of speech sounds, is most clearly evident beginning around six months. By the time children are seven or eight months of age, most parents can correctly identify different cries by an infant as indicating hunger cries, request cries, or cries of surprise (Ricks, 1975). Between six and nine months of age, infants are able to produce all of the basic speech sounds (phonemes) that make up a language.

The emission of speech sounds, even at this early age, can be controlled to some extent by an adult. For example, the rate at which infants emit speech sounds can be increased by having an adult repeat the sounds after the infant. These responses, called *echoic responses*, can be trained or shaped in the sense of increasing their rate just like other instrumental responses. Language learning is not, however, the simple result of reinforcement of particular speech sounds and sequences. Language involves learning to use complex rules of grammar.

One of the striking features of language acquisition is that children of various cultures learn their unique languages in similar ways. For example, children of different cultures acquire speech sounds at about the same time. Later on, they develop syntactic patterns at about the same time. These regularities in language development suggest that some features of language learning are *universal* (Slobin, 1973), and thus perhaps innate. In fact, several studies have shown similar patterns of language development in hearing and deaf children, even though the learning of sign language by the latter is delayed due to the lack of early exposure to language (e.g., Marschark, West, Nall, & Everhart, 1986). For convenience, we henceforth will refer to "speech" and "sounds" in discussing language development, but our points generally extend to "sign language" and "signs" as well.

Making speech sounds is only the first step in acquiring language. The sounds must come to represent objects, symbols, and events in the child's environment. This is simply to say that the sounds must acquire *meaning* for the child. Moreover, children must learn to associate particular sound symbols with particular aspects of their environment. Children are familiar with many aspects of their environment before they learn to speak. Their parents are familiar stimuli; toys, pets, siblings, and household objects are also familiar stimuli. At this early stage of language development, their task is one of learning to associate particular environmental stimuli with particular responses. For example, they must learn to associate the sight of mother with the sound of *mama*. Similarly, the sight, feel, and taste of a cookie must become associated with the sound of *cookie*. Only when such associations are acquired can the speech sound come to represent or symbolize a specific object or event for the child. Thus, the development of meaning begins with the acquisition of associations between objects and events on the one hand, and speech sounds on the other hand.

One popular view of the acquisition of word meanings is that children learn semantic features and then attempt to apply an original word that includes the features to objects that share features in common. For example, a child may learn the word *ball* and then overgeneralize it to other round objects such as moon, grapefruit, and the like.

The association of speech sounds with environmental stimuli is, of course, only a part of language development. Once children acquire a rudimentary vocabulary, they must then begin to form sentences. At first young children form quite simple sentences, usually consisting of two or three words, such as, "Want drink." These sentences are quite systematic, are usually understood by the parent, and are similar to adult English sentences with the unessential words omitted (cf. Brown, 1973). For these reasons, they are usually referred to as *telegraphic speech,* likening such productions to the concise, economical language of telegrams. Even as the vocabulary expands, short sentences continue to be used. The very first words that children produce often combine saying a word with a gesture such as "bye-bye" accompanied by a hand wave. Similarly, the speech act of asserting something is often accompanied by a pointing gesture, such as saying "Mama" and pointing toward the mother (Greenfield & Smith, 1976).

Gradually the child begins to construct more complex sentences that take on the characteristics of adult language. This is an enormously complex task (Brown, 1973). Children must learn to construct increasingly complex sentences, most of which they have never heard. Thus any type of imitation theory of language learning seems quite inadequate. Another possibility is that children might learn language by way of reinforcement principles. According to this view, children learn new utterances by being encouraged by their parents or other adults. But there is little support for the reinforcement view. Indeed, Brown reports that there is almost no evidence that parents make approval contingent upon the grammaticality of what their children say. In addition, there is an almost infinite number of possibilities in constructing sentences, so that we cannot regard the process of sentence construction as resulting from reinforcement of grammatically correct sentences.

What the child learns are sets of *grammatical , semantic,* and *pragmatic* rules for constructing sentences. Usually, children are unable to verbalize the rules, but their linguistic *performance* indicates that they do possess linguistic *competence,* the knowledge necessary to produce all and only those sentences of a given language. Indeed, many adults who speak grammatically acceptable English are unable to specify the rules they use. But these rules allow us to generate an almost infinite number of different sentences. One of the best pieces of evidence for learning syntactic rules is the phenomenon of overgeneralization (syntactic). For example, children learn to say *went* correctly, apparently by rote, then learn the rule of forming the past tense by adding *ed,* and then incorrectly say *goed.* They later learn the exception to the rule and go back to saying *went.* Similar overgeneralizations occur in the deaf child's acquisition of sign language.

This brief description only begins to sketch some of the complexities of language development. What is clear is that young children have an enormously complex task in learning to speak, read, and use language in a meaningful fashion. The fact that human beings can acquire and use language emerges as a remarkable achievement.

SOME ISSUES IN LANGUAGE

In this section a few issues in language are examined. Included are the topics of language and thought, language in animals, cultural differences in language, and language and the brain.

Language and Thought

Language and thought are related events. The ability of children to handle concepts is related to their language development. Indeed, children who can verbalize relationships such as "nearer than" or "larger than" are better able to deal with problems involving relationships among stimuli than children who cannot yet verbalize such relationships.

Nevertheless, language does not seem to be *essential* for complex mental processes, despite the fact that language facilitates problem solving. The most explicit attempt to relate language and thought is seen in the *linguistic relativity hypothesis,* sometimes called the *Whorfian hypothesis,* developed by Benjamin Lee Whorf (1956). Whorf argued that the structure of one's language leads one to perceive and conceive of the world in particular ways—ways that differ from another individual using a different language. This is simply to say that a person's language imposes a particular view of the world. Presumably, cognitive processes are in some way inevitably affected by the structure of language. The notion of *linguistic relativity* is emphasized because thought is presumed to be relative to the particular language used.

Vocabulary differences provide one instance of how language is presumably related to thought. For instance, Eskimos have several different words for labeling snow, depending upon its characteristics, whereas only one is widely used in English. Downhill skiers, of course, do distinguish between several different kinds of snow, using words that describe its consistency (e.g., "cornstarch" or "powder"). Cross-country skiers distinguish even more kinds of snow, using color words that refer to the kind of wax applied to the bottom of a ski under different conditions (e.g., "green" or "violet" snow). Does this mean that nonskiers, downhill skiers, and cross-country skiers have different *perceptions* of snow? Some cultures have many words for the colors of the spectrum; other cultures have only a few. For Whorf, the range of words or labels available influences the range of cognitive activities in which human beings may engage. Persons having a number of different descriptive labels that they can apply to a range of events are presumably able to think about these events in more different ways than are persons having only a few labels.

There are two versions of Whorf's hypothesis. The *strong version* emphasizes that language *invariably* influences thought, whereas the *weak version* emphasizes that language affects thought when the particular task directly depends upon properties of the language system. There is little support for the strong version of the hypothesis. For example, if the strong version of the Whorf hypothesis is true, we would expect that persons who have many different words for different colors (parts of the visual spectrum) would perceive more distinctions among colors than persons who have only a few words. But this is not the case. Rosch (1973) compared the performance of the Dani, a primitive people of New Guinea, who use only two words for colors, with English-speaking subjects who use many different color terms. Despite differences in color terms, the two groups appear to perceive colors in much the same way. In short, just because a language lacks a range of terms for various stimuli does not mean that the user of the language cannot perceive the various features of the stimuli. The lack of particular adjectives in a language may indicate the relative unimportance of those dimensions in the culture and thus speakers of the language may simply ignore those features or fail to report them as significant even when noticed.

The evidence consistent with this weaker version of Whorf's hypothesis comes from research on the effects of verbal labels on perception and recognition memory of visual patterns. In his summary of this research, Ellis (1973) noted that verbal labeling of visual patterns can affect the ease with which they are subsequently perceived and remembered. For example, if different visual patterns are all labeled with the same term, the patterns then become more difficult to recognize. Conversely, if the patterns are given different and meaningful verbal labels, they become more recognizable compared with control tests.

An example of the typical results of Ellis's studies in which subjects label visual (or tactual) shapes with verbal labels and then are tested for recognition of the shapes is shown in figure 11.2. The figure shows that subjects who are instructed to label shapes with unique, *distinctive* labels do better in subsequently recognizing the shapes than do subjects who attach *common* verbal labels. Subjects who simply observe the shapes but are allowed to covertly label them do as well as those who give them distinctive

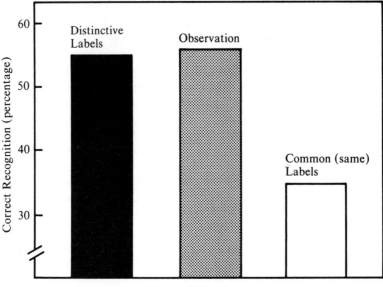

Figure 11.2 Shape recognition following practice in labeling and observation of shapes. (Adapted from "Stimulus Encoding Processes in Human Learning and Memory" by H. C. Ellis, in G. H. Bower, Ed., *The Psychology of Learning and Motivation,* Vol. 7. New York: Academic Press, 1973.)

labels. Ellis contends that the common verbal labels lead the subject to attend to the more common or similar features of the pattern. Hence the subjects achieve a *less* distinctive encoding for each pattern and thus have greater difficulty in recognizing the patterns.

Not all studies have shown that observation of shapes leads to as good recognition as does uniquely labeling them. Ellis (1968, 1973) also reports that if the labels are *representative* of the shapes, then labeling itself leads to superior recognition.

Language in Animals

Many people have raised this question: Do animals have language? The answer depends upon how one defines language. Animals clearly communicate with each other, and in this sense animals can be said to have language. But communication is not synonymous with language, although it is part of language. Language is composed of symbols which stand for other concepts. The word *dog* stands for the object dog; the word *joy* stands for an emotional experience. Words are used in accordance with complex rules of grammar, and the intent is to convey meaning.

Psychologists have made a number of attempts to teach language to chimpanzees. Early attempts by language researchers were largely unsuccessful, with only limited evidence for language being learned. In one of the most famous studies, the Kelloggs raised their son with a chimpanzee named Gua. The chimpanzee learned to understand a number of commands but never produced a single word. In a similar study a chimpanzee raised by the Hayeses learned to speak only three identifiable words, *mama, papa,* and *cup,* and only after great difficulty and extended training. As a result of these failures, many psychologists conclude that chimpanzees lack the vocal chord structures necessary for humanlike speech and that such efforts are doomed to failure.

The vocal inability of chimpanzees was recognized in more recent attempts to teach chimpanzees language by Gardner and Gardner (1969, 1975) and Premack (1971) who took a different approach to the problem. Their approach was to teach chimpanzees a *nonverbal* version of language. The Gardners attempted to teach their subject, Washoe, the sign language used by the deaf, which consists of making signs for different words. Using her hands, Washoe eventually learned over 150 signs. Of even greater importance was that Washoe learned to string signs together to make up primitive sentences. The fact that Washoe was able to produce simple strings is suggestive of a very primitive form of language. Premack's approach was to teach another chimpanzee, Sarah, a form of sign language using colored plastic chips displayed on a board, where each chip stood for a word. For example, a red square stood for *banana.* Sarah learned to "write" by placing chips on a magnetized board and with practice learned to construct simple sentences. But does this mean that Sarah uses language like human beings do? Probably not. Indeed, the language that is learned may be restricted to skills in word substitution, that is, transforming a phrase like "Mary eat banana" to "Mary wash banana."

More recently Terrace and colleagues continued this research in animal language with a chimp named Nim Chimpsky (Terrace, 1979). Nim was raised in a very rich social environment something like that of a young child. For example, he was bottle fed, praised, and given affection. Like Washoe, Nim was taught the American Sign Language and gradually learned a total of 125 signs. But after almost four years of research, Terrace came to doubt that Nim was learning language in the same sense that a child does. For instance, when a human child learns a language, the average length and complexity of the utterances increase, whereas the average length of Nim's utterances showed little growth. Moreover, Nim gave no indication of an expanding grasp of syntax.

Do these studies allow the conclusion that chimpanzees possess language? What we can say is that chimpanzees do show the ability to produce simple sentences, which is *one* criterion of language. But they have not shown other features characteristic of human language. For example, when these animals produce strings of three or four signs, the strings are repetitive rather than sentencelike, according to Terrace and colleagues (Terrace, Pettito, & Bever, 1976). Some linguists contend that the uniquely human aspect of language is its *reflexive* quality (another of Hockett's design features), the fact that it can refer to itself in language about language. Thus far, chimpanzees have not used language to discuss the language system itself, even though they have created new lexical units ("water-bird" for a duck, "juicefruit" for a watermelon), satisfying Hockett's (1963) productivity requirement for language.

Two more recent findings from research with language-trained chimpanzees are even more significant for those researchers who think that these ape productions approach human language. One is that chimpanzees who have not been specifically trained in language nonetheless pick up signs spontaneously from other chimps who were trained and appear to use them instrumentally (Fouts, Fouts & Schoenfield, 1984). (Incidentally, this finding satisfies Hockett's (1963) requirement that a true language have *traditional transmission,* that is, that the experienced teach those who are inexperienced.) The second important discovery is that, as with humans, language-trained chimpanzees appear to have a variety of problem-solving abilities not possessed by chimps who are not language trained (Premack, 1983). The implications of these findings are not yet clear, but while we attempt to determine the limits of nonhuman primates' abilities in using symbolic communication systems, the debates on whether chimpanzees truly have language and the precise definition of "language" will continue.

Cultural Differences in Language

One of the fascinating issues in language is the question of how individual differences in language are to be explained. More specifically, one issue is the development of cultural, regional, and ethnic differences in language. Well-known regional variations in the dialect of English in the United States include dialects associated with the South, New England, New York City, Texas, and the Midwest. The midwestern dialect is frequently referred to as standard, and this accent is sometimes preferred for radio and television broadcasting. Some natives of the Outer Banks of North Carolina and Appalachia speak with a sixteenth-century English accent (similar to a cockney accent). It is not clear how all these variations are maintained other than the general conclusion that we each learn the language patterns typical to our particular culture.

Many black Americans speak a dialect different from standard American English as spoken by midwesterners and television announcers. Black American dialect is different in several ways from standard American English, including slight differences in sound and important differences in grammar. For example, the expressions "I do," "I did," and "I have done" are the accepted forms of the verb *to do* in standard English; however, a black child might say "I do," "I done," and "I have did." While these forms depart from standard English, some linguists have recently recognized that such forms are grammatical.

Until quite recently the use of nonstandard English by blacks has been assumed by some white educators to be a reflection of the cultural deprivation of blacks. Some have felt that the use of nonstandard English may be the principal basis for blacks scoring lower than whites on the average on standard intelligence tests and for school performance of blacks to reflect slower progress than whites. While there may be a relation between language and scholastic performance, recent evidence argues that nonstandard English is logical, orderly, and grammatical. It has been proposed that if whites were required, for example, to take an IQ test based on black culture and language, they would also show poorer performance.

This issue can be placed in another perspective. Is nonstandard black English like any other dialect, or is it a less optimal form of language that may possibly limit the intellectual functioning of those who use it? Although we do not have a full and complete answer to this and similar questions, the recent arguments of some linguists lead us to consider the position of regarding black English as a dialect in its own right, having its own rules and its own sense of time.

Language and the Brain

Language is clearly dependent upon brain functioning and in this section we will consider two issues: hemispheric specialization and brain disorders.

Hemispheric Specialization

The human brain is divided into two hemispheres which are not functionally equivalent. Each hemisphere receives information from the senses, but the two hemispheres generally receive separate information. Information from the visual environment is usually divided, with information from the right visual field being projected to the left hemisphere and information from the left visual field being projected to the right hemisphere. Nevertheless, information which reaches each half of the brain is usually coordinated or integrated in some fashion.

The fact that the human brain is asymmetrical is especially important for language. For most human adults, the left cerebral hemisphere controls the functions of language which include production of both spoken and written language and comprehension of verbal information. In contrast, the right cerebral hemisphere is frequently unable to produce language or to comprehend abstract words. In turn, the right hemisphere is concerned with perceptual processes such as picture recognition and comprehension and learning of visual forms. This physiological distinction has been taken as an important source of support for the dual-coding theory of memory, discussed in chapter 5 (see Paivio, 1986, for discussion). Recently, however, this picture has been clouded by evidence suggesting that image generation, unlike imaginal manipulation (e.g., mental rotation), may have its locus in the occipital region of the left hemisphere (used in visual perception) rather than, or in addition to, the temporal region of the right hemisphere (Farah, Peronnet, & Weisberg, 1987).

The knowledge of this dual functioning of the brain stems from what is called the *split-brain* experiment. A split brain usually results from surgery which severs the corpus callosum, fibers connecting the two hemispheres, in order to alleviate symptoms of certain rare forms of epilepsy. Since the normal interaction between the two hemispheres is eliminated by this operation, it is possible to observe the function of each largely independent hemisphere. Important differences in how the two hemispheres are involved in language behaviors have been discovered. For example, when a split-brain patient held an object in the right hand, allowing sensory information to be sent to the left cerebral hemisphere, the patient was able to name and describe the object. In contrast, when the patient held the object in the left hand, allowing sensory information to go primarily to the right hemisphere, he was unable to describe the object verbally although he could match the object to an identical one in a recognition task. Similarly, when a split-brain patient was shown a picture of an object so that sensory information went to the right hemisphere, he was unable to label the object in the picture; however, he was able to pick out the object in a recognition test when it was presented with others (Gazzaniga, 1970, 1977).

A number of systematic studies have begun to reveal the functioning of the two hemispheres. This separation of language and perceptual functions is the beginning of an important line of work.

Brain Disorders: Aphasia

Two diseases involving language function loss caused by damage to the left hemisphere of the brain are *Broca's aphasia* and *Wernicke's aphasia*. Broca's Aphasia is caused by damage to the brain's premotor area, responsible, in part, for controlling motor commands used in speech production. A person suffering from Broca's aphasia exhibits speech containing excess pauses, slips of the tongue and has trouble finding words when talking. They also fail to make use of function words such as "a, the, of", etc. For this reason, they also produce ungrammatical sentences (Tartter, 1987). Further, Broca's aphasics also have trouble using syntactic information when understanding sentences (Just & Carpenter, 1987). For example, while a Broca's aphasic has no trouble understanding a sentence such as "The bicycle that the man is holding is blue," they have great trouble comprehending a sentence such as "The dog that the woman is biting is grey." This difference is due to fact that while the first sentence can be understood using real world knowledge (e.g., bicycles are blue, not people), the second sentence cannot (because it is unlikely that a woman would bite a dog). Because understanding the second sentence requires correctly using syntactic information, which Broca's aphasics have difficulty doing, the sentence poses problems for them (Berndt & Caramazza, 1980).

People with Wernicke's aphasia suffer from damage to the left temporal lobe of the brain. They have generally fluent phonetic and syntactic but semantically incoherent speech. This incoherence is exhibited through the creation of nonsense words for real world concepts and improper substitutions of function words for content words (e.g., nouns, verbs). In contrast with Broca's aphasics, Wernicke's aphasics also exhibit problems using semantic structure, in categorization and picture-word processing tasks (see Tartter, 1987). Diseases like Broca's and Wernicke's aphasia, while tragic, tell us much about the critical functions of certain regions of the brain. Notably, their symptoms suggest that (at least certain) phonological, syntactic and semantic language information is stored and processed separately in the brain.

SUMMARY

In chapter 11 some of the main features of language were described. As was seen, language is the principal means of human communication. The three functions of language discussed were speech acts, propositional content, and thematic structure. Speech acts involve ordering, questioning, and telling others; propositional content refers to the actual content surrounding a speech act; and thematic structure involves keeping track of what listeners understand.

The basic units of language are phonemes. In order to understand adult language the structure of sentences must be examined. Sentences possess both a surface structure and a deep structure which can be related by transformational grammar.

The important processes of language production, speech perception, and language development were examined. Language production involves five phases: discourse plans, sentence plans, constituent plans, articulatory programs, and articulation. Speech perception begins with the production of speech sounds and ends with their interpretation in memory. Speech perception is not a matter of one-to-one correspondence between the sounds of speech and the perceptions of listeners. Rather, speech perception is heavily dependent upon content, intentions, and knowledge. Language development is a progressive and orderly process in which children learn general rules of language so that they can communicate.

Language and thought are related processes; however, the evidence does not support a strong version of the Whorf hypothesis. Animals such as chimpanzees can be taught certain features of language, but do not appear to possess all the complex features of human language. Language is heavily dependent upon the left cerebral hemisphere, whereas perception is predominantly dependent on the right cerebral hemisphere.

Broca's and Wernicke's aphasias are language disorders caused by left hemispheric damage to the premotor and temporal lobe regions of the brain, respectively. Broca's aphasia affects syntactic information processing whereas Wernicke's aphasia affects more semantic information processing.

MULTIPLE-CHOICE ITEMS

1. A sentence can serve several functions including a request for information, a command, a description, and so forth. These functions refer to
   a. speech acts
   b. grammar
   c. syntax
   d. semantics

2. The function of language which most clearly involves the role of the listener is
   a. propositional content
   b. thematic structure
   c. speech acts
   d. phonemes

3. The phrase structure of sentences emphasizes the way human beings
   a. associate single words
   b. group information for thinking
   c. transform information from deep structure to surface structure
   d. derive meaning

4. The production of language is basically concerned with
   a. phonemes
   b. emotions
   c. planning
   d. conditioning

5. The idea that language leads us to perceive and think about the world in particular ways is called the
   a. distinctive-feature hypothesis
   b. cultural hypothesis
   c. transformational hypothesis
   d. linguistic relativity hypothesis

6. The fact that children produce sentences which they have never in fact heard is taken as support of which conception of language?
   a. grammatical rules are learned
   b. imitation
   c. reinforcement-learning theory
   d. linguistic relativity

TRUE–FALSE ITEMS

1. The consideration of thematic structure by a speaker involves making judgments about the listener's current state of knowledge.

2. Language development is largely a matter of simple imitation.

3. Black English is a less grammatical form of English.

4. Split-brain studies suggest the same locus for language and perceptual functions.

5. Language production is viewed as a five-stage affair beginning with the planning of a sentence.

6. Phonemic restoration refers to the tendency of a listener to "fill in" a missing phoneme while hearing sentences.

DISCUSSION ITEMS

1. Outline several major features of language development.

2. What is the role of context and expectations in the interpretation of speech?

3. Suppose that you had language for only four colors of the visual spectrum, say, red, yellow, green, and blue. Speculate as to how this might affect the way you think about colored objects in the environment.

4. Summarize the basic issues and findings regarding language in chimpanzees.

5.   If it is assumed that various dialects of English are all grammatical, are there advantages to learning standard English? Discuss.

6.   What do brain disorders like Broca's and Wernicke's aphasias tell us about how a healthy brain processes phonological, syntactic and semantic information?

ANSWERS TO MULTIPLE-CHOICE ITEMS

1.   (a)   All utterances or sentences can be classified as to the type of speech act they represent.

2.   (b)   Good speakers pay careful attention to their listeners, judging their level of knowledge and comprehension. This process takes into account thematic structure.

3.   (b)   Phrases appear to be the way in which information is naturally grouped for thinking as well as for memory. Pauses in speech allow for the effective grouping or chunking of phrases in memory.

4.   (c)   Prior to speaking, the speaker decides what kind of discourse to initiate, which involves planning. This is followed by planning at the sentence level and then at the constituent level of the sentence.

5.   (d)   The idea that language influences perceptual and cognitive processes is called the linguistic relativity hypothesis, developed by Whorf.

6.   (a)   The production of novel sentences is thought to occur as the result of using the rules of grammar.

ANSWERS TO TRUE–FALSE ITEMS

1.   (True)   Consideration of thematic structure by speakers means that they are aware of the listeners and make fairly accurate judgments of their level of understanding.

2.   (False)   Imitation appears to be at best only a small part of language learning. Learning a language is very much a matter of learning the set of rules which govern the use of language.

3.   (False)   Many linguists now regard black English as a dialect whose grammatical form is quite lawful.

4.   (False)   Split-brain studies do suggest a separate locus for language and perceptual functions.

5.   (False)   Language production is viewed as a five-stage affair; however, it begins with overall discourse plans and is followed by sentence plans.

6.   (True)   Phonemic restoration is the process of "filling in" a missing phoneme in a word when a sentence is heard.

12

COGNITION, EMOTION AND MEMORY

U p to this point we have described the important characteristics of memory and cognition. We have discussed the basic processes as they operate in normal people, as usually studied under typical laboratory or other conditions. We have, however, said very little about how these processes depend on emotional states, including stress, depression, temporary moods, or other similar conditions. Even without research evidence, there are impressive reasons to suspect that prevailing emotional states can influence memory and other cognitive processes.

Most of us are personally aware that under certain emotional states, such as feeling sad or depressed, we are less attentive to our environment and are less likely to process information in an effective fashion. Similarly, newspaper reports of aircraft accidents have noted that pilot error can be a factor when a pilot is operating under stress. Likewise, aircraft traffic controllers have been observed to make mistakes, such as briefly forgetting to attend to two closely flying aircraft, when under high levels of stress or tension, a characteristic of the job. In another context, clinical observations of depressed patients reveal that they frequently show memory deficits, and severe stress or trauma can lead to temporary or even prolonged amnesia. Thus personal experiences, everyday observations of events, and clinical reports all attest to the idea that emotional states can affect cognitive processes. In this chapter we shall examine some of the recent research on the effects of emotional states on cognitive processes and some of the theoretical accounts of emotion-cognition relationships. This area of research is sometimes referred to as "hot" cognition because emotional variables are seen as determinants of performance.

Research on the relation between emotional states and cognitive processes has burgeoned since about 1975. Ellis and Ashbrook (1988) have noted that although this area of research had a much earlier history of activity, it lay dormant for many years. One reason for this was due to a lack of interest on the part of many cognitive psychologists. For a long period researchers in memory and cognition were preoccupied with understanding how basic processes in memory operate with little regard for the role of emotional variables. Another reason for this lack of activity was the absence of acceptable experimental procedures for producing or manipulating emotional states in the laboratory. It was not until appropriate research procedures were available that cognitive psychologists became more interested in this area. A third reason for delay in research progress was the fact that concepts, theories, and methods in the two areas, cognition and emotion, developed to a large extent independent of each other despite occasional efforts to describe their interrelations (e.g., Antrobus, 1970; Mandler, 1975, 1985). In recent years this area has accelerated and developed to the stage where it has now become a prominent domain of research activity (e.g., Blaney, 1986; Bower, 1981; Ellis, 1986; Ellis & Ashbrook, 1991; Fiedler & Forgas, 1988; Hertel & Narvaez, 1986; Hertel & Rude, 1991; Ingram, 1986; Isen, 1984; Kihlstrom, 1991; Kuiken, 1989, 1991; Riskind, 1991.)

IMPORTANCE OF COGNITION AND EMOTION

Ellis (1986) has outlined several reasons why this area has become increasingly significant to cognitive psychologists, as well as to clinical, developmental, educational, and social psychologists. One straightforward reason is that it is apparent that emotional or affective states can very much influence cognitive processes in important ways. It is therefore essential that psychology understand what these influences are and how they come about. A second reason is that useful ways for inducing temporary emotional states have been developed, thus allowing the experimental manipulation of emotional states as a class of independent variables. For example, subjects in an experiment can be induced, by way of hypnosis or verbal-induction procedures, into a particular mood state such as happiness or sadness. Thus increased methodological sophistication has permitted the expansion of emotion-cognition research. A third factor has been the recognition of the limitations of clinical studies, valuable as they are. Until about ten years ago, the majority of studies of depressed mood states on memory and other cognitive processes used clinical patient populations. Leight and Ellis (1981) have noted an issue in this research:

> Although it is important to understand memory processes of clinically diagnosed depressives, there is an inherent limitation in this endeavor; it does not involve the explicit manipulation of mood state. And without a direct manipulation of mood state, there is no clear way of separating these effects from any confounding related to the general syndrome associated with the clinical entity of depression. Moreover, we believe that it is equally important to investigate how learning and memory are affected by the relatively common occurrence of more transient fluctuations in mood. (p. 251)

Finally, there is the growing belief that theoretical accounts of memory and cognition must explain the influences of affective states such as stress, anxiety, depression, values, arousal, and the like. A complete theory of cognition must ultimately account for the role of these factors. In summary, for these as well as other reasons, the area of cognition, memory, and emotion has developed into an exciting and active research enterprise.

EXPERIMENTAL FINDINGS:
MOOD AND MEMORY

In this section we shall examine some important representative experimental findings relating emotion and cognition. The majority of studies reviewed deal with mood effects on memory and we will focus on studies that experimentally manipulate mood states. We describe the following effects: mood-congruent effects; mood-state dependency; general effects of mood on encoding; mood and elaborative encoding; mood and effortful processing; mood effects on organization; retrieval and mood; focused attention, depression and memory; and moods, thoughts and memory.

Mood-Congruent Effects

The idea of *mood congruence* refers to the finding that people are more likely to remember information that is congruent with their own mood state when they learned the material. Simply put, mood congruence means that a happy person is more likely to remember happy rather than sad material, and conversely, a sad person is more likely to remember sad than happy material.

A good demonstration of mood-congruent effects is seen in a study by Bower, Gilligan, and Monteiro (1981). In one experiment subjects were made either happy or sad by hypnotic suggestion as they read a short story about two college men, Jack and Andre, who get together to play a friendly game of tennis. Andre is happy because everything is going well with him; things are great in school, great with his girlfriend, and he is good at tennis. In contrast, Jack is sad because he has problems with school, with his girlfriend, and with his tennis game. The events of the two men's lives and their emotional reactions (happiness or sadness) were vividly portrayed in the stories. When the subjects had completed reading the story they were assigned, they were first asked to tell who they thought was the central character and who they identified with. Bower et al. (1981) found that the subjects who were happy identified with the happy character, thought the story was about him, and thought the story contained more statements about him. In contrast, subjects who were sad identified with the sad character and thought that the stories contained more statements about him. These findings pertain to mood-identification effects.

On the following day the subjects were required to recall the stories while in a neutral mood. The subjects recalled more facts about the character with whom they identified. Specifically, subjects in a sad mood recalled 80 percent of the facts about the sad character, Jack, and only 20 percent of the facts were recalled about the happy character, Andre. Here the effect of mood congruence is very pronounced. The effect is still present but less prominent with subjects who were in a happy mood during hypnosis. Here, subjects in a happy mood recalled 55 percent of the facts about the happy character and 45 percent of the facts about the sad character. Thus mood congruence was demonstrated because there was selectivity in recall produced by the mood state during learning.

How is mood congruity to be explained? Bower (1981) proposed two possible explanations, and we shall consider the one that is best supported. This is the *selective reminding* interpretation, which contends that when one is sad, a sad incident in a story is more likely than a happy incident to remind the person of a related incident in one's own life. Similarly, when one is happy, then a happy aspect of a story is likely to remind the person of a similar incident in his or her personal life. In addition, the process of reminding is an event that acts to strengthen one's memory of the material which was read. One way this can occur is that the old memory allows a person to enrich or elaborate upon the emotional content of the story.

The mood-congruity effect has been investigated by many researchers and has received considerable support (Blaney, 1986). A number of issues still remain and many aspects need to be worked out in detail. It is a robust finding of mood-memory research which stands in contrast to the next issue, mood-state-dependent effects in memory.

Mood-State-Dependent Effects

Mood-state-dependent effects occur when material learned in a particular mood is recalled or recognized best when a person is tested under that same mood state. For example, if you learned a prose passage while in a happy mood, mood-state dependency would occur if you recalled the material better in a happy mood than in a neutral or sad mood. It is assumed that the mood at encoding will subsequently serve as an effective retrieval cue for the information during recall (Mayer & Bower, 1986; Bower & Mayer, 1989).

Although there is considerable evidence for state-dependent effects in memory involving *drug*-induced states (e.g., Eich, 1980; Peters & McGee, 1982), a recent review of the mood-state-dependent research involving elation and depression observed that the evidence for this effect was neither strong nor consistent (Blaney, 1986) and similar conclusions were reached by Mayer and Bower (1985).

The typical study of mood-state-dependency is outlined below. This table shows the simplest conditions under which state-dependent effects are studied. An experimental group of subjects learns and recalls material in the same mood while a control condition learns and recalls material in a different mood. If recall is superior in the experimental group (same mood) then we infer that a state-dependent effect has been produced. Of course, such an experiment must demonstrate that the control group is not showing a decrement in recall simply because there has been a *change* in context.

	Learning	*Recall*
Experimental Group	Mood A	Mood A
Control Group	Mood B	Mood A

In an early study, Bower, Monteiro, and Gilligan (1978) studied mood-state dependency in three experiments. Hypnotized subjects were asked to produce happy or sad moods by imagining a scene from their lives in which they had experienced a happy or sad emotion. Subjects were required to learn a list of meaningful words and were given either an immediate recall (experiment 1) or a one-day delayed recall (experiment 2). In neither case did they obtain state-dependent memory for the recall of word lists. In a third experiment the researchers made the task more difficult by having the subjects learn two lists with interference involved. They learned one list while happy and the other while sad. Moreover, when subjects were asked to reinstate the appropriate mood at recall, they were asked to imagine a different happy or sad scene from the one they used while learning the material. With this procedure, Bower et al. (1978) were able to obtain mood-state-dependent effects.

Unfortunately, additional studies have failed to replicate this finding. Most importantly, Mayer and Bower (1985) have failed to replicate the results of the third experiment just described. In addition, Mayer and Bower (1986) in a series of four experiments found no support for state-dependent effects except in one study.

Leight and Ellis (1981, experiment 2) conducted a study in which mood-state dependency was examined using both recognition and recall measures. Subjects were presented a task requiring them to learn a list of consonant-vowel-consonant sequences such as *CAMREP*. One day later they were tested for recall or recognition while in the same mood or in a different mood. Subjects were given a mood induction using the Velten (1968) procedure in which they read a list of statements designed to induce either a neutral or a sad mood. The experiment was designed so that state-dependent effects could appear under eight possible conditions. However, in only one condition that involved recognition for the items was a state-dependent effect found. Again, this experiment demonstrates that the effect appears to be fragile and not easily obtained.

Mood-state-dependent effects in memory have appeared in isolated clinical studies (e.g., Weingartner, Miller, & Murphy, 1977), in studies with children (Bartlett, Burleson, & Santrock, 1982), and in right hemisphere studies of face recognition (Gage & Safer, 1985). Overall, however, there have been substantially more failures to produce mood-state-dependent effects.

Given the difficulty in obtaining state-dependent effects, it is important to try to specify those conditions under which the effect is most likely to occur. At least four conditions have been noted as possible contributors to this effect, when it does appear: (1) Mayer and Bower (1986) have suggested that mood-state dependency is most likely to occur when the mood state is perceived as "causally belonging" to the material being remembered. The idea is that somehow, during learning, the mood state and the material being learned must become connected in the sense of belonging to each other. This position argues that if the mood state is to be an important retrieval cue for the target material, it must become integrated in some fashion at the time of learning. The proposal is quite similar to Tulving's idea of encoding specificity, discussed earlier in this book. (2) Leight and Ellis (1981) have proposed that mood-state effects are likely to depend on the nature of the material being learned. They have suggested that meaningful materials, because of their organized structure and more ready accessibility in memory, are less like to show state-dependent effects. They propose that such effects are more likely to be pronounced with poorly structured, unorganized, or less meaningful materials because mood is more likely to become an effective cue with these materials. (3) Eich (1980) has suggested that mood-state dependency is more likely to occur when there are relatively few other cues available to the person. Thus mood-state dependency would be less likely to occur with cued recall, where explicit retrieval cues are presented, than, say, in free recall. (4) Finally, Isen (1984) has suggested that mood-dependent effects are more likely to occur when the material to be remembered is ambiguous or equivocal, as in interference-learning paradigms.

In summary, we conclude that the mood-state-dependent effect in memory does not appear to be robust and is not easy to obtain in laboratory studies. We do have some ideas as to the conditions important for this effect, and we believe that our understanding of this effect will increase as researchers develop better control of these experimental conditions. For the moment, mood-state dependency in memory presents more puzzles than solutions. Fortunately, recent work by Eich (1989) and Eich and Metcalf (1989) promises to clarify some of the earlier puzzles, in that they have found good evidence for state-dependent memory when few cues for memory were available.

Mood Effects on Encoding

In this section we turn our attention to the effects of mood states on the encoding of information. At one level we can ask what effects mood states such as being happy or sad have on the encoding of information. At another level we can delineate the memory processes that are importantly affected by mood states. And at a third level we can develop theoretical accounts of the effects of mood on memory.

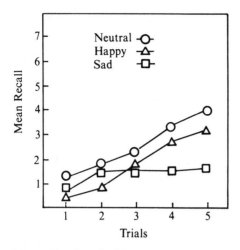

Figure 12.1 Recall of letter sequences following a neutral, elated, or depressed mood-induction procedure. (From "Emotional Mood States, Strategies, and State-dependency in Memory" by K. A. Leight and H. C. Ellis, *Journal of Verbal Learning and Verbal Behavior,* 1981, *20,* 251–256. Copyright 1981 by Academic Press. Reprinted by permission of Academic Press.)

As an example of the first level of experiments, Leight and Ellis (1981, experiment 1) examined the effects of experimentally induced mood states on learning of lists of consonant-vowel-consonant pairs. College students served as subjects and were given a mood induction using the Velten (1968) procedure. The subjects were placed in one of three mood states, happy, sad, or a neutral mood, by having them read a list of 60 self-referent statements from Velten's procedure. Subjects who were placed in a happy mood read a series of happy self-referent statements which dealt with feeling good and being competent, to being extremely happy. Sad subjects read a series of sad self-referent statements and neutral subjects read statements designed to induce or maintain a neutral state. After mood induction was given, subjects were administered a questionnaire to be sure that the induction procedure was effective, which it was. Subjects were then given five trials on the list-learning task and the results are shown in figure 12.1.

As the figure clearly shows, subjects in the neutral mood induction showed the best performance, whereas subjects in the sad mood showed the poorest performance. Moreover, subjects in the sad mood failed to show any improvement in recall after the second trial, indicating the pronounced impairment of these subjects. The happy subjects were intermediate, and they continued to show improvement over trials but were always below the neutral group. This latter finding indicates that being happy, at the level induced by the Velten procedure, has a slight interfering effect on learning the list. This does not mean that being mildly happy is undesirable, but indicates that the high level of emotion induced by the elation procedure does produce some lowering of performance.

These results indicate clearly that mood states can affect the encoding of neutral information, that sadness interferes with encoding, and that even high levels of elation have some interfering effects. Now let us examine some experiments that look at the effects of mood states on important memory processes.

Mood and Elaborative Encoding

In this section we shall examine the effects of an experimentally induced depressed mood state on elaborative encoding. Elaboration is an important process in memory and, therefore, it is important to understand how depression affects this process.

Ellis, Thomas, and Rodriguez (1984) addressed this issue in the first of a series of experiments. They asked the question, How would a sad mood state affect the performance of subjects in a memory task that encourages elaborative encoding? The task required that subjects read a set of ten sentences and rate each sentence as to its comprehensibility. The sentences were either simple, base sentences or they were elaborated sentences containing information that enriched and elaborated upon a target adjective in the sentence. For example, the sentence *The hungry child opened the door* is a base sentence. There is nothing in the sentence that relates to or elaborates on the adjective *hungry*. In contrast, *The hungry child opened the door of the refrigerator* contains the phrase *of the refrigerator* which precisely elaborates upon the to-be-target word for testing in the sentence, *hungry*. Previous experiments (e.g., Stein & Bransford, 1979) have shown that if subjects are then presented the sentences without the target word *hungry* and asked to recall the word, they do substantially better if they had seen the word embedded in the elaborated rather than the base sentence. This occurs because of the information presented during study and is not dependent on having a more elaborated sentence during recall testing.

Given that elaboration of information in a sentence aids recall, Ellis et al. (1984) were primarily interested in how a depressed mood state would affect memory for this type of material. They reasoned that since elaboration would activate a greater level of encoding, depression should have a greater impact on the processing of material in elaborative rather than base, simple sentences.

Subjects were given either a sad mood or neutral mood induction as well as a set of either base or elaborated sentences to rate on comprehensibility. This was an *incidental* memory procedure; thus subjects did not know that they would be asked to recall target words in the sentences after

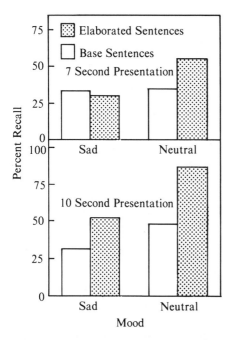

Figure 12.2 Recall of target words in elaborated or base sentences following a sad or neutral mood induction. (From "Emotional Mood States and Memory: Elaborative encoding, semantic processing, and cognitive effort" by H. C. Ellis, R. L. Thomas, and A. I. Rodriguez, *Journal of Experimental Psychology: Learning, Memory and Cognition,* 1984, 10, 470–481. Copyright 1985 by the American Psychological Association. Reprinted by permission of the publisher).

they had rated them. Subjects were presented the sentences for either a 7- or 10-second rate in order to examine the role of time to process the information. Immediately following the sentence-rating procedure, subjects were presented the sentences with the target word removed, for example, "The _____ child opened the door," and asked to recall the missing word.

The results are shown in figure 12.2, which is broken down into two panels. The top panel shows recall of the target words under sad or neutral mood states and for elaborated or base sentences for the 7-second presentation. The striking finding, and the most important one, was that subjects who were sad showed a clear reduction in recall of words in the elaborated condition, but being sad had no effect whatsoever on the recall of words in the base sentence conditions. Figure 12.2 presents a clear interaction between mood states and sentence conditions, that is, the effect of a sad mood induction is greatest when the task is more demanding, in the sense of requiring more elaborative encoding.

The bottom panel of figure 12.2 shows, as expected, that recall is much higher when subjects have longer to process the sentences. This is not surprising and is not of particular interest. What is of interest is that while there is some suggestion of a mood-state interaction with the sentence conditions, the effect is much less pronounced at the 10-second presentation level.

What these findings show is that the induction of a sad mood state has a somewhat complex effect on memory. First, being sad will reduce memory but not in all conditions. The sad and neutral mood subjects perform equally well when recalling words from the base sentences under the faster (7-second) presentation rate. However, sad mood subjects do poorer in the remaining three comparisons. And second, as noted above, there is clear evidence that elaborative processing is more impaired by depression than is processing of base sentences.

Mood and Effortful Processing

This second finding supported more generally the idea that depression is most likely to affect the processing of more difficult, demanding material. *Ellis et al. (1984) proposed that as the encoding demands of a task become greater, the interfering effects of disruptive mood states increase.* With simple tasks that require fewer encoding demands or less effort, being sad may have little or no effect on performance. However, as the task becomes more complex, difficult, or demanding, the effects of sadness become greater. Ellis et al. (1984, experiment 3) directly examined this hypothesis in a study in which variations in the effortful demands on subjects were made. This was accomplished by presenting subjects with sentences in which a single word (the object noun) had been omitted. The incomplete sentence was followed by a pair of nouns from which the subject was to select the word that correctly completed the sentence. In each sentence, only one word (the target) fit meaningfully into the sentence. The amount of effort required in making the decision was varied as follows: For a low-effort word the missing item was quite obvious and virtually self-evident, such as, "The girl was awakened by her frightening _____ ." In the high-effort condition, the missing word was not obvious but was one of several possible solutions: "The man was alarmed by the frightening _____ ." For both sentences, the appropriate target word was *dream,* which easily fits into the low-effort sentence, but requires some deliberation for selection in the high-effort sentence.

It was known that in such a task subjects recall more of the high-effort items in an incidental memory task. The experimenters were interested in the effects of being sad on recall of high- and low-effort items, with the prediction that depressed subjects would show greater impairment of the

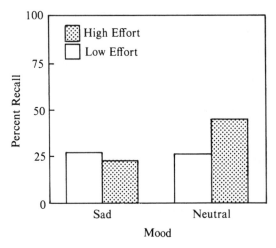

Figure 12.3 Recall of words in an incidental memory task involving high- and low-effort tasks following a sad or neutral mood induction. (From "Emotional Mood States and Memory: Elaborative Encoding, Semantic Processing, and Cognitive Effort" by H. C. Ellis, R. L. Thomas, and A. I. Rodriguez, *Journal of Experimental Psychology: Learning, Memory, and Cognition,* 1984, *10,* 470–481. Copyright 1985 by the American Psychological Association. Reprinted by permission of the publisher.)

high-effort items. Following the task of selecting an appropriate word for each sentence, subjects were given a surprise free-recall test for the words and the results are shown in figure 12.3. The figure shows two important findings. First, as indicated by the neutral mood conditions, subjects show better recall for the high-effort items. Second, the effect of being sad on recall is to reduce performance only on the high-effort items. In contrast, being sad had no effect on the recall of low-effort items whatsoever. Again, this study supports the idea that being sad has its greatest impairment on more effortful tasks.

There is also clinical-study evidence that is consistent with the idea that depression has its greatest effects on more demanding tasks. For example, Weingartner, Cohen, Murphy, Martello, and Gerdt (1981) found a decrement in the recall of depressed patients, compared with nonpatient control subjects, in three experiments that required the processing of words. They asked subjects to process concrete nouns, either semantically or acoustically, by generating semantic associates or rhymes for the to-be-remembered words. Free recall of the target words was measured a day later. Making the assumption that the semantic-processing task requires more cognitive effort or capacity than the acoustic task, then a decrease in recall of semantically processed items should be greater than that of the rhymes for the depressed patients, when compared with the nonpatient controls. They found that the depressed patients recalled fewer of the semantically processed items than the control subjects, whereas free recall for the rhymes was essentially identical for the two groups.

In another study by Weingartner et al. (1981, experiment 3), they examined the effects of depression on recall of highly organized versus unorganized word lists. Depressed patients and control subjects did not differ in the recall of the highly-organized word lists. In contrast, depressed patients were much poorer in recall of the unorganized lists. Making the assumption that unorganized lists require more capacity or effort to process than do the highly structured lists, these results are consistent with the interactions between mood and task demands in the Ellis et al. (1984) experiments examining elaboration and effort. Similarly, Cohen, Weingartner, Smallberg, Pickar, and Murphy (1982) have proposed that the greatest impairment by depressed patients on cognitive tasks is found in those tasks that require *sustained effort.*

Why is it that depressed mood states have greater effects on the processing of more difficult or demanding tasks? An explanation developed by Ellis and Ashbrook (1988), which depends upon the allocation of processing capacity, can account for these findings and will be described in detail later, after our review of general theories and models.

Mood Effects on Organization

It is certainly reasonable to assume that emotional states such as depression, anxiety, or similar sources of stress interfere with organizational processes in memory. Certainly common experience suggests that when we are stressed or in a poor mood we find ourselves forgetful, and our ability to think clearly and in an organized fashion seems impaired. Fortunately, our personal impressions are borne out in both laboratory and clinical studies; however, the results again depend upon characteristics of the task.

We noted in the previous section that depressed patients showed difficulty in remembering word lists that were unorganized (Weingartner et al. 1981, experiment 3). Depression impairs the ability to organize material that is poorly structured, although no impairment was found with highly organized materials. More specifically, it was found that depressed subjects employ less subjective organization of randomly organized materials than do normal control subjects. Other clinical studies of depressive subjects have found deficits in the ability to organize information. For example, Russell and Beekhuis (1976) found that depressed patients showed poorer free recall and reduced clustering in free recall, a measure of organization.

Experimental studies have also found deficits in organizational processes due to depression. For example, Leight and Ellis (1981, experiment 2) found a marked reduction in both recall and organizational measures

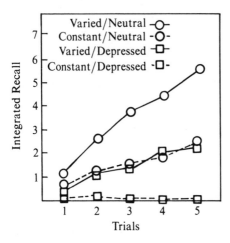

Figure 12.4 Integrated recall (chunking) of letter sequences under conditions of varied versus constant presentation of letter sequences following depressed or neutral mood induction. (From "Emotional Mood States, Strategies, and State-dependency in Memory" by K. A. Leight and H. C. Ellis, *Journal of Verbal Learning and Verbal Behavior,* 1981, *20,* 251–256. Copyright 1981 by Academic Press. Reprinted by permission of Academic Press.)

for college students given the Velten depressed mood induction. In their study subjects learned lists of eight consonant-vowel-consonant pairs (e.g., *CAMREP, BONKID, GAMLUX*). The letter sequences were broken up into grouping structures (e.g., *CA MR EP*) that masked the pronounceable units (e.g., *CAM, REP*). In one case the grouping structures were the same on each presentation, a *constant* presentation condition. In the second case, the structures were *varied* on each presentation which encouraged subjects to look for pronounceable (organized) units (See Ellis, Grah, Parente, & Spiering, 1975). Subjects were given either a depressed or neutral mood induction and either a varied or constant presentation of the letter sequences.

The results were quite striking and are shown in figure 12.4. The figure shows recall of the letter sequences as integrated units, a measure of organization, over five successive trials. The important results were that the depressed subjects showed no improvement whatsoever over five learning trials when the material was presented in constant fashion. In contrast, with varied presentation the depressed groups did show some improvement, and performed virtually identical to neutral mood subjects who learned constant sequences. The figure also shows that subjects in the varied-neutral condition performed best and showed the most rapid improvement in performance.

What was most striking was the inability of the constant-depressed group to show any gain in performance over five trials. Given a task that is difficult to organize, the induction of a depressed mood severely impairs performance in this perceptual grouping task, an organizational task that depends upon the subject being able to chunk or group the letter sequences. Note that these findings parallel those of Weingartner et al. (1981), who found that depressed patients showed reduced recall and organizational ability when required to learn poorly structured materials. Thus it appears that depression has its greatest negative impact on organizational processes when the materials are inherently difficult to organize.

Retrieval and Mood

Another issue that has been examined is the role of mood on retrieval as distinct from the encoding of information. Studies of mood effects on retrieval require the induction of a mood state *after* subjects have processed some information. The basic sequence involves having subjects first process some material, then placing them in a mood state, and finally testing for their recall of the information. As you can see, this differs from studies of mood on encoding where subjects are given a mood induction *prior* to performing some cognitive task. Thus studies of the effects of mood on retrieval examine the effects of mood on the *output* of information.

Experimental studies of mood effects on retrieval show basically two sets of results. One group of studies have failed to find effects of mood on retrieval, and others have reported that mood states do have an effect on retrieval. This difference is not a matter of unreliable findings but is likely due to different experimental conditions used in the various studies.

Two studies have reported no effects of mood on retrieval. First, Bower, Gilligan, and Monteiro (1981, experiment 2) failed to obtain retrieval effects when a hypnotic mood induction was administered 5 hours after reading a story. The delayed retention interval, as well as delay of mood induction, may be one factor that precluded the researchers from finding an effect of mood on retrieval. As Ellis, Thomas, McFarland, and Lane (1985) suggest, it is possible that any potential effects of mood on retrieval will be attenuated after a 5-hour retention interval, and that any mood state will have its major effect when induced immediately or soon after a study session rather than when it is delayed.

Similarly, Goldstein (1983) found no retrieval effects of a depressed mood state on the recall of personal memories. He had subjects attempt to recall early childhood memories after being given either a neutral or depressed mood induction. His procedure was to bring subjects to the laboratory and have them recall their earliest, (or one of their earliest) childhood memories. Two days later they returned to the laboratory and were given

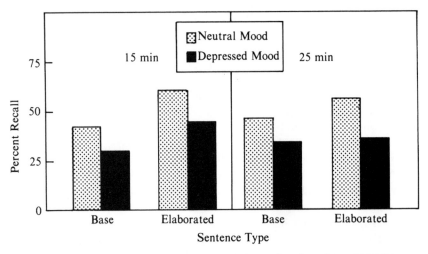

Figure 12.5 Percentage of target words recalled as a function of mood conditions, elaborated and base sentences, and retention interval. (From "Emotional Mood States and Retrieval in Episodic Memory" by H. C. Ellis, R. L. Thomas, A. D. McFarland, and J. W. Lane, *Journal of Experimental Psychology: Learning, Memory, and Cognition,* 1985, *11,* 363–370. Copyright 1985 by the American Psychological Association. Reprinted by permission of the publisher.)

a mood induction and then required to recall the early memory. His null effects may have been because early childhood memories are quite likely part of a highly integrated memory system relatively impervious to a depressed mood state.

In contrast, clear effects of a depressed mood induction on the retrieval of target words in sentences have been reported by Ellis et al. (1985). In this study, they used the base and elaborated sentences used by Ellis et al. (1984). As described earlier in this chapter, in the section on mood and elaborative encoding, subjects processed sentences and were later tested with an incomplete sentence with the target adjective removed. Again using this procedure, Ellis et al. (1985) required subjects first to process the list of ten sentences, then to undergo a neutral or depressed mood induction, and finally were tested for recall of the target words. Subjects were given either a full Velten mood induction requiring 25 minutes or a partial induction procedure requiring 15 minutes.

The basic results are shown in figure 12.5. Regardless of the type of sentence processed or the duration of the mood induction, depressed mood subjects recalled fewer target words than neutral control subjects. These results establish the general point that a depressed mood can impair the retrieval of information. Much is yet to be understood about retrieval effects, including how they depend on type of material, instructions to subjects, the mood induction itself, and other factors.

How does the induction of a depressed mood state interfere with retrieval? Ellis et al. (1985) and Ellis and Ashbrook (1988) have proposed a model to account for these results. They propose that emotional states can be viewed as conditions that regulate the allocation of capacity of resources in cognitive tasks. A depressive or, more generally, a disruptive mood state interferes with the retrieval of information because it preempts some capacity that would normally be allocated to retrieving information. Ellis et al. (1985) also note that an additional account is possible in that the cognitive activities associated with retrieval may interfere in a more direct sense, in that the negative cognitions of the depressed subject compete directly with the cognitive activities necessary for successful retrieval. In this account, emphasis is placed upon the potential competition of cognitive activities in working memory. These two accounts are complementary and both sets of processes may occur during retrieval.

Focused Attention, Depression, and Memory

Depression does not always impair memory. Although deficits in memory have been shown in a number of experiments (e.g., Ellis & Ashbrook, 1988; Hertel & Hardin, 1990; Kuiken, 1991), it is also the case that such deficits can be eliminated by procedures requiring depressed subjects to pay focused attention to the task. This has been demonstrated by Hertel and Rude (1991) whose subjects were given a surprise recall test after they had read incomplete sentence frames in which they determined if a word properly completed a sentence. In one condition subjects simply read the sentence and decided if the word fit; in the other condition subjects were required to read aloud the word both at the beginning and end of the presentation, forcing the subjects to attend to the task. Figure 12.6 shows total recall for both attention conditions (focused and unfocused) and depressed versus neutral mood states. The figure shows that having to pay attention eliminated the deficits in memory typically found. What is clear is that depressives do not necessarily have to suffer impaired memory and their recall can be considerably improved if they are required to perform a task that encourages their focused attention.

Moods, Thoughts, and Memory

Several theoretical accounts of the effects of emotional states on memory have proposed the idea that mood states produce a prevailing pattern of thoughts that influence performance in a variety of cognitive tasks (e.g., Beck, Rush, Shaw, & Emery, 1979; Ellis & Ashbrook, 1988; Ingram, 1984). An important assumption in these theories is that a depressed mood state produces its effect on memory and cognition via negative or unfavorable

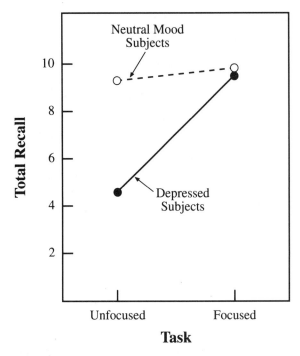

Figure 12.6 Recall as a function of depression and focused versus unfocused attention on the memory task. (From "Depressive deficits in memory: Focusing attention improves subsequent recall" by P. T. Hertel and S. S. Rude. *Journal of Experimental Psychology: General,* 1991, *120,* 301–309. Copyright 1991 by the American Psychological Association. Reprinted by permission of the publisher and author.)

self-thoughts that interfere with performance. For example, two assumptions of the Ellis-Ashbrook (1988) model deal with the role of irrelevant, distracting thoughts. The model proposes that the production of irrelevant thoughts increases under emotional duress and that these irrelevant, distracting thoughts interfere with a person's ability to encode and organize information in memory, thus explaining poorer recall. What is particularly important about these assumptions is that they contend that disruptive emotional states produce their effects on memory and other cognitive processes not directly by emotion per se, but by way of distracting, irrelevant thoughts that compete with thoughts relevant to encoding the pertinent information in the memory task.

Seibert and Ellis (1991) have directly tested this idea. College students were tested in two mood-memory experiments in which they were asked to produce all their thoughts, which were tape recorded, while they were studying a set of items. They were subsequently asked to judge their reported thoughts as being relevant or irrelevant, on a five-point scale, to the criterion memory task. Subjects were given either a sad, happy, or neutral mood induction. In a second experiment subjects were asked to list and judge their thoughts at the end of the study session. Both experiments required students to recall the study items, providing a measure of recall for each student and a measure of judged relevance of thoughts. Using either the first procedure, concurrent verbalization, or the second procedure, thought listing, the production of irrelevant thoughts was strongly negatively correlated with recall. These results, while correlations, provide support for the view that mood effects on memory are the results of thoughts, that is, the cognitive activity which intervenes between the subjects' mood state and performance on the memory task.

THEORETICAL APPROACHES

There are three somewhat independent theoretical frameworks that account for the effects of emotional states on memory and cognition. The first is *network theory* developed largely by Gordon Bower and his colleagues (Bower, 1981; Bower & Cohen, 1982; Gilligan & Bower, 1984). The second approach is *schema theory* which contends that a person's mood state functions as a schema (conceptual framework) for processing and organizing incoming information as well as guiding the retrieval process (e.g., Beck, 1967; Kuiper, McDonald, & Derry, 1983). The third approach consists of the *resource allocation model* developed largely by Henry Ellis and his colleagues (e.g., Ellis & Ashbrook, 1988; Ellis, Thomas, & Rodriguez, 1984; Ellis, Thomas, McFarland, & Lane, 1985). This model is based on the idea of allocating attentional capacity to an appropriate task, and will be discussed in more detail shortly. Several variations of each theory or model have been developed but our intent is to describe briefly a representative example of each. These approaches are not to be regarded as competing but are properly seen as complementary.

Network Theory

An elaborately developed approach is *network theory* and it is based upon the general idea that emotional states are represented as nodes, or components, of semantic memory. There are several alternative models of network theory (e.g., Bower, 1981; Clark & Isen, 1982; Isen, 1984; Teasdale, 1983), and Bower's (1981) theory is currently the most comprehensive of these. His description of the semantic network captures the most essential features of his theory as follows:

> The semantic-network approach supposes that each distinct emotion such as joy, depression, or fear has a specific node or unit in memory that collects together many other aspects of

the emotion that are connected to it by associative pointers. . . . [Around each] emotion node are its associated autonomic reactions, standard role and expressive behaviors . . . , and descriptions of standard evocative situations which when appraised lead to sadness. . . . [Each] emotion unit is also linked with propositions describing events from one's life during which that emotion was aroused. . . . These emotion nodes can be activated by many stimuli—by physiological or symbolic verbal means. When activated above a threshold, the emotion unit transmits excitation to those nodes that produce the pattern of autonomic arousal and expressive behavior commonly assigned to that emotion. . . . Activation of an emotion node also spreads activation throughout the memory structures to which it is connected, creating subthreshold excitation at those event nodes. Thus, a weak cue that partially describes an event, such as "kindergarten days," may combine with activation from an emotion unit to raise the total activation of a relevant memory above a threshold of consciousness. . . . This recall constitutes reactivation of a sad memory and sends feedback excitation to the sadness node, which will maintain activation of that emotion and thus influence later memories retrieved (p. 135).

The network model has been applied to an understanding of a variety of mood effects including mood-congruent effects, remembering personal episodes, similarity of emotions, mood-state-dependent effects, and general emotional effects on cognitive processes. For instance, mood-congruent effects in memory are the result of activation of emotion nodes by some emotional event that is consistent with one's network of emotional memories. If a person is in a happy mood, then the semantic network system is activated and is therefore more receptive to materials that have a happy tone to them.

Schema Theory

The second approach, schema theory, is somewhat similar to network theory and also accounts for the effects of emotional states on memory and cognitive processes. Schema theory proposes that people in a typical or characteristic prevailing mood have a generalized framework or schema that is congruent with that mood state. Thus a sad person has a prevailing sad or depressive schema for organizing information. For instance, a sad person characteristically perceives and remembers negative experiences, sad episodes, and tends to interpret the world from a negative perspective. Not only does a sad schema predispose a person to encode unhappy, negative events more readily than happy events, the schema also directs their retrieval of specific memories that have a sad content.

The idea of a negative schema is part of general cognitive theories of depression. A leading developer of cognitive theories of depression is Aaron Beck who proposes that depression is produced by specific stressful situations that activate a prevailing schema. The activated schema selectively encodes negative information and thereby maintains the depressive state of the individual.

Schema and semantic-network theories are conceptually very similar in that they both propose that knowledge structures (semantic networks or schemas) predispose a person to selectively encode and retrieve information that is consistent with one's knowledge structure. There are, however, two important distinctions that have been noted (Ingram, 1984). First, network theories typically adopt the assumption of spreading activation (Collins & Loftus, 1975), whereas schema theories have not typically adopted this assumption. Second, some have noted that the schema concept is less well developed than the semantic-network concept. Nevertheless, the status of the schema concept has become much developed in recent years and it is clearly a useful and important concept (Mandler, 1984).

Resource Allocation Model

The third general approach to accounting for the effects of emotional states on cognitive processes is called resource allocation or capacity models. We have briefly referred to this idea in this chapter and will develop it here. In general, resource allocation models, designed to explain the effects of emotional states on memory and cognition, have considered two features: (1) the role of emotional states in regulating the amount capacity allocated to some cognitive task and (2) the demands on processing capacity made by the cognitive task itself. This approach has been most fully developed by Ellis and Ashbrook (1988) who characterize their model as follows:

> The model adopts the concept of capacity or resource allocation which is part of general capacity models of attention. . . . [These models] have assumed that there is a limited, momentary pool of capacity (attentional resources) which can be allocated to any given task. . . . From this perspective, it is our position that emotional states can affect the amount of attentional capacity that can be allocated to a given cognitive or motor task. Thus we are considering the effect of emotion on attention but from the view of capacity (resource) models of attention as distinct from other conceptions of attention. The essence of the resource allocation model, in accounting for the effects of generally disruptive mood states on memory, is to assume that emotional states regulate the amount of capacity

that can be allocated to some criterion task. Most tasks involving memory of information require some allocation of capacity and thus the effect of a disruptive mood state is to reduce the amount of capacity available for processing the criterion task (p. 26).

This model makes five principal assumptions in order to account for the effects of emotional states on memory and cognitive tasks: (1) emotional states produce their effects on cognitive activities by regulating the amount of capacity available to be allocated to a given task; (2) the encoding of information usually requires some allocation of cognitive capacity or effort; (3) memory performance is frequently correlated with the amount of capacity allocated to the cognitive task, an assumption based on the empirical findings regarding cognitive effort (e.g., O'Brien & Myers, 1985; Swanson, 1984; Tyler, Hertel, McCallum, & Ellis, 1979). Assumptions (4) and (5) deal with mood effects on irrelevant-task processing and extra-task processing and propose that emotional states increase the production of irrelevant thought, which, in turn, impairs memory for criterion tasks. These latter two assumptions have been found valid by Seibert and Ellis (1991), as noted earlier in this chapter.

A wide range of research findings support the Ellis-Ashbrook (1988) model. These include the results from studies on overall decrements in recall due to depression, the effects of depression on the encoding of easy versus demanding tasks, and the effects of depression on retrieval, personal memories, organization, and schema recall.

One of the most important predictions of the model is that depression will have its greatest impairment in the recall of demanding or difficult tasks. As noted earlier, this finding has appeared in a number of experiments. The model explains this outcome by assuming that a depressed mood state or, more generally, any disruptive mood state can interfere with the encoding of material because it takes away some resources that might otherwise be allocated to the memory task. When a task is very demanding, there will be fewer resources available to process the task and if a person is already depressed, then insufficient resources are available. In contrast, if one is processing an easy task, then adequate resources are available to process the task and little or no decrements in recall should occur (Ellis & Ashbrook, 1988; Ellis et al., 1984).

The three general approaches we have described are seen as complementary and not competing. Network and schema theories approach the issue of mood effects on memory from the perspective of how organized knowledge structures, such as semantic-network models or schemas, influence the encoding and retrieval of information. In turn, the resource allocation model approaches this from the viewpoint of how mood affects the allocation of resources, which ultimately is correlated with memory. We believe that a complete model of how mood affects memory will see an integration of these two conceptual approaches and Ingram (1984) has, similarly, argued for such an integration.

SPECIFIC ISSUES IN EMOTION AND COGNITION

In the final section of this chapter we shall consider four special issues that go beyond the usual research on mood and memory. These issues are mood states and judgments of contingency, emotion and eyewitness testimony, flashbulb memory, and anxiety and performance.

Mood States and Contingency Judgments

The mood of a person not only affects memory, but it also influences other cognitive processes such as judgment. Since depression has been shown to interfere with memory in a variety of settings, we might suspect that depression would similarly impair the accuracy of judgments a person makes. In a surprising series of experiments, however, Alloy and Abramson (1979) have shown that students who were depressed were actually more accurate in contingency judgments than nondepressed students!

In their studies, they examined the ability of depressed and nondepressed college students to detect the degree of contingency between their responses and environmental outcomes. The students were presented a contingency problem in which the subject made one of two responses (pressing a button or not pressing it) and received one of two outcomes (a green light or no green light). At the end of a series of trials, the subject was asked to judge the degree of contingency (relationship) that existed between pressing a button and onset of the green light.

In one study (Alloy & Abramson, 1979, experiment 2), students were presented with one of two problems in which responses and outcomes were *noncontingently* related (unrelated) but differed in the overall frequency with which the green light came on. If people use the rule of percentage of reinforcement (percentage of time the green light comes on), then they will believe they have more control in the problem in which the green light occurs more frequently than in the situation in which the green light occurs less frequently. In one problem, designated 25–25, the subjects had no control over the green light, but the green light was presented 25 percent of the time. In the second problem, called 75–75, the subjects also had no control, but the green light was presented 75 percent of the time.

The basic results are shown in figure 12.7, which shows judged control for the two problems for depressed and nondepressed subjects and also shows separate results for male and female subjects. Any judgment of perceived control is in error in a noncontingent situation, because pressing a button

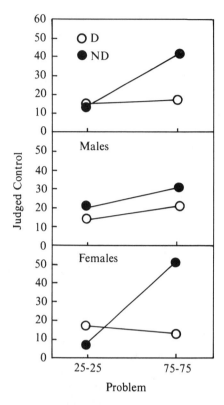

Figure 12.7 Judged degree of control for depressed (D) and nondepressed (ND) students as a function of problem type. (From "Judgment of Contingency in Depressed and Nondepressed Students: Sadder but Wiser?" by L. B. Alloy and L. Y. Abramson, *Journal of Experimental Psychology: General,* 1979, *108,* 441–485. Copyright 1979 by the American Psychological Association. Reprinted by permission of the publisher.)

did not cause the green light to appear, so the greater the degree of judged control the greater the actual error in judgment. As you can see from the top panel of the figure, nondepressed subjects thought they had little control in the 25–25 problem, but considerably overestimated their degree of control in the 75–75 problem. In contrast, the depressed subjects made relatively accurate judgments for both problems. Looking at male-female results, it is clear that the females overestimated the 75–75 problem, that is, they thought they had greater control than did the males.

The most important issue is why depressed subjects should be more accurate in judging contingencies. Or, the alternative issue is why nondepressives are less accurate in making contingency judgments. Alloy and

Abramson (1979) suggest several alternative hypotheses. They favor a generalized motivational account in which it is assumed that nondepressed people have a more self-enhancing attributional style, that is, they tend to attribute success or good outcomes to themselves and are more likely, therefore, to develop the illusion of control in a situation when none actually exists. Depressives in contrast do not have this self-enhancing attributional style, and hence suffer fewer illusions. As Alloy and Abramson suggest, depressives may be "sadder but wiser" in these judgmental tasks.

This issue of the illusion of control was subsequently examined by Alloy, Abramson, and Viscusi (1981). They selected nondepressed and depressed subjects, according to a depression inventory, and then induced a mood of depression or elation. Naturally nondepressed subjects who were made temporarily depressed by a Velten (1968) mood induction gave accurate judgments of control, whereas naturally depressed subjects who were made temporarily elated showed an illusion of control and made overestimates in judgments.

More generally, these studies reveal the important effects of mood states on judgments and the illusion of control over events. They further indicate the importance of emotional factors in influencing cognitive processes and yield findings that were surprising and unexpected in the initial Alloy and Abramson (1979) studies.

Emotion and Eyewitness Testimony

Since about 1970 there has been a renewed interest in eyewitness testimony, both with respect to basic questions about memory and perception, and practical issues concerning the application of knowledge about eyewitness testimony to the courtroom situation (e.g., Kassin, Ellsworth, & Smith, 1989; Loftus, 1986; McCloskey, Egeth, & McKenna, 1986). A fairly large body of information about eyewitness testimony has developed, much of it associated with the issue of unreliability of eyewitness testimony. Some of the important findings include the lack of any substantive correlation between the accuracy of an eyewitness and the degree of confidence expressed by the witness (Wells & Murray, 1984), the role of postevent misleading information in producing distortions of memory or perception (Loftus, Burns, & Miller, 1978), the role of bias in cross racial identification (Brigham & Malpass, 1985), and the limited amount of information that jurors have about eyewitness perception and memory (Deffenbacker & Loftus, 1982).

In this section we shall briefly comment on the role of emotional states in eyewitness testimony. A frequent claim has been that emotional stress produces an impairment in memory such that witnesses to a traumatic emotional event will be less accurate in recall. Indeed, experts in the field tend to believe that very high levels of stress impair the accuracy of eyewitness testimony (Kassin, Ellsworth, & Smith, 1989).

In a review of this literature, Christianson (1991) indicates that the results are somewhat complex. For instance, some studies have shown that unpleasant emotional events are poorly remembered compared with neutral events (e.g., Loftus & Burns, 1982; Neisser & Harsch, in press). Neisser and Harsch found that in studies of college students' memories of the Challenger space shuttle disaster, that poorer recall was associated with stronger negative emotions, as remembered. Similarly, Baddeley (1972) has shown that strong emotion impairs memory. Servicemen were taken on a plane flight and led to believe that an emergency situation had arisen; when tested, the results indicated that the simulated emergency impaired ability to remember detailed instructions. Other studies, however, have shown that unpleasant events can be remembered fairly well (e.g., Heuer & Reisberg, 1990; Reisberg & Heuer, in press).

It is not possible to resolve the divergence in findings in any brief or simple fashion. The results seem to depend on the type of task used, what kind of information is required in memory, and a variety of other features. One resolution of these differences may lie in Easterbrook's (1959) cue-utilization hypothesis. According to this position, as emotional arousal increases there is a progressive restriction in the range of cues utilized or attended. At a moderate level of arousal, a restriction in attention to environmental cues can benefit performance because relevant cues will still be attended to whereas irrelevant or unimportant cues will receive little attention. However, at high arousal levels, as seen in high stress or anxiety, even fewer cues would receive attention including relevant ones, thus degrading performance. Thus whether emotion helps or hinders would, according to Easterbrook's hypothesis, ultimately depend upon the level of arousal. These findings can also be accounted for by Ellis and Ashbrook's (1988) model, in which it is proposed that moderate levels of emotional arousal are unlikely to impair memory, especially with easy tasks. In contrast, strong levels of emotion are likely to impair memory, especially if the task is more difficult.

Flashbulb Memory: Personal Memories Revisited

Flashbulb memory refers to the recall of very important, vivid, and often emotionally arousing events. The term flashbulb memory was used by Brown and Kulik (1977) who asked their subjects if they could recall how they heard the news about President John Kennedy's assassination as well as other striking events. Many subjects reported a very vivid and personal recollection of these events with a lot of attendant details. The focus of flashbulb memory is on memory for one's own personal circumstances, such as where one was, what one was doing, and how one felt about the shocking news of Kennedy's death as distinct from memory about the event itself (Pillemer, in press). Much of the research concerns memory for shocking public events such as the attempted assassination of President Reagan (Pillemer, 1984), the space shuttle disaster (Bohannon, 1988) and President Nixon's resignation (Winograd & Killinger, 1983).

An initial interpretation of flashbulb memory, proposed by Brown and Kulik (1977), was that a surprising and important event produces an initial registration in memory that is automatic. However, the subsequent recollections that people produce are constructed from their imagery of the events and their covert rehearsal and overt retelling of the event. They further assumed that automatic encoding of shocking events would have some kind of survival value for people in that the memories contained information about how to act when having similar shocking, presumably threatening experiences in the future. Subsequently, Neisser (1982) argued that one value of flashbulb memories is that the ability to convey rich memorial detail to others was important in facilitating social communication. For example, answering questions on the basis of personal memories by citing anecdotes enables the speaker and listener to relate in a more empathetic manner. Moreover, by retelling an event in a personal manner, the speaker gains greater interest and may be more convincing in his or her recollection.

Descriptions of personal details that are usually contained in flashbulb memories can have a very persuasive effect in communication. This point has been nicely illustrated by David Pillemer (in press) and reveals how the personal activities and feelings of a person in recalling an event act to increase the acceptance of the recollection. Pillemer (in press) describes the testimony of George Schultz, who was Secretary of State in 1988, before the Senate and House committees concerning covert military assistance to Iran. Schultz's testimony contained frequent references to personal details:

> So I picked up the phone Sunday morning, and I called the President. I said "Mr. President, I have something I should bring over here and tell you about now." So he said "Fine, come over." . . . I went up to the family quarters, and Al Keel, who was then Acting National Security Advisor, went with me at my request. And I told the President the items on this agenda, including such things as doing something about the Dawa prisoners, which made me sick to my stomach that anybody would talk about that as something we would consider doing. And the President was astonished, and I have never seen him so mad. He is a very genial, pleasant man and doesn't——very easy going. But his jaws set and his eyes flashed, and both of us, I think, felt the same way about it, and I think that in that meeting I finally felt that the President deeply understands that something is radically wrong here! (From Pillemer, in press, quoting the Select Committees on the Iran-Contra Investigation, 1988.)

As you can see, this type of testimony helps to communicate the sense of things as George Schultz remembered them and adds face validity to his recollection. Moreover, Pillemer (in press) points out that the sharing of detailed memories of personal circumstances sets an intimate stage for communication. A personal recollection can draw in the listener and evoke a more empathetic response than abstract, generalized recollections.

What about the accuracy of flashbulb memories? Here the evidence is complex with some reports showing low accuracy and others showing high accuracy. Even though a memory may be very vivid, it may also contain many errors (Neisser, 1982). In a study by Neisser and Harsch (in press) they interviewed subjects one day after the Challenger space shuttle explosion and then again three years later. They found relatively little agreement between the initial and delayed recollections, even with respect to such items as who delivered the news and other details. Nevertheless, the subjects were highly confident of their delayed recollections. In another study of the space-shuttle disaster, McCloskey, Wible, and Cohen (1988) also report many errors in their subjects' recollections, but they nevertheless recalled a good deal of information. After a nine-month delay, 67% of the subjects' reports matched their reports given immediately after the disaster.

Is there a special mechanism underlying flashbulb memory? Brown and Kulik (1982) have proposed that there is a special neural mechanism that is activated by striking and vivid events. This neural mechanism causes the whole scene or event to be "printed" on the memory, making it a different kind of memory. Moreover, such memories have a particular structure in that people remember such details as location (where they were), activity (what they were doing), affect (how they felt), and aftermath (what happened next).

As you might suspect, another view of flashbulb memories has been proposed. Although agreeing that a flashbulb memory is a subjectively compelling account of some important event, Neisser (1982) contends that there is no need for a special interpretation of flashbulb memories. Neisser contends that the vividness and persistence of such memories is the result of rehearsal and frequent retelling after the event rather than any special neural mechanism activated at the time of the event. Similarly, Rubin and Kozin (1984) suggest that flashbulb memories are not necessarily different from other vivid memories. In both cases, Neisser and Rubin argue that flashbulb memories do not require special mechanisms and are to be explained by usual memory processes involving rehearsal, elaboration, and organization. At present, the evidence seems to support the views of Neisser, Rubin, and others who share this position.

Anxiety and Performance

Anxiety and depression are somewhat related in that depressed individuals are frequently anxious (cf. Ellis & Hertel, in press; Eysenck, 1991). In the studies described so far, depression tends to impair memory performance by reducing the appropriate processing of the information, that is, by reducing the resources allocated to some task, and by increasing the number of distracting, irrelevant thoughts, which are usually negative self-referent thoughts (Ellis & Ashbrook, 1988; Seibert & Ellis, 1991). Anxiety can also increase the number of distracting, irrelevant thoughts but it can also produce distortions in people's perceptions of events (cf. Eysenck, 1991; Williams, Watts, MacCleod, & Mathews, 1988). The research on anxiety and performance provides strong evidence that anxiety, as well as stress in general, produces performance decrements in a variety of situations, especially so with tasks that make high demands on resources (e.g., Darke, 1988).

One feature of anxious people is that they tend to expect unpleasant outcomes. Butler and Mathews (1983) investigated this issue by having normal people and anxious or depressed patients rate the likelihood of occurrence of a number of pleasant and unpleasant events. The subjects were asked to estimate the likelihood that each event would happen to themselves and to other people. The three groups were similar in their estimates of positive events but differed in their estimates of negative events. Both the anxious and depressed subjects thought that the unpleasant events were more likely to happen to themselves, but not to other people.

Classical studies of anxiety and learning proposed that anxiety can interfere or facilitate learning depending upon the complexity of the task. If the task was complex, meaning that many alternative responses were available to the person in learning the task, then anxiety usually interfered with learning. In contrast, if the task was relatively simple, allowing few alternative responses, such as in eyelid conditioning, then anxiety could facilitate learning. For practical purposes, anxiety is more likely to impair our important everyday activities because they do allow for multiple response alternatives.

In an important review of the research on anxiety and performance, Eysenck (1983) reported that anxiety generally impairs performance but he also found exceptions; sometimes it has no effect and sometimes it can actually facilitate performance. He attributes this divergence in findings to two different processes. First, he notes that anxiety tends to increase worry which leads to an increase in distracting thoughts which interfere or compete with relevant thoughts. Recall that Seibert and Ellis (1991) have reported direct confirmation of this idea. Second, Eysenck proposed that anxiety increases the overall arousal level of people, thus inducing them to allocate more effort to the task. Additional effort, however, may or may not enable the anxious individuals to overcome the negative effects of worry and the associated distracting thoughts. Hertel and Rude (1991) have provided some evidence for support of this second process in that individuals can be assisted in overcoming performance deficits by allocating more effort to the task; their subjects were, however, depressed rather than anxious.

Eysenck's (1983) two-process idea may help to explain the divergent effects of anxiety on performance. For example, many people report that a *little* anxiety is actually helpful in preparing for a test, giving a speech, or undertaking some other important task, whereas excessive anxiety impairs performance. What is reported is that a little anxiety is motivating, in that it arouses us to do our best, which is the arousal aspect of anxiety. In turn, too much anxiety can overwhelm us so that performance is poorer.

Finally, another approach toward studying the effects of stress and anxiety on performance attempts to produce the emotional state under highly realistic conditions or examines performance in work settings. In an unusual experiment, Keinen, Friedland, and Arad (1991) simulated stress, and the attendant anxiety, in a realistic and convincing manner. Subjects were assigned to a high-or low-stress condition and then were given a classification task. In the high-stress condition, subjects were trainees in a parachuting course, just learning to jump. They were sitting on a runway, harnessed with their parachutes, waiting to board an airplane for their first night parachute jump. Parachute jumping, at least for novices, is a stressful experience and the prospect of parachuting in the night would add to the subject's anxiety. Under the low-stress situation, subjects simply performed the criterion task during a break in training. The criterion task was a classification procedure in which subjects categorized a list of objects. The results revealed that high-stress subjects categorized the objects more rapidly but used fewer groups to categorize the objects than did low-stress subjects. The results suggested that high-stress subjects pay less attention to distinctive features and/or that they tend to show greater overgeneralization due to stress.

SUMMARY

This chapter indicates that emotional states can play an important role in memory and cognition. This research area has become very active since about 1975, with several factors contributing to its development. There is strong evidence for mood-congruent effects in memory, in which memory for affectively toned material is best when one is in a mood like that of the material to be learned. In contrast, the evidence for mood-state-dependent memory is limited and the effect is not robust.

Mood influences a range of encoding effects as well as retrieval. Subjects in a sad mood show learning decrements. Subjects who are given a sad mood induction show greater impairment in tasks that require elaborative encoding and enhanced cognitive effort. The induction of a sad mood interferes with organizational processes in perceptual grouping and free recall tasks. Finally, depressed subjects make more accurate judgments of contingency, that is, they have fewer illusions of control in contingency judgments.

Network and schema theories represent two approaches to accounting for the effects of emotional states on memory, approaches based upon knowledge structures. The third major approach is that of a resource allocation model, which assumes that emotional states govern or regulate the amount of capacity that can be allocated to some cognitive task. Finally, we examined four special issues: mood states and judgments of contingency, emotion and eyewitness testimony, flashbulb memory, and anxiety and performance.

MULTIPLE-CHOICE ITEMS

1. Research on emotional influences in memory and cognition has increased since 1975 because
   a. the area is recognized as important
   b. methodological approaches have developed
   c. there is a need to explain how emotion influences memory and cognition
   d. all of the above

2. In the Bower, Gilligan, and Monteiro (1981) study on mood congruence, the mood-congruence effect was greatest when the subjects were in
   a. a happy mood
   b. both a happy and a sad mood
   c. a sad mood
   d. an angry mood

3. Bower (1981) explained the mood-congruent findings by way of
   a. mood enhancement
   b. selective reminding
   c. schema theory
   d. state dependency

4. Mood-state-dependent effects in memory are best seen as
   a. strong
   b. fragile
   c. schematic
   d. organized

5. Studies on depressed mood states that vary the effortfulness of the task show the greatest decrements in recall performance when the task is
   a. easy
   b. difficult
   c. intense
   d. problem solving

6. Alloy and Abramson (1981) show that depressed subjects, when making judgments of contingency, that is, estimates of their control over the occurrence of an event, are _____ neutral mood subjects.
   a. less accurate than
   b. equally accurate with
   c. more accurate than
   d. none of the above

TRUE–FALSE ITEMS

1. Being in an elated mood can interfere with the learning of certain tasks.

2. In studies of cognitive effort, depression does not impair performance when the task is low in effort.

3. Depression will always reduce recall in tasks requiring retrieval.

4. Normal-mood subjects who make noncontingent judgments show no impairment in judgment accuracy when the green light follows a button press 75 percent of the time.

5. Schema theory and network theory are both similar, and they both assume the operation of spreading activation.

6. The resource allocation model predicts that people in a depressed mood will show the greatest impairment in recall when the task is of moderate difficulty.

DISCUSSION ITEMS

1. How does selective reminding explain mood-congruent effects in memory?

2. Why is it that depressed subjects are more accurate in judgments of contingency?

3. How does the resource allocation model account for greater decrements in tasks that are more effortful?

4. Why are mood-state-dependent effects difficult to obtain in laboratory studies?

5. What role does the organized structure of material to be learned play in deficits due to depressed moods?

6. How can we account for flashbulb memories?

7. What does the Easterbrook hypothesis predict about the role of emotion in eyewitness testimony?

8. How might Eysenck's two-process idea explain both the facilitating and interfering aspects of anxiety on human performance?

ANSWERS TO MULTIPLE-CHOICE ITEMS

1. (d) All of these influences have been important.
2. (c) Sad-mood subjects showed a much greater effect than happy-mood subjects.
3. (b) Selective reminding is the major interpretation Bower proposed.
4. (b) These findings are difficult to obtain, hence fragile.
5. (b) Depressed moods do have their greatest impact on performance when the task is difficult.
6. (c) These subjects are actually more accurate than neutral mood subjects.

ANSWERS TO TRUE–FALSE ITEMS

1. (True) Too much elation can also interfere with cognitive processing.
2. (True) Depression appears to impair performance in high-effort but not in low-effort tasks.
3. (False) Depression sometimes will reduce recall during retrieval but not always.
4. (False) Normal- (neutral-) mood subjects do show impairment of accuracy in judgments in a 75 percent situation, but not in a 25 percent situation.
5. (False) They are both similar, but schema theory does not make the assumption of spreading activation.
6. (False) The model predicts that the greatest impairment will occur with tasks of high difficulty.

GLOSSARY

Algorithm: A solution rule or procedure which ensures a solution.

Analysis-by-synthesis: A theory of pattern recognition which advocates the decomposition of the sensory pattern into component features prior to matching with long-term memory.

Aphasia: Disorder involving loss of language function.

Articulatory loop: The verbal storage system of working memory.

Associative network models: Models of semantic memory which describe the structure of semantic memory as an interrelation of nodes in a complex network.

Associative strength theory: Theory of the effectiveness of retrieval cues which says that a cue is effective depending on how strongly associated it is with the to-be-remembered item of information.

Attention: Process of focusing selectively on some part of the environment while ignoring other aspects.

Automatic processing: Processing of information that appears to occur without involvement of resources or central capacity requirements.

Backward masking: Process in which previously presented information is erased from sensory memory.

Basic-level category: The level of a category in which it has the clearest perceptual features *and* is most readily distinguished from other categories.

Brown-Peterson paradigm: Famous distractor paradigm for measuring short-term retention.

Capacity model: Model of attention which assumes that attention is the process of allocating resources or capacity to various sensory inputs.

Categorization: Process in which people acquire categories.

Categorization, theories of: Theories developed to explain how people develop categories. The major ones are attribute, prototype, and exemplar theories.

Category size effect: Prediction from semantic memory models that larger categories require more search time than do smaller categories.

Central executive: Controlling, decision-making mechanism such as that in working memory.

Clustering in recall: The tendency of human beings to organize items in free recall so that they are recalled according to conceptual or other categories. Items from a particular category tend to be recalled adjacently.

Coding: Process by which external stimulation is transformed into a representation for purposes of memory.

Cognition: A class of symbolic mental activities such as thinking, reasoning, problem solving, memory search, and so forth.

Cognitive effort: Concept referring to the amount of capacity allocated to a given task. Concept is typically measured in the secondary-task paradigm used in attention.

Conceptually-driven processes: Psychological processes initiated by meaning.

Connectionism: Memory strucure in which elements are connected by associations differing in strength. Combined with paralled distributed processing in theories of pattern recognition and memory.

Constructive processes: The tendency of human beings to construct or reconstruct information in memory, altering the information to make it more consistent with a schema.

Control processes: Term which refers to all regulatory processes in memory models such as attention, search, organization, coding, retrieval, and so forth.

Convergent thinking: Thinking that moves in a direct fashion toward a specific answer.

Cue-dependent forgetting: A failure in retrieval due to ineffectiveness of the cue.

Data-driven processing: Psychological processes corresponding to the physical features of the stimulus.

Decay theory: Theory of forgetting which says that forgetting is due to an autonomous weakening or decay of the memory trace.

Dichotic listening: A laboratory procedure used primarily for the study of attention in which two different messages are played simultaneously.

Distinctiveness hypothesis: Hypothesis which emphasizes that information is better retained in memory when the memory traces or representations are more distinctive.

Divergent thinking: Thinking that moves outward from a problem in a variety of directions.

Dual-code theory: Theory which says that information stored in memory may be in two forms: verbal codes and imaginal codes.

Early selection theory: A theory of central attention which presumes that attentional filtering occurs prior to pattern recognition.

Echoic memory: The sensory register for audition.

Elaboration: Process by which information to be remembered is linked or related to information already known.

Encoding: Process by which the to-be-remembered information is transformed into a form suitable for storage in memory.

Encoding specificity theory: Theory which says that a cue is effective only if it was specifically encoded with the to-be-remembered item of information.

Episodic memory: Memory for specific events that happened at a particular time or place.

Expertise: Refers to level of competence, skill, and/or knowledge a person has.

Feature set theory: Model of semantic memory which emphasizes that semantic memory can be described in terms of bundles or sets of features.

Filter model: Model of attention which assumes that some or all of the information presented to one sensory channel is filtered or blocked.

Flashbulb memory: Recall of especially important, vivid events that are often emotionally arousing.

Forgetting: Process in which failure to access stored information occurs.

Free recall: Task requiring a person to recall items of information in any order.

Functional fixedness: Tendency to think of objects as functioning in a particular way and failing to perceive other ways the object might be useful.

Generate-test method: A problem-solving strategy in which a possible solution is first generated and then tested to see if it works.

Generation effect: The empirical finding that self-generated material is better remembered than externally provided material.

Generation-recognition model of retrieval: Model which involves two stages in retrieval: first, the generation of candidates for retrieval and, second, the decision process in which the candidates are evaluated.

Grice's Maxims: Guidelines that speakers and listeners follow in order to foster good communication during a conversation.

Heuristic: A rule of thumb or approximation which helps in solving a problem but does not ensure its solution.

Ill-defined problems: Problems in which the original state, the objectives, or the rules to be used are poorly defined.

Implicit memory: Use of prior experience without intent to remember.

Inference: Drawing conclusions that may or may not be valid.

Interference theory: Theory of forgetting which contends that events are forgotten because other learning interferes with those events or prevents them from being remembered.

Late selection theory: A theory of attention which presumes that attentional filtering occurs following pattern recognition.

Levels of processing: Principle which proposes that the depth at which information is processed determines its accessibility in memory.

Linguistic relativity hypothesis: Idea that a peoples' language structure affects the way they perceive the world and represent information.

Memory code: The stored representation of an event in memory.

Mental rotation: The process of rotating mental images so that they are imaged in a new orientation.

Method of loci: A mnemonic technique in which different to-be-remembered items are imagined in different locations of some familiar scene.

Modality effect: Better recall of the last few items of a list with auditory presentation as opposed to visual presentation.

Modal model of memory: General or typical memory model which assumes several stages in memory.

Mood congruence: Finding that people tend to remember information that is consistent with their prevailing mood state during the encoding of that information.

Mood-state dependency: Finding that memory is facilitated when mood is the same during learning and recall.

Network theory of mood: Theory explaining the effects of mood states on memory based upon the assumption that emotions are stored as nodes in semantic memory.

Organization: Process by which information to be placed in memory is grouped or rearranged in a new and more optimal manner.

Orienting tasks: Tasks used in human memory experiments which orient the subject to a particular task.

Parallel distributed processing: A model of pattern recognition and memory that assumes simultaneous processing of input and nonlocalized representations.

Parallel processing: Model of information processing which assumes that events are processed at the same time.

Partial report technique: Technique used in studies of sensory memory in which subjects produce only part of the information presented.

Pattern recognition: Process in which patterns of sensory signals are translated into psychological experience, that is, the process by which meaning is derived.

Perceptual grouping: Type of organization in which human beings chunk or organize spatially or temporally grouped information into a higher-order or more meaningful structure.

Phonemic restoration: Tendency to perceive speech patterns correctly even when part of the pattern is masked.

Precategorical: Of or relating to information in the sensory register that is assumed to be stored without meaning.

Preconscious processing: Information which is processed below the level of awareness but which can become available to awareness.

Preprocessing: A process of "cleaning-up" or reorienting a sensory pattern prior to matching with long-term memory in pattern recognition.

Presupposition: An assumption that is made in order to understand an assertion.

Prior Knowledge: Refers to the body of knowledge a person has prior to engaging in some specific task.

Proactive interference: The forgetting of currently learned material produced by interference from previously learned material.

Problem space: The way a person mentally represents a problem.

Propositional code: Abstract representation of both verbal and pictorial materials considered by some theorists to be the language of thought.

Propositional network models: Models of semantic memory which use associative networks and propositions as the basic units stored.

Propositional reasoning: Type of reasoning that involves reasoning from if . . . then . . . statements. The four basic arguments in propositional reasoning are *modus ponens, modus tollens,* affirming the consequent, and denying the antecedent.

Prototype: The best example of a concept.

Reality monitoring: Discrimination between thought and perception.

Rehearsal, elaborative: The repeating of information aloud or to oneself in the attempt to relate the information to already known events or to other information.

Resource allocation model: Model explaining the effects of mood states on memory based upon the allocation of cognitive resources.

Response competition: Process in forgetting in which different responses made to the same stimuli compete with each other at the time of recall.

Retrieval: Process of accessing information in memory.

Retroactive interference: Process in which an event learned during a retention interval leads to forgetting a previously learned event.

Schema: An organized body of knowledge about a class of events, ideas, objects, and so on.

Schema theory: Class of theories designed to explain how people acquire, develop, and use schematic representations.

Semantic memory: General knowledge of the world.

Semantic priming: Facilitation of word recognition in lexical decision provided by a prior word meaningfully related to the target.

Sensory register: Memory system designed to store information received by the sensory receptors.

Serial position curve: Finding that in the free recall of serially presented items, items at the beginning and end of a list are best retained and items in the middle of a list are poorly retained.

Serial processing: Model of information processing which assumes that events are processed serially in time.

Shadowing: Procedure in which a listener in an attention study is required to repeat aloud a message presented to one ear.

Spreading activation: The idea that activity in an associative network will spread to related concepts.

Spreading-activation model: Model of semantic memory based on associative networks which incorporates the notion of associative distance.

State-dependent memory: Idea that memory may be dependent upon reinstatement of the original state in which information was encoded.

Storage: The process by which memory representation is held in memory.

Strategy: The cognitive approach used in dealing with a task involving memory, reasoning, problem solving, and so forth.

Subjective organization: Tendency of human beings to organize unrelated items in accord with a self-developed mode of organization.

Suffix effect: Poor recall of the last word of an auditorially presented list when followed by another speech sound.

Teachable Language Comprehender (TLC): The earliest of the major modern models of semantic memory.

Template theory: Class of pattern recognition theories which assume that a literal copy of experience is stored in memory.

Theme: A theme is the central or general topic of a passage.

Unlearning: Loss or weakening of first-list associations during the learning of a second list.

Visuospatial sketchpad: The visual storage system of working memory.

Whole report technique: Technique used in studies of sensory information in which subjects are asked to produce all of the to-be-remembered material.

Working memory: An active system of memory in which information is assembled and organized prior to recall.

REFERENCES

Aaronson, D., & Scarborough, H. (1976). Performance theories for
    sentence coding: Some quantitative evidence. *Journal of
    Experimental Psychology: Human Perception and Performance, 2,*
    56–70.

Alba, J. W., & Hasher, L. (1983). Is memory schematic? *Psychological
    Bulletin, 93,* 203–231.

Allen, S. W., & Brooks, L. R. (1991). Specializing the operation of an
    explicit rule. *Journal of Experimental Psychology: General, 120,*
    3–19.

Alloy, L. B., & Abramson, L. Y. (1979). Judgment of contingency in
    depressed and nondepressed students: Sadder but wiser? *Journal of
    Experimental Psychology: General, 108,* 441–485.

Alloy, L. B., Abramson, L. Y., & Viscusi, D. (1981). Induced mood and
    the illusion of control. *Journal of Personality and Social
    Psychology, 41,* 1129–1140.

Amabile, T. M. (1983). *The social psychology of creativity.* New York:
    Springer-Verlag.

Anderson, J. R. (1983). *The architecture of cognition.* Cambridge,
    Mass.: Harvard University Press.

Anderson, J. R. (1976). *Language, memory, and thought.* Hillsdale,
    N.J.: Erlbaum.

Anderson, J. R., & Bower, G. H. (1973). *Human associative memory.*
    Washington, D.C.: Winston.

Antrobus, J. S. (1970). *Cognition and affect.* Boston: Little, Brown.

Ashcraft, M. H. (1987). Children's knowledge of simple addition: A
    developmental model and simulation. In J. Bisanz, C. G. Brainerd,
    & R. Kail (Eds.), *Formal methods in developmental psychology:
    Progress in cognitive development research,* pp. 302–338. New
    York: Springer-Verlag.

Ashcraft, M. H. (1989). *Human memory and cognition.* Glenview, IL.:
    Scott, Foresman.

Atkinson, R. C., & Shiffrin, R. M. (1968). Human memory: A proposed system and its control processes. In K. W. Spence & J. T. Spence (Eds.), *The psychology of learning and motivation: Advances in theory and research* (Vol. 2). New York: Academic Press.

Averbach, E., & Coriell, A. S. (1961). Short-term memory in vision. *Bell System Technical Journal, 40,* 309–328.

Baddeley, A. D. (1966). The influence of acoustic and semantic similarity on long-term memory for word sequences. *Quarterly Journal of Experimental Psychology, 18,* 302–309. (a)

Baddeley, A. D. (1966). Short-term memory for word sequences as a function of acoustic, semantic, and formal similarity. *Quarterly Journal of Experimental Psychology, 18,* 362–365. (b)

Baddeley, A. D. (1986). *Working memory.* Oxford: Oxford University Press.

Baddeley, A. D. (1990). *Human memory: Theory and practice.* Needham Heights, MA: Allyn and Bacon.

Baddeley, A. D., & Hitch, G. (1974). Working memory. In G. H. Bower (Ed.), *The psychology of learning and motivation* (Vol. 8). New York: Academic Press.

Baddeley, A. D., & Hitch, G. J. (1977). Recency reexamined. In S. Dornic, (Ed.), *Attention and Performance, 6,* 647–667. Hillsdale, N. J.: Lawrence Erlbaum Associates.

Baddeley, A. D., & Warrington, E. K. (1970). Amnesia and the distinction between long- and short-term memory. *Journal of Verbal Learning and Verbal Behavior, 9,* 176–189.

Baggett, P. (1975). Memory for explicit and implicit information in picture stories. *Journal of Verbal Learning and Verbal Behavior, 14,* 538–548.

Bahrick, H. P., Bahrick, P. O., & Wittlinger, R. P. (1975). Fifty years of memory for names and faces: A cross-sectional approach. *Journal of Experimental Psychology: General, 104,* 54–75.

Bahrick, H. P., & Hall, L. K. (1991). Lifetime maintenance of high school mathematics content. *Journal of Experimental Psychology: General, 120,* 20–33.

Baron, J. B., & Sternberg, R. J. (1987). *Teaching thinking skills: Theory and practice.* New York: Freeman.

Barsalou, L. W. (1982). Context-independent and context-dependent information in concepts. *Memory and Cognition, 10,* 82–93.

Barsalou, L. W. (1983). Ad hoc categories. *Memory and Cognition, 11,* 211–227.

Barsalou, L. W., & Medin, D. L. (1986). Concepts: Static definitions or context-dependent representations? *Cahiers de Psychologie Cognitive, 6* (2), 187–202.

Barsalou, L. W., & Sewell, D. R. (1984). Constructing representations of categories from different points of view. In *Emory Cognition Project Report No. 2.* Atlanta, Ga.: Emory University.

Bartlett, F. C. (1932). *Remembering: An experimental and social study.* Cambridge: Cambridge University Press.

Bartlett, J. C., Burleson, G., & Santrock, J. W. (1982). Emotional mood and memory in young children. *Journal of Experimental Child Psychology, 34.* 59–76.

Beck, A. T. (1967). *Depression: Clinical, experimental, and theoretical aspects.* New York: Harper & Row.

Beck, A. T., Rush, A. J., Shaw, B. S., & Emery, G. (1979). *Cognitive therapy of depression.* New York: Guilford.

Begg, I. (1978). Similarity and contrast in memory for relations. *Memory and Cognition, 6,* 509–517.

Begg, I., & Snider, A. (1987). The generation effect: Evidence for generalized inhibition. *Journal of Experimental Psychology: Learning, Memory, & Cognition, 13,* 553–563.

Berkerian, D. A., & Bowers, J. M. (1983). Eyewitness testimony: Were we misled? *Journal of Experimental Psychology: Human Learning and Memory, 9,* 139–145.

Bernbach, H. A. (1975). Rate of presentation in free recall: A problem for two-stage memory theories. *Journal of Experimental Psychology: Human Learning and Memory, 1,* 18–22.

Berndt, R. S., & Caramazza, A. (1980). A redefinition of the syndrome of Broca's aphasia: Implications for neuropsychological models of language. *Applied Psycholinguistics, 1,* 225–278.

Bierwisch, M. (1970). Semantics. In J. Lyons (Ed.), *New Horizons in linguistics.* Baltimore: Penguin Books.

Bjork, R. A., & Richardson-Klavehn, A. (1989). On the puzzling relationship between environmental context and human memory. In C. Izawa (Ed.), *Current issues in cognitive processes.* Hillsdale, N.J.: Lawrence Erlbaum Associates.

Blaney, P. (1986). Affect and memory: A review. *Psychological Bulletin, 99,* 229–246.

Blaxton, T. A. (1989). Investigating dissociations among memory measures: Support for a transfer-appropriate processing framework. *Journal of Experimental Psychology: Learning, Memory, & Cognition, 15,* 657–668.

Bohannon, J. N. (1988). Flashbulb memories for the space shuttle disaster: A tale of two stories. *Cognition, 29,* 179–196.

Bourne, L. E., Jr. (1982). Typicality effects in logically defined concepts. *Memory and Cognition, 10,* 3–9.

Bourne, L. E., Jr., Dominowski, R. L., & Loftus, E. F. (1979). *Cognitive processes*. Englewood Cliffs, N.J.: Prentice-Hall.

Bower, G. H. (1970). Organizational factors in memory. *Cognitive Psychology, 1,* 18–46.

Bower, G. H. (1981). Mood and memory. *American Psychologist, 36,* 129–148.

Bower, G. H., & Cohen, P. R. (1982). Emotional influences in memory and thinking: Data and theory. In S. Fiske & M. Clark (Eds.), *Affect and social cognition.* Hillsdale, N. J.: Lawrence Erlbaum Associates.

Bower, G. H., & Karlin, M. B. (1974). Depth of processing pictures of faces and recognition memory. *Journal of Experimental Psychology, 103,* 751–757.

Bower, G. H., & Mayer, J.D. (1989). In search of mood-dependent memory. In D. Kuiken (Ed.), Mood and memory: Theory, research, and applications [Special Issue]. *Journal of Social Behavior and Personality, 4*(2), 121–156.

Bower, G. H., Gilligan, S. G., & Monteiro, K. P. (1981). Selectivity of learning caused by affective states. *Journal of Experimental Psychology, 110,* 451–473.

Bower, G. H., Monteiro, K. P., & Gilligan, S. G. (1978). Emotional mood as a context of learning and recall. *Journal of Verbal Learning and Verbal Behavior, 17,* 573–585.

Bransford, J. D., & Franks, J. J. (1971). The abstraction of linguistic ideas. *Cognitive Psychology, 2,* 331–350.

Bransford, J. D., & Johnson, M. K. (1973). Consideration of some problems of comprehension. In W. G. Chase (Ed.), *Visual information processing.* New York: Academic Press.

Bransford, J. D., Barclay, J. R., & Franks, J. J. (1972). Sentence memory: A constructive versus interpretative approach. *Cognitive Psychology, 3,* 193–209.

Brewer, W. F., & Nakamura, G. V. (1984). The nature and function of schemas. In R. S. Wyer & T. K. Srull (Eds.), *Handbook of social cognition,* Vol I. Hillsdale, N. J.: Lawrence Erlbaum Associates.

Brewer, W. F., & Treyens, J. C. (1981). Role of schemata in memory for places. *Cognitive Psychology, 13,* 207–230.

Brigham, J. C., & Malpass, R. S. (1985). The role of experience and contact in the recognition of faces of own- and other-race persons. *Journal of Social Issues, 41,* 139–155.

Britton, B. K., & Tesser, A. (1982). Effects of prior knowledge on use of cognitive capacity in three complex cognitive tasks. *Journal of Verbal Learning and Verbal Behavior, 21,* 421–436.

Britton, B. K., Glynn, S. M., Meyer, B. J., & Penland, M. J. (1982). Effects of text structure on use of cognitive capacity during reading. *Journal of Educational Psychology, 74,* 51–61.

Britton, B. K., Westbrook, R. D., & Holdredge, T. S. (1978). Reading and cognitive capacity usage: Effects of text difficulty. *Journal of Experimental Psychology: Human Learning and Memory, 4,* 582–591.

Broadbent, D. E. (1958). *Perception and communication.* London: Pergamon Press.

Brooks, L. R. (1978). Non-analytic concept formation and memory for instances. In E. Rosch & B. Lloyd (Eds.), *Cognition and categorization.* Hillsdale, N.J.: Erlbaum.

Brown, J. A. (1958). Some tests of the decay theory of immediate memory. *Quarterly Journal of Experimental Psychology, 10,* 12–21.

Brown, J. S., & Burton, R. R. (1978). Diagnostic models for procedural bugs in basic mathematical skills. *Cognitive Science, 2,* 155–192.

Brown, R. (1973). *A first language: The early stages.* Cambridge, Mass.: Harvard University Press.

Brown, R., & Kulik, J. (1977). Flashbulb memories. *Cognition, 5,* 73–99.

Bruner, J. S., Goodnow, J., & Austin, G. A. (1956). *A study of thinking.* New York: Wiley.

Bugelski, B. R., & Alampay, D. A. (1961). The role of frequency in developing perceptual sets. *Canadian Journal of Psychology, 15,* 205–211.

Butler, G., & Mathews, A. (1983). Cognitive processes in anxiety. *Advances in Behavior Therapy, 5,* 51–62.

Charness, N. (1981). Aging and skilled problem solving. *Journal of Experimental Psychology: General, 110,* 21–38.

Chase, W. G., & Simon, H. A. (1973). The mind's eye in chess. In W. G. Chase (Ed.), *Visual information processing.* New York: Academic Press.

Cherry, C. (1953). Some experiments on the recognition of speech with one and two ears. *Journal of the Acoustical Society of America, 23,* 915–919.

Chi, M. T. H., & Glaser, R. (1985). Problem solving ability. In R. J. Sternberg (Ed.), *Human abilities: An information processing approach.* New York: Freeman.

Chi, M. T. H., Glaser, R., & Rees, E. (1982). Expertise in problem solving. In. R. J. Sternberg (Ed.), *Advances in the psychology of human intelligence* (Vol. 1). Hillsdale, N.J.: Erlbaum.

Chiesi, H. L., Spilich, G. J., & Voss, J. F. (1979). Acquisition of domain-related information in relation to high- and low-domain knowledge. *Journal of Verbal Learning and Verbal Behavior, 18,* 257–273.

Chipman, S. F., Segal, J. W., & Glaser, R. (Eds.), (1985). *Thinking and learning skills: Research and open questions* (Vol. 2). Hillsdale, N.J.: Erlbaum.

Chomsky, N. (1965). *Aspects of the theory of syntax.* Cambridge, Mass.: M.I.T. Press.

Chomsky, N. (1975). *Reflections on language.* New York: Pantheon Books.

Chomsky, N. (1985). *Knowledge of language: Its nature, origin, and use.* New York: Praeger.

Christianson, S. A. (in press). Emotional stress and eyewitness memory: A critical review. *Psychological Bulletin.*

Clark, H. H., & Clark, E. V. (1977). *Psychology and language.* New York: Harcourt, Brace, & Jovanovich.

Clark, M. S., & Isen, A. M. (1982). Toward understanding the relationship between affect and social behavior. In A. Hastorf & A. M. Isen (Eds.), *Cognitive social psychology.* New York: Elsevier/North Holland.

Cohen, J. (1971). *Thinking.* Chicago: Rand McNally.

Cohen, R. M., Weingartner, H., Smallberg, S. A., Pickar, D., & Murphy, D. L. (1982). Effort and cognition in depression. *Archives of General Psychiatry, 39,* 593–597.

Cole, R. A. (1979). Navigating the slippery stream of speech. *Psychology Today,* 77–87.

Cole, R. A. (1980). *Perception and production of fluent speech.* Hillsdale, N.J.: Erlbaum.

Collins, A. M., & Loftus, E. F. (1975). A spreading activation theory of semantic processing. *Psychological Review, 82,* 407–428.

Collins, A. M., & Quillian, M. R. (1969). Retrieval time from semantic memory. *Journal of Verbal Learning and Verbal Behavior, 8,* 240–247.

Conrad, C. (1972). Cognitive economy in semantic memory. *Journal of Experimental Psychology, 92,* 149–154.

Conrad, F. G., & Rips, L. J. (1986). Conceptual combination and the given/new distinction. *Journal of Memory and Language, 25,* 255–278.

Conrad, R., & Hull, A. J. (1968). Input modality and the serial position curve in short-term memory. *Psychonomic Science, 10,* 135–136.

Cooper, L. A., & Shepard, R. N. (1973). Chronometric studies of the rotation of mental images. In W. G. Chase (Ed.), *Visual information processing.* New York: Academic Press.

Craik, F. I. M., & Jacoby, L. L. (1979). Elaboration and distinctiveness in episodic memory. In L. Nilsson (Ed.), *Perspectives on memory research: Essays in honor of Uppsala University's 500th anniversary.* Hillsdale, N.J.: Erlbaum.

Craik, F. I. M., & Lockhart, R. S. (1972). Levels of processing: A framework for memory research. *Journal of Verbal Learning and Verbal Behavior, 11,* 671–684.

Craik, F. I. M., & Tulving, E. (1975). Depth of processing and the retention of words in episodic memory. *Journal of Experimental Psychology, 104,* 268–294.

Crowder, R. G. (1976). *Principles of learning and memory.* Hillsdale, N.J.: Lawrence Erlbaum Associates.

Daniel, T. C. (1972). The nature of the effect of verbal labels on recognition memory for form. *Journal of Experimental Psychology, 96,* 152–157.

Darke, S. (1988). Anxiety and working memory capacity. *Cognition and Emotion, 2,* 145–154.

Darwin, C. T., Turvey, M. T., & Crowder, R. G. (1972). An auditory analogue of the Sperling partial report procedure: Evidence for brief auditory storage. *Cognitive Psychology, 3,* 255–267.

Davis, G. A. (1973). *Psychology of problem solving: Theory and practice.* New York: Basic Books.

DeCasper, A. J., & Spence, M. J. (1986). Prenatal maternal speech influences newborns' perception of speech sounds. *Infant Behavior and Development, 9,* 133–150.

Deffenbacher, K. A., & Loftus, E. F. (1982). Do jurors share a common understanding concerning eyewitness behavior? *Law and Human Behavior, 6,* 15–30.

DeGroot, A. D. (1965). *Thought and choice in chess.* The Hague: Mouton.

DeGroot, A. D. (1966). Perception and memory versus thought. In B. Kleinmuntz (Ed.), *Problem solving.* New York: Wiley.

Deutsch, J. A., & Deutsch, D. (1963). Attention: Some theoretical considerations. *Psychological Review, 70,* 80–90.

Devitt, M., & Sterely, K. (1989). *Language and reality.* Cambridge, Mass: M.I.T. Press.

Dominowski, R. L. (1972). Effects of solution familiarity and number of alternatives on problem difficulty. *Journal of Experimental Psychology, 95,* 223–225.

Dominowski, R. L. (1977). Reasoning. *Inter-American Journal of Psychology, 11,* 68–77.

Donaldson, W., & Bass, M. (1980). Relational information and memory for problem solutions. *Journal of Verbal Learning and Verbal Behavior, 19,* 26–35.

Dreyfus, H. L. (1979). *What computers can't do: The limits of artificial intelligence.* New York: Harper & Row.

Duncker, K. (1945). On problem solving. *Psychological Monographs,* No. 270, *58.*

Easterbrook, J. A. (1959). The effect of emotion on cue utilization and the organization of behavior. *Psychological Review, 66,* 183–201.

Eckhardt, B. B. (1990). *Elements of schema theory.* Unpublished paper, University of New Mexico.

Eckhardt, B. B. (1991). *The impact of retrieval interval and emotion on comprehension of film.* Doctoral dissertation, University of New Mexico.

Eich, J. E. (1989). Theoretical issues in state-dependent memory. In H. L. Roediger & F.I.M. Craik (Eds.) *Varieties of memory and consciousness,* pp. 331–354. Hillsdale, N. J.: Lawrence Erlbaum Associates.

Eich, J. E. (1980). The cue-dependent nature of state-dependent retention. *Memory and Cognition, 8,* 157–173.

Eich, J. E., & Metcalf, J. (1989). Mood dependent memory for internal versus external events. *Journal of Experimental Psychology: Learning, Memory, and Cognition, 15,* 443–455.

Einstein, G. O., & Hunt, R. R. (1980). Levels of processing and organization: Additive effects of individual item and relational processing. *Journal of Experimental Psychology: Human Learning and Memory, 6,* 588–598.

Ellis, H. C. (1968). Transfer of stimulus predifferentiation to shape recognition and identification learning: Role of properties of verbal labels. *Journal of Experimental Psychology, 78,* 401–409.

Ellis, H. C. (1973). Stimulus encoding processes in human learning and memory. In G. H. Bower (Ed.), *The psychology of learning and motivation* (Vol. 7). New York: Academic Press.

Ellis, H. C. (1978). *Fundamentals of human learning, memory, and cognition.* Dubuque, Iowa: Wm. C. Brown Company.

Ellis, H. C. (1986). *Emotional mood states and memory.* Presidential Address to the Division of Experimental Psychology, APA, Washington, D.C.

Ellis, H. C. (1987). Recent developments in human memory. In V. P. Makosky (Ed.), *The G. Stanley Hall Lecture Series* (Vol. 7), pp. 159–206. Washington, D.C.: American Psychological Association.

Ellis, H. C., & Ashbrook, P. W. (1988). Resource allocation model of the effects of depressed mood states on memory. In K. Fiedler & J. Forgas (Eds.), *Affect, cognition and social behavior.* Toronto:

Ellis, H. C., & Ashbrook, P. W. (1991). The "state" of mood and memory research: A selective review. In D. Kuiken (Ed.), Mood and memory: Theory, research, and applications. Newbury Park, CA: Sage.

Ellis, H. C., Bennett, T. L., Daniel, T. C., & Rickert, E. J. (1979). *Psychology of learning and memory.* Monterey, Calif.: Brooks/ Cole.

Ellis, H. C., & Daniel, T. C. (1971). Verbal processes in long-term stimulus recognition memory. *Journal of Experimental Psychology, 90,* 18–26.

Ellis, H. C., & Hertel, P. T. (in press). Cognition, emotion and memory: Some applications and issues. In C. Izawa (Ed.), *Cognitive psychology applied.* Hillsdale, N. J.: Lawrence Erlbaum Associates.

Ellis, H C., McFarland, A. D., Ashbrook, P. W., McDermott, M. J., Kline, J. S., Hayden, S. R., & Lane, J. W. (1987). Emotion and memory: Depressed mood states and memory for schematically organized events. In preparation.

Ellis, H. C., Parente, F. J., Grah, C. R., & Spiering, K. (1975). Coding strategies, perceptual grouping, and the "variability effect" in free recall. *Memory and Cognition, 3,* 226–232.

Ellis, H. C., Thomas, R. L., McFarland, A. D., & Lane, J. W. (1985). Emotional mood states and retrieval in episodic memory. *Journal of Experimental Psychology: Learning, Memory, and Cognition, 11,* 363–370.

Ellis, H. C., Thomas, R. L., & Rodriguez, I. A. (1984). Emotional mood states and memory: Elaborative encoding, semantic processing, and cognitive effort. *Journal of Experimental Psychology: Learning, Memory, and Cognition, 10,* 470–482.

Epstein, M. L., Phillips, W. D., & Johnson, S. J. (1975). Recall of related and unrelated word pairs as a function of processing level. *Journal of Experimental Psychology: Human Learning and Memory, 1,* 149–152.

Eysenck, M. W. (1979). Depth, distinctiveness, and elaboration. In L. Cermak & F. I. M. Craik (Eds.), *Levels of processing: An approach to memory.* Hillsdale, N.J.: Lawrence Erlbaum Associates.

Eysenck, M. W. (1982). *Attention and arousal: Cognition and performance.* Berlin: Springer.

Eysenck, M. W. (1983). Anxiety and individual differences. In G. R. J. Hockey (Ed.), *Stress and fatigue in human performance.* Chichester: John Wiley & Sons.

Farah, M. J., Peronnet, F., & Weisberg, L. (1987). Brain Activity underlying mental imagery: An ERP study. Paper presented at the annual meetings of the Psychonomic Society, Seattle, Washington, November 6–8.

Ferreira, F., & Clifton, C. (1986). The independence of syntactic processing. *Journal of Memory and Language, 25,* 348–368.

Fiedler, K., & Forgas, J. (1988). *Affect, cognition, and social behavior.* Toronto: Hogrefe.

Fodor, J. A., Garrett, M. F., Walker, E.C.T. & Parkes, C. H. (1980). Against definitions. *Cognition, 8,* 263–367.

Foley, M. A., & Johnson, M. K. (1985). Confusions between memories for performed and imagined actions: A developmental comparison. *Child Development, 56,* 1145–1155.

Fouts, R., Fouts, D., & Schoenfield, D. (1984). Sign language conversational interaction between chimpanzees. *Sign Language Studies, 42,* 1–12.

Francik, E. P., & Clark, H. H. (1985). How to make requests that overcome obstacles to compliance. *Journal of Memory and Language, 24,* 560–568.

Gage, D. F., & Safer, M. A. (1985). Hemispheric differences in the mood state-dependent effect for recognition of emotional faces. *Journal of Experimental Psychology: Learning, Memory, and Cognition, 11,* 752–763.

Gardner, B. T., & Gardner, R. A. (1975). Evidence for sentence constituents in the early utterances of child and chimpanzee. *Journal of Experimental Psychology: General, 104,* 244–267.

Gardner, R. A., & Gardner, B. T. (1969). Teaching sign language to a chimpanzee. *Science, 165,* 664–672.

Gazzaniga, M. S. (1970). *The bisected brain.* New York: Appleton-Century-Crofts.

Gazzaniga, M. S. (1977). Consistency and diversity in brain organization. *Annals of the New York Academy of Sciences, 299,* 415–423.

Gee, J. P., & Grosjean, F. (1983). Performance structures: A psycholinguistic and linguistic appraisal. *Cognitive Psychology, 15,* 411–458.

Gibbs, R. W. (1985). Situational conventions and requests. In J. P. Forgas (Ed.), *Language and social situations.* New York: Springer-Verlag.

Gibbs, R. W. (1986). What makes some indirect speech acts conventional? *Journal of Memory and Language, 25,* 181–196.

Gick, M. L., & Holyoak, K. J. (1980). Analogical problem solving. *Cognitive Psychology, 12,* 306–355.

Gick, M. L., & Holyoak, K. J. (1983). Schema induction and analogical transfer. *Cognitive Psychology, 15,* 1–38.

Gilligan, S. G., & Bower, G. H. (1984). Cognitive consequences of emotional arousal. In C. Izard, J. Kagan, & R. Zajonc (Eds.) *Emotions, cognitions, and behavior.* New York: Cambridge University Press.

Glanzer, M., & Cunitz, A. R. (1966). Two storage mechanisms in free recall. *Journal of Verbal Learning and Verbal Behavior, 5,* 351–360.

Glaser, E. M. (1985). Critical thinking: Educating for responsible citizenship in a democracy. *National Forum, 65,* 24–27.

Glisky, E. J., & Rabinowitz, J. C. (1985). Enhancing the generation effect through repetition of operations. *Journal of Experimental Psychology: Learning, Memory & Cognition, 11,* 193–205.

Glucksberg, S., & Danks, J. (1968). Effects of discriminative labels and of nonsense labels upon availability of novel function. *Journal of Verbal Learning and Verbal Behavior, 7,* 72–76.

Glucksberg, S., & Weisberg, R. W. (1966). Verbal behavior and problem solving: Some effects of labeling in a functional fixedness problem. *Journal of Experimental Psychology, 71,* 659–664.

Graesser, A. C. (1981). *Prose comprehension beyond the word.* New York: Springer.

Graesser, A. C. & Bower, G. H. (1990). *Inferences and text comprehension.* San Diego, CA: Academic Press.

Graesser, A. C., & Riha, J. R. (1984). An application of multiple regression techniques to sentence reading times. In D. Kieras & M. A. Just (Eds.), *New methods in reading comprehension research,* p. 183–218. Hillsdale, N.J.: Lawrence Erlbaum Associates.

Graf, P. (1980). Two consequences of generating: Increased inter- and intraword organization of sentences. *Journal of Verbal Learning and Verbal Behavior, 19,* 316–327.

Graf, P., & Schacter, D. L. (1985). Implicit and explicit memory for new associations in normal and amnesic subjects. *Journal of Experimental Psychology: Learning, Memory, and Cognition, 11,* 501–518.

Graf, P., Squire, L. R., & Mandler, G. (1984). The information that amnesic patients do not forget. *Journal of Experimental Psychology: Learning, Memory, & Cognition, 10,* 164–178.

Greene, R. L., & Crowder, R. G. (1986). Recency effects in delayed recall of mouthed stimuli. *Memory and Cognition, 14,* 355–360.

Greenfield, P. M., & Smith, J. H. (1976). *The structure of communication in early language development.* New York: Academic Press.

Greeno, J. G. (1978). A study of problem solving. In R. Glaser (Ed.), *Advances in instructional psychology* (Vol. 1). Hillsdale, N.J.: Erlbaum.

Grice, H. P. (1975). Logic and conversation. In P. Cole & J. L. Morgan (Eds.), *Syntax and semantics: 3. Speech acts.* New York: Academic Press.

Guilford, J. P. (1959). The three faces of intellect. *American Psychologist, 14,* 469–479.

Guilford, J. P. (1967). *The nature of human intelligence.* New York: McGraw-Hill.

Halpern, D. F. (1984). *Thought and knowledge: An introduction to critical thinking.* Hillsdale, N. J.: Erlbaum.

Harris, R. J. (1977). Comprehension of pragmatic implications in advertising. *Journal of Applied Psychology, 62,* 603–608.

Hasher, L., & Zacks, R. T. (1979). Automatic and effortful processes in memory. *Journal of Experimental Psychology: General, 108,* 356–388.

Hayes, J. R. (1981). *The complete problem solver.* Philadelphia: Franklin Institute Press.

Hayes-Roth, B., & Thorndyke, P. W. (1979). Integration of knowledge from texts. *Journal of Verbal Learning and Verbal Behavior, 18,* 91–108.

Hebb, D. O. (1960). The American Revolution. *American Psychologist, 15,* 735–745.

Hertel, P. T., & Hardin, T. S. (1990). Remembering with and without awareness in a depressed mood: Evidence of deficits in initiative. *Journal of Experimental Psychology: General, 119,* 45–59.

Hertel, P. T., & Narvaez, A. (1986). Confusing memories for verbal and nonverbal communication. *Journal of Personality and Social Psychology, 50,* 478–481.

Hertel, P. T., & Rude, S. S. (1991). Depressive deficits in memory: Focusing attention improves subsequent recall. *Journal of Experimental Psychology: General, 120,* 301–309.

Heuer, F., & Reisberg, D. (1990). Vivid memories of emotional events: The accuracy of remembered minutiae. *Memory & Cognition, 18,* 496–506.

Hockett, C. F. (1963). The problem of universals in language. In J. H. Greenberg (Ed.), *Universals of language.* Cambridge, Mass.: M.I.T. Press.

Holding, D. H., & Reynolds, R. I. (1982). Recall or evaluation of chess positions as determinants of chess skill. *Memory and Cognition, 10,* 237–242.

Holyoak, K. J. (1985). The pragmatics of analogical transfer. In G. H. Bower (Ed.), *The psychology of learning and motivation.* Vol. 19, pp. 59–87. Orlando: Academic Press.

Holyoak, K. J., & Koh, K. (1987). Surface and structural similarity in analogical transfer. *Memory and Cognition, 15,* 332–340.

Homa, D., Sterling, S., & Trepel, L. (1981). Limitations of exemplar-based generalization and the abstraction of categorical information. *Journal of Experimental Psychology: Human Learning and Memory, 7,* 418–439.

Hubel, D. H., & Wiesel, T. N. (1962). Receptive fields, binocular interaction, and functional architecture in the cat's visual cortex. *Journal of Physiology, 160,* 106–154.

Hunt, E. B. (1962). *Concept learning: An information-processing problem.* New York: Wiley.

Hunt, R. R. (1975). How similar are context effects in recognition and recall? *Journal of Experimental Psychology: Human Learning and Memory, 1,* 530–537.

Hunt, R. R. (1976). List context effects: Inaccessibility or indecision? *Journal of Experimental Psychology: Human Learning and Memory, 2,* 423–430.

Hunt, R. R. (1985). No generation effect, but source information facilitates event retrieval. Paper presented to the Psychonomic Society, Boston.

Hunt, R. R., & Einstein, G. O. (1981). Relational and item-specific information in memory. *Journal of Verbal Learning and Verbal Behavior, 20,* 497–514.

Hunt, R. R., & Elliott, J. M. (1980). The role of nonsemantic information in memory: Orthographic distinctiveness effects upon retention. *Journal of Experimental Psychology: General, 109,* 49–74.

Hunt, R. R., Elliott, J. M., & Spence, M. J. (1979). Independent effects of process and structure on encoding. *Journal of Experimental Psychology: Human Learning and Memory, 5.* 339–347.

Hunt, R. R., & Ellis, H. C. (1974). Recognition memory and degree of semantic contextual change. *Journal of Experimental Psychology, 103,* 1153–1159.

Hunt, R. R., & Mitchell, D. B. (1978). Specificity in nonsemantic orienting tasks and item specific information in memory. *Journal of Experimental Psychology: Human Learning and Memory, 4,* 121–135.

Hunt, R. R., & Mitchell, D. B. (1982). Independent effects of semantic and nonsemantic distinctiveness. *Journal of Experimental Psychology: Learning, Memory, and Cognition, 8,* 81–87.

Hunt, R. R., & Toth, J. P. (1990). Perceptual identification, fragment completion, and free recall: Concepts and data. *Journal of Experimental Psychology: Learning, Memory, and Cognition, 16,* 282–290.

Ingram, R. E. (1984). Toward an information-processing analysis of depression. *Cognitive Therapy and Research, 8,* 443–478.

Ingram, R. E. (1986). Processing of depressive and anxious information by depressive and anxious individuals. In P. H. Blaney (chair), *Mood and memory: Current research issues.* Symposium conducted at the meeting of the American Psychological Association, Washington, D.C.

Isen, A. M. (1984). Toward understanding the role of affect in cognition. In R. S. Wyer & T. K. Srull (Eds.), *Handbook of social cognition*. Hillsdale, N.J.: Erlbaum.

Izawa, C. (1989). *Current issues in cognitive processes*. Hillsdale, N.J.: Lawrence Erlbaum Associates.

Izawa, C. (in press). *Cognitive psychology applied*. Hillsdale, N.J.: Lawrence Erlbaum Associates.

Jacoby, L. L. (1983). Perceptual enhancement: Persistent effects of an experience. *Journal of Experimental Psychology: Learning, Memory, & Cognition. 9*, 21–38.

Jacoby, L. L. (1991). A process dissociation framework: Separating automatic from intentional uses of memory. *Journal of Memory and Language, 30*, 513–541.

Jacoby, L. L., & Brooks, L. R. (1984). Nonanalytic cognition: Memory, perception and concept learning. In G. H. Bower (Ed.), *The psychology of learning and motivation: Advances in research and theory* (Vol. 18). New York: Academic Press.

Jacoby, L. L., & Dallas, M. (1981). On the relationship between autobiographical memory and perceptual learning. *Journal of Experimental Psychology: General, 3*, 306–340.

Jacoby, L. L. & Witherspoon, D. (1982). Remembering without awareness. *Canadian Journal of Psychology, 32*, 300–324.

Jacoby, L. L., Woloshyn, V., & Kelley, C. M. (1989). Becoming famous without being recognized: Unconscious influences of memory produced by dividing attention. *Journal of Experimental Psychology: General, 118*, 115–125.

Jakobson, R., & Halle, M. (1956). *Fundamentals of language*. The Hague: Mouton.

James, W. (1890). *The principles of psychology*. Boston: Henry Holt.

Johnson, M. K., Bransford, J. D., & Solomon, S. (1973). Memory for tacit implications of sentences. *Journal of Experimental Psychology, 98*, 203–205.

Johnson, M. K. (1988). Discriminating the origin of information. In T. F. Oltmans & B. A. Maher (Eds.), *Delusional beliefs: Interdisciplinary Perspectives*. (pp. 34–65). New York: John Wiley & Sons.

Johnson, N. F. (1986). On looking at letters within words: Do we "see" them in memory? *Journal of Memory and Language, 25*, 558–570.

Johnson-Laird, P. N., & Steedman, M. (1978). The psychology of syllogisms. *Cognitive Psychology, 10*, 64–99.

Johnston, W. A., Greenberg, S., Fisher, R., & Martin, D. (1970). Divided attention: A vehicle for monitoring memory processes. *Journal of Experimental Psychology, 83*, 164–171.

Just, M. A., & Carpenter, P. A. (1984). Using eye fixations to study reading comprehension. In D. Kieras & M. A. Just (Eds.), *New methods in reading comprehension research,* pp. 151–182. Hillsdale, N.J.: Lawrence Erlbaum Associates.

Just, M. A., & Carpenter, P. A. (1987). *The psychology of reading and language comprehension.* Boston: Allyn and Bacon.

Kahneman, D. (1973). *Attention and effort.* Englewood Cliffs, N.J.: Prentice-Hall.

Kahneman, D., & Henik, A. (1981). Perceptual organization and attention. In M. Kubovy & J. R. Pomerantz (Eds.), *Perceptual organization.* Hillsdale, N.J.: Lawrence Erlbaum Associates.

Kahneman, D., & Triesman, A. (1984). Changing views of attention and automaticity. In R. Parasuraman & D. R. Davies (Eds.), *Varieties of attention.* New York: Academic Press.

Kassin, S. M., Ellsworth, P. C., & Smith, V. L. (1989). The "General Acceptance" of psychological research on eyewitness testimony. *American Psychologist, 44,* 1089–1098.

Katz, J. (1972). *Semantic theory.* New York: Harper & Row.

Keenan, J. M., & Moore, R. E. (1979). Memory for images of concealed objects: A reexamination of Neisser and Kerr. *Journal of Experimental Psychology: Human Learning and Memory, 5,* 374–385.

Keinan, G., Friedland, N., & Arad, L. (1991). Categorization and integration: Effects of stress on the structuring of information. *Cognition and Emotion, 5,* 133–145.

Keppel, G., & Underwood, B. J. (1962). Proactive inhibition in short-term retention of single items. *Journal of Verbal Learning and Verbal Behavior, 1,* 153–161.

Kerr, B. (1973). Processing demands during mental operations. *Memory and Cognition 1,* 401–412.

Kerr, N. H. (1983). The role of vision in "visual imagery" experiments: Evidence from the congenitally blind. *Journal of Experimental Psychology: General, 112,* 265–277.

Kihlstrom, J. F. (1991). On what does mood-dependent memory depend? In D. Kuiken (Ed.), *Mood and memory.* Newbury Park, CA: Sage.

Kintsch, W. (1974). *The representation of meaning in memory.* Hillsdale, N.J.: Lawrence Erlbaum Associates.

Kintsch, W., & van Dijk, T. A. (1978). Toward a model of text comprehension and production. *Psychological Review, 85,* 363–394.

Klein, S. B., & Loftus, J. (1988). The nature of self-referent encoding: The contributions of elaborative and organizational processes. *Journal of Personality and Social Psychology, 55,* 5–11.

Kosslyn, S. M., Ball, T. M., & Reiser, B. J. (1978). Visual images preserve spatial metric information: Evidence from studies of image scanning. *Journal of Experimental Psychology: Human Perception and Performance, 4,* 47–60.

Kuiken, D. (1989)(Ed.). Mood and memory: Theory, research, and applications [Special Issue]. *Journal of Social Behavior and Personality, 4*(2), 1–192.

Kuiken, D. (Ed.)(1991). *Mood and memory.* Newbury Park, CA: Sage Publications.

Kuiper, N. A., MacDonald, M. R., & Derry, P. A. (1983). Parameters of a depressive self-schema. In J. Suls & A. G. Greenwald (Eds.), *Psychological perspectives on the self.* (Vol. 2, pp. 191–217). Hillsdale, NJ: Lawrence Erlbaum Associates.

Labov, W. (1973). The boundaries of words and their meanings. In C. J. N. Bailey & R. W. Shuy (Eds.), *New ways of analyzing variations in English.* Washington, D.C.: Georgetown University Press.

Lachman, R., Lachman, J. L., & Butterfield, E. C. (1979). *Cognitive psychology and information processing.* Hillsdale, N.J.: Lawrence Erlbaum Associates.

Lakoff, G. (1987). *Women, fire, and dangerous things: What categories tell us about the nature of thought.* Chicago: University of Chicago Press.

Larkin, J. H. (1981). Enriching formal knowledge: A model for learning to solve textbook physics problems. In J. R. Anderson (Ed.), *Cognitive skills and their acquisition.* Hillsdale, N.J.: Lawrence Erlbaum Associates.

Leight, K. A., & Ellis, H. C. (1981). Emotional mood states, strategies, and state-dependency in memory. *Journal of Verbal Learning and Verbal Behavior, 20,* 251–266.

Lesgold, A. M. (1984). Acquiring expertise. In J. R. Anderson & S. M. Kosslyn (Eds.), *Tutorials in learning and memory.* W. H. Freeman: San Francisco.

Lesgold, A. M., Roth, S., & Curtis, M. B. (1979). Foregrounding effects in discourse comprehension. *Journal of Verbal Learning and Verbal Behavior, 18,* 291–308.

Lettvin, J. Y., Maturana, H. R., McCulloch, W. S., & Pitts, W. H. (1959). What the frog's eye tells the frog's brain. *Proceedings of the IRE, 47,* 1940–1951.

Levelt, W. J. M. (1989). *Speaking.* Cambridge, Mass: M.I.T. Press.

Levine, M. (1987). *Effective problem solving.* Englewood Cliffs, N.J.: Prentice-Hall.

Lewis, C. L., & Anderson, J. R. (1976). Interference with real world knowledge. *Cognitive Psychology, 8,* 311–335.

Light, L. L. (1991). Memory and aging: Four hypotheses in search of data. In M. R. Rosenzweig & L. W. Porter (Eds.). *Annual Review of Psychology, 42,* 333–376.

Light, L., & Carter-Sobell, L. (1970). Effects of changed semantic context on recognition memory. *Journal of Verbal Learning and Verbal Behavior, 9,* 1–12.

Linton, M. (1982). Transformations of memory in everyday life. In U. Neisser (Ed.), *Memory observed: Remembering in natural contexts,* pp. 77–91. San Francisco: Freeman.

Linton, M. (1986). Ways of searching and the content of memory. In D. C. Rubin (Ed.), *Autobiographical memory,* pp. 50–67. New York: Cambridge University Press.

Loftus, E. F. (1986). Experimental psychologist as an advocate or impartial educator. *Law and Human Behavior, 10,* 63–78.

Loftus, E. F., & Burns, T. (1982). Mental shock can produce retrograde amnesia. *Memory & Cognition, 10,* 318–323.

Loftus, E. F., Donders, K., Hoffman, H. G., & Schooler, J. W. (1989). Creating new memories that are quickly assessed and confidently held. *Memory and Cognition, 17,* 607–616.

Loftus, E. F., & Loftus, G. R. (1980). On the permanence of stored information in the human brain. *American Psychologist, 35,* 409–420.

Loftus, E. F., Miller, D. G., & Burns, H. J. (1978). Semantic integration of verbal information into a visual memory. *Journal of Experimental Psychology: Human Learning and Memory,* 1978, *4.*

Loftus, E. F., & Palmer, J. C. (1974). Reconstruction of automobile destruction: An example of the interaction between language and memory. *Journal of Verbal Learning and Verbal Behavior, 13,* 585–589.

Loggie, R. H., & Baddeley, H. D. (1987). Cognitive processes in counting. *Journal of Experimental Psychology: Learning, Memory, & Cognition, 13,* 310–326.

Luchins, A. S. (1942). Mechanization in problem solving. *Psychological Monographs, 54,* (6, Whole No. 248).

Maki, R. (1990). Memory for script actions: Effects of relevance and detail expectancy. *Memory and Cognition, 18,* 5–14.

Mandler, G. (1967). Organization and memory. In K. W. Spence & J. T. Spence (Eds.), *The psychology of learning and motivation* (Vol. 1). New York: Academic Press.

Mandler, G. (1975). *Mind and emotion.* New York: Wiley.

Mandler, J. M. (1984). *Stories, scripts, and scenes: Aspects of schema theory.* Hillsdale, N.J.: Lawrence Erlbaum Associates.

Mantyla, T. (1986). Optimizing cue effectiveness: Recall of 500 and 600 incidentally learned words. *Journal of Experimental Psychology: Learning, Memory, and Cognition, 12,* 66–71.

Marcel, A. J. (1980). Conscious and preconscious recognition of polysemous words: Locating the selective effects of prior verbal context. In R. S. Nickerson (Ed.), *Attention and performance VIII*. Hillsdale, N.J.: Lawrence Erlbaum Associates.

Marcus, S. L., & Rips, L. J. (1979). Conditional reasoning. *Journal of Verbal Learning and Verbal Behavior, 18*, 199–223.

Marschark, M. (1979). The syntax and semantics of comprehension. In G. Prideaux (Ed.), *Perspectives on experimental linguistics*. Amsterdam: John Benjamins.

Marschark, M., Everhart, V. S., Martin, J., & West, S. A. (1987). Identifying linguistic creativity in deaf and hearing children. *Metaphor and Symbolic Activity, 2*, 281–306.

Marschark, M., West, S. A., Nall, L., & Everhart, V. S. (1986). Development of creative linguistic devices in signed and oral production. *Journal of Experimental Child Psychology, 41*, 534–550.

Massaro, D. W. (1975). *Experimental psychology and information processing*. Chicago: Rand McNally.

Mayer, J. D., & Bower, G. H. (1985). Naturally occurring mood and learning: Comment on Hasher, Rose, Zachs, Sanft, and Doren. *Journal of Experimental Psychology: General, 14*, 396–403.

Mayer, J. D., & Bower, G. H. (1986). Detecting mood-dependent retrieval. In P. H. Blaney (chair), *Mood and memory: Current research issues*. Symposium conducted at the meeting of the American Psychological Association, Washington, D.C.

Mayer, R. E. (1983). *Thinking, problem solving, cognition*. New York: Freeman.

McClelland, J. L., & Rumelhart, D. E. (1981). An interactive activation model of context effects in letter perception: Part 1. An account of basic findings. *Psychological Review, 88*, 375–407.

McClelland, J. L., Rumelhart, D. E., & Hinton, G. E. (1986). The appeal of parallel distributed processing. In D. E. Rumelhart & J. L. McClelland (Eds.) *Parallel distributed processing*. Cambridge, Mass.: M.I.T. Press.

McCloskey, M., Egeth, H., & McKenna, J. (1986). The experimental psychologist in court: The ethics of expert testimony. *Law and Human Behavior, 10*, 1–13.

McCloskey, M., Wible, C. G., & Cohen, N. J. (1988). Is there a special flashbulb-memory mechanism? *Journal of Experimental Psychology: General, 117*, 171–181.

McCloskey, M., & Zaragoza, M. S. (1985). Misleading postevent information and memory for events: Arguments and evidence against memory impairment hypotheses. *Journal of Experimental Psychology: General, 114*, 1–16.

McDaniel, M. A., Riegler, G. L. & Wadill, P. J. (1990). Generation effects in free recall: Further support for a three-factor theory. *Journal of Experimental Psychology: Learning, Memory, and Cognition, 16*, 789–798.

McDaniel, M. A., Waddill, P. J., & Einstein, G. O. (1988). A contextual account of the generation effect: A three-factor theory. *Journal of Memory and Language, 27*, 521–536.

McElroy, L. A., & Slamecka, H. J. (1982). Memorial consequences of generating nonwords: Implications for semantic memory interpretations of the generation effect. *Journal of Verbal Learning and Verbal Behavior, 21*, 249–259.

McEwan, N. H., & Yuille, J. C. (1987). The effects of training and experience on eyewitness testimony. Paper presented at the meeting of the Canadian Psychological Association.

McFarland, A. D. (1986). *Cognitive effort during reading: Effects of topic knowledge.* Unpublished doctoral dissertation, University of New Mexico.

McGeoch, J. A. (1942). *The psychology of human learning.* New York: McKay.

McKoon, G., & Ratcliffe, R. (1979). Priming in episodic and semantic memory. *Journal of Verbal Learning and Verbal Behavior, 18*, 463–480.

McKoon, G., Ratcliff, R., & Dell, G. S. (1986). A critical evaluation of the semantic-episodic distinction. *Journal of Experimental Psychology: Learning, Memory, and Cognition, 12*, 295–306.

McNeill, D. (1985). So you think gestures are nonverbal? *Psychological Review, 92*, 350–371.

Medin, D. L. (1989). Concepts and conceptual structure. *American Psychologist, 44*, 1469–1481.

Medin, D. L., & Schaffer, M. M. (1978). Context theory of classification learning. *Psychological Review, 85*, 207–238.

Medin, D. L., & Shoben, E. J. (1988). Context and structure in conceptual combination. *Cognitive Psychology, 20*, 158–190.

Miller, G. A. (1956). The magical number seven, plus or minus two: Some limits on our capacity for processing information. *Psychological Review, 63*, 81–97.

Miller, G. A., Galanter, E., & Pribram, K. H. (1960). *Plans and the structure of behavior.* New York: Holt.

Miller, J. R., & Kintsch, W. (1980). Readability and recall of short prose passages: A theoretical analysis. *Journal of Experimental Psychology: Human Learning and Memory, 6*, 335–354.

Milner, B. (1970). Memory and the medial temporal regions of the brain. In K. H. Pribram and D. E. Broadbent (Eds.), *Biology of memory.* New York: Academic Press.

Mitchell, D. B., & Brown, A. S. (1988). Persistent repetition priming in picture naming and its dissociation from recognition memory. *Journal of Experimental Psychology: Learning, Memory, & Cognition, 14,* 213–222.

Mitchell, D. B., Brown, A. S., & Murphy, D. R. (1990). Dissociations between procedural and episodic memory: Effects of time and aging. *Psychology and Aging, 5,* 264–276.

Mitchell, D. B., & Richman, C. L. (1980). Confirmed reservations: Mental travel. *Journal of Experimental Psychology: Human Perception and Performance, 6,* 58–66.

Mitchell, D. B., Hunt, R. R., & Schmitt, F. A. (1986). The generation effect and reality monitoring: Evidence from dementia and normal aging. *Journal of Gerontology, 41,* 79–84.

Moates, D. R., & Schumacher, G. M. (1980). *An introduction to cognitive psychology.* Belmont, Calif.: Wadsworth.

Moray, N. (1970). *Attention: Selective processes in vision and hearing.* New York: Academic Press.

Morrell, R. W., Park, D. C., & Poon, L. W. (1989). Quality of instructions on prescription drug labels: Effects on memory and comprehension in young and old adults. *Gerontologist, 29,* 345–354.

Morris, C. D., Bransford, J. D., & Franks, J. J. (1977). Levels of processing versus test-appropriate strategies. *Journal of Verbal Learning and Verbal Behavior, 16,* 519–533.

Morrison, F. J., Giordani, B., & Nagy, J. (1977). Reading disability: An information processing analysis. *Science, 199,* 77–79.

Murphy, G. L., & Medin, D. L. (1985). The role of theories in conceptual coherence. *Psychological Review, 92,* 289–316.

Murray, D. J. (1966). Vocalization at presentation and immediate recall, with varying recall methods. *Quarterly Journal of Experimental Psychology, 18,* 9–18.

Nakamura, G. V., & Graesser, A. C. (1985). Memory for script-typical and script-atypical actions: A reaction time study. *Bulletin of the Psychonomic Society, 23,* 384–386.

Neisser, U. (1964). Visual search. *Scientific American, 210,* 94–107.

Neisser, U. (1967). *Cognitive psychology.* New York: Appleton-Century-Crofts.

Neisser, U. (1982). Snapshots or benchmarks? In U. Neisser (Ed.), *Memory observed* (pp. 43–48). San Francisco: Freeman.

Neisser, U. & Harsch, N. (in press). False recollections on hearing news about the Challenger. In E. Winograd & U. Neisser (Eds.), *Affect and flashbulb memories.* New York: Cambridge University Press.

Neisser, U., & Kerr, N. (1973). Spatial and mnemonic properties of visual images. *Cognitive Psychology, 5,* 138–150.

Nelson, D. L., Schreiber, T. A., & McEvoy, C. L. (1992). Processing implicit and explicit representations. *Psychological Review, 99,* 322–348.

Nelson, D. L., Walling, J. R., & McEvoy, C. L. (1979). Doubts about depth. *Journal of Experimental Psychology, Human Learning and Memory, 5,* 24–44.

Newell, A., & Simon, H. (1972). *Human problem solving.* Englewood Cliffs, N.J.: Prentice-Hall.

Nickerson, R. S. (1987). Why teach thinking? In J. B. Baron & R. J. Sternberg (Eds.), *Teaching thinking skills: Theory and practice.* New York: Freeman.

Nickerson, R. S., Perkins, D.N., & Smith, E. E. (1985). *The teaching of thinking.* Hillsdale, N.J.: Lawrence Erlbaum Associates.

Norman, D. A. (1968). Toward a theory of memory and attention. *Psychological Review, 75,* 522–536.

Norman, D. A., & Bobrow, D. G. (1975). On data-limited and resource-limited processes. *Cognitive Psychology, 7,* 44–64.

Norman, D. A., & Rumelhart, D. E. (1975). *Explorations in cognition.* San Francisco: Freeman.

Nosofsky, R. M. (1989). Further tests of an exemplar-similarity approach to relating identification and categorization. *Cognition and Psychophysics, 45,* 279–290.

O'Brien, E. J., & Myers, J. L. (1985). When comprehension difficulty improves memory for text. *Journal of Experimental Psychology: Learning, Memory, and Cognition, 11,* 12–21.

Paivio, A. (1969). Mental imagery in associative learning and memory. *Psychological Review, 76,* 241–263.

Paivio, A. (1971). *Imagery and verbal processes.* New York: Holt.

Paivio, A. (1986). *Mental representations.* Oxford: Oxford University Press.

Paivio, A., & Begg, I. (1981). *Psychology of language.* Englewood Cliffs, NJ: Prentice-Hall.

Palmer, S. E. (1975). Visual perception and world knowledge: Notes on a model of sensory cognitive interaction. In D. A. Norman, D. E. Rumelhart, and the LNR Research Group, (Eds.), *Explorations in cognition.* San Francisco: Freeman.

Pellegrino, J. W. (1985). Inductive reasoning ability. In R. J. Sternberg (Ed.), *Human abilities: An information processing approach.* San Francisco: Freeman.

Penfield, W. (1959). Consciousness, memory, and man's conditioned reflexes. In K. Pribram (Ed.), *On the biology of learning.* New York: Harcourt, Brace, & World.

Peters, R., & McGee, R. (1982). Cigarette smoking and state-dependent memory. *Psychopharmacology, 76,* 232–235.

Peterson, L. R., & Peterson, M. J. (1959). Short-term retention of individual verbal items. *Journal of Experimental Psychology, 58,* 193–198.

Pillemer, D. (in press). Remembering personal circumstances: A functional analysis. In. E. Winograd & U. Neisser (Eds.), *Affect and accuracy in recall: The case of flashbulb memories.* New York: Cambridge University Press.

Pinker, F., & Prince, A. (1988). On language and connectionism: Analysis of a parallel distributed processing model of language acquisition. *Cognition, 28,* 73–193.

Poincaré, H. (1929). *The foundations of science.* New York: Science House.

Pollack, I., & Pickett, J. M. (1963). The intelligibility of language from conversations. *Language and Speech, 6,* 165–171.

Polya, G. (1957). *How to solve it.* Garden City, N.Y.: Doubleday Anchor.

Posner, M. I. (1973). *Cognition: An introduction.* Glenview, Ill.: Scott, Foresman.

Posner, M. I., & Boies, S. J. (1971). Components of attention. *Psychological Review, 78,* 391–408.

Postman, L., and Underwood, B. J. (1973), Critical issues in interference theory. *Memory and Cognition, 1,* 19–40.

Premack, D. (1971). Language in chimpanzees? *Science, 172,* 808–822.

Premack, D. (1983). The codes of man and beasts. *The Behavioral and Brain Sciences, 6,* 125–167.

Pylyshyn, Z. W. (1973). What the mind's eye tells the mind's brain: A critique of mental imagery. *Psychological Bulletin, 80,* 1–24.

Quillian, M. R. (1968). Semantic memory. In M. Minsky (Ed.), *Semantic information processing.* Cambridge, Mass.: M. I. T. Press.

Quillian, M. R. (1969). The teachable language comprehender: A simulation program and theory of language. *Communications of the Association for Computing Machinery, 12,* 459–476.

Rabinowitz, J. C., Mandler, G., & Patterson, K. E. (1977). Determinants of recognition and recall: Accessibility and generation. *Journal of Experimental Psychology: General, 106,* 302–329.

Rabinowitz, M., & Mandler, J. M. (1983). Organization and information retrieval. *Journal of Experimental Psychology: Learning, Memory, and Cognition, 9,* 430–439.

Reed, S. K. (1972). Pattern recognition and categorization. *Cognitive Psychology, 3,* 382–407.

Reicher, G. M. (1969). Perceptual recognition as a function of meaningfulness of stimulus material. *Journal of Experimental Psychology, 81,* 275–280.

Reisberg, D., & Heuer, F. (in press). Remembering the details of emotional events. In G. Winograd & U. Neisser (Eds.), *Affect and accuracy in recall: The case of flashbulb memories.* New York: Cambridge University Press.

Reitman, J. S. (1971). Mechanisms of forgetting in short-term memory. *Cognitive Psychology, 2,* 185–195.

Reitman, J. S. (1974). Without surreptitious rehearsal, information in short-term memory decays. *Journal of Verbal Learning and Verbal Behavior, 13,* 365–377.

Reitman, W. R. (1964). Heuristic decision processes, open constraints, and the structure of ill-defined problems. In M. W. Shelley & G. L. Bryan (Eds.), *Human judgements and optimality.* New York: Wiley.

Reitman, W. R. (1965). *Cognition and thought: An information procesing approach.* New York: Wiley.

Richman, C. L., Mitchell, D. B., & Reznick, J. S. (1979). Mental travel: Some reservations. *Journal of Experimental Psychology: Human Perception and Performance, 5,* 13–18.

Ricks, D. M. (1975). Vocal communication in preverbal normal and autistic children. In N. O'Connor (Ed.), *Language, cognitive deficits, and retardation.* London: Butterworth.

Rips, L. J. (1983). Cognitive processes in propositional reasoning. *Psychological Review, 90,* 38–71.

Riskind, J. H. (1991). Will the field ultimately need a more detailed analysis of mood-memory? In D. Kuiken (Ed.) *Mood and memory* Newbury Park, CA: Sage.

Roediger, H. L. (1990). Implicit memory: Retention without remembering. *American Psychologist, 45,* 1043–1056.

Roediger, H. L., & Blaxton, T. A. (1987). Retrieval modes produce dissociations in memory for surface information. In D. S. Gorfein & R. R. Hoffman (Eds.), *Memory, and Learning: The Ebinghaus Centennial Conference,* pp. 349–379. Hillsdale, N. J.: Lawrence Erlbaum Associates.

Roediger, H. L. & Craik, F. I. M. (Eds.) (1989). *Varieties of memory and consciousness.* Hillsdale, N.J.: Lawrence Erlbaum and Associates.

Roediger, H. L.., Weldon, M. S., & Challis, B. A. (1989). Explaining dissociations between implicit and explicit measures of retention: A processing account. In H. L. Roediger III & F.I.M. Craik (Eds.), *Varieties of memory and consciousness: Essays in honor of Endel Tulving* pp.3–41. Hillsdale, N. J.: Lawrence Erlbaum Associates.

Rogers, T. B., Kuiper, N. A., & Kirker, W. S. (1977). Self-reference and the encoding of personal information. *Journal of Personality and Social Psychology, 35,* 677–688.

Roland, P. E., & Friberg, L. (1985). Location of cortical areas activated by thinking. *Journal of Neurophysiology, 53,* 1219–1243.

Rosch, E. (1975). Cognitive representations of semantic categories. *Journal of Experimental Psychology: General, 104,* 192–233.

Rosch, E. (1973). Natural categories. *Cognitive Psychology, 4,* 328–350. (a)

Rosch, E. (1973). On the internal structure of perceptual and semantic categories. In T. E. Moore (Ed.), *Cognitive development and the acquisition of language.* New York: Academic Press. (b)

Rosch, E., & Mervis, C. B. (1975). Family resemblances: Studies in the internal structure of categories. *Cognitive Psychology, 7,* 573–605.

Rosch, E. H., Mervis, C. B., Gray, W. D., Johnson, D. M., & Boyers-Braem, P. (1976). Basic objects in natural categories. *Cognitive Psychology, 8,* 382–439.

Roth, E. M., & Shoben, E. J. (1983). The effect of context on the structure of categories. *Cognitive Psychology, 15,* 346–378.

Rubin, D. C. (1977). Very long-term memory for prose and verse. *Journal of Verbal Learning and Verbal Behavior, 16,* 611–621.

Rubin, D. C., & Kozin, M. (1984). Vivid memories. *Cognition, 16,* 81–95.

Rubin, D. C., & Wallace, W. T. (1989). Rhyme and reason: Analyses of dual retrieval cues. *Journal of Experimental Psychology: Learning, Memory, & Cognition, 15,* 698–709.

Russell, P. N., & Beekhuis, M. E. (1976). Organization in memory: A comparison of psychotics and normals. *Journal of Abnormal Psychology, 85,* 527–534.

Sachs, J. (1967). Recognition memory for syntactic and semantic aspects of connected discourse. *Perception and Psychophysics, 2,* 437–442.

Samuel, A. G. (1987). Lexical uniqueness effects on phonemic restoration. *Journal of Memory and Language, 26,* 36–56.

Sanford, A. J., & Garrod, S. C. (1981). *Understanding written language.* New York: Wiley.

Schacter, D. L. (1992). Understanding implicit memory: A cognitive neuroscience approach. *American Psychologist, 47,* 559–569.

Schacter, D. L., Harbluk, J. L., & McLachlan, D. R. (1984). Retrieval without recollection: An experimental analysis of source amnesia. *Journal of Verbal Learning and Verbal Behavior, 23,* 593–611.

Schank, R., & Abelson, R. (1977). *Scripts, plans, goals, and understanding.* Hillsdale, N.J.: Lawrence Erlbaum Associates.

Searle, J. R. (1969). *Speech acts.* Cambridge: Cambridge University Press.

Searle, J. R. (1975). Indirect speech acts. In P. Cole & J. L. Morgan (Eds.), *Syntax and semantics* (Vol. 3). New York: Seminar Press.

Segal, J. W., Chipman, S. F., & Glaser, R. (Eds.), (1985). *Thinking and learning skills: Relating instruction to research* (Vol. 1). Hillsdale, N.J.: Lawrence Erlbaum Associates.

Seibert, P. S., & Ellis, H. C. (1991). Irrelevant thoughts, emotional mood states and cognitive task performances. *Memory and Cognition, 19,* 507–513.

Selfridge, O. G. (1959). Pandemonium: A paradigm for learning. In *The mechanization of thought processes.* London: H. M. Stationary Office.

Shallice, T., & Warrington, E. K. (1970). Independent functioning of verbal memory stores: A neuropsychological study. *Quarterly Journal of Experimental Psychology, 22,* 261–273.

Simon, H. A. (1973). The structure of ill-structured problems. *Artificial Intelligence, 4,* 181–201.

Simon, H. A. (1978). Information-processing theory of human problem solving. In W. K. Estes (Ed.), *Handbook of learning and cognitive processes.* Hillsdale, N.J.: Lawrence Erlbaum Associates.

Simon, H. A., & Kotovsky, K. (1963). Human acquisition of concepts for sequential patterns. *Psychological Review, 70,* 534–546.

Slamecka, N. J., & Fevreiski, J. (1983). The generation effect when generation fails. *Journal of Verbal Learning and Verbal Behavior, 22,* 153–163.

Slamecka, N. J., & Graf, P. (1978). The generation effect: Delineation of a phenomenon. *Journal of Experimental Psychology: Human Learning and Memory, 4,* 592–604.

Slamecka, N. J., & Katsaiti, L. T. (1987). The generation effect as an artifact of selective displaced rehearsal. *Journal of Memory and Language, 26,* 589–607.

Slobin, D. I. (1973). Cognitive prerequisites for the acquisition of grammar. In C. A. Ferguson & D. J. Slobin (Eds.), *Studies of child language development.* New York: Holt.

Sloman, S. A., Hayman, C. A. G., Ohta, N., Law, J., & Tulving, E. (1988). Forgetting in primed fragment completion. *Journal of Experimental Psychology: Learning, Memory, & Cognition, 14,* 223–239.

Smith, E. E., Shoben, E. J., & Rips, L. J. (1974). Structure and process in semantic memory: A featural model for semantic decision. *Psychological Review, 81,* 214–241.

Smith, D. A., & Grasser, A. C. (1981). Memory for actions in scripted activities as a function of typicality, retention interval, and retrieval task. *Memory and Cognition, 9,* 550–559.

Smith, S. M. (1988). Environmental context-dependent memory. In D. M. Thomson & G. M. Davies (Ed.) *Memory in context: Context in memory.* New York: Wiley.

Solso, R. L. (1991). *Cognitive Psychology,* Boston: Allyn & Bacon.

Sperling, G. (1960). The information available in brief visual presentations. *Psychological Monographs, 74* (Whole No. 498).

Spilich, G. J., Vesonder, G. T., Chiesi, H. L., & Voss, J. F. (1979). Text processing of domain-related information for individuals with high- and low-domain knowledge. *Journal of Verbal Learning and Verbal Behavior, 18,* 275–290.

Standing, L., Conezio, J., & Haber R. N. (1970). Perception and memory for pictures: Single trial learning of 2560 visual stimuli. *Psychonomic Science, 19,* 73–74.

Stein, B. S. (1978). Depth of processing reexamined: The effects of the precision of encoding and test appropriateness. *Journal of Verbal Learning and Verbal Behavior, 17,* 165–174.

Stein, B. S., & Bransford, J. D. (1979). Constraints on effective elaboration: Effects of precision and subject generation. *Journal of Verbal Learning and Verbal Behavior, 18,* 769–777.

Sternberg, S. (1966). High-speed scanning in human memory. *Science, 153,* 652–654.

Sulin, R. A., & Dooling, D. J. (1974). Intrusions of a thematic idea in retention of prose. *Journal of Experimental Psychology, 103,* 255–262.

Swanson, H. L. (1984). Effects of cognitive effort and word distinctiveness on learning disabled and nondisabled reader's recall. *Journal of Educational Psychology, 76,* 894–908.

Tartter, V. C. (1987). *Language processes.* New York: Holt, Rinehart and Winston.

Teasdale, J. D. (1983). Negative thinking in depression: Cause, effect, or reciprocal relationship? *Advances in Behavioral Research and Therapy, 5,* 3–25.

Terrace, H. S. (1979). How Nim Chimpsky changed my mind. *Psychology Today,* November.

Terrace, H. S., Pettito, L. A., & Bever, T. G. (1976). *Project Nim, Progress Report I.* New York: Columbia University Press.

Torrance, E. P. (1968). Examples and rationales of test tasks for assessing creative abilities. *Journal of Creative Behavior, 2* (3).

Toth, J. P., & Hunt, R. R. (1990). Effect of generation on a word-identification task. *Journal of Experimental Psychology: Learning, Memory, & Cognition, 16,* 993–1003.

Treisman, A. M. (1960). Contextual cues in selective listening. *Quarterly Journal of Experimental Psychology. 12,* 242–248.

Treisman, A. M. (1964). Selective attention in man. *British Medical Bulletin, 20,* 12–16.

Treisman, A. M., & Geffen, G. (1967). Selective attention: Perception or response? *Quarterly Journal of Experimental Psychology, 19,* 1–17.

Tulving, E. (1962). Subjective organization in free recall of "unrelated" words. *Psychological Review, 69,* 344–354.

Tulving, E. (1972). Episodic and semantic memory. In E. Tulving & W. Donaldson (Eds.), *Organization of memory.* New York: Academic Press.

Tulving, E. (1974). Cue-dependent forgetting. *American Scientist, 62,* 74–82.

Tulving, E. (1983). *Elements of episodic memory.* New York: Oxford University Press.

Tulving, E. (1985). Memory and consciousness. *Canadian Psychology, 26,* 1–12.

Tulving, E. (1986). What kind of hypothesis is the distinction between episodic and semantic memory? *Journal of Experimental Psychology: Learning, Memory, and Cognition, 12,* 307–311.

Tulving, E., & Psotka, J. (1971). Retroactive inhibition in free recall: Inaccessibility of information available in the memory store. *Journal of Experimental Psychology, 87,* 1–8.

Tulving, E., & Thomson, D. M. (1971). Retrieval processes in recognition memory: Effects of associative context. *Journal of Experimental Psychology, 87,* 116–124.

Tulving, E., & Thomson, D. M. (1973). Encoding specificity and retrieval processes in episodic memory. *Psychological Review, 80,* 352–373.

Turner, M. L., LaPointe, L. B., Cantor, J., Reeves, C. H., Griffeth, R. H., & Engle, R. (1987). Recency and suffix effects found with auditory presentation and with mouthed visual presentation: They're not the same thing. *Journal of Memory and Language, 26,* 138–164.

Tyler, L. K., & Marslen-Wilson, W. (1986). The effects of context on the recognition of polymorphemic words. *Journal of Memory and Language, 25,* 741–752.

Tyler, S. W., Hertel, P. T., McCallum, M. C., & Ellis, H. C. (1979). Cognitive effort and memory. *Journal of Experimental Psychology: Human Learning and Memory, 5,* 607–617.

van Dijk, T. A., & Kintsch, W. (1983). *Strategies of discourse comprehension.* New York: Academic Press.

Velten, E. (1968). A laboratory task for induction of mood states. *Behavior Research and Therapy, 6,* 473–482.

von Wright, J. M. (1968). Selection in visual immediate memory. *Quarterly Journal of Experimental Psychology, 20,* 62–68.

Voss, J. F., Greene, T. R., Post, T. A., & Penner, B. C. (1983). Problem solving skill in social sciences. In G. H. Bower (Ed.), *The psychology of learning and motivation,* Vol 17. New York: Academic Press.

Voss, J. F., Tyler, S. W., & Yengo, L. A. (1983). Individual differences in the solving of social science problems. In R. F. Dillon & R. R. Schmeck (Eds.), *Individual differences in cognition,* New York: Academic Press.

Wallace, W. T., & Rubin, D. C. (1988). Memory of a ballad singer. In M. M. Grunesberg, P. E. Morris, & R. E. Sykes (Eds.), *Practical aspects of memory: Current research and issues: Vol 1. Memory in everyday life,* pp. 257–262. New York: Wiley.

Warren, R. M., & Obusek, C. J. (1971). Speech perception and phonemic restorations. *Perception and Psychophysics, 9,* No. 3B.

Warrington, E. K., Logue, V., & Pratt, R. T. C. (1971). The anatomical localization of selective impairment of auditory verbal short-term memory. *Neuropsychologia, 9,* 377–387.

Warrington, E. K., & Weiskrantz, L. (1968). New method of testing long-term retention with special reference to amnesic patients. *Nature, 217,* 972–974.

Wason, P. C., & Johnson-Laird, P. N. (1972). *Psychology of reasoning.* Cambridge, Mass.: Harvard University Press.

Watkins, O. C., & Watkins, M. J. (1980). The modality effect and echoic persistence. *Journal of Experimental Psychology: General, 109,* 251–278.

Weingartner, H., Cohen, R. M., Murphy, D. L., Martello, J., & Gerdt, C. (1981). Cognitive processes in depression. *Archives of General Psychiatry, 38,* 42–47.

Weingartner, H., Miller, H., & Murphy, D. L. (1977). Mood state-dependent retrieval of verbal associations. *Journal of Abnormal Psychology, 86,* 276–284.

Weisberg, R. W. (1986). *Creativity: Genius and other myths.* New York: W. H. Freeman

Wells, G. L., & Murray, D. M. (1984). Eyewitness confidence. In G. L. Wells & E. F. Loftus (Eds.), *Eyewitness testimony: Psychological perspectives.* New York: Cambridge University Press.

Whorf, B. L. (1956). Science and linguistics. In J. B. Carroll (Ed.), *Language, thought and reality: Selected writings of Benjamin Lee Whorf.* Cambridge, Mass.: M. I. T. Press.

Wickelgren, W. A. (1974). *How to solve problems.* San Francisco: Freeman.

Williams, J. M. G., Watts, F. N., MacLeod, C., & Mathews, A. (1988). *Cognitive psychology and emotional disorders.* New York: Wiley.

Winograd, E. (1981). Elaboration and distinctiveness in memory for faces. *Journal of Experimental Psychology: Human Learning and Memory, 7,* 181–190.

Winograd, E., & Killinger, W. A. Jr. (1983). Relating age at encoding in early childhood to adult recall: Development of flashbulb memories. *Journal of Experimental Psychology: General, 112,* 413–422.

Winograd, E., & Neisser, U. (in press). *Affect and accuracy in recall: The case of "flashbulb" memories.* New York: Cambridge University Press.

Wood, M. R. (1990). *Contributions of context and inferencing on cognitive capacity during television viewing.* Doctoral dissertation, University of New Mexico.

Woodworth, R. S., & Sells, S. B. (1935). An atmosphere effect in formal syllogistic reasoning. *Journal of Experimental Psychology, 18,* 451–460.

Zadah, L. A., Fu, K. S., Tanaka, K., & Shimura, M. (1975). *Fuzzy sets and their applications to cognitive and decision processes.* New York: Academic Press.

Zaragoza, M. S., & McCloskey, M. (1989). Misleading postevent information and the memory impairment hypothesis: Comment on Belli and a reply to Tversky and Tuchin. *Journal of Experimental Psychology: General, 118,* 92–99.

NAME INDEX

SUBJECT INDEX

Dichotic listening, 54–56
Direct memory test, 148
Distinctiveness, 113–15, 119–21, 146–47, 162–63
Dual-code theory, 127–29

Echoic memory, 25–29
Effortful processing, 341–43
Elaboration, 111–12
  and mood, 339–41
Emotion and Cognition, 333–61
  anxiety, 359
  depression, 347
  effect on encoding, 337–41
  effects on retrieval, 345–47
  and eyewitness testimony, 355–56
  flashbulb memory, 356–59
  and judgment, 353–55
  state dependence, 335–37
  theories, 349–52
Encoding, 238
  and mood, 337–41
Encoding specificity, 138, 140
Episodic memory, 141, 149–50, 153, 189–92
Exemplar theory, 193–95, 218–19
Expertise, 170–71, 282–84
Eyewitness testimony, 232–34, 355–56

Family resemblances, 215
Feature set theory, 181–84
Features, 37–39, 181–84, 211, 216, 218
Filter models of attention, 52–58
Flashbulb memory, 356–59
Focus gambling, 208
Forgetting, 87–89, 157–63
Functional fixedness, 275–77
Fuzzy categories, 212–13

Generate-test problem solving, 268
Generation effect, 122–23
Generation-recognition model, 142–46
Gestalt psychology, 288
Goals, 2
Graded structure, 213
Grammar, 310, 313–14
Grice's maxims, 315–16

Hedges, 183
Hemispheric specialization, 325–26
Heuristic strategy, 267

Ill-defined problems, 283–84
Imagery, 125–33
Implicit memory, 91–93, 148–57
Incidental memory, 99, 339–40
Incubation, 271–72
Indirect memory test, 148, 190–92
Inductive reasoning, 295–96
Inferences, 235–37
  in advertising, 236–37
  inductive inference, 219
  logical, 235
  pragmatic, 235
Information processing, 8–9, 289–90
Integration in memory, 227–30
Intentionality, 2
Interference, 80, 88
  theory, 160–61

Language, 304–27
  in animals, 322–24
  and brain, 325–27
  comprehension of, 316–17
  and culture, 324–25
  development of, 318–20
  functions of, 305–8
  production of, 314–16
  structure of, 308–14
  and thought, 320–22
Levels of processing, 98–101, 110–11
Lexical content, 309
Linguistic relativity, 320
Logical concepts, 205–6
Long-term memory, 12, 86–87, 108–34
  and aging, 133
  autobiographical, 109–10
  distinctiveness, 113–15, 120–21
  elaboration, 111–12
  imagery, 125–32
  organization, 115–21

Means-end analysis, 268–70
Memory systems, 140–42, 149–50, 153, 189
Mental representation, 216, 263–64
Mental rotation, 35
Mental travel, 125–27
Mind, 6
Mnemonics, 132–33
Modality effects, 26, 150
Model, 7
Mood and memory, 334–49